ENGAGING
THE CHRISTIAN
SCRIPTURES

SECOND EDITION

ENGAGING THE CHRISTIAN SCRIPTURES

An Introduction to the Bible

Andrew E. Arterbury,
W. H. Bellinger Jr.,
and Derek S. Dodson

Baker Academic

a division of Baker Publishing Group
Grand Rapids, Michigan

© 2014, 2021 by Andrew E. Arterbury, W. H. Bellinger Jr., and Derek S. Dodson

Published by Baker Academic
a division of Baker Publishing Group
PO Box 6287, Grand Rapids, MI 49516-6287
www.bakeracademic.com

Printed in the United States of America

Library of Congress Cataloging-in-Publication Data
Names: Arterbury, Andrew E., author. | Bellinger, W. H. (William H.), Jr., 1949– author. | Dodson, Derek S., author.
Title: Engaging the Christian scriptures : an introduction to the Bible / Andrew E. Arterbury, W. H. Bellinger Jr., and Derek S. Dodson.
Description: Second edition. | Grand Rapids, Michigan : Baker Academic, a division of Baker Publishing Group, [2021] | Includes bibliographical references and index.
Identifiers: LCCN 2020038299 | ISBN 9781540962256 (paperback) | ISBN 9781540964373 (casebound)
Subjects: LCSH: Bible—Introductions.
Classification: LCC BS475.3 .A78 2021 | DDC 220.6/1—dc23
LC record available at https://lccn.loc.gov/2020038299

21 22 23 24 25 26 27   7 6 5 4 3 2 1

To our students—past, present, and future—who inspire us.

Contents

Preface

We intend for this volume to serve as an introductory textbook to the Christian Scriptures for students who are engaging in an informed reading of the Bible within an academic setting. Because we believe the biblical texts should function as the primary texts in such a setting, we have crafted this textbook to function as a supplemental resource. For example, we have focused our readers' attention on the prevailing conversations and leading opinions within the field of biblical studies on most subjects. In other words, we have not attempted to provide exhaustive descriptions of every academic conversation about the Bible, but rather we have striven to introduce the most important conversations for students who are encountering the field of biblical studies for the first time. In the process, we have intentionally created a manageable, accessible, and affordable textbook that aims first and foremost to benefit students rather than their professors.

Methodologically, we have employed a contextual approach to the Christian Scriptures, giving attention to historical, literary, and theological contexts. Rather than telling students about the Bible, we aim to help students become educated readers of the Bible. Furthermore, while introducing critical perspectives and approaches, we have simultaneously attempted to highlight and to underscore the theological claims found within the Christian Scriptures rather than to critique or to deconstruct those claims. Consequently, our title reflects our aim. We hope beginning students will "engage" the Christian Scriptures. Ideally, this textbook will function as the supplemental resource that empowers students to do just that.

In this second edition of *Engaging the Christian Scriptures*, we have added a glossary (terms that appear there are bolded on first use in the main text), introduced some new material, updated previous material, and sought to improve the overall flow of the book. As a result, this new or updated material equates to about twenty percent of the book.

We want and need to thank many people who have helped us envision and publish this second edition of *Engaging the Christian Scriptures*. For starters, we are grateful to the fine people at Baker Academic. In particular, Bryan Dyer, our acquisitions editor, provided encouragement and wise counsel from the first to the last. In addition, James Korsmo, the project editor, kept us on schedule and greatly enhanced the readability and layout of this second edition. Furthermore, Sarah Gombis assembled a robust marketing strategy for the book. Thanks to all of you. Likewise, we are grateful for B. J. Parker's creative illustrations, the feedback and proofreading work that Rebecca Whitten Poe Hays, Amanda Brobst-Renaud, Kim Williams Bodenhamer, and Josiah Hall provided, and the assistance that Rebecca Whitten Poe Hays and Valerie Fisk provided in the compilation of teacher resources. We also wish to thank Baylor University for the means and resources that allowed us to tackle a project like this one, and we are grateful for the support provided by President Linda Livingstone, Provost Nancy Brickhouse, Dean Lee Nordt, Dean Todd Still, and the faculty of the Department of Religion and the George W. Truett Theological Seminary.

Visit www.bakeracademic.com/professors
to access study aids
and instructor materials for this textbook.

Abbreviations

General

BCE	before the Common Era	LXX	Septuagint
c.	century	MT	Masoretic Text
ca.	circa	NIV	New International Version
CE	Common Era	NLT	New Living Translation
col(s).	column(s)	NRSV	New Revised Standard Version
e.g.	*exempli gratia*, for example	NT	New Testament
esp.	especially	OT	Old Testament
GNT	Good News Translation	//	parallel(s)

Old Testament

Gen.	Genesis	Eccles.	Ecclesiastes
Exod.	Exodus	Song	Song of Songs
Lev.	Leviticus	Isa.	Isaiah
Num.	Numbers	Jer.	Jeremiah
Deut.	Deuteronomy	Lam.	Lamentations
Josh.	Joshua	Ezek.	Ezekiel
Judg.	Judges	Dan.	Daniel
Ruth	Ruth	Hosea	Hosea
1 Sam.	1 Samuel	Joel	Joel
2 Sam.	2 Samuel	Amos	Amos
1 Kings	1 Kings	Obad.	Obadiah
2 Kings	2 Kings	Jon.	Jonah
1 Chron.	1 Chronicles	Mic.	Micah
2 Chron.	2 Chronicles	Nah.	Nahum
Ezra	Ezra	Hab.	Habakkuk
Neh.	Nehemiah	Zeph.	Zephaniah
Esther	Esther	Hag.	Haggai
Job	Job	Zech.	Zechariah
Ps(s).	Psalm(s)	Mal.	Malachi
Prov.	Proverbs		

New Testament

Matt.	Matthew	1 Tim.	1 Timothy
Mark	Mark	2 Tim.	2 Timothy
Luke	Luke	Titus	Titus
John	John	Philem.	Philemon
Acts	Acts	Heb.	Hebrews
Rom.	Romans	James	James
1 Cor.	1 Corinthians	1 Pet.	1 Peter
2 Cor.	2 Corinthians	2 Pet.	2 Peter
Gal.	Galatians	1 John	1 John
Eph.	Ephesians	2 John	2 John
Phil.	Philippians	3 John	3 John
Col.	Colossians	Jude	Jude
1 Thess.	1 Thessalonians	Rev.	Revelation
2 Thess.	2 Thessalonians		

Places to Begin

Why read the Bible? For some, this may seem like a very odd question. Practicing Jews and Christians regard the Bible as divine revelation, and so reading the Bible is a spiritual practice that fosters formation and provides guidance. Communities of faith read the Bible as part of their worship services, and the Bible usually provides the basis for sermons or homilies presented in these services. We suspect, however, that this textbook is being used primarily in an academic setting, which approaches the Bible with an additional set of questions and modes of inquiry. With good reason, many people believe we live in a post-Christian and postmodern world that is characterized by increasing secularization and pluralism. The Christian tradition and its Bible can no longer be assumed to have unquestioned authority in society. Even religiously affiliated colleges and universities are experiencing more diverse student populations that reflect society's pluralism. So why include the study of the Bible as part of an academic curriculum? Why study the Bible if you do not identify yourself as Jewish or Christian? And if you are Jewish or Christian, why study the Bible in an academic setting?

First, the Bible offers a window into the ancient world, both ancient Near Eastern and Greco-Roman civilizations. History and cultural studies are integral to a liberal arts education, and the Bible can contribute to these studies. The Bible is a historical source that reveals how successive empires of the ancient world—Assyrian, Babylonian, Persian, Seleucid, and Roman—influenced and shaped cultures and societies. The Bible also provides a unique cross-cultural study that illustrates ancient conceptions of war, social structures, religion, ritual, cosmology, and cultural dynamics (e.g., honor/shame). The Bible serves as a rich resource for a variety of academic interests.

Second, the Bible has significantly influenced Western civilization. The stories of the Bible have inspired centuries of literature, music, and art. Biblical precepts have guided ethics, legal theory, and political policies. European and American histories are intimately linked with the history of biblical interpretation. Now certainly the histories of Europe and America are histories of political, social, geographical, and economic factors as well, but often the events of these histories were interpreted and justified by an appeal to the Bible (e.g., divine right of kings, Protestant Reformation, divine destiny of American expansion, and slavery). To engage in a study and reading of the Bible is to encounter one of the most significant influences on Western culture.

Third, the Bible continues to be viewed as authoritative by a majority of the world's population. Despite our previous allusion to a post-Christian world, for many people the Bible still has an aura of solemnity, if not a sense of the sacred. Appeals to the Bible continue to be made in political and cultural debates, often from opposing perspectives. Popular news and information websites regularly assert what the Bible says about this or that issue. Books, movies, and television productions about the Bible consistently succeed in sales and viewer ratings. Why study the Bible? In part, to evaluate contemporary interpretations of the Bible that one may encounter in various ways: in church-related and religious literature, in sermons, in politics, through the media, and in informal conversations with family and friends.

Finally, the academic study of the Bible is not at odds with more devotional readings of the Bible that are practiced privately or communally. Giving attention to the Bible's historical and literary contexts contributes to the meaning of the text, though it certainly does not exhaust its meaning. For those who hold the Bible to be authoritative for their faith and practice, studying the Bible in an academic setting can illuminate and deepen their understanding of the Bible.

We intend for this textbook to give beginning students the tools and information to become better-informed readers of the Bible. We want the reader not only to know the contents of the Bible but also to gain a critical appreciation and respect for the historical distance between us as modern readers and the ancient contexts of the Bible. We want the reader to consider how these texts were heard or read by their ancient audiences by asking historical, literary, and theological questions of the texts. We hope this study of the Bible initiates a journey of both discovery and intellectual curiosity, and thus deepens engagement with the biblical text.

How Did We Get the Bible?

For centuries, perhaps even from its earliest origins, the Bible has circulated in multiple forms. Anyone who has attempted to purchase a Bible has likely been overwhelmed with choices. We can speak not only of diverse Bible translations but also of diverse forms of the Bible: Jewish Bibles, Roman Catholic Bibles, Protestant Bibles, and Eastern Orthodox Bibles (including the Greek Orthodox Bible and the Russian Orthodox Bible). Below, we will briefly narrate the history of the Bible in terms of **canon**, text, and translation in an effort to explain the factors that have led to this immense diversity.

Canons of the Bible

Building on the Latin term for "covenant" (*testamentum*), the Christian Bible divides between the Old and New Testaments. The Old Testament (a Christian title) contains the same texts as the Jewish Bible. The New Testament consists of writings from the earliest history of Christianity. Yet how did the Old Testament canon and the New Testament canon come into existence?

Definitions. We begin with terminology. The term *scripture* refers to those writings that function authoritatively for the faith and practice of a religious group. The word does not necessarily refer to a formal, fixed number of texts. The term *canon* comes from the Greek word *kanōn*, which originally referred to a reed or rod used for measuring or keeping straight. Eventually, *canon* began denoting what is "normative" or "standard" in a metaphorical sense. For our purposes, *canon* refers to the normative list of authoritative texts that function as scripture, and it reflects a religious community's attempt to discern and single out the writings that function authoritatively for their faith tradition. Notice, however, that by definition a canon not only identifies the authoritative texts but also excludes other religious texts from serving in an authoritative capacity. The following examples illustrate these concepts.

Second Kings 22 recounts a story about the renovation of the temple in Jerusalem in the seventh century BCE. During the repairs, the high priest discovers a lost text referred to as "the book of the law" (22:8). When the book is read to the king, he recognizes its authority and initiates a campaign of religious reforms based on the commands of the book. Most scholars believe the discovered book was an early version of the book of Deuteronomy. For the king and the high priest, this book became scripture, functioning authoritatively for the faith and practice of the Jerusalem temple and the **kingdom of Judah**. At that point, however, "the book of the law" functioned as a solitary text. No canon had yet been assembled—no Bible as we know it. And even when Deuteronomy became part of a larger authoritative corpus known as the Torah, the complete Jewish canon that we have today was still centuries away from being finalized.

The second example comes from the New Testament. The apostle Paul wrote letters to individual churches in the 50–60s CE. By the end of the first century, however, these letters began circulating as small collections of letters among many churches. These collections of letters became authoritative for matters of Christian faith and practice among those churches. As a result, early Christians deemed these Pauline letter collections to be scripture. For example, the writer of 2 Peter affords Paul's letters the same authority as the Jewish Scriptures early in the second century CE (2 Pet. 3:15–16). At a much later point, perhaps two centuries later, Christians began making official lists (or canons) of what became known as the New Testament as they dialogued among themselves regarding which books should be authoritative and which should not.

At this point, it is important to note the significance of collected writings in the process of canonization. Once a collection of writings began to function as scripture, the process toward a canon was well under way, because adding to or taking away from that collection involved a discernment of what constituted Scripture. As a matter of fact, the Jewish and Christian canons are actually a collection of collections.

Hebrew Bible and Old Testament. The Christian Old Testament is in essence identical to the **Hebrew Bible**, because Christianity began as a Jewish movement. The Jewish Scriptures were authoritative for the Christian movement from its very inception. Any discussion of the Old Testament canon is dependent on the development of the Hebrew canon.

The Hebrew Bible is arranged into three parts: the **Torah**, the **Prophets**, and the **Writings**. Accordingly, the Hebrew canon of Scripture is often referred to as the "Tanakh," which is an acronym based on the Hebrew titles for the three parts—*Torah*, *Nevi'im*, and *Ketuvim*. The order of these three parts also reflects the chronological development of the Hebrew canon. As a corpus, the Torah came into existence first, and by the end of the fifth century BCE its authority gained wide acceptance. (We will explain the Torah's compositional history in chapter 2.) The development of the Prophets is more vague, but by the second century BCE we see references to the Prophets as a collection along with the Torah: "the Torah and the Prophets." Most likely the emerging book of Psalms was first grouped with the Prophets. Eventually, though, the Psalms were clustered with the last category of the Hebrew canon to develop, the Writings. This final collection of sacred texts remained fluid in its content during the first centuries BCE and CE before being finalized in the second century CE.

The primary difference between the Hebrew Bible and the Christian Old Testament is the arrangement of the books, in particular the arrangement of the Prophets. Whereas all of the Prophets constitute the second division of the Hebrew Bible, the Christian canon separates the **Former Prophets** (Joshua–2 Kings) and the **Latter Prophets** (Isaiah–Malachi). It places the Latter Prophets at the conclusion of the Old Testament and groups the Former Prophets with other biblical books that resemble historical narratives, thereby creating a "Historical Books" category.

When talking about the Christian Old Testament, though, we need to distinguish between the Catholic Old Testament and the Protestant Old Testament. Even though the Catholic Old Testament shares the same arrangement as the Protestant Old Testament, it contains additional writings not found in the Protestant Old Testament and the Hebrew Bible. These differences derive from the **Septuagint**, the Greek translations of the Hebrew Scriptures. In the first half of the third century BCE, probably in Alexandria, Egypt, Greek-speaking Jews began translating the Hebrew Scriptures, particularly the **Pentateuch**, into Greek. By the end of the second century BCE, the Septuagint expanded to include the Prophets, most of the Writings, and some additional Jewish religious texts. It is important to remember that at this point in the development of the Hebrew canon there was no third part known as the Writings, and therefore no fixed distinction existed between the books that eventually composed the Writings and these "additional texts." These "additional texts" are included in the Catholic Old Testament but not in the Hebrew Bible (which took its final form in the second century CE). We should also note that the Greek Orthodox and Russian Orthodox canons also include the additional writings found in the Catholic Old Testament as well as a few extra texts (1 Esdras, Prayer of Manasseh, Psalm 151, and 3 Maccabees; plus 2 Esdras in the Russian canon). All of these extra texts also originated from the Septuagint.

The Septuagint served as the primary form of Scriptures for many Jewish communities both inside and outside **Palestine** in the first centuries BCE and CE. The Septuagint—with its "additional" writings—also became the most common version of the Jewish Scriptures used by early Christians. The Catholic Old Testament simply follows early Christian traditions in having the Septuagint as its Old Testament canon, both in its arrangement and its content. The Protestant Reformers (sixteenth century CE), however, decided that the Old Testament should correspond to the content of the Hebrew Bible, which in its final form excluded the additional Septuagint writings. So the Protestant tradition separated the additional writings from the traditional Christian Old Testament, put them in an appendix, and called them the **Apocrypha**. The Catholic tradition refers to these writings as deuterocanonical ("second canon"), indicating their continued authoritative status. Thus, the Christian Old Testament—both Catholic and Protestant versions—followed

CANONS OF THE HEBREW BIBLE AND OLD TESTAMENT

The Hebrew Bible (Tanakh)	Protestant Old Testament	Catholic Old Testament
Law (*Torah*)	**Pentateuch**	**Pentateuch**
Genesis	Genesis	Genesis
Exodus	Exodus	Exodus
Leviticus	Leviticus	Leviticus
Numbers	Numbers	Numbers
Deuteronomy	Deuteronomy	Deuteronomy
Prophets (*Nevi'im*)	**Historical Books**	**Historical Books**
Former Prophets	Joshua	Joshua
Joshua	Judges	Judges
Judges	Ruth	Ruth
1–2 Samuel	1–2 Samuel	1–2 Samuel
1–2 Kings	1–2 Kings	1–2 Kings
Latter Prophets	1–2 Chronicles	1–2 Chronicles
Isaiah	Ezra	Ezra
Jeremiah	Nehemiah	Nehemiah
Ezekiel	Esther	*Tobit*
The Twelve	**Poetry & Wisdom Books**	*Judith*
Hosea	Job	Esther (*with additions*)
Joel	Psalms	*1–2 Maccabees*
Amos	Proverbs	**Poetry & Wisdom Books**
Obadiah	Ecclesiastes	Job
Jonah	Song of Songs	Psalms
Micah	**Prophetic Books**	Proverbs
Nahum	Isaiah	Ecclesiastes
Habakkuk	Jeremiah	Song of Songs
Zephaniah	Lamentations	*Wisdom of Solomon*
Haggai	Ezekiel	*Ecclesiasticus*
Zechariah	Daniel	**Prophetic Books**
Malachi	Hosea	Isaiah
Writings (*Ketuvim*)	Joel	Jeremiah
Psalms	Amos	Lamentations
Proverbs	Obadiah	*Baruch*
Job	Jonah	Ezekiel
Song of Songs	Micah	Daniel (*with three additions: the Prayer*
Ruth	Nahum	*of Azariah and the Song of the Three*
Lamentations	Habakkuk	*Young Men, Susanna, and Bel and the*
Ecclesiastes	Zephaniah	*Dragon*)
Esther	Haggai	Hosea
Daniel	Zechariah	Joel
Ezra	Malachi	Amos
Nehemiah		Obadiah
1–2 Chronicles		Jonah
		Micah
		Nahum
		Habakkuk
		Zephaniah
		Haggai
		Zechariah
		Malachi

Note: The Hebrew Bible and Protestant Old Testament are identical in content but differ in arrangement. Italics indicate additional writings included in the Catholic Old Testament.

the arrangement of biblical books found in the Septuagint; but whereas the Catholic Old Testament included the additional writings found in the Septuagint, the Protestant Old Testament excluded these writings, instead opting to match the content of the Hebrew Bible.

New Testament canon. Most of the writings of the New Testament originated in the first century CE, and a few originated in the early second century, but the canon of the New Testament may not have been finalized until the fifth or sixth century. Instead, small clusters or collections of New Testament texts provided the developmental bridge from individual scriptural writings to an official New Testament canon. In other words, in different times and places Christians began assembling their writings into collections. Paul's letters came first. As noted earlier, by the beginning of the second century Paul's letters were being circulated and used in a collected form as Scripture. Our earliest evidence of this collection was a ten-letter collection that included 1–2 Corinthians, Romans, Ephesians, 1–2 Thessalonians, Galatians, Philippians, Colossians, and Philemon. Eventually in the second century, the Pauline collection grew to a thirteen- or fourteen-letter collection to include 1–2 Timothy and Titus, along with Hebrews for those who thought Paul wrote Hebrews.

Next, the four-**Gospel** collection provided another building block for what eventually became the New Testament canon. The four-Gospel collection included Matthew, Mark, Luke, and John. This collection came into existence no later than the latter half of the second century and quickly gained wide acceptance as authoritative.

The third collection became known as the "Catholic Letters." It included James, 1–2 Peter, 1–3 John, and Jude. The term *catholic* is a transliteration of the Greek word *katholikos*, which simply means "universal" or "general." The earliest reference to the catholic collection comes from a Christian writer named Eusebius in the early fourth century CE. Only 1 Peter and James were known widely before the formation of this collection.

The earliest canon lists most likely emerged in the third century CE. These canon lists derive from different regions and represent various attempts to identify which Christian writings were authoritative. Though the differences are certainly of interest, the consistencies are especially telling. The four-Gospel collection and the Pauline Letters (with or without Hebrews) consistently formed a kind of core canon. Acts, 1 Peter, and 1 John frequently appeared on canon lists as well. Revelation was favored in Western Christianity but was more controversial in the East. More variety of opinion existed with James, Jude, 2 Peter, 2–3 John, Epistle of Barnabas, Apocalypse of Peter, and Shepherd of Hermas. The latter three writings were eventually excluded from the increasingly stable New Testament canon. Jude, 2 Peter, and 2–3 John were likely adopted in part because of their inclusion in a collection with 1 John and 1 Peter.

Early Christians relied on various criteria while attempting to discern the parameters of the New Testament canon. They highly valued texts with apostolic connections—meaning either written by an **apostle** (one closely associated with Jesus), written in the time of the apostles, or simply in agreement with apostolic teaching. Early Christians also placed great value on writings that were universally relevant and adaptable to all Christian churches in all places and in all times. Finally, writings that had early and widespread

SAMPLING OF NT CANON LISTS

Muratorian Canon (3rd/4th c.)	Claromontanus Catalog (4th c.)	Athanasius, bishop of Alexandria (367)[a]
[Matthew][b]	**Four Gospels**	**Four Gospels**
[Mark]	Matthew	Matthew
Luke	John	Mark
John	Mark	Luke
Acts of the Apostles	Luke	John
Pauline Letters	**Pauline Letters**	Acts of the Apostles
1–2 Corinthians	Romans	**Catholic Letters**
Ephesians	1–2 Corinthians	James
Philippians	Galatians	1–2 Peter
Colossians	Ephesians	1–3 John
Galatians	(Philippians and 1–2 Thessalonians	Jude
1–2 Thessalonians	were accidentally omitted, and	**Pauline Letters**
Romans	probably Hebrews as well)	Romans
Philemon	1–2 Timothy	1–2 Corinthians
Titus	Titus	Galatians
1–2 Timothy	Colossians	Ephesians
Jude	Philemon	Philippians
1–2 John	1–2 Peter	Colossians
Wisdom of Solomon	James	1–2 Thessalonians
Revelation	1–3 John	Hebrews
Apocalypse of Peter	Jude	1–2 Timothy
	Epistle of Barnabas	Titus
	Revelation	Philemon
	Acts of the Apostles	Revelation
	Shepherd of Hermas	
	Acts of Paul	
	Apocalypse of Peter	

Note: Writings in italics were eventually excluded from the New Testament canon.

[a] The canon of Athanasius is the earliest known canon list that corresponds to the New Testament canon as we have it today, though the arrangement is different.

[b] The brackets indicate the manuscript is fragmented, but the missing section most certainly included Matthew and Mark.

use and had consistently proved to be beneficial either in communal worship settings or in matters of faith and practice were perceived to have an intrinsic authority. Not all the writings of the New Testament have all these qualities, but in general Christians affirmed the authority of the New Testament because of its **apostolicity**, universality, and traditional use.

Textual Traditions of the Bible

Modern Bibles are based on the study and comparison of thousands of ancient **manuscripts**. The original texts of the Bible—referred to as "**autographs**"—have long since disappeared. The manuscripts that are in existence are copies of copies of copies exponentially. Prior to the invention of the printing press in the fifteenth century, scribes copied and produced these manuscripts by hand (the term *manuscript* literally means handwritten). Given the human element of this process, it should come as no surprise that these manuscripts differ from one another; in fact, no two manuscripts agree exactly. The majority of the variations involve minor differences in spelling or grammar, but some discrepancies represent significant differences. So the situation needs repeating: there are no original manuscripts; instead we have thousands of copies of copies that differ from one another.

Textual criticism. When scholars study the manuscript traditions of the Bible, they engage in a discipline called *textual criticism*. The traditional purpose of textual criticism is to reconstruct the earliest form of the text—ideally the original form—by analyzing and comparing diverse manuscripts. The methods of this textual analysis can be quite technical and detailed. A basic overview of textual criticism follows.

Discrepancies among manuscripts are called *variant readings*. Differences among copies of the same literary work came about because of both unintentional errors on the part of scribes while copying (e.g., accidental omissions or repetitions) and intentional changes created by scribes (e.g., harmonizing divergent elements or clarifying ambiguous aspects).

When faced with variant readings among manuscripts of a given book of the Bible, scholars consider both external evidence and internal evidence to discern which of the variant readings best represents the earliest form of the text. External evidence pertains to the historical traits of the manuscripts themselves. For example, what is the date of the manuscript? Earlier manuscripts are usually given preference. Does the manuscript exhibit a particular text type? Manuscripts that share common textual and scribal characteristics are identified as text types. Text types, in turn, can be dated and analyzed for distinguishing textual and theological characteristics. Can any scribal tendencies be identified within the manuscript? Sometimes variant readings resulted from a scribe's idiosyncrasies or theological preferences.

In terms of internal evidence, scholars have developed some general principles or guidelines to assist them in discerning the earliest reading. First, scholars tend to identify the shortest reading as the earliest version of the text, because scribes had a tendency to conflate the different readings into one harmonized passage, which usually results in a longer reading. Second, the more difficult reading is most likely the earliest version, because scribes frequently smoothed out problematic readings—both grammatical and theological difficulties. Finally, the reading that best explains how the other variant readings originated is to be preferred. This principle is like "checking your work" in mathematics. After identifying the earliest form of the text, scholars must explain how the other variations of the text entered the manuscript tradition. If an explanation is lacking, then perhaps the decision should be reconsidered.

Knowledge of these scribal practices allows scholars to resolve most variant readings and to establish the earliest form of the text with a high degree of certainty. Based on the manuscript evidence available today, we affirm that modern translations represent a close approximation to the earliest forms of the biblical text, especially now that most modern translations provide notes when significant variant readings are present. These notes represent transparency in the work of text-critical scholars and translators, and they provide readers with more information about the textual traditions of the Bible (see the text box "Notations about Variant Readings" on p. 11).

Old Testament textual criticism. The practices of textual criticism for the Old Testament and for the New Testament differ in their basic approach. Textual criticism for the Old Testament begins with a "base text" to which all other manuscripts are compared. This base text is called the **Masoretic Text** (MT). The Masoretic Text is named for generations of scribes—known as Masoretes—who worked between 500 and 1000 CE to standardize and preserve the Hebrew text. The text type of the Masoretic Text, however, can be traced back to the third century BCE. The primary representatives of the Masoretic Text are the manuscripts **Codex** Leningradensis (1008 CE) and the Aleppo Codex (930 CE). These manuscripts were the oldest Hebrew manuscripts available until the discovery of the **Dead Sea Scrolls** in the mid-twentieth century. The Dead Sea Scrolls include Hebrew biblical manuscripts dating from the mid-third century BCE to the first century CE, which now represent the oldest known Hebrew manuscripts of the Hebrew Bible / Old Testament. These Dead Sea Scrolls manuscripts represent a variety of text types: some reflect a precursor of the Masoretic Text; some reflect similarities to the **Samaritan** (Hebrew) Pentateuch; and some reflect a text type found in the Greek translations (Septuagint). So the Masoretic Text serves as a base text

NOTATIONS ABOUT VARIANT READINGS

Modern translations of the Bible provide notes on significant textual variants. To become an informed reader of the Bible, it is necessary to know how to read these notes. The following examples come from the New Revised Standard Version of the Bible.

Old Testament Example: Genesis 36:2

> Esau took his wives from the Canaanites: Adah daughter of Elon the Hittite, Oholibamah daughter of Anah son[d] of Zibeon the Hivite.
>
> [d] Sam Gk Syr: Heb *daughter*

The superscript *d* after the word *son* points to a corresponding note. The note indicates that the word *son* is found in three manuscript traditions: Sam (= Samaritan Pentateuch [Hebrew]), Gk (= ancient Greek translation of the OT, Septuagint), and Syr (= ancient Syriac translation of the OT, Peshitta). Heb (= Hebrew, the Masoretic Text), however, reads "daughter." (The abbreviations for these notes are found in the front of Bibles under "Abbreviations.") So the translators of the NRSV simply indicate that at Genesis 36:2 they chose to print the word *son*, which is found in other manuscript traditions, rather than the Hebrew (MT) manuscript tradition of *daughter*. The reading "daughter" most likely came about by a scribe's unintentional error of repetition: accidentally repeating the term *daughter* from the series of previous daughters ("Adah *daughter* of Elon the Hittite, Oholibamah *daughter* of Anah . . .").

New Testament Example: Ephesians 3:14–15

> For this reason I bow my knees before the Father,[a] from whom every family in heaven and on earth takes its name.
>
> [a] Other ancient authorities add *of our Lord Jesus Christ*

The superscript a after the word *Father* points to a corresponding note. The note indicates that some ancient Greek manuscripts ("authorities") add the phrase "of our Lord Jesus Christ" after the word *Father* whereas others do not. Based on text-critical methods, the translators of the NRSV decided that the shorter reading best represents the earliest or original text of Ephesians. The longer reading probably originated from a scribe's attempt to harmonize 3:14 with 1:3 and other places (1:2, 17; 5:20), where God "the Father" is usually connected with "Lord Jesus Christ."

with which scholars compare other Hebrew manuscripts and ancient translations. The other Hebrew manuscripts include primarily the texts of the Dead Sea Scrolls and the Samaritan Pentateuch. The ancient translations include the ancient Greek translations (Septuagint), the ancient Syriac translation (Peshitta), and the ancient Latin translation (Vulgate). Where there is a variance between the Masoretic Text and any of these other manuscript traditions, scholars weigh external and internal evidence to decide which reading best represents the earliest form of the text. All this information—the Masoretic Text with comparisons—is made available for scholars and translators in a printed critical edition called the *Biblia Hebraica Stuttgartensia*.

New Testament textual criticism. The textual tradition of the New Testament consists of more than five thousand Greek manuscripts in addition to quotations from early Christian writers and ancient translations of the New Testament (Syriac, Coptic, Latin, Armenian, and Georgian). Traditionally, in order to make this quantity of manuscripts more manageable, scholars grouped New Testament manuscripts according to text types. The idea was that when a variant reading appears in more than one text type, there is a higher probability that it represents the earliest reading. More recently, textual scholars have used computer-generated models that take into account all the manuscript evidence (eliminating the need for identifying text types), resulting in a more detailed representation of the relationship and history of the New Testament texts and their variant readings.

New Testament textual critics rely most heavily on two kinds of Greek manuscripts. First, there are the fourth- and fifth-century codices (plural of *codex*, which is an ancient book form). These important manuscripts are the earliest mostly complete copies of the New Testament and include the following:

- Codex Sinaiticus (fourth c.)—all of the New Testament; also contains the Greek OT
- Codex Vaticanus (fourth c.)—most of the New Testament, missing the latter half of Hebrews and the books of 1–2 Timothy, Titus, Philemon, and Revelation; also contains the Greek OT
- Codex Bezae (fifth c.)—most of the Gospels and Acts with a small Latin fragment of 3 John
- Codex Alexandrinus (fifth c.)—all of the New Testament, missing most of Matthew as well as portions of John and 2 Corinthians; also contains the Greek OT

Second, the **papyri** are the earliest manuscripts of the New Testament and date back to the second and third centuries. Only coming to light in the last hundred years, they reveal a notable fluidity of the New Testament text in the earliest centuries. These manuscripts, written on paper-like material made from papyrus plants, are very important witnesses to the earliest forms of the New Testament, but they are now fragmentary and incomplete because of natural decomposition. For an extreme example, Papyrus 101 (third century CE) is a scrap containing only Matthew 3:10–12 on one side and 3:16–4:3 on the reverse side. Similarly, the oldest manuscript of the New Testament is Papyrus 52 (mid-second century CE), but it measures only two and a half by three and a half inches and preserves portions of John 18:31–33, 37–38. The most significant papyri include the following ($\mathfrak{P}$ = papyrus):

- $\mathfrak{P}$45 (third c.)—Gospels and Acts; only two fragmentary pages for each of Matthew and John survive; only six pages of Mark, seven of Luke, and thirteen of Acts
- $\mathfrak{P}$46 (ca. 200)—Pauline Letters and Hebrews, though 1–2 Timothy and Titus were never included; portions of Romans and 1 Thessalonians are missing, and all of 2 Thessalonians is missing
- $\mathfrak{P}$47 (third c.)—Revelation; only 9:10–17:2 survives
- $\mathfrak{P}$66 (ca. 200)—Gospel of John; portions are missing; chapters 14–21 are quite fragmentary
- $\mathfrak{P}$72 (third c.)—Jude and 1–2 Peter (along with other, noncanonical texts)
- $\mathfrak{P}$75 (early third c.)—Luke and John; portions are missing from both Gospels, including the last seven chapters of John

New Testament textual criticism does not use a base text like Old Testament textual criticism but collates and compares all the manuscripts. Where variant readings occur in this comparison, each variant is considered individually based on both external and

Figure 1.1. **New Testament papyrus, a page from $\mathfrak{P}$46**

internal evidence. The result of this "eclectic" approach is a reconstructed text that is not actually represented by any single extant manuscript. This reconstructed text with the manuscript evidence is made available for scholars and translators in the printed critical edition of the Nestle-Aland *Novum Testamentum Graece*, 28th revised edition, and the United Bible Society's *The Greek New Testament*, 5th edition.

Translations of the Bible

The original language of the Old Testament was Hebrew (with some portions in Aramaic), and the original language of the New Testament was Greek. We have already mentioned several ancient translations of the Hebrew Bible / Old Testament and the New Testament. In the late fourth century, the Christian theologian Jerome began translating the Old Testament and New Testament into Latin. The resulting translation became known as the Latin **Vulgate,** which served as the Bible for Western Christianity for nearly a thousand years. The term *vulgate* means "common," and so the title Latin Vulgate refers to the common version of the Latin Bible that came to be used in the Western church. At the Council of Trent (1545–63), the Roman Catholic Church designated the Latin Vulgate as its official canon of the Bible.

With the invention of the printing press (fifteenth century) and the Protestant Reformation (sixteenth century), the history of Bible translations changed significantly and flourished. The Protestant Reformers believed the Bible should be in the language of the people. Thus **Martin Luther** translated the Bible into German, publishing the New Testament in 1522 and the entire Bible in 1534. Because of the printing press, Luther's German Bible was widely disseminated and became greatly influential in German literature and theology.

In the same way, the English Bible originated out of a spirit of reform and benefited from the printing press. **John Wycliffe**, with the help of some associates, translated the Latin Vulgate into English and produced the first English translation of the Bible in manuscript form (1384). Using a printing press, **William Tyndale** produced the first *printed* English Bible, known as the Tyndale Bible, when he published the New Testament in 1526 and the Pentateuch in 1530. Tyndale never finished his translation of the Bible, because he was burned at the stake for his translating activities. Notably, Tyndale translated from Greek and Hebrew rather than Latin, and his New Testament translation became the basis for a number of subsequent English Bibles. The King James Bible, however, became the most enduring and influential of all English translations. It was also known as the **Authorized Version**. Produced by a committee of translators from Oxford, Cambridge, and Westminster, the **King James**

Version was translated from Hebrew and Greek and first appeared in 1611. It exerted tremendous influence on both British and American cultures, shaping language, literature, and Protestant theology. Yet after almost three centuries, the King James Version was in need of revision. The discovery of earlier and better Greek manuscripts meant that the New Testament of the King James Version was based on what are now known to be inferior manuscripts. Moreover, advances in Hebrew philology clarified meanings in the Hebrew text about which the King James translators were forced to guess. And finally, the Shakespeare-like English of the King James Version was becoming archaic. Multiple revisions appeared both in England and America. The New Revised Standard Version (1989) and the English Standard Version (2001) are two recent translations that trace their revision history back to the King James Version. Unlike the singular prominence that their predecessor once held, however, the New Revised Standard Version and the English Standard Version are simply two translations among a multiplicity of modern translations.

The most reliable modern translations of the Bible are produced by translation committees, which provide proper vetting of the translations and guard against an independent translator's idiosyncrasies. At the beginning of the translation process, translation committees decide which translation principle will guide their work: **formal correspondence** or **dynamic equivalence**. Formal correspondence takes a more literal approach to translation—a "word for word" translation. This approach to translation seeks to stay as close as possible to the *form* of the original language both in its grammar and word order. So if the source language contains a noun, it will be translated as a noun in the target language; a prepositional phrase, as a prepositional phrase; an infinitive, as an infinitive; and so on. Also, biblical idioms are usually translated literally. On the other hand, dynamic equivalence focuses on the *function* of the original language and attempts to "re-create" that reading experience in the target language. Usually described as a "meaning for meaning" translation, dynamic equivalence is concerned with faithfully expressing the message of the original language in the words and structure of the target language. Instead of alternative options, these translation principles often serve as poles of a spectrum. So, for example, the committee that translated the New Revised Standard Version adopted the maxim "As literal as possible, as free as necessary," which intends to be primarily a formal correspondence translation but with some openness in making the translation understandable in modern English.

Modern translations are not produced in a vacuum with only these principles at work. Translations are often guided by other considerations as well, like theology, literacy, and the evolution of the English language. Protestant evangelicals published the very popular New International Version (NIV) in the 1970s as an alternative to the Revised Standard Version (1952), which was perceived as theologically liberal. Translation committees also take into account the reading level of the general public, which can considerably affect a translation's final form. In the case of the United States, the general public on average reads at a fifth- to seventh-grade level. Finally, gender-inclusive

FORMAL CORRESPONDENCE AND DYNAMIC EQUIVALENCE

The following examples of translations begin with formal correspondence and move along a spectrum toward dynamic equivalence. The first example is called an interlinear translation, in which English words are given underneath the Greek words. The progression from formal correspondence to dynamic equivalence can be seen in the more stilted "And Jesus said unto them" (KJV) to simply "Jesus answered" (NIV) or "Jesus replied" (NLT). Also, notice how the idiom "children of the bridechamber" (KJV) is rendered more comprehensively with "guests of the bridegroom" (NIV) or "wedding guests" (NRSV, NLT). And finally, notice the inclusion of the terms "celebrating" (NLT) and "wedding party" (GNT), which are attempts to convey the meaning or sense of the text even if the literal, corresponding words are absent. *Mark 2:19a*

καὶ	εἶπεν	αὐτοῖς	ὁ	Ἰησοῦς·	μὴ	δύνανται	οἱ	υἱοὶ	τοῦ
and	said	to-them	the	Jesus	not	are-able	the	sons	of-the

νυμφῶνος	ἐν	ᾧ	ὁ	νυμφίος	μετ'	αὐτῶν	ἐστιν	νηστεύειν
bridechamber	in	which	the	groom	with	them	is	to-fast?

King James Version (KJV)—"And Jesus said unto them, Can the children of the bride-chamber fast, while the bridegroom is with them?"

New American Standard Bible (NASB)—"And Jesus said to them, 'While the bridegroom is with them, the attendants of the bridegroom cannot fast, can they?'"

New Revised Standard Bible (NRSV)—"Jesus said to them, 'The wedding guests cannot fast while the bridegroom is with them, can they?'"

New International Version (NIV)—"Jesus answered, 'How can the guests of the bridegroom fast while he is with them?'"

New Living Translation (NLT)—"Jesus replied, 'Do wedding guests fast while celebrating with the groom? Of course not.'"

Good News Translation (GNT)—"Jesus answered, 'Do you expect the guests at a wedding party to go without food? Or course not!'"

language has also become an issue for Bible translations. Though some criticize the use of inclusive language as succumbing to political correctness, others advocate that gender-inclusive language provides a more accurate translation while also recognizing the evolution of the English language. For example, based on substantial research on the current state of the English language, translators of the 2011 updated edition of the New International Version (NIV) decided to use gender-inclusive language. Translators of the New Revised Standard Version (NRSV) employed gender-inclusive language, but they also sought to preserve the historical, patriarchal situation often embedded in the texts. The NRSV translators often found these dual goals in tension with one another. Ultimately, all translations are an act of interpretation. Therefore, a good method of Bible study includes a comparison of several modern translations.

How Shall We Read the Bible?

The Bible is likely the most read of all sacred books. One of the important tasks for students is to think about how to become better, more informed readers of this text; only then will readers perceive its greatest impact. What are the tools that can help students delve even more deeply into the Bible? One approach to this task begins by acknowledging gratefully that faithful readers have interpreted the Bible for centuries. That history of interpretation is a remarkable gift, and we can learn much from it. The earliest interpreters of the Bible were those scribes who shaped the canon of Scripture. Job 7 and Hebrews 2, for example, both allude to Psalm 8 and read the psalm from a particular perspective as part of their proclamation. The writers of the New Testament often interpret the Old Testament from the perspective of their Christian faith. Matthew and Mark, for example, use Psalm 22 as a text to narrate the suffering of Jesus in the crucifixion with the question "My God, my God, why have you forsaken me?" The tradition of interpreting the Scriptures has continued throughout the history of Judaism, Christianity, and Islam.

Early Christian Interpretation

In the early history of the Christian church and in the medieval era, those who wrote about the Bible spent a great deal of time working on the language of the Bible and finding ways to communicate the message of the Bible to their communities. Some of these interpreters understood the text to have hidden meanings and thus great symbolic value for readers. That approach we label *allegory*. For example, the character of Aslan functions as an allegory for Jesus Christ in C. S. Lewis's book *The Lion, the Witch and the Wardrobe* and in the larger series the Chronicles of Narnia. Another example that is more historical is that of Jonah and the great fish. Many medieval interpreters read this narrative as an allegory of Jesus's death, burial, and resurrection. Others took a more literal approach to the biblical text, and that approach, focusing on the more plain sense of the text, continues to influence readers today.

Post-Reformation Interpretation

With the coming of the Renaissance and the Protestant Reformation, readers of the Bible in the Western world began to pay special attention to the cultures of the ancient world. With the rise of the Enlightenment, interpreters began to apply methods of historical analysis to the Bible, as they had to other texts. These interpreters saw history and culture as the key elements of interpretation, and so the emphasis was on how the Bible originated. Two questions were at the heart of the interpretive task: What *did* the Bible mean, and what *does* the Bible mean? This process of interpretation has come to be known as **hermeneutics** (the art of interpretation), and these questions suggest a hermeneutic focusing on historical matters related to the origin of the text. So interpreters began with the issue of the historical meaning of the text and, based on that, asked about the significance of the text for contemporary readers. Scholars have developed a number of tools or methods of interpretation to seek this historical meaning. A number of these methods use the term *criticism* in their title. For many readers that term carries a negative connotation, but in the context of biblical scholarship, the term is borrowed from the wider world of literary studies and means the serious, analytical study of a text.

New Trends in Interpretation

In recent decades, many interpreters have suggested that scholars have given too much attention to questions of the origin of the text and should balance those concerns with attention to literary qualities in the text itself. Reading the text closely with attention to matters of plot and portrayal of characters or with careful attention to the poetic imagery or the repetition of terms or synonyms can be helpful in crafting an account of a biblical text. These interpretations focus on how the text itself communicates via language. Other recent interpreters have focused on how ancient and contemporary readers might receive the biblical text. How would readers in the Greco-Roman world respond to literary patterns in the Gospels or to particular topics in the Pauline Epistles? What do contemporary readers bring with them when they read the book of Job and its dialogue between approaches to wisdom? How does the scientific mindset of today's readers influence the reading of ancient texts from a very different culture?

In summary, when we consider the question of how to read the Bible, many approaches have been used in the past, and we can learn from them. We might think of this history of hermeneutics in terms of the readings prior to the Enlightenment (premodern) and then readings focusing on history (modern) and then recent interpretations that begin with the text and pay attention to readers ancient and contemporary (postmodern). Today's biblical scholarship grew out of the concerns of modernity, and thus a great deal of scholarship focuses on the history and origins of texts. Recent attention to a literary and theological approach has provided some helpful ways forward.

The task of this volume is to help you journey toward becoming more informed readers of the Bible or practitioners of hermeneutics (the art of interpretation). The question is how careful and imaginative we will be in this practice. One way to proceed is to think of the questions we might ask when seeking to understand the Bible faithfully. Three categories come to the fore.

1. Questions of origin. The Bible originated in the **ancient Near East** and the ancient Mediterranean world. If we are to grasp the full sense of these texts, it will be enormously helpful to explore the cultural codes of the world in which the text originated (the world behind the text). **Archaeology** is one of the essential tools to help interpreters. It reveals the material culture and life of those whose experience the text portrays. Geography also comes into play. It had an impact on ancient Israel's move from groups with no central authority, such as the ones we see in the period of the **judges**, toward central monarchy in Jerusalem, and it also had an impact on the life of the early church. Awareness of cultural customs can be helpful to us as readers of these ancient texts. For example, Genesis 15 narrates Abram and **YHWH** (the divine name, often represented in Bible translations as "LORD"; see the text box "The Divine Name" on p. 52) taking part in a **covenant** ceremony with animals cut in two and "a smoking fire pot and a flaming torch." What can historical studies tell us about the significance of such a ceremony? A central act in Ruth 4 is the giving of a sandal. Why is that important to the story? Ancient hospitality is in the background of Acts 10. How can that custom inform our interpretation? In addition to questions about cultural codes, exploration of how biblical texts came to be is also important—questions of authorship and sources and redaction. Careful readers of the **book of Isaiah** will notice that beginning with chapter 40, the text relates to a different era

CRITICAL TOOLS

Source Criticism. The analysis of a biblical text to determine what sources (usually written) were used in its composition. Identifying a text's sources (along with their possible "authors" and dates) allows interpreters to reconstruct the text's compilation history and/or analyze the intent of the biblical author(s). For examples of source criticism, see "The Composition of the Pentateuch" on p. 45 and "The Literary Tradition of the Gospels" on p. 162.

Form Criticism. The analysis and classification of literary types according to their form—such as hymns, laments, sagas, parables, and miracle stories. These literary types are studied for their rhetorical functions within a text. Older form-critical approaches attempted to reconstruct the history of a literary form within various settings of Israel's institutions or the various activities of early Christianity. See "Form Criticism and the Psalms" on p. 114 for an example of this approach.

Tradition History. The study of the development and reconfiguration of key events, institutions, and ideas in the Old and New Testaments. For example, How has the tradition of the **exodus event** been reappropriated in Isaiah 40–55? or, How did the hope of a Davidic king develop in **postexilic** Judaism, and do the Gospels reflect this tradition or not?

Redaction Criticism. The analysis of how a text's sources have been adapted and edited, so that an author's literary and theological emphases can be detected. For example, a study of how the author of the Gospel of Luke edited his source (the Gospel of Mark) reveals an emphasis on prayer in Luke's portrayal of Jesus (cf. Luke 3:21 // Mark 1:9–10 and Luke 9:28–29 // Mark 9:2–3).

Narrative Criticism. An analysis that pays close attention to the way narrative features such as character and characterization, narration, plot development, point of view, and literary techniques (e.g., irony and hyperbole) shape meaning in the text.

in ancient Israel's history. How does that affect our reading? There are four Gospels in the New Testament. Careful readers will notice that each Gospel portrays the story of Jesus from its particular perspective. How can asking questions of the origin of the Gospels help us in understanding the distinctive characteristics of each Gospel?

2. Questions of literature. Faithful readers of texts pay attention to literary forms. Genesis 1, for example, has a distinctive literary structure (seven days of creation) that is important in the message it communicates. The hymns of praise in the book of Psalms take a typical form; awareness of the form will enliven the reading of those texts. The epistles in the New Testament interact

Rhetorical Criticism. An analysis of how a text persuades or affects its readers. Attention is given to rhetorical features such as structural patterns, repetition, wordplays, forms of argumentation, and type scenes.

Canonical Criticism. A variety of approaches that emphasize the final form of a biblical book and how that book has been received and interpreted as authoritative (or "canonical") by the believing community (Jewish or Christian). A text's historical process of canonization and its location in the canon are also contexts for interpretation. For Christian interpreters, a canonical approach may also include how the Old and New Testaments are read as a unified text.

Reader-Response Criticism. An approach that emphasizes the construction of meaning by the reader as opposed to the text itself or its historical circumstances. Attention is given to a reader's social location, gender, and ideology. For example, a peasant farmer in Colombia will read the parables of Jesus differently than a corporate accountant in the United States.

Feminist Criticism. An approach to the text that emphasizes the perspectives and experiences of women. Feminist readings detect forms of patriarchy in the text and in the history of interpretation, but they also highlight positive portrayals of the feminine in the text that have often been ignored or even deliberately suppressed in the history of interpretation.

Postcolonial Criticism. An approach that pays attention to issues of imperial power and domination both in the text and in the history of interpretation. The texts of the Old and New Testaments were compiled or produced in times and circumstances of imperial domination (Babylonian, Persian, Greek, or Roman). Postcolonial criticism looks at how these texts reflect the various ways a people negotiate the reality of their oppression and their religious identity, and even appropriate and mimic images and language of imperial power for their own message and theology. It also investigates how contemporary postcolonial populations interpret these texts differently from their colonial masters who used these texts to promote their domination.

with the standard form of ancient letters in crafting their message. Much of the primary history in the Old Testament and the Gospels in the New Testament take the form of narratives. Accounting for the plot of these stories and the portrayal of characters in the stories will provide much raw material for us as we seek to understand the significance of the stories. A large portion of the Old Testament is poetic in form, especially the Psalms, the **Wisdom literature**, and the Prophets. How does that poetry communicate its message? The use of repetition and of poetic imagery is important in these texts. Some interpreters would use the term *rhetoric* to describe these questions—how a text persuasively communicates its message.

3. Questions of reception. How would readers, ancient and contemporary, receive these texts? What was the cultural context in which ancient readers/hearers would have encountered these texts? What do readers today bring to the text? How does that have an impact on interpretation?

The task of this volume is to give us enough information and context to begin the process of forming us as careful and creative interpreters. The tools of interpretation begin with questions to ask as readers:

- *Historical questions* of cultural backgrounds and the origin of texts
- *Literary questions* of genre and use of language
- *Theological questions* of how the text speaks to the divine-human relationship and to the life of faith, ancient and contemporary

Reading the biblical text carefully with these questions in mind, reviewing a good study Bible and several translations, studying an introductory volume like this one, consulting Bible dictionaries and commentaries, and learning about how others have read the Bible—all these things and others can help us become better readers of the text. Along with the hermeneutical work we have been discussing, it is important for readers to think about biblical texts in light of the whole story the canon narrates. That overarching narrative provides a full context in which readers can consider the significance of texts.

SUGGESTED READING

Brown, William P. *A Handbook to Old Testament Exegesis*. Louisville: Westminster John Knox, 2017.

Hull, Robert F., Jr. *The Story of the New Testament Text: Movers, Materials, Motives, Methods, and Models*. Society of Biblical Literature Resources for Biblical Study 58. Atlanta: Society of Biblical Literature, 2010.

McDonald, Lee Martin. *The Biblical Canon: Its Origin, Transmission, and Authority*. Peabody, MA: Hendrickson, 2007.

Metzger, Bruce M. *The Bible in Translation: Ancient and English Versions*. Grand Rapids: Baker Academic, 2001.

Nida, Eugene A. "Theories of Translation." In *The Anchor Bible Dictionary*, edited by David Noel Freedman, 6:512–15. New York: Doubleday, 1992.

Tate, W. Randolph. *Biblical Interpretation: An Integrated Approach*. 3rd ed. Grand Rapids: Baker Academic, 2008.

PART ONE

THE OLD TESTAMENT

Pentateuch

Our look at the Old Testament will follow the three parts of the Hebrew canon: the Torah (Pentateuch), the Prophets, and the Writings, with some attention paid to the category of Historical Books. We begin with the Pentateuch and the book of Genesis, with its look at origins. The story continues with books that focus on the covenant relationship between ancient Israel and YHWH. It will be helpful first to put the story in the context of the ancient world.

The Old Testament World

Geography provides important contextual information for readers of the Old Testament or Hebrew Bible. The Old Testament world has been dubbed the **Fertile Crescent**, because of its crescent-like shape when viewed from afar. The area curves from the Persian Gulf westward toward Syria and down through Palestine into Egypt. The strip of land is arable because water is available to support life. We will consider each area of the region.

Mesopotamia

This area begins on the east at the Persian Gulf and moves north and west toward the Mediterranean Sea. Mountains border the area in the north. The name **Mesopotamia** means "in the midst of rivers" or "between rivers." The rivers that make the land arable and provide water to support civilization are the Tigris and Euphrates. Today this area is the swathe of land from Kuwait and southern Iraq up to northern Syria and southeastern Turkey. It is the land of the origins of the biblical Hebrews as the note of migration in Genesis 11:27–32 and the memory of origins in Joshua 24:2 indicate.

Prior to the biblical accounts of the ancestors in Genesis (Abraham and Sarah; Isaac and Rebekah; Jacob, Rachel, and Leah; and the Joseph generation), the empires of the Sumerians and Akkadians in the third millennium BCE built strong cultures in the region. The Sumerians invented the earliest known form of writing (cuneiform), and the Akkadians come into play in the biblical narrative by way of their descendants, the **Assyrians** and **Babylonians**. The Akkadians were Semites, the group of peoples to which the Hebrews belonged. In the second millennium BCE, Amorites or "westerners" migrated to the Fertile Crescent and established important kingdoms in Mesopotamia. The most famous of these kingdoms was Babylonia, whose most famous king was Hammurabi, known for his law codes. The Mesopotamian cultures have provided rich treasures of archaeological materials. In addition to law codes, there are important creation accounts such as the **Enuma Elish** and the **Epic of Gilgamesh**, which includes a flood story. Mesopotamia provides significant background to explore the cultural context from which the Old Testament or Hebrew Scriptures arose. While the area is beyond the Fertile Crescent, it is worth noting that Asia Minor and its Hittite Empire had some connections to the biblical story.

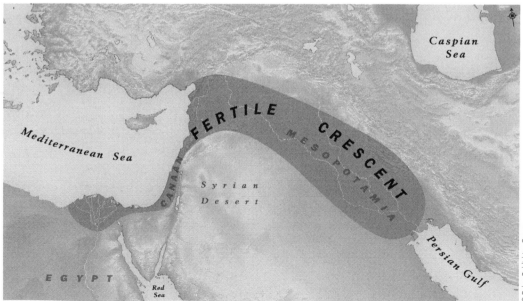

Figure 2.1. The Fertile Crescent

Syria-Palestine

Moving farther south along the coast of the Mediterranean Sea, we find a land bridge called Syria-Palestine or **Canaan**. To its east is desert, to its west the sea. Today this area consists of Syria, Lebanon, Israel, and Jordan. The Old Testament often speaks of Canaanites, and in the northern part of this area important Canaanite texts have been discovered at Ugarit, a cultural center of the second millennium BCE. In northern Syria in the third and second millennia BCE, an important empire flourished at Ebla, where archaeologists have excavated significant treasures. The ancient Israelites (or Hebrews) had frequent economic interactions with these Canaanite cultures set in an area with ports and with considerable natural resources.

Much of the Old Testament narrative takes place in Palestine, to the south of what is today Lebanon. Through this land runs the Jordan River, lifeblood to the peoples of the area, between the Sea of Galilee and the Dead Sea. Today this area is known as the "Holy Land" for the Abrahamic faiths (Judaism, Christianity, and Islam claim Abraham as an ancestor), but in the ancient world its primary value was strategic. Those who sought to trade between the major civilizations of Egypt and Mesopotamia had to travel by way of one of the highways through Palestine. The two major roads between Damascus (in Syria) and Egypt were the **Via Maris**, or Way of the Sea, which followed the coast, and the **King's Highway** along the **Transjordan Platcau** east of the Jordan River. These roads were valuable for military and trade purposes. The strategic location of Palestine explains why the empires of Egypt and Mesopotamia so often sought to control the area.

Egypt

To the south is the land of Egypt with the Nile River. The northern part of the land included fertile areas; here the Nile breaks up into many branches that reach the Mediterranean. Egypt was somewhat separated from the rest of the Fertile Crescent, and so, fed by the Nile, it developed powerful civilizations. Egypt at times sought to expand and control Palestine and in the second millennium BCE faced a number of conflicts and connections with Palestine and Mesopotamia. Thus, Egyptian background has an impact on our reading of the Old Testament in terms of historical connections with ancient Israel and literary connections that we will discover in the upcoming chapters. Significant archaeological discoveries from Egypt, such as the **Rosetta Stone** (see the text box "Significant Archaeological Finds" on p. 30), also provide helpful information for biblical interpretation.

Palestine

Coastal plain. We move now from the broad view of the Old Testament world to a slightly more detailed account of the world of Palestine, because most of the Old Testament narratives take place in this land. The land is slightly smaller than the state of New Jersey, approximately 150 miles long and 70 miles wide. Moving from west to east, the land reveals four major geographical areas. The **coastal plain** begins in the south with the broad Plain of Philistia, named after the seafarers who settled there. Gaza and Ashdod are familiar biblical names from this area (see, e.g., Josh. 10:41; Amos

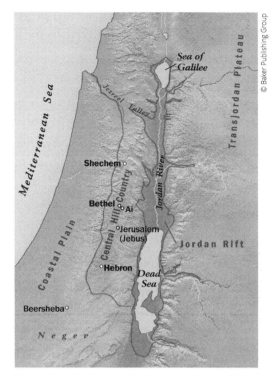

Figure 2.2. **The four regions of ancient Palestine**

1:6–8). The plain narrows as it moves north toward the Plain of Sharon and Mount Carmel.

Central hill country. The second major geographical division is the **central hill country**. In the north the Galilee hills give way to the Plain of Megiddo, which leads to the hills of what was later the Northern Kingdom. As one moves farther south, one encounters the Shephelah, or low-lying hills, and the plateau where Jerusalem is located, a position that holds many advantages for those defending it. Farther to the south is the Negev, which leads to the Sinai Desert.

Jordan Rift. The third division is the **Jordan Rift**. It begins near Mount Hermon in the north and provides the location for the Jordan River, which flows from the Sea of Galilee in the north to the Dead Sea in the south. The Jordan, the "down rusher," meanders and rushes from a high elevation to a low elevation at the Dead Sea. The Jordan is not as advantageous to agriculture as are the Mesopotamian rivers and the Nile. The Dead Sea is a saltwater lake well below sea level and thus befitting of its name. Beyond the Dead Sea, the rift is known as the Arabah.

Transjordan Plateau. The final division is the Transjordan Plateau. The area of Bashan, today's Golan Heights, in the north was known for its cattle

(Ezek. 39:18; Amos 4:1). Moving from north to south, the hills of Gilead give way to the broad plateau of Moab, where sheep grazed, leading to the more rugged territory of the Edomites to the south.

These geographical features have significance for our reading of the Scriptures. They are reflected in the texts. They also show that in ancient Israel hopes for unity and cooperation would not be easy with the diversity of geography and topography. Most of the Hebrew settlements were initially in the central hill country and so were not in lands friendly to agriculture. More broadly, information about the Old Testament world reveals some of the cultural context in which these texts originated. Ancient Near Eastern texts from other peoples in the region often help in the task of interpreting the texts from ancient Israel. The cultures of Mesopotamia and Egypt and of the Canaanites set the background for the Old Testament; for example, ancient Israel's paradigmatic story, the exodus, centers on time spent in Egypt. What historians and archaeologists can teach us about this world reveals the kind of life the Hebrews lived and can illuminate our understanding of Old Testament texts. Central to life in the ancient Near East was religion and its rituals. Most of the cultures were polytheistic (worshiping multiple deities), though there were some exceptions. In this context, the distinctiveness of the faith revealed in the Hebrew Scriptures is remarkable.

Archaeology

Our discussion of geography relates to the work of archaeologists. Archaeologists are those who study the material remains of ancient cultures such as pottery, animal bones, remains of buildings, or written texts.

The concern here is with archaeological work related to the ancient Near East and the ancient Mediterranean world. The purpose of this work is to help us understand such ancient cultures and peoples. Sites in the areas related to the biblical story are often tells, mounds built up over the centuries as communities were destroyed and new ones were built on the same site. The need for natural resources, especially water, limited the sites that were settled.

Archaeologists determine which sites might hold significant evidence, divide the area into squares, and begin carefully to excavate the site. The task is a painstaking one that requires much attention to detail. Those who do the digging look both for major finds such as city gates and for the homes of common people to see what can be learned of the community's organization and its way of life. They remove and sift earth, and scholars seek to interpret the findings. Contemporary archaeologists use a variety of basic tools, such as picks and brushes, and modern electronic tools, such as computers and radar that penetrates beneath the surface. Carbon-14 dating is important in this work, but pottery styles and writing styles are also important when archaeologists seek to date their finds. Archaeological evidence does not in itself solve questions for understanding biblical texts, but when interpreted carefully, archaeological remains can provide vital information to assist readers.

The goal of archaeologists is neither to prove nor to disprove anything about the Bible and historicity. It is rather to provide as much information as possible for reconstructing the lives of ancient peoples in the context from which the Bible originated. Archaeological finds often relate to ancient religious practices. All of this information can be most helpful in the interpretation of biblical texts. The social and historical contexts of ancient Israel and

SIGNIFICANT ARCHAEOLOGICAL FINDS

Our look at biblical texts will on occasion refer to textual finds of archaeologists. Here is a brief list of some of these important discoveries.

The Rosetta Stone. This inscription on black granite, discovered around 1800, made it possible to translate many previously undecipherable Egyptian inscriptions. The inscription is in three languages. The comparison of the Greek version to the two Egyptian languages of demotic and hieroglyphics unlocked the key to understanding these Egyptian texts.

The Gilgamesh Epic. An ancient Assyrian library in Nineveh, discovered in the middle of the nineteenth century, included a number of clay tablets. Among them was an epic poem about a hero, Gilgamesh. This ancient epic included a flood story and therefore provides important background to the Genesis story of Noah.

The Ugaritic Materials. Beginning in the late 1920s, archaeologists discovered clay tablets from the ancient city of Ugarit in Syria. These texts provide much information about Canaanite religion, often opposed by Hebrew prophets.

The Mari Tablets. These texts come from Mari, a capital city in northern Mesopotamia on the Euphrates River. The excavations began in the 1930s, and the texts reveal third- and second-millennium-BCE customs of people who were ancestors of the Hebrews.

The Dead Sea Scrolls. These texts were discovered in the mid-twentieth century in caves near the Dead Sea. A treasure of biblical and nonbiblical manuscripts is among the scrolls. This find is the most famous of all archaeological discoveries related to the Bible. It provides much background information to the New Testament and provides many texts to help in the task of textual criticism in Old Testament studies.

the early church are important to informed readers of biblical texts. To these texts we now turn.

Primeval History

Having considered the introductory materials, we are now prepared to begin reading the Old Testament. The first division of the Hebrew canon is the Pentateuch, the first five books of the Old Testament. We will consider these books in four sections: the **primeval history**, the ancestral stories, the exodus and covenant, and the sojourn in the wilderness. The first two sections relate to the book of Genesis, appropriately labeled as a book about various kinds of "origins." The primeval history, or the history of the first age, makes up Genesis 1–11; the **ancestral narratives** about Abraham and Sarah and their descendants come in Genesis 12–50. Not surprisingly, the primeval history begins at the beginning, with creation portrayed in texts that are both familiar and challenging.

In the Beginning

One of the important strategies for readers is to see the overall literary structure of texts. A first read of the beginning chapters of Genesis reveals that the book begins with a creation account organized around seven days. That literary structure continues through Genesis 2:3. There is a clear pattern to the seven days, and it will be helpful to read the text along with the table titled "The Literary Structure of Genesis 1." An introduction announcing the creation in Genesis 1:1–2 and a conclusion of the process with the seventh day in Genesis 2:1–3 frame the creation account. The introduction sets up the body of the account by portraying the creation as unformed (Hebrew *tohu*) and unfilled (*bohu*). The accounts of days one through three, the left-hand column of the table, deal with the *unformed* character of creation, and the accounts of days four through six, the right-hand column of the table, deal with the *unfilled* character of creation. In days one through three the creation is by division and takes place effortlessly with a divine command. First is the division of light and darkness, then of the sky with its waters above (rain) and surface waters, and then the division between water and dry land. Each section contains common elements and concludes with a summary statement. The left-hand column concludes with the "forming" of creation with two divine commands in day three and the appearance of vegetation. God pronounces the parts of creation to be "good" (*tov*), conforming to the divine intention.

The accounts of days four through six deal with the matter of "filling" the creation with the sun, moon, and stars and then with fish and birds. This right-hand column of the table reaches its conclusion in the sixth day with three divine commands: the creation of earth creatures and humans and the provision of food. At the end of this section, God pronounces these parts of creation as *very* good. The structural goal of the chapter comes in verse 27 with the thrice-emphasized creation of woman and man in the image of God. Humans are clearly not divine, but they are able to relate to God and represent God in caring for the creation (v. 28), just as images or statues in the ancient Near East were understood to represent rulers in looking over kingdoms.

Perceptive readers may have noticed another dimension of our table on the structure of Genesis 1. The table also runs from left to right. That is, the parts of creation formed in day one are filled in day four: the heavens are

THE LITERARY STRUCTURE OF GENESIS 1

Tohu (Unformed)	*Bohu* (Unfilled)

Day One (1:3–5)
Divine Command (1:3–5a)
  Appearance of Light (1:3)
  Division of Light from Darkness (1:4)
  Naming of Night and Day (1:5a)
Summary Phrase (1:5b)
	Day Four (1:14–19)
	Divine Command (1:14–18)
	  The Command (1:14–15)
	    Command That Lights Appear (1:14a)
	    Their Purposes Stated (1:14b–15)
	  Its Execution (1:16–18)
	    Making the Lights (1:16)
	    Their Purposes Fulfilled (1:17–18)
	Summary Phrase (1:19)

Day Two (1:6–8)
Divine Command (1:6–8a)
  Making of Sky (1:6–7a)
  Division of Lower Waters from Upper (1:7b)
  Naming of Heaven (1:8a)
Summary Phrase (1:8b)
	Day Five (1:20–23)
	Divine Command (1:20–22)
	  Command to Produce Fish and Birds (1:20)
	  Resultant Creation of Fish and Birds (1:21)
	  Blessing of Fish and Birds (1:22)
	Summary Phrase (1:23)

Day Three (1:9–13)
Two Divine Commands (1:9–12)
  Command One (1:9–10)
    Division of Lower Waters from Dry Land (1:9)
    Naming of Earth and Seas (1:10)
  Command Two (1:11–12)
    Command to Produce Vegetation (1:11)
    Resultant Production of Vegetation (1:12)
Summary Phrase (1:13)
	Day Six (1:24–31)
	Three Divine Commands (1:24–30)
	  Command One (1:24–25)
	    Command to Produce Earth Creatures (1:24)
	    Resultant Production of Earth Creatures (1:25)
	  Command Two (1:26–28)
	    Decision to Make Humanity (1:26)
	    Resultant Creation Thrice Emphasized (1:27)
	    Blessing of Humanity (1:28)
	  Command Three: Provision of Vegetation as Food (1:29–30)
	Summary Phrase (1:31)

filled with the sun, moon, and stars. The sky and surface waters, formed in day two, are filled with birds and fish in day five. The earth, formed in day three, is filled with earth creatures and humans in day six. Reading Genesis 1 with the question of literary structure in mind, as reflected in the table, makes clear that this creation account has been carefully shaped to communicate a perspective about God as creator and humans as created in the image and likeness of God.

The Garden of Eden

The first sentence of Genesis 2:4 suggests that the shapers of the book of Genesis understood the seven-day account as introducing the creation and that beginning with chapter 2 we will hear the story of the "generations of the heavens and the earth." The narrative of the **garden of Eden** in chapters 2–3 has a different style and feel than does Genesis 1. It portrays God in human terms—that is, in anthropomorphic language. The text narrates the creation of the land, and then, in the style of a potter, the Lord God makes

CREATION IN THE ANCIENT NEAR EAST

The first chapters of Genesis, part of the primeval history, have a complex relationship with other creation narratives, especially those from ancient Mesopotamia. These texts help us to understand some of the cultural codes reflected in the biblical texts. The Babylonian creation epic goes back to the Akkadians in the third millennium BCE and is often called Enuma Elish after its first words. That epic narrates the creation in terms of a soap opera–like war among the gods and goddesses. The earth is shaped from the defeated body of the goddess Tiamat. This story exhibits some parallels to Genesis 1. They both begin with a watery chaos and with a deity creating by speaking. There are six divisions followed by divine rest, and creation begins with light. The order of creation follows a similar sequence, though in the Babylonian text the parts of creation are often related closely to gods and goddesses. These parallels indicate that Genesis 1 reflects the cultural codes of its origin. If we are to understand fully the text of Genesis, having a sense of the social and historical setting from which it came is part of our responsibility as informed readers. At the same time, readers can see differences between Genesis 1 and Enuma Elish. The creation account in Genesis 1 is much more peaceful and orderly. Also, the Genesis account speaks of only one God rather than a host of deities; the divine name *Elohim* occurs frequently in the text. In Enuma Elish, humans are the slaves of the gods and goddesses to do the demeaning labor the world requires. In Genesis 1, God creates humans in the image of God as divine representatives caring for the world.

the man (*'adam*), a man from the dust of the ground (*'adamah*). The creation of the animals and the search for human community lead to the creation of a woman, the mother of all living people. God places the man and woman in a garden to care for it.

Along with the provision for life in the garden came the prohibition against eating of the tree of the knowledge of good and evil. In chapter 3 readers encounter the story of the serpent, simply described as the craftiest of all the wild animals, that tempts Eve to eat of the fruit of the tree. The two humans break the divine prohibition. When the Lord God comes walking in the garden in the cool of the evening, the consequences of this sin become clear. God curses the serpent to crawl in the dust, and the man and woman, because they have sought to substitute their own way for God's way of living, will suffer the difficulty of working the cursed ground and will endure the pain of childbirth. God then expels them from the garden to find their own way in the world.

Most interpreters would agree that Genesis 1 and 2 provide two creation accounts. Genesis 1 begins with a watery chaos that becomes an ordered creation. Genesis 2 begins with land that is watered by a mist. Both the names for God and the portrayal of God are different in the two accounts. The place of humans in the order of creation and the creation of man and woman are different. We have already noted the diversity of styles, with a patterned, repetitive litany of the seven days of creation in Genesis 1 and with a vivid story that unfolds in Genesis 2. The shapers of the book of Genesis saw these accounts not as contradictory but as providing two perspectives on creation, one from the broad angle of the whole universe and the other from the narrow angle of a story in the garden of Eden.

Genesis 4–11

Another helpful strategy for readers of texts like the book of Genesis is to consider the types of literature in the text and how these literary types relate. We have already labeled Genesis 1–11 as primeval history and Genesis 12–50 as ancestral stories. We will return to the relationship between the two. Genesis 1–11 also contains two types of materials: narratives and genealogies. We will consider the two in order. The four narratives in these chapters are the garden of Eden (Gen. 2–3), Cain and Abel (Gen. 4), Noah and the flood (Gen. 6–9), and the tower of Babel (Gen. 11). The basic story line is clear from the table "The Narrative Structure of Genesis 2–11."

We have already briefly recounted the story in the garden. The woman and man violate the divine prohibition of eating the fruit of the tree of the knowledge of good and evil. The consequence for not respecting the divine prohibition in the midst of this garden full of provision for life is expulsion from it. This narrative has given rise to many interpretations through the centuries. The prohibition first comes in Genesis 2:16–17: "You may freely eat of every tree of the garden; but of the tree of the knowledge of good and evil you shall not eat, for in the day that you eat of it you shall die." The eating of the fruit brings awareness of good and evil (perhaps a word pair suggesting knowledge of "all things") and makes the humans "like God" (3:5, 22). Still, the woman and man are allowed to continue the human adventure, but now outside the provision of the garden. Before they are expelled, however, in an act of kindness God clothes the woman and the man (3:21).

Genesis 4 recounts the story of Cain and Abel, two sons of Adam and Eve. Cain becomes enraged that God accepts the **sacrifice** of Abel, and he kills his brother. The text associates this violent act with sin (4:7). God's confrontation with Cain brings forth the pointed question "Am I my brother's keeper?" The consequence of the murder is ostracism from the clan to be "a fugitive and a wanderer on the earth." When Cain complains that this punishment is severe and that anyone could then kill him without the protection of the clan or extended family, God provides a mark of protection. The story reflects the custom of blood vengeance in which a death is avenged by the next of kin. The mark of protection suggests that God will serve as the next of kin for Cain.

Genesis 6–9 brings the familiar story of Noah and the flood. Chapter 6 makes it clear that evil has become pervasive in the human community and the consequence of this insidious evil is the flood. Noah and his family have, however, found favor in God's eyes, and so God instructs him to build an ark in which he and his family and representatives of the animals can survive

FLOOD NARRATIVES IN THE ANCIENT NEAR EAST

Archaeology has brought to light various flood stories from Mesopotamia. In the Gilgamesh Epic, the Noah-like Babylonian character named Utnapishtim narrates the flood to Gilgamesh, the ruler who searches for eternal life. There is divine warning of an impending flood and instruction to build a boat for family and animals. The parallels to the Genesis story at the conclusion of the flood are striking, as the boat comes to rest on a mountain and the hero releases three birds. The **Atrahasis Epic** also recounts a form of the flood narrative and may provide the basis for the Gilgamesh Epic. The story of Noah has its distinctive message in the Genesis primeval history, but there are similarities to these Mesopotamian texts. These texts provide readers with clues about the cultural codes through which Genesis originated and communicates. Responsible and informed readers of the primeval history will attend both to these cultural backgrounds and to the distinctive import of the Noah story.

the deluge. Following the flood, God renews the creation with the promise (and the sign of the rainbow) that God will not again "destroy every living creature" (8:21).

The primeval history's concluding narrative is the story of the tower of Babel in Genesis 11. Following the flood, the human community enjoys one language, and they decide to build a city and a tower to storm the heavens in order to "make a name for [them]selves" (11:4). YHWH decides to frustrate this ambition, scattering the people "abroad from there over the face of all the earth" (11:8) and confusing their language. The story likely originated as an *etiology*, an explanation of a current reality by narrating its origins. The story explains the presence of many nations and languages; it also explains the name of the place Babel as related to the Hebrew verb meaning "to confuse." The story also reflects Babylonian culture, and the tower likely connotes Babylonian structures called ziggurats. In the primeval history this story shows the movement of ongoing human rebellion against God. It also plays an important part in the relation between the primeval history and the ancestral stories to follow.

Interpreters have seen a pattern in these four stories that make up the primeval history (the garden of Eden, Cain and Abel, Noah and the flood, and the tower of Babel). Each story narrates disobedience against God and consequences that follow, as noted in the chart above; the stories focus on sin and punishment. The theme of these narratives seems to be the growing power of sin in the world; the human problem is at base a problem of relationship with the divine that works out in human relationships. Careful readers will then notice that the punishment of disobedience is not the end of the story. The story of the garden, of Cain and Abel, and of Noah all conclude with an act of divine grace or kindness. So the countertheme to the growing power of sin is the (almost secret) growing power of grace in the world. The full sequence is sin-punishment-grace (see the text box "The Narrative Structure of Genesis 2–11" below), a sequence present in many biblical narratives. So

THE NARRATIVE STRUCTURE OF GENESIS 2–11

Narrative	Sin	Punishment	Grace
Genesis 2–3: Garden of Eden	Eating the Fruit	Expulsion	Clothes/Life
Genesis 4: Cain and Abel	Murder	Ostracism	Mark of Protection
Genesis 6–9: Noah and the Flood	Pervasive Sin	Flood	Noah/Ark
Genesis 11: Tower of Babel	Storming Heaven	Dispersion/Confusion	?

in the midst of these primeval narratives that reflect on the pervasiveness of human fallibility, God continues to bring hope. The fourth narrative raises a significant question. Where is the sign of grace or hope? A number of interpreters have suggested that the sign is in the call of Abram introduced at the end of Genesis 11 and narrated at the beginning of Genesis 12, where divine engagement with the human community centers on Abram and Sarai and their descendants.

At the beginning of this section, we noted that Genesis 1–11 contains two types of texts—narratives and genealogies. We have considered the narratives. The genealogies are the lists of generations found in Genesis 5, 10, and 11. Genesis 5 begins by introducing Seth, who is in the "image and likeness" of his father Adam, and leads eventually to Noah. The list also introduces Enoch—who "walked with God; then he was no more, because God took him" (5:24)—and his son, the long-living Methuselah. Following the story of Noah and the flood, Genesis 10 presents the Table of Nations listing the descendants of Noah's sons, including the first hunter, Nimrod. Following the story of the tower of Babel, Genesis 11 presents a list of descendants of Shem that leads to Terah, the father of Abram, Nahor, and Haran. This genealogy at the end of the primeval history leads to Abram and his wife, Sarai, who are the focus of the narratives to follow in the ancestral stories and the means of divine engagement with the world. These genealogies are not usually considered interesting reading today, but they serve important functions in Genesis 1–11. In them, additional characters become part of the story. These texts also show God's continuing relationship with humans through the generations. In some ways the genealogies are the glue that holds together the narratives and bridges the gaps between them. Most interpreters suggest that these lists hold a literary relationship with the creation account in Genesis 1 and so move forward the account of the generations of the heavens and the earth and the humans who inhabit the earth.

Summary

Genesis 1–11 has been a source of much fascination and much controversy for readers through the centuries. These texts reflect the ancient Near Eastern culture of their origins, and yet they seem to have a different character than other biblical texts. Perhaps it is helpful to label the primeval history as universal history. The texts narrate the origin of the world and of humans and represent the human condition and context to begin the biblical story. Many interpreters suggest that these texts, with their names and language and types of narratives and connections with other ancient Near Eastern traditions, are more representative of women and men than they are about specific persons.

That approach takes seriously the historical context of the texts and their distinctiveness. Our exploration of Genesis 1–11 has focused on literary and theological issues, with attention paid to historical clues and questions in order to encourage responsible and informed reading. The invitation is to read these texts with these suggestions in mind as a way to treat the texts with genuine seriousness and to take them on their own terms. These texts continue to exert enormous influence in the Abrahamic faiths and in Western culture; they have been central to Christian history. Such influential texts deserve the careful attention of readers who use all the resources available. Fruitful reading of these texts also calls on the creative abilities of readers, for the texts reflect cultural codes from a world very different from the world of readers in twenty-first-century Western culture. The conceptions of creation and the world and the divine and human place in life are articulated quite differently than they are in cultures determined by modern science and industry. Reading Genesis 1–11 in a way that brings all these things to bear can transform life.

Ancestral Stories

The genealogy in Genesis 11 leads to the family of Abram and Sarai, whose story begins the second major division of the book of Genesis, the ancestral narratives in Genesis 12–50. Our discussion of these stories will consider the stories in the context of the book of Genesis and review the narratives of the four generations portrayed. First, it will be important to consider some historical matters.

The Ancestors and History

We have reviewed the universal history in Genesis 1–11, with its broad view of the beginnings of the human story. At the end of the genealogy in Genesis 11, the story narrows to Abram and Sarai and their descendants. While the broader implications are ever in view, the story now narrows to this family, so readers can detect a different kind of history in the texts. Many interpreters would suggest that the cultural world of this family history fits in the first half of the second millennium BCE. The text box "Outline of the History of the Hebrew People" provides a simple overview for such historical questions. The outline may provide a convenient reference point as we move through the history of the Hebrew people. Although the matter is debated, the Bronze Age—perhaps the Middle Bronze Age (2100–1550 BCE)—seems to fit the sociohistorical world portrayed in the ancestral stories. Social and religious customs reflected in the texts connect with customs and artifacts discovered by archaeologists. In the first half of the twentieth century, major excavations in Mesopotamia brought light on this cultural setting. Genesis names Ur, in contemporary Iraq near the Persian Gulf, as the place of origin for the ancestral family, and archaeologists excavated it in the early twentieth century along with Nuzi near the Tigris River in Mesopotamia (contemporary Iraq). Texts there seem to reflect some of the marriage and inheritance customs in Genesis. Texts from Mari, near the Euphrates in contemporary Syria, come from the first half of the second millennium BCE and reveal the use of names such as those found in Genesis 12–50. The excavation of Ras Shamra or Ugarit on the Syrian coast also reveals religious practices and divine names that connect to the ancestral stories in Genesis.

The exact nature of the parallels between the biblical stories and these ancient Near Eastern texts is complicated. Some scholars take the stories to be anachronistic and suggest that the background is much later; others simply ignore the questions of history, seeing them as unhelpful. Many interpreters suggest, however, that these texts from the ancient Near East and the customs reflected in the ancestral stories

OUTLINE OF THE HISTORY OF THE HEBREW PEOPLE

I. Beginnings of human history
II. Patriarchs and matriarchs, 2000–1500 BCE
  A. Abraham and Sarah
  B. Isaac and Rebekah
  C. Jacob, Rachel, and Leah
  D. Joseph Generation
III. Exodus: thirteenth century BCE
  A. Moses and Joshua
  B. Canaan
IV. Judges
V. United kingdom
  A. Saul, 1020–1000 BCE
  B. David, 1000–961 BCE
  C. Solomon, 961–922 BCE
VI. Divided kingdom
  A. Israel
    1. Jeroboam I
    2. Omri
    3. Ahab
    4. Jehu
    5. Jeroboam II
    6. Syro-Ephraimite Crisis
    7. Fall of Samaria, 722/721
  B. Judah
    1. Rehoboam
    2. Athaliah
    3. Uzziah
    4. Hezekiah
    5. Manasseh
    6. Josiah
    7. Jehoiakim
VII. Babylonian period
  A. Fall of Jerusalem, 587/586
  B. Exile
VIII. Persian age
  A. Ezra
  B. Nehemiah
IX. Greek period
  A. Maccabean Revolt

reveal a background for the patriarchs (first fathers) and matriarchs (first mothers) in Genesis. Archaeologists have not found direct evidence of the person Abram or the person Sarai, but the texts portray the family of Abram and Sarai and their descendants as itinerant herders living in extended families in the Middle Bronze Age. These historical clues will be helpful to readers when encountering seemingly unusual customs in these texts.

The Context in Genesis

Genesis 12–50 recounts narratives from four generations:

Abraham and Sarah	Genesis 12–25
Isaac and Rebekah	Genesis 24; 26
Jacob, Rachel, and Leah	Genesis 25–36
Joseph Generation	Genesis 37–50

The stories overlap at times. As we saw with the narratives in the primeval history, stories also have a particular literary context in Genesis. The primeval history narratives recounted the beginnings of the human adventure and revealed continuing human fallibility. As the wide angle of those stories narrows at the end of Genesis 11 to the story of one family, divine engagement with the world continues with a focus on the family of Abram and Sarai as a means of engaging all the families of the earth. Divine initiation of this relationship answers the question of the place of divine grace following the scattering and confusion of languages in the story of the tower of Babel. The opening text of the ancestral stories, Genesis 12:1–3, recounts the call of Abram and provides a preface and context for the narratives to follow. YHWH here calls Abram to journey to a "land that I will show you" and makes three promises: to make Abram a great people, to provide blessing, and to make Abram's name great in order to bring blessing to "all the families of the earth." The universal implications of the story never disappear. Abram then receives this divine call that includes the ancestral covenant promise and initiates the ancestral journey of blessing. This promise articulates the primary theme of the ancestral stories, a promise that is often expressed in terms of descendants, land, and blessing. The theme comes to light in each of the ancestral generations:

Abraham and Sarah: Genesis 12:1–3; 15:5–7; 17:2, 7, 19, 21
Isaac and Rebekah: Genesis 26:24
Jacob, Rachel, and Leah: Genesis 28:3–4, 13–15
Joseph Generation: Genesis 48:16

As with all gripping literature, there is also a countertheme, that of threat to this ancestral covenant promise; the question driving the narratives is whether the blessing will come to fruition. Several threats come to the fore.

- *Barrenness* threatens the promise of children. This problem drives the plot in the Abraham and Sarah story (e.g., Gen. 16).
- *Compromise of the matriarchs* threatens the promise, for the blessing is also tied to them. Sarah is endangered in Genesis 12:10–20; 20.
- *The sibling rivalry between Jacob and Esau* threatens the future of the family and the promise (e.g., Gen. 27).
- *Conflicts with local citizenry* also threaten the future of the promise (e.g., Gen. 34).

The Joseph story also recounts a number of threats to the promise: the jealousy of Joseph's brothers, the suggestive encounter with Potiphar's wife, and famine in the land.

The book concludes with the hope of the promise still intact (Gen. 50:20). This theme of the ancestral covenant promise and countertheme of threats to the promise provide the tension that drives the plot of this section of Genesis and will provide a context to help readers in their work as interpreters.

Abraham and Sarah

Genesis 12 brings readers into the story of Abram and Sarai, whom God calls to journey to a new land with a new promise. This itinerant family goes down to Egypt because of famine, and there Abram puts his wife in danger by seeking to pass her off as his sister so that the Egyptians will not kill him to take her. YHWH delivers the patriarch and matriarch from this danger, and the promise continues. Abram becomes a wealthy man and deals with family matters such as the conflicts with his nephew Lot (Gen. 13–14). Genesis 15 provides readers with a glimpse of customs of that era. Despite the promise of progeny, Abram still does not have a child. This text suggests that Abram's lead house servant will receive Abram's inheritance if there is no child. YHWH then repeats the promise and confirms it with a covenant custom that will be unusual for contemporary readers. Sacrificial animals are brought and cut in two, and "a smoking fire pot and a flaming torch passed between the pieces" (15:17). The smoke and flame are symbols of the divine presence, and so the scene includes a theophany, an appearance of God to humans, in this case to Abram. Here YHWH is the one who makes the commitment by passing between the pieces, an act that says, "If I do not in due time keep this commitment of land and progeny, may I be cut in two as these animals have been."

Chapter 16 reveals another custom of that culture. When Sarai is barren, she instructs the servant Hagar to have a child with Abram, and so Ishmael is born. Chapter 17 repeats the promise, and in this chapter the names are changed from Abram ("great father") to Abraham ("father of a multitude") and from Sarai to Sarah ("princess"). This chapter also describes a physical sign of the covenant relationship between this family and God, the sign of **circumcision**. Finally, in chapter 21 a son, Isaac, is born to Abraham and Sarah. Hagar and Ishmael are sent away; the promise will not flow through them, but God does make provision for them. Remarkably, in the very next chapter, Abraham hears God instruct him to offer Isaac as a sacrifice. Abraham follows this instruction faithfully, and in the end God provides a ram for the sacrifice and Isaac is spared. The text becomes the occasion for the repetition of the divine blessing of children and land. Sarah and Abraham then come to the end of their lives. Their journey has been one of learning to trust the ancestral covenant promise from YHWH in the face of threats and distractions from the customs of their culture.

Isaac and Rebekah

The brief narratives about Isaac and Rebekah serve as a transition from the Abraham and Sarah generation to that of Jacob and Rachel/Leah. Chapter 24 recounts the marriage of the long-awaited son of Abraham and Sarah to a woman from the country and kindred of the parents. The beginning of chapter 26 reaffirms the ancestral covenant promise of progeny, land, and blessing for this generation.

Jacob, Rachel, and Leah

The stories of the next generation make up the next block of Genesis, chapters 25–36. Twins Jacob and Esau are born to Isaac and Rebekah, and sibling rivalry between the two boys is evident from the beginning. The conflict between the two very different personalities comes to a boil when Jacob plays the role of the trickster and procures both the birthright and the blessing of his older brother, Esau, through deceptive means. Jacob's mother has colluded with him, and with her help he flees to his uncle Laban's to escape the murderous threat of his rival brother. On the way to Haran, Jacob encounters YHWH in a dream that has come to be labeled as "Jacob's Ladder." In this dream at Bethel, God gives the ancestral covenant promise to Jacob.

The narrative of Jacob's time with Laban's family also centers on deception. Jacob seeks to marry Rachel, Laban's daughter, but Laban tricks him into marrying the older daughter Leah first, and then to stay and work yet longer for the opportunity to marry Rachel. Jacob does stay and marry Rachel according to Laban's plan, but in the process manipulates things so that he becomes wealthy, and under the dark of night he leaves with his family and belongings. Rachel takes her father's household gods without permission and conceals them from Jacob; possession of these household gods apparently relates to customs of inheritance. Genesis 31 labels the small idols as *teraphim*.

The journey back toward Canaan raises the specter of the unresolved relationship with Jacob's older twin, Esau. Jacob makes various preparations for this encounter with his twin brother and in Genesis 32 finds himself alone near the ford of the Jabbok where he endures a mysterious encounter with the divine in which his name is changed from Jacob, the trickster, to Israel, one who strives with God. Jacob comes away from this encounter with a limp and with a new name for the one who carries the ancestral covenant promise. The encounter with Esau is peaceful, and Jacob and his family journey on to Bethel, where the promise of divine blessing is repeated at the close of this cycle of stories. Jacob's relationship with Esau and the concern with the covenant promise frame these narratives. The story of Jacob's marriages to Rachel and Leah and their relationship with Laban is folded into that frame. This section of Genesis contains a variety of traditions organized around the question of the future of the covenant promise.

The story of Shechem and Dinah in chapter 34 and the story of Judah and Tamar in chapter 38 narrate encounters with local Canaanite peoples and conflicts that could threaten the family of Jacob and his children. These narratives again demonstrate the diversity of materials in the ancestral stories and the presence in the narratives of cultural customs of the era.

The Joseph Generation

The story of the Joseph generation in Genesis 37–50 is somewhat different from the preceding ancestral narratives. This section is more of a self-contained unit, and its Egyptian background comes to the fore. The story takes the form of a novella, or short novel, in which God communicates with the characters in a different way. The previous sections of Genesis recount divine appearances to the patriarchs and matriarchs, but now God seems to communicate by way of the natural processes of life. A number of interpreters have also suggested that Joseph is a wisdom character who interprets dreams and perceives the way forward for the future of the divine promise.

The novella opens in the context of the twelve sons of Jacob/Israel, with Joseph recounting dreams in which he rules over his brothers. The recurring scene of sibling rivalry suggests another threat to the promise in the young Joseph. His brothers sell him into slavery in Egypt and tell his distraught father that an animal has killed his favorite son. In Egypt, Joseph enters the house of Potiphar as a servant and is falsely accused of sexually assaulting Potiphar's wife. He is incarcerated but again rises to the top of the heap, and eventually, by way of his interpretation of dreams, he is introduced in the **pharaoh**'s court. Joseph rises to be the prime minister of Egypt and will make it possible for the kingdom to survive severe famine, a threat to both Egyptians and the family of Jacob. Sons of Jacob journey to Egypt seeking food, and in a complicated plot including several deceptions, Joseph is reunited with his family, and the whole of the Jacob clan migrates to Egypt. Jacob comes to the end of his life and passes on the promise to Joseph's children. The Joseph story and the book of Genesis conclude with the reconciliation of Joseph with his brothers in the context of God's providential use of all manner of events for the sake of the future of the ancestral covenant promise and those who carry it into that future. The book of Genesis ends with the death of Joseph.

As noted above, some scholars have suggested that Joseph is a wisdom character who follows the basics of wisdom as preserved in the book of Proverbs. He interprets dreams and is able to discern the way forward in daily life. In his story, the wise and faithful grow and thrive in the world. In that sense, Joseph is a teaching character for the young in ancient Israel. He demonstrates how to live wisely. Beyond this educational goal, the narrative of the Joseph generation also relates to the ancestral covenant promise central to the earlier chapters of Genesis. The focus of the narrative in the Joseph generation is on threats to the promise: famine, sibling rivalry, and other conflicts. The promise is not repeated until the end of the Joseph story, because Jacob is still alive to bear it. The promise is passed to Jacob's grandchildren in chapter 48. At the end of the book of Genesis, with all its twists and turns, the promise is still alive and well.

Conclusion

The ancestral stories in Genesis focus on the divine promise of progeny, land, and blessing and narrate the history of that promise through the generations of the patriarchs and matriarchs. The history takes many twists and turns and reveals multiple threats to the promise. The narratives thrive on the question of whether the promise will find a future. In the end, Genesis 12–50 portrays the God of ancient Israel as one who makes and keeps promises and in so doing brings a faith community to fullness of life. The imperfect characters in these narratives represent the human community and its history of learning to trust the divine promise, for therein is lasting hope. The story continues in the book of Exodus.

One of the clues for readers of Genesis is the etiologies often given in the text, especially for place names. The text narrates the origin of names, such as Babel ("confusion," in Gen. 11), Beer-Sheba ("well of the oath," in Gen. 21), Bethel ("house of God," in Gen. 28), and Peniel ("the face of God," in Gen. 32). True to its name Genesis ("origins"), the book addresses etiological questions on behalf of the community: Who are we, and where did we originate? What is the significance of the name "Israel"? Who is this God YHWH with whom our community's life is so intimately intertwined? How do we view ourselves, others, the world, and God? How do we live? Genesis narrates a script for the faith community as it recounts the memory of God's involvement with this community.

The Composition of the Pentateuch

Our journey through the book of Genesis has provided enough background for us to pause and consider the question of how the first five books of the Old Testament, the Pentateuch or Torah, came to be. This issue has been a major subject in biblical studies.

The Books of Moses

Tradition has tied the first five books of the Bible to Moses, and that tradition has been interpreted in some circles to suggest Mosaic authorship. These books pass on the faith centered on the Mosaic covenant, but they nowhere explicitly claim Mosaic authorship. They are anonymous. There are indications in the text of these books that writers have recounted the past from a later time and perspective. Genesis 12:6, for example, includes the note, "At that time the Canaanites were in the land," and Genesis 36:31 reads, "These are the kings who reigned in the land of Edom, before any king reigned over the Israelites." The conclusion of the book of Deuteronomy also comes after the death of Moses. Much of the perspective of the Pentateuch is from those who are already living in Jerusalem at a later time. Numbers 21:14 provides a glimpse into the process of composition with a biblical version of a footnote; it gives the source of the quotation in verses 14–15 as "The Book of the Wars of the LORD." Careful readers of the book of Genesis will have noticed the two creation accounts in Genesis 1–2 and the differences in parts of the account of Noah and the flood—in chapter 6, the instruction is to take two of every living thing onto the ark; in chapter 7, the instruction is to take seven pairs of clean animals and one pair of unclean animals. In addition, Genesis 15 and 17 articulate two Abrahamic covenant traditions of a rather different character; and the narrative of the Joseph generation appears to be a self-contained unit. So it is important to see that the text itself provides a good bit of evidence that the first five books of the Bible came about by way of a process of composition over a period of time.

The Documentary Hypothesis

Those who studied these biblical books through the centuries suggested from time to time that some of the composition of these books came after the time of Moses, but it was in the seventeenth century, with a renewed emphasis on human reason, that scholars began to develop a number of hypotheses to explain how the books originated. In that era, scholars often questioned traditional views in the context of historical studies of ancient cultures. The view that came to dominate the discussion is called the **Documentary Hypothesis**, the theory that the Pentateuch developed from the combination of several documents. The classic statement of this hypothesis came from Julius Wellhausen in 1878 and reigned in scholarship on the Hebrew Bible for the next century.

A brief summary of the view is that one of ancient Israel's theologians in the tenth century BCE brought together a number of the narratives in the Pentateuch to begin to tell the story of ancient Israel's origins. Scholars often label this writer with the letter *J* because of the use of the divine name YHWH ("LORD"); that name was spelled with a *J* (*Jahweh*) in Germany, where the theory originated. An additional set of texts was added a century later and is called "E" because of the use of the divine name *Elohim* (God). These sources were then redacted together. The book of Deuteronomy (D) became the next stage in the development of the Pentateuch and relates to Josiah's reform in the seventh century (2 Kings 22). The concluding stage is the Priestly material (P) following the beginning of the **Babylonian exile** in the sixth century. The Priestly theologians redacted together the J and E material with Deuteronomy and the Priestly material. This account of the origin of the Pentateuch is the classic example of **source criticism** in scholarship on the Hebrew Scriptures. The sources of the Pentateuch are the JEDP documents. **Redaction criticism** also becomes part of the picture as the sources are edited together. Some scholars suggest that the formation process was less mechanical and so, rather than talking about sources or documents, talk about the process in terms of traditions or memories coming together, an example

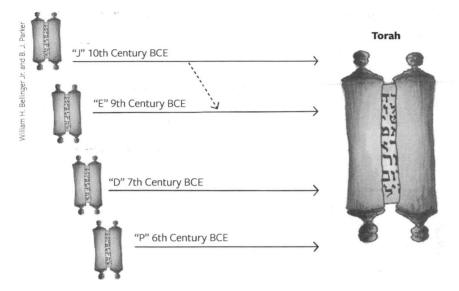

"J" 10th Century BCE

"E" 9th Century BCE

"D" 7th Century BCE

"P" 6th Century BCE

Torah

Figure 2.3. **The proposed sources of the Pentateuch and their relationship**

of what was labeled "**tradition history**" (see the text box "Critical Tools" on p. 20). The table titled "Pentateuchal Traditions" describes the sources or traditions of the standard Documentary Hypothesis.

Scholars developed the Documentary Hypothesis to make sense of the evidence the text reveals, but it is not the only approach. Alternatives arise because of challenges to the classic hypothesis, which reflects an account of the history of ancient Israel that is now dated. The so-called documents have not ever been found, and scholars at times disagree about which texts belong with which documents. In addition, source criticism tends to divide the text into documents but not help with making sense of the current text as a whole. In recent decades, the classic Documentary Hypothesis has undergone considerable revision. Most interpreters would still suggest the influence of D and P documents or traditions in relation to the Babylonian exile and its aftermath (see "Exile and Beyond" on p. 98). Discussion of E has virtually disappeared, and discussion of the Yahwist's work (J) is now very different, with a later date often suggested. Currently there is not much consensus on whether there was a collection or collections of narratives prior to the works labeled D and P. The other current question is whether the Priestly theologians or the Deuteronomists gave the Pentateuch its final form.

Some scholars would suggest that the traditional Documentary Hypothesis, which in the twentieth century dominated the question of the origin of the Pentateuch, is now defunct. Others would say that the hypothesis has

PENTATEUCHAL TRADITIONS

Tradition	Characteristics	Date
J (Yahwist)	Uses *YHWH* for God Vivid, concrete style Storyteller Begins with creation (Gen. 2:4b) Uses term *Mount Sinai* for place where Mosaic covenant was concluded Related to the Southern Kingdom (Judah) Hopeful tone	Ca. 950 BCE
E (Elohist)	Uses *Elohim* for God Style more abstract, less picturesque than J's Uses term *Horeb* for covenant mountain Begins with story of Abraham Related to northern Israel (Ephraim) "Prophetic" tone	Ca. 850 BCE
D (Deuteronomist)	Reflects literary style and religious attitudes of Josiah's reform (ca. 621 BCE) Insists that only one central sanctuary is acceptable to YHWH Composed in the north (?) Related to the Former Prophets Covenant theology	Ca. 650–621 BCE
P (Priestly)	Emphasizes priestly concerns, law, and worship aspects of religion Precise style Lists censuses and genealogies Derived from priestly preservation of Mosaic traditions in the Babylonian exile (following 587 BCE)	Ca. 550 BCE

reinvented itself, especially in European scholarship. Consider the following possibility. In the aftermath of the fall of Jerusalem in the sixth century BCE and the Babylonian captivity, Jewish scribes sought to preserve the historical and theological traditions of their community. A community of priestly scribes collected earlier stories of the ancestors and connected them with stories their own scribal community held in its cultural memory. The question of whether the earlier stories were part of a preexisting collection is an open question, though many now doubt that. One prominent view is that the priestly scribal community was the first to connect the ancestral stories in Genesis with the Moses story in Exodus, Leviticus, and Numbers. These books emphasize priestly perspectives. This community also shaped the creation traditions in Genesis. Another scribal community was also working in this time. Their emphasis was on the covenant traditions such as those in Deuteronomy. It was the combination of the work of these two scribal communities that shaped the Pentateuch or Torah, the first section of the Hebrew canon. Scholars who follow this path appeal to textual evidence and recent research on scribalism in that culture to support this revision of the Documentary Hypothesis. The traditions of Deuteronomy came to have considerable impact in the shaping of the historical traditions in the Former Prophets. In the Pentateuch read today, Deuteronomy and its covenant traditions have the last word, but the beginning and the center of the content of these five books is solidly priestly in its concerns and its subject matter.

Other Approaches

Some interpreters do not think the search for the compositional sources of the Pentateuch will succeed. Others prefer an approach that emphasizes the final text of these books, rather than hypothetical original sources or traditions, as the basis of interpretation. These interpreters focus on the literary forms or patterns in the text. They may be form critics or rhetorical critics. The Pentateuch reveals a plot with characters, and narrative critics follow those clues to articulate the significance of the text. Some of these interpreters also follow the clues of **canonical criticism**, which seeks the context in which the text took its final form. (For review of these methods, see the text box "Critical Tools" on p. 20.)

The approach followed in the treatment of Genesis in this part of our textbook was a holistic one that attended both to questions of origin and to questions of the shape of the final text of the Pentateuch. The treatments of the primeval history and the ancestral stories followed the movements of the text with an emphasis on literary issues. History came into the picture with attention to cultural customs. This approach will typify this volume. Historical questions of origin will also come into play when they have a reasonable basis and can help with the task of interpretation. For example, the creation account in Genesis 1 and the genealogies in the book of Genesis are commonly tied to the Priestly traditions that deal with the crisis of exile and its aftermath. That connection suggests that the hopeful provision for life in Genesis 1 could also apply to those returning from exile. The returnees are authorized to be fruitful and multiply and again fill the land (the Hebrew word means both "earth" and "land"). The latter part of the book of Exodus, the book of Leviticus, and the first part of the book of Numbers are also often connected to the Priestly traditions. The book of Deuteronomy provides another example. Scholarship on the origins of the book provides insights that have implications for interpreting the book. As we have seen, historical and literary questions can help readers interact with the biblical text in more significant ways.

Summary

The first five books of the Bible are traditionally labeled "the **books of Moses**," because they pass on to readers the authoritative Mosaic faith. Moses is the fountainhead of the covenant faith established in Exodus. The text also makes clear that later writers and editors have shaped this tradition. Thoughtful readers of these books will notice the repetitions and tensions in the text and the different literary styles. The Pentateuch is not the kind of literature an author writes in one sitting. It brings together a variety of traditions to pass down this covenant faith through the generations. Such a process fits the practices of the ancient Near East. Based on this evidence, scholars developed the Documentary Hypothesis to account for the different strands in the text. The sometimes-complicated efforts to reconstruct the origin and history of the Pentateuch continue today and sometimes take rather different directions from the classic documentary theory. It is clear, however, that the Torah derives from a process that has brought together a variety of traditions to compose this first section of the Bible, a section that in its current form also has a plot, characters, and literary features that communicate to readers. Those who seek the full import of the text will do well to explore all these aspects.

The image of the Pentateuch as a river fed by tributaries is a helpful one. The various traditions contribute to the whole. We have already noted a number of the major themes in the text: the ancestral covenant promise, creation, calls for faithfulness, and Mosaic covenant traditions (such as those in the book of Deuteronomy). Perhaps these major themes reflect some of the traditions that have come to compose the Pentateuch. Perhaps the other helpful image is that of the memory of a people. The various dimensions of ancient Israel's memory have come together to form these books to reveal the Mosaic covenant faith.

Exodus and Covenant

The second book of the Bible is titled Exodus, meaning "a going out." It tells the story of the Hebrew exodus from Egyptian bondage, a story central to the shape of the Hebrew Scriptures. We will first consider the historical and literary setting of the narrative in the first half of the book of Exodus and then come to the various dimensions of covenant in the latter part of Exodus and in Leviticus. The narrative continues with the wilderness experience in Numbers and concludes with Deuteronomy.

Exodus in Context

The book of Genesis began with the creation of the world; Exodus begins with the creation of the people of God and moves toward the fulfillment of the ancestral covenant promise. The ancestral stories in Genesis provide the beginnings of the literary context. Joseph rises to power in Egypt, and his family joins him. Egyptian records provide accounts of others entering Egypt to escape famine and succeeding there. The story of Joseph is often related to the reign of the **Hyksos**, a Semitic group who came to power in Egypt (1700–1550 BCE), and so might have been sympathetic to fellow Semites (the Hebrews were Semites). Such times of change and upheaval were part of Egyptian history. The **Amarna Age**, named after a new capital city, witnessed a time of radical change by Pharaoh Akhnaton (fourteenth century BCE), including a monotheistic religion. Letters from that era document the activities of **Habiru**. These groups caused considerable conflict and could well have included rebellious elements among slave labor in Egypt and in Mesopotamia and among groups in Palestine. The evidence does not support an ethnic connection between the Habiru and the Hebrews, but the escape of Hebrew slaves from Egypt typifies the activities of these groups. While there are not explicit Egyptian records recounting the Hebrew story of the exodus, the biblical account fits what we know of Egyptian history and culture.

The book of Exodus opens with Israel in Egypt. The Hebrew people have been fruitful and multiplied and filled the land of Egypt. The promise of progeny has come to pass, and the narrative moves toward the promise of land. A political change comes in Egypt, and the new rulers are not sympathetic to the descendants of Joseph. The new rulers begin a public-works program and collect money from taxation. The workers for these building projects are the Hebrews, who become slaves in a harsh and oppressive environment. The account in Exodus 1:8–14 is brief but clear in recounting the tyrannical attempts to harness the prolific Hebrews. The story of the Hebrew midwives in Exodus 1 introduces the element of Hebrew resistance to this oppression.

The Story of Moses

Exodus 2 introduces Moses, the one who will lead the Hebrew people out of Egyptian bondage. He is born and preserved in the midst of oppression and even given an Egyptian name (2:10), and he grows up in the pharaoh's court with all its advantages. He begins to see how the Hebrew people are oppressed and kills an Egyptian who is beating a Hebrew. In fear he flees to the wilderness and marries into the family of Jethro. While shepherding for Jethro at Mount Horeb, or Sinai, he encounters the God YHWH in the strange sight of a bush that burns but that the fire does not consume. In that theophany, that appearance of YHWH, Moses encounters a divine call to go back to Egypt to lead the Hebrews out of oppression. Moses resists this call first with questions about who this YHWH is and then with questions about his own ability to lead. The Divine One answers these objections with confirmations of power to bring about this deliverance and with the choice of Aaron to assist an ineloquent Moses. Moses—with the assistance of Aaron—is now prepared for this daunting task of liberation and so returns to Egypt to face the most powerful military-industrial complex of the ancient Near Eastern world, led by the pharaoh.

The struggle in Egypt. Exodus 7–12 recounts the struggle of the Hebrews to escape oppression in Egypt. Central to this narrative is the account of the plagues oppressing the Egyptians. The plagues are a series of progressively intensifying mighty acts designed to establish the authority of YHWH for

THE DIVINE NAME

It is in the context of this theophany that the divine name YHWH is revealed in Exodus 3. The name is at times called the **tetragrammaton**, because it is composed of four letters. The name became so **holy** to ancient Israel that they came to the practice of not pronouncing it or writing out the whole name. From our understanding of Hebrew and other Semitic languages, it is most likely that the name was pronounced "Yah-weh." It is the proper, personal name for ancient Israel's God. When vowels were added to the Hebrew words of the text, the vowels of *Adonai* ("Lord") were added as a clue to say *Adonai* or "Lord" rather than "Yahweh." Eventually, the use of the vowels along with the original four consonants led to the creation of the name *Yehowah*, rendered as *Jehovah* with influences from German spelling and used in some English translations; see, for example, Genesis 22:14 in the King James Version. Most contemporary English versions render the name "Lord." In the encounter with Moses, YHWH self-identifies as "the God of your father, the God of Abraham, the God of Isaac, and the God of Jacob" (Exod. 3:6), tying the story of the exodus to the Genesis ancestral stories. Further in the conversation about divine authority to deliver the oppressed Hebrews comes the self-revelation of the divine name YHWH (Exod. 3:14): God said to Moses, "I am who I am." He said further, "Thus you shall say to the Israelites, 'I am has sent me to you.'" The phrase can be translated in a variety of ways: "I am who I am," "I am what I am," and "I will be what I will be" are all reasonable renderings. This revelation associates the divine name with the verb *to be*, suggesting that this God is the one who causes things to be and the one who, in the context of Exodus, will come to deliver the Hebrews. The phrase also suggests that this God is not one who will be manipulated, but who has the authority to call Moses to lead the Hebrews out of Egyptian bondage.

both Israel and Egypt and to persuade the pharaoh to let the Hebrews go. The narrative asserts that YHWH is above all gods: "For this time I will send all my plagues upon you yourself, and upon your officials, and upon your people, so that you may know that there is no one like me in all the earth" (9:14). YHWH is not shaken by magic or equaled by any power, and YHWH is Israel's God. The plagues YHWH sends attack the Egyptian pantheon. For example:

- The turning of the water of the Nile River to blood bests the god of the Nile.
- The plagues of the frogs and of lice and flies defeat the insect deities.
- The death of cattle challenges Hathor.
- The solar deity Ra fails to prevent darkness.
- The final, overpowering plague of the death of the firstborn Egyptians defeats the creator god Ptah and leads to the tradition of the Hebrew festival of **Passover** to remember that the angel of death brought death to Egypt and not Israel.

YHWH sends a total of ten plagues:

1. The water of the Nile turns to blood.
2. Frogs come and cover the land.
3. Gnats or mosquitoes cover the land.
4. Flies swarm everywhere.
5. Cattle die of disease.
6. Festering boils afflict humans and animals.
7. Extreme hail destroys everything in its path.
8. Locusts destroy what is left of crops.
9. Darkness covers the land.
10. The death of firstborn Egyptians.

The account of the plagues is organized in series of threes. The first, fourth, and seventh plagues begin at the Nile River with the pharaoh present. Plagues two, five, and eight are narrated at the palace with the pharaoh present; and plagues three, six, and nine begin with a gesture and no warning.

This narrative technique adds to the drama and shows that the text has been carefully constructed to reach the high point of the final plague of the death of the firstborn Egyptians and the defeat of the powerful empire and its pantheon. As a result, the Hebrews escape the formative experience of oppression in Egypt. Led by Moses, they head out of oppression and toward

Sinai, where YHWH called Moses to instigate this act of liberation. The text emphasizes the beginning of the Passover festival so that future generations will remember the story of how YHWH spared the Hebrews in the death of the firstborn and liberated them from Egyptian oppression.

But there is more to the story. Moses leads the Hebrews away from Egypt but toward the sea (traditionally labeled the **Red Sea** but more accurately translated as "the sea characterized by reeds/vegetation"). Apparently acting on a change of heart, the pharaoh leads his powerful army after the escaping Hebrews, and so the Hebrews are caught between the Egyptian army and the sea. YHWH uses the wind to push back the waters of the sea, and the Hebrews cross on dry land to escape, leaving the Egyptian army with its heavy chariots mired in the sea as the waters cover them (14:21–31). The God who delivers, YHWH of Israel, brings the Hebrews out of oppression and creates a people through mighty acts and the leadership of Moses, Aaron, and Miriam. Human leadership in the narrative is essential. It is worth noting that women play a significant role in the movement of the exodus narrative—from the Hebrew midwives Shiphrah and Puah; to Moses's mother and sister; to Pharaoh's daughter; to Moses's wife, Zipporah; to the leader Miriam (called a **prophet**), sister to Moses and Aaron.

History and faith. This narrative account of the exodus from Egypt leaves a number of questions. The account attests to the mighty acts of the plagues and the deliverance at the sea. Interpreters have from time to time attempted to explain these miracles by natural means. The text includes statements that indicate divine use of natural elements to accomplish mighty acts. The narrative, however, seems to be uninterested in human questions of causation but centers on mighty acts that accomplish the announced purposes of the Hebrew God YHWH. Readers of these narratives will understand that while the Egyptians saw frogs on the ground, the eyes of faith see a mighty act that contributes to the purpose of divine liberation of the oppressed Hebrews.

The story continues at Sinai, but the event of the exodus from Egypt creates a people and forms its identity and history. Some have attempted to date the exodus from Egypt in the fifteenth century BCE, but the consensus among scholars is that the events likely come in the thirteenth century BCE during the time of Pharaoh Ramesses II. The picture of Canaan derived from ancient Near Eastern texts and what we know of Egyptian history from that time suggest the thirteenth century. The first extrabiblical mention of Israel comes from that time period in a victory stele (a monument) erected by Pharaoh Merenptah. Following the exodus narrative, that piece of evidence would place the liberation from Egypt in the reign of Ramesses II (mid-thirteenth century BCE) and the oppression of the Hebrews in the reign of Seti I. In that context, the interweaving of faith and history in the first half of the book of Exodus creates the people of YHWH named Israel.

Covenant at Sinai

The liberation from Egypt eventually leads to the defining theophany in the Hebrew Scriptures, the encounter of YHWH with Israel at **Mount Sinai** leading to a covenant relationship. Exodus 19:4–6 summarizes the exodus narrative, and then Moses leads the people to prepare to encounter YHWH, whose presence is symbolized with trumpet sound, thunder, lightning, smoke, and fire. From Sinai, YHWH reveals the shape of life for this community. Exodus 20 presents the familiar **Ten Commandments**, or the Decalogue, the "ten words" central to the shape of Old Testament faith. Readers will note that the first instruction comes in verse 3. The opening two verses provide important context for this law code. The instructions are in the context of divine self-revelation from the God who has delivered this community from oppression in Egypt; that context is central to the import of this instruction. The instruction gives the basic shape of Israel's relationship with their liberating God in the first half of the code and then the shape of their relationship with each other in the last half. This law code articulates a vision of life for a people in covenant relationship with YHWH.

The **Covenant Code** follows the Decalogue in Exodus 20:22–23:19. This law code expands the basic statements of the Decalogue and applies them to daily life. For example, the Covenant Code expands the prohibition of

---

THE DECALOGUE

This list provides a basic understanding of the commandments:

1. Worship of YHWH only.
2. Prohibition of images that give a fixed point of contact with the deity and thus the impression of controlling the deity.
3. Prohibition of use of the name YHWH in spells supporting evil.
4. Setting aside of the Sabbath day for worship and rest.
5. Support for aging parents in the extended family.
6. Prohibition of premeditated murder in the context of a blood-vengeance society.
7. Prohibition of adultery.
8. Prohibition of stealing.
9. Prohibition of perjury in the legal system.
10. Prohibition of coveting what others have.

murder to deal with a variety of settings and circumstances in which people are injured or die (21:12–14, 18–25, 28–32; 22:2–3). Following this law code, YHWH and Israel formally enter into a covenant relationship.

The revelation at Sinai consists of two types of law—apodictic and casuistic. **Apodictic law** is given on the authority of the lawgiver and is a basic, universal statement; most of the Ten Commandments fit this description. **Casuistic law** is case law applying basic principles to various contexts in the community's life and usually in the form of "If this thing happens, then this consequence follows." Much of the Covenant Code is in this form. These Old Testament law codes are often compared to other ancient Near Eastern law codes, most of which are in casuistic form. Assyrian law codes are very strict, moderated somewhat by Babylonian law codes such as the **Code of Hammurabi**. The story of the early Babylonian emperor Hammurabi (eighteenth century BCE) has some parallels to that of Moses. The law code with his name remains the best known of the ancient Near Eastern codes; it reflects a society with clear social stratification. Israel's codes seem to center more on the sacredness of life, perhaps reflecting the traditions of YHWH as creator of life. Historical and cultural context is important in understanding these codes. For example, the ***lex talionis*** (law of retaliation) appears in the Code of Hammurabi and in the Pentateuch. In this principle of "an eye for an eye," punishments should fit crimes (Exod. 21:22–25; Lev. 24:19–22; Deut. 19:15–21). In this context, these legal assertions serve to ensure that offenders are not executed because of accidental injuries.

Old Testament law codes are cast in the context of divine revelation. Contemporary readers will have various responses to the term *law*, but in the context of the book of Exodus, the law can be characterized as follows:

- An avenue of response to God's deliverance from Egyptian bondage
- Revelation of the divine view of life in a covenant relationship
- A means of deepening relationship—with YHWH and with each other in the community

The Hebrew word typically translated "law" is *torah*. Better translations understand the term in the sense of instruction or guidance or direction or teaching. The divine revelation of the Torah is a gift, a gracious act of the deity in shaping life together for this covenant community. Ancient Israel was not called to keep Torah in order to become YHWH's people but to live according to Torah because they are YHWH's covenant people delivered in the exodus from Egyptian bondage. Covenant is a way of articulating the relationship between YHWH and Israel, initiated by YHWH, in which YHWH declares "I will be your God" and the people respond with "We will be your people."

God then instructs the people in how to live in this relationship (Torah) and articulates the consequences of obedience and disobedience. The narrative of the deliverance from Egypt provides the context and initiates a covenant relationship that shapes Israel's life as YHWH's people.

Covenant and Worship

The latter half of Exodus transitions to the implications of the covenant relationship in terms of worship and ritual. Such matters are central for organizing life as a people defined by relationship with a deity; all parts of the community's life come into view. These concerns were central to the priests who shaped this part of the Pentateuch. The context in the latter half of Exodus is important. Chapters 26–27 give instructions for building the mobile wilderness sanctuary (or **tabernacle**), and chapters 28–29 give instructions for ordaining the priests of the line of Aaron to lead the worship at the sanctuary. In the concluding chapters of Exodus, the people build the tabernacle and God accepts it as a fitting place for the worship of YHWH (Exod. 40:34–38). The **priests** are ordained and worship begins in Leviticus 8–10. Prior to the

Figure 2.4. **Diagram of the tabernacle**

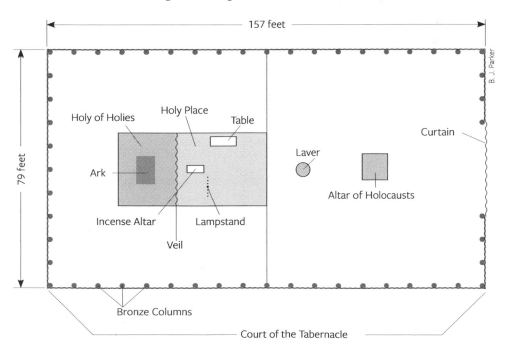

worship, instruction in the offering of sacrifice is essential, and it is with that task that the book of Leviticus begins.

Leviticus

Ritual codes determine the shape of the book of Leviticus. The title means "the Levitical book," reflecting the task of the **Levites** to teach about worship in their role of supporting the priests, the leaders of worship.

Manual of Sacrifice (Lev. 1–7). The **Manual of Sacrifice** presents the ritual for five sacrifices for both laity and priests:

- *Whole burnt offering* dedicating one's whole life to YHWH, an atoning sacrifice
- *Cereal offering* suggesting that everyday life is from YHWH
- *Shared offering* in which YHWH and worshipers share the sacrificial meal
- *Purification offering* bringing cleansing from sin and uncleanness
- *Compensation/reparation offering* making amends for guilt

Sacrifice is understood in the text to be a genuine act of faith in a variety of ways. At times the sacrifice is an act of communion between deity and the covenant community. At other times it is a gift indicating thanksgiving for life provisions. Other sacrifices center on atonement, putting back "at one" a fractured relationship with the deity. The character of at-one-ment is a matter of considerable discussion. Some have taken a negative view of these acts and seen them as a means of bribing an angry deity. The best picture suggests that the sacrificial ritual constitutes an arena for the communication between the human and the divine in which the one offering the sacrifice engages in the risky business of taking the life of another (the sacrificial animal), a role that is properly assigned to God. The deity mysteriously honors that risk and wipes clean the slate of the divine-human relationship. Worship at the tabernacle centered on sacrifice begins in the historical narrative of Leviticus 8–10.

Manual of Purity (Lev. 11–16). The first ten chapters of Leviticus institute worship; the remainder of the book speaks to preparation for that worship. The definition of purity in terms of clean and unclean is important. Clean suggests a state acceptable for worship; unclean suggests what is unacceptable for worship. Uncleanness is contagious, and encountering the unclean ostracizes one from the central community act of worship; so causes of uncleanness are listed, whether eating unclean food (Lev. 11), giving birth (Lev. 12), suffering from flaky skin diseases (Lev. 13–14), or experiencing bodily emissions (Lev. 15). Scholars have made various attempts to articulate the concepts of purity and impurity that underlie these chapters. Some would emphasize health concerns or the attempt to distinguish Israel from other communities or the call to obedience of YHWH. It seems likely that the underlying concepts reflect categories of creation relating to Genesis 1 and applying to various life settings. The ritual of the **Day of Atonement** follows in Leviticus 16 and fits with the **Manual of Purity** because it has to do with the cleansing of impurity. First there is the purification offering for the priest who is conducting the ritual. Then two goats are presented as a purification offering to cleanse the sanctuary of the effects of sin and uncleanness. With a cleansed sanctuary, the perfectly holy deity can continue to "tabernacle" in the center of the community and give life. The second goat is labeled the **scapegoat**. The priest confesses the sin of the people over the goat, and it is taken away from the community. This ancient ritual is central to the continuity of ancient Israel's worship in their covenant relationship with YHWH. The Priestly view is that sin and uncleanness can fracture the relationship; the atonement rituals provide a means of restoring and renewing the relationship for the life of the community.

Holiness Code (Lev. 17–26). These last chapters in Leviticus instruct the community in how to reflect the holiness of YHWH in their worship and community life, again with a view to preparation for worship in the tabernacle. YHWH is understood to be holy in the sense of completely distinct, and so the **Holiness Code** calls the community to live in a distinct (holy) way. Holiness is not a way to separate from the world but a way to relate to the world based on the distinct covenant relationship of Israel with YHWH. Leviticus 18 illustrates this understanding with its introduction and conclusion urging the community to live as covenant people of YHWH rather than as the Egyptians or Canaanites. In that context, the remainder of the chapter instructs the people on matters of incest. The Holiness Code addresses holiness in both worship and ethics. Worship includes both regular worship (Lev. 24:1–9) and the special feasts:

- Spring—Passover and Unleavened Bread
- Summer—Festival of Weeks and **Pentecost**
- Fall—New Year, Feast of Tabernacles, Day of Atonement

The festivals reflect the patterns of harvest but also include attention to the faith of ancient Israel with the memory of Passover (Exod. 12), the giving of the law codes (Pentecost), and the wilderness experience in tabernacles. Ethical implications of holiness are central to Leviticus 25 and the customs of rest for servants, animals, and land in the Sabbath pattern and in the possibility of beginning again in the face of debt and servitude with the Year of Jubilee.

The divine presence with the covenant community provides the center for the book of Leviticus. Because this deity is perfectly holy (distinct), it is imperative that the community embody that holiness; thus the book provides instruction in how to live that way. Sacrifice and cleansing rituals make it possible to renew the relationship when it is fractured by the effects of sin and uncleanness. All of this instruction is a gift from the covenant God YHWH given at Sinai and constitutes what it means for ancient Israel, delivered from Egypt, to be for YHWH "a priestly kingdom and a holy nation" (Exod. 19:6).

Sojourn in the Wilderness

The Book of Numbers

The book of Numbers is named for the "numbering" of the people with which it begins; chapter 26 recounts a second census. In broad outline, the narrative action of the book occurs in three places: Sinai in chapters 1–10, the wilderness in chapters 10–20, and the Transjordan for the remainder of the action.

Two themes. The book exhibits two primary themes. The first is the right ordering of life as the covenant people of YHWH. The previous section on Leviticus demonstrates that worship was central to the shape of life for this covenant community, and thus the organization of worship is important in the priestly texts ranging from Exodus 25 through Leviticus and the first ten chapters of Numbers. The tabernacle as the community's central, movable sanctuary is at the heart of that organization. In the most holy place of the tabernacle stood the **ark of the covenant**, a container for the Decalogue and the most important visible symbol of the divine presence with the community. YHWH was understood to be invisibly enthroned above the ark with its winged cherubs overlooking it. Those who cared for the tabernacle and its worship regalia were the Levites, a priestly clan whose origin reminded the community of the defining story of the Passover. These priestly texts operate on a very concrete basis. They do not articulate a conceptual sense of the ordering of life as a covenant people; rather, they give concrete embodiment to that reality. The second arena for that organization is the shape of the camp itself. Included in this organization of the community are the **Nazirites**, who are to embody the holiness of the community by following the vow of not cutting their hair, avoiding strong drink with its evil fermentation, and avoiding the uncleanness of corpses. In the initial taking of the vow, their hair is cut and offered to YHWH as a symbol of the giving of life to the deity. With this theme of the right ordering of life, the covenant people of YHWH are now prepared to depart from Sinai with their identity set. Because they are YHWH's covenant people, they are now organized to live in a distinct way.

The second primary theme of the book of Numbers is the wilderness rebellions. This theme reaches back into earlier pentateuchal narratives. Following the community's deliverance at the sea celebrated in Exodus 15 and prior to reaching Sinai, the people complain that they do not have provision of food and water and will die in the wilderness. YHWH provides for them, including water and quail and manna, a bread-like substance. Later, while Moses has disappeared onto Mount Sinai and into its divine presence, the people become bewildered and complain. Aaron crafts for them an idol reminiscent of their life in Egypt, and the people indulge in the golden calf rebellion. This rebellious scene leads to a rupture in the covenant relationship, a rupture that must be healed. The covenant is renewed with Moses's intense intercession and considerable angst. The theme of rebellion surfaces

Figure 2.5. **The encampment of ancient Israel**

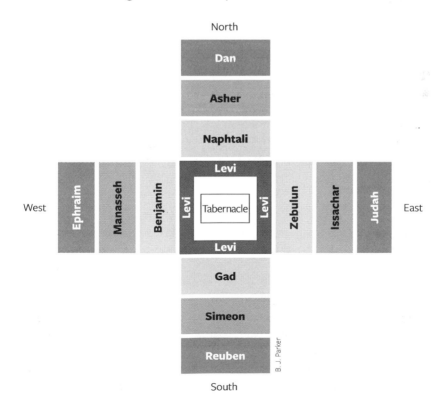

in the book of Numbers when the community breaks camp and departs from Sinai. The first complaints begin on the edge of the camp and again concern food provisions, but the complaints move toward the center of the camp and focus on issues of authority. In Numbers 12, Aaron and Miriam challenge Moses's authority; in Numbers 16, Korah, Dathan, and Abiram and their allies challenge the authority of Moses and Aaron. In the story of the spies in Numbers 13–14, the people distrust their leaders when spies sent to report on the promised land of Canaan suggest that possessing the land will be too difficult. These rebellions are all challenges to the authority of the covenant Lord YHWH, and they lead to prolonged wanderings in the wilderness. In the course of time, the wilderness generation dies and the "numbering" of a new generation comes to pass (Num. 26). The camp looks toward the destination of the land of Canaan promised in the ancestral covenant.

The route of the exodus. Numbers 33 recounts the itinerary of the ancient Israelites from Egypt to the edge of Canaan in the Transjordan Plateau. Scholars have long debated the identification of the sea that was crossed and the route that was taken. The locations of the places along the way are literally

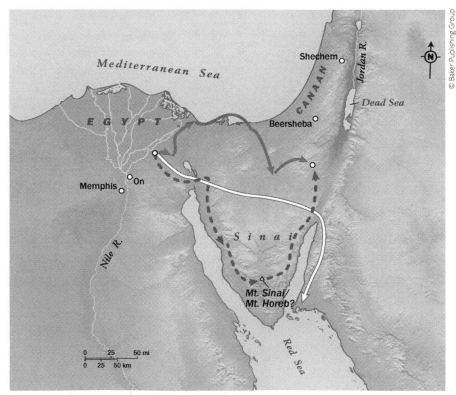

Figure 2.6. **The proposed routes of the exodus**

lost in the sands of time. Regarding the sea, some place that location along the Mediterranean coast, while others suggest that the sea was either in the region of the Bitter Lakes farther south or at the northern end of the Gulf of Suez. Regarding the route, some suggest that the community took the route along the coast, the Via Maris or Way of the Sea. A second route proposed for the wilderness journey would take the people through trade routes in the central Sinai. A third proposed route of the exodus (the traditional one) moves over into the Sinai Peninsula and south toward the traditional location of the mountain of Moses, Mount Sinai, the location of the famous Saint Catherine's Monastery to this day. From there the group turns north and wanders in the wilderness for a generation. The oasis of Kadesh-Barnea becomes a place of camp for some of this time. They eventually pass over into the Transjordan Plateau as they haltingly move toward crossing the Jordan into Canaan.

Numbers 22–24 narrates the story of Balaam and illustrates some of the conflict the ancient Israelites endured during this journey. Balaam appears to be a regional figure combining the characteristics of prophet or seer, judge, sage, and magician. Archaeologists have found at Deir Alla in the eastern Jordan Valley extrabiblical texts suggesting Balaam's presence in the region. In Numbers, a local ruler, Balak, hires Balaam to hurl a curse on Israel. Balaam instead pronounces a blessing on Israel, showing the inevitability of the victory of Israel and YHWH. The account suggests that groups in the region have begun to fear Israel and their God YHWH. These narratives provide some comic relief in a book centered in troubles of the wilderness and provide a picture of an ancient cultural setting and Israel's progress toward entering the land.

The Book of Deuteronomy

The Pentateuch concludes with the lengthy book of Deuteronomy (meaning "second law"), another recounting of the Mosaic tradition of Torah. The book takes the form of farewell addresses from Moses to the covenant community as it stands on the edge of a new place and a new era in the land promised to the ancestors. It calls the community to covenant faithfulness on the cusp of a new day. The literary style of the book is distinct. It recounts the Torah but does so in a sermonic context calling the people to embody the Torah as the covenant people of YHWH, who has delivered this people in the exodus from Egypt. YHWH delivered the people with powerful hand and outstretched arm (Deut. 4:34; 5:15; 7:19; 11:2; 26:8) and has journeyed with this people to a place which YHWH has chosen to make the divine name dwell (Deut. 12:5, 11, 21; 14:23, 24; 16:2, 6, 11; 26:2). Deuteronomy commands this community, "Love [YHWH] your God with all your heart, and with all your soul, and with all your might" (6:5). The book's organization accords with the notion of covenant and calls for covenant faithfulness at a time of decision for ancient Israel. The book begins with a historical recounting of the events from Sinai to the edge of the Jordan to provide a context for the recounting of the law codes that provide the center of the book. That section concludes with an exhortation for the people to decide "this very day" (26:16) to keep covenant. The consequences of blessing or cursing found in keeping or breaking covenant follow in chapters 27–28 along with concluding texts (chapters 29–34) that countenance the future of new generations. This covenant book articulates the basis of the Mosaic covenant in the exodus history and mighty acts of YHWH and calls the people to respond with covenant fidelity on the verge of a new era.

Covenant formularies. Twentieth-century scholars became aware of ancient treaty formulas from the Hittites that give a particular shape to suzerainty relationships (relationships between overlords and vassals) as opposed to parity treaties, between equals. These suzerainty treaties characteristically take the following shape:

- Preamble introducing the suzerain or overlord
- An account of the previous history of beneficence from the suzerain for the vassals
- Basic principles of the treaty relationship
- Detailed instructions in the shape of the relationship
- Witnesses to the agreement (typically divine witnesses)
- Blessings and cursings as consequences of keeping or breaking the treaty

The book of Deuteronomy broadly follows this pattern, again emphasizing the covenant nature of the book. Some things, however, are different in Deuteronomy, such as the absence of gods and goddesses as witnesses. This basic covenant pattern also appears in the book of Exodus with the preamble to the Decalogue in Exodus 20 and the following articulation of the Torah in the Ten Commandments and then the Covenant Code. The basic structure is divine acts of beneficence followed by response of fidelity in a covenant relationship shaped by instruction.

Deuteronomic influence. The book of Deuteronomy addresses the covenant community "today" and calls for a decision for or against covenant (Deut. 30:15–20). Its narrative setting in the Pentateuch is preparation for entering a new era in the land of Canaan promised to the ancestors. Later, in the seventh century BCE, Deuteronomy serves to address Jerusalem with a call to covenant faithfulness. Josiah is on the throne, and a scroll of law is found when the temple is being renovated (2 Kings 22). The female prophet Huldah authenticates the scroll, and it becomes the basis of Josiah's grand reform, a covenant renewal that included the following features:

- Centralization of worship
- Abolition of astral worship
- Removal of sacred prostitutes
- Prohibition of child sacrifice
- Removal of necromancers
- Reinstitution of the Passover in the temple

These features are important in Deuteronomy (12:13–18; 16:1–8; 17:3; 18:10–12; 23:17–18), and so most would suggest that the scroll found during Josiah's reign was the basic law code of Deuteronomy. We noted in the discussion of the composition of the Pentateuch that many scholars consider the Josianic reform to be the background for the shaping of the book of Deuteronomy. The book was also important when the kingdom of Judah fell and sought to come to terms with its covenant infidelity and how that might be remedied. As a result, Deuteronomy is central to the story of ancient Israel and begins the notion of a canon for the community, an abiding guide for the community's life as a covenant people.

Deuteronomy brings the Pentateuch to a close with an ardent formulation of a God whose mighty acts bring into being a people called Israel, those who strive with God. This YHWH is fiercely zealous that this people might have wholeness of life found only in faithful relationship with YHWH. Other gods lead to death; YHWH gives life and so acts to bring Israel to wholeness because they are the ones chosen from the ancestors of old. Deuteronomy 6:4 articulates the distinctiveness of YHWH: "Hear, O Israel: The Lord is our God, the Lord alone." The text, called the Shema for its first word *shema'* ("hear"), continues to be central to Jewish faith. The proper response to this YHWH is covenant loyalty.

Deuteronomy illustrates this fierceness of YHWH in the command for one place of worship; one God suggests one sanctuary with loyal worship. The fierceness of YHWH also comes into play in the instructions for wars against those loyal to other deities. We shall return to the issue of warfare in the next chapter. The central issue in Deuteronomy, however, begins with the reality that in the deliverance from Egypt, Israel becomes the covenant people of YHWH. The question in Deuteronomy is whether Israel will live out that covenant relationship. Their future depends on their decisions, and those decisions are enacted in ethical living, in which the book gives extensive instruction: "Then Moses and the levitical priests spoke to all Israel, saying: Keep silence and hear, O Israel! This very day you have become the people of the LORD your God. Therefore obey the LORD your God, observing his commandments and his statutes that I am commanding you today" (Deut. 27:9–10). The book of Deuteronomy is an extensive sermon on covenant faithfulness put in the context of the exodus from Egypt and thus appropriately concludes the books of Moses.

Theological Reflection: Creation and Covenant

The Pentateuch composes the first section of the Hebrew canon, and its conclusion with the treatise of Deuteronomy provides an appropriate place to pause and take stock of the import of this literature that articulates ancient Israel's purpose by telling the faith community's foundational story. The story provides a script for life—especially in the arenas of worship and ethics—and as the community practices the story, it encounters the fullness that YHWH provides. Thus central to the script is relationship with YHWH. The Pentateuch is thus a multidimensional, identity-forming narrative placing ancient Israel in the community of peoples.

This first part of the Hebrew canon begins with creation and moves through the early struggles of humans. With the ancestral narratives, the community of ancient Israel comes into focus with a promise of future and place as blessing from YHWH. In the book of Exodus, the paradigmatic event of liberation sets the community on the road toward this future. The law codes and the priestly texts in Exodus, Leviticus, and Numbers articulate a shape for life together as a covenant community. By the end of Deuteronomy, the community looks forward to life in the land of Canaan.

The two theological themes that run through this first section of the Hebrew canon are creation and covenant. The Old Testament begins with God as creator of the world and of humans and as the one who provides for life (Gen. 1:28–30). That provision carries through the primeval era and on through the ancestral narratives as YHWH promises the blessing of divine presence leading to a future in a land. That provision is also seen in the shaping of institutions of worship so that the holy divine presence could continue with the community and provide for life. The Pentateuch concludes by looking forward to life in the land as central to the divine blessing from this creator deity. This God is the one who is present to bless, to provide vitality for growth and thriving in the world.

The second theological theme is covenant. The Pentateuch contains various expressions of covenant. The Noachic covenant and the ancestral covenant promise are important in Genesis. The focus in this textbook will be on the Mosaic or Sinaitic covenant. In the context of the deliverance from bondage in Egypt, YHWH reveals a covenant pattern of life for the community of ancient Israel. That covenant holds ethical dimensions and liturgical dimensions. The various law codes specify these implications. This covenant revelation comes at Sinai and runs through the priestly texts in the latter part of Exodus and on through the instruction in worship and holiness in Leviticus and in the first part of Numbers. The Pentateuch's concluding book of Deuteronomy is an extensive exhortation on the nature of covenant with the fierce God YHWH. The beginning point for this covenant tradition is the confession that YHWH is the God who comes to deliver when the people cry out in the midst of oppression (Exod. 3:7–9). God delivers the people and begins a new life for them by offering them a covenant relationship. Ancient Israel enters into this relationship and hears the divine instruction for the shape of covenant life and the consequences of keeping and breaking covenant. The shape and hope of this covenant survive the struggles of the wilderness journey, and with the major exhortation to covenant loyalty in Deuteronomy, the first section of the Hebrew canon comes to a close looking forward to the embodiment of covenant in this community in the land toward which they move.

SUGGESTED READING

Blenkinsopp, Joseph. *The Pentateuch: An Introduction to the First Five Books of the Bible*. New York: Doubleday, 2000.

Clines, David J. A. *The Theme of the Pentateuch*. 2nd ed. Sheffield: Sheffield Academic Press, 1997.

Coogan, Michael D. *A Reader of Ancient Near Eastern Texts: Sources for the Study of the Old Testament*. New York: Oxford University Press, 2013.

Dozeman, Thomas B. *The Pentateuch: Introducing the Torah*. Minneapolis: Fortress Press, 2017.

Hallo, William W., and K. Lawson Younger, eds. *The Context of Scripture: Canonical Compositions, Monumental Inscriptions and Archival Documents from the Biblical World*. 3 vols. Leiden: Brill, 2003.

McEntire, Mark. *Struggling with God: An Introduction to the Pentateuch*. Macon, GA: Mercer University Press, 2008.

Sakenfeld, Katharine Doob. *Journeying with God: A Commentary on the Book of Numbers*. Grand Rapids: Eerdmans, 1995.

3

Former and Latter Prophets

Covenant is one of the major themes of the Torah or Pentateuch, the first division of the Hebrew Scriptures. That theme continues in the second division, the Prophets. The Former and Latter Prophets narrate the story of the covenant community in the form of history and in the form of proclamations from the prophets, vital interpreters of the covenant history.

Historical and Social Contexts of the Prophets

The second division of the Hebrew canon continues the story of ancient Israel. The promise of progeny (or descendants) has come to pass, and the promise of a land in which to live out a future is at hand. This next part of the canon remembers the story of the people in the land, from the beginnings of their time in the land through the time of the monarchy with a united kingdom and with two kingdoms and beyond. The Former Prophets (Joshua, Judges, 1–2 Samuel, and 1–2 Kings) are often popularly labeled as historical books. They are called the Former Prophets because they include significant characters who are prophets and because they espouse the same view of ancient Israel's history as do the Latter Prophets. The Latter Prophets come after the Former Prophets and carry the names of Isaiah, Jeremiah, and Ezekiel (also known as the Major Prophets) as well as the twelve texts sometimes titled Minor Prophets. Our look at these books will begin with the Former Prophets and proceed to the Latter Prophets as they arise in their historical contexts.

The Former Prophets recount history from the time of Joshua to the fall of the Southern Kingdom of Judah. History is always written backward; that is, historians look back on history and then recount it. History is not recounted *in medias res* (in the middle of it). Part of what that literary reality suggests is that history is recounted from a perspective. The narrative in the Former Prophets, for example, remembers this part of ancient Israel's story from a perspective inside the land of Canaan. These books of Joshua, Judges, 1–2 Samuel, and 1–2 Kings also recount history from a theological perspective, and that theological perspective comes from the book of Deuteronomy with its emphasis on covenant. The language and theological approach of these books can fairly be called **Deuteronomic** or Deuteronomistic (they are sometimes referred to as the **Deuteronomistic History**). Most scholars who study these texts suggest that the heirs to the tradition of Deuteronomy have compiled various historical and literary sources and put together these historical books. Although the Former Prophets recount the history from Joshua to the fall of Jerusalem, they speak to their readers of the relationship between the covenant community of ancient Israel and the covenant God YHWH. In a sense, the book of Deuteronomy both concludes the Pentateuch and introduces the Former Prophets with its theological language and agenda. Thus some scholars suggest reading the books of Genesis through 2 Kings as one unit called the Primary History, since all the books exhibit connections.

The Former Prophets constitute a good example of redaction criticism. Various historical and literary sources have been brought together for a purpose. Many interpreters would suggest that the collection of these sources began in the seventh century BCE, in the time of King Josiah, or perhaps even earlier. The unit as a whole, however, concludes at the end of 2 Kings in the middle of exile. German scholar Martin Noth, who wrote the definitive

OUTLINE OF THE HISTORY OF THE HEBREW PEOPLE

  I. Exodus: thirteenth century BCE
   A. Moses and Joshua
   B. Canaan
 II. Judges
III. United kingdom
   A. Saul, 1020–1000 BCE
   B. David, 1000–961 BCE
   C. Solomon, 961–922 BCE
IV. Divided kingdom
   A. Israel and Jeroboam I
      1. Syro-Ephraimite Crisis
      2. Fall of Samaria, 722/721 BCE
   B. Judah and Rehoboam
 V. Babylonian period
   A. Fall of Jerusalem, 587/586 BCE
   B. Exile
VI. Persian age
   A. Ezra
   B. Nehemiah
VII. Greek period
   A. Maccabean Revolt

study, indicates that a redactor edited the books of the Former Prophets together around 550 BCE in the midst of exile. Other scholars would suggest that these historical books came together in stages. The American scholar Frank Moore Cross suggests a double redaction—in the time of Josiah and in the time of exile. Central to the redaction of these texts is the question of why the kingdom of Judah fell to Babylon in the sixth century, with the Deuteronomic theology of these texts providing the answer. The community has broken covenant and now is encountering the consequences of their faithlessness. YHWH, however, may not be finished with this covenant community, for time after time in the story of the Former Prophets, Israel repents and comes back to YHWH and the life-giving covenant relationship YHWH seeks for them. Indeed, the book of 2 Kings ends in exile, but with the release of the Davidic heir from prison. Does that suggest hope for the future? As we journey through these books, we will see this Deuteronomic theme of covenant faith as a means to articulating the significance of this part of Israel's history.

Settlement in the Land

The Book of Joshua

The book of Joshua recounts the entry of Israel into the land of Canaan in three parts.

- Joshua's leading Israel across the Jordan and into Canaan (Josh. 1–12)
- The division of the land among the tribes (Josh. 13–21)
- The Shechem assembly (Josh. 22–24)

Joshua's leadership. The book begins with YHWH's commission for Joshua, who succeeds Moses as the leader of Israel, to lead the people into the land of Canaan. The people cross the Jordan River into the land in a similar fashion to the crossing of the sea in the exodus from Egypt, though now the community is organized as a covenant community and the ark of the covenant leads their procession into the land. They set up a memorial of stones to remember the crossing into the land. Then the males of the community are circumcised, a physical sign of their covenant relationship with YHWH. The wilderness generation has passed from the scene, and this new generation entering the land needs to demonstrate the covenant relationship with this physical symbol. The community then observes Passover. Joshua encounters an angelic commander of YHWH's armies, and in this theophany comes confirmation of his leadership in the conquest of the land. Chapter 6 recounts the battle of Jericho, the first military challenge for the community of ancient Israel. Earlier in the book, Joshua had sent spies to reconnoiter the area. They had gone to the establishment of Rahab the prostitute as a way of not drawing too much attention to themselves. Rahab had protected them when the leaders of Jericho sought them, and Rahab's loyalty is rewarded with her life and a place with Israel when Jericho falls. The account of the battle of Jericho shows the ritual nature of the warfare with its processions and trumpets and priestly involvement.

After Israel conquers Jericho, they move on to the city of Ai.

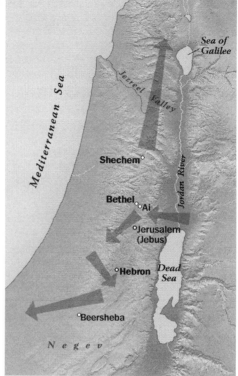

Figure 3.1. **The conquest of Canaan**

Here they encounter a new difficulty as they are not successful. The text makes it clear that the reason for the defeat lies with Israel. One of the community, Achan of the tribe of Judah, keeps for himself some of the booty from the Jericho victory. Because these battles are dedicated to the covenant deity YHWH, all that is captured goes to YHWH. Because of Achan's transgression, the people face defeat. Achan is executed when his sin is discovered, and eventually the city of Ai is captured with a clever military stratagem. This story demonstrates the idea of corporate solidarity. Because someone in Israel has violated the divine instruction, the whole community faces the consequences. Achan's whole family and all his possessions are destroyed; they are all understood to be in solidarity with the transgressor Achan.

After the Gibeonites become Israel's servants rather than being destroyed in battle, the text recounts victories over the kings of the south and over the kings of the north. Chapters 11–12 then summarize Joshua's conquests. Chapters 13–21 recount the division of the land among the tribes, and the final section of the book of Joshua recounts the assembly of the people at Shechem to renew their covenant with YHWH and with one another. The book's concluding chapter recounts the mighty acts of YHWH on behalf of the people and calls them to "serve the LORD" in covenant faithfulness. The basis of the renewal of covenant here at the end of the book is the covenant theology articulated in the book of Deuteronomy.

The question of conquest. Joshua 1–12 recounts faithful Israel taking possession of the land of Canaan by way of a military incursion in three prongs—the central hill country, the south, and the north.

Many popular accounts of this era of ancient Israel's history take these chapters simply as the description of how Israel came to possess the land. At the same time, attention paid to a variety of texts in Joshua and Judges suggests that the historical picture may be more complicated. Joshua 11:13, 22; 15:63; 16:10; 17:11–13; and the opening chapters of Judges make clear that parts of the land have not been conquered. Some gradual settlement seems to be part of the picture. The text also gives hints of indigenous Canaanites, such as those from Gibeon, joining with Israel. So the text suggests that there are at least three aspects to Israel's emergence in the land: military incursion, gradual settlement, and defections from the Canaanite population. Three major models of how Israel emerged in Canaan have thus come to the fore:

1. *Military invasion.* This model follows the first half of the book of Joshua in recounting Israel's military victories and is especially associated with the twentieth century American archaeologist W. F. Albright.

2. *Peaceful infiltration.* The German Old Testament scholar Albrecht Alt developed this model more in line with the text of Judges and in line with considerable archaeological evidence.

3. *Peasant revolt.* The American scholars George Mendenhall and Norman Gottwald developed a model focusing on how indigenous Canaanites joined with Israel in rebellion against their oppressive overlords.

The work of archaeologists is important in seeking to reconstruct how Israel emerged in the land. The record of this time in Palestine (thirteenth century BCE) indicates that it was a time of upheaval and change. Military destruction occurred at Hazor in the north as well as at Bethel and Debir. The excavation of Jericho demonstrates the difficulties, however. Apparently, the city was not occupied during that time. Contemporary archaeologists suggest that the material remains indicate a time of change to which oversimplified historical accounts do not do justice. It is clear that Israel's emergence in the land is a complicated process with the Moses/Joshua group gaining a foothold and eventually coming to possess the land. Others joined them in this time of considerable upheaval in Canaan, a time of change in all the social dimensions of life in this land. Archaeologists and historians emphasize the importance of the entrance of the

Sea Peoples (the Philistines) into Canaan as part of the upheaval. The text also focuses on the covenant faithfulness (or lack thereof) of Israel.

Wars of YHWH. One of the major issues that surface in the accounts of battles in Joshua and Judges surrounds the customs of battle taken up in the name of the covenant deity. The battle of Jericho in Joshua 6 provides a good example of the procedure outlined in Deuteronomy 20. First, the people must prepare for the battle. YHWH will be present in the act of war, and so the community must ritually prepare to encounter the divine. Because the battle belongs to YHWH, who determines the outcome, the covenant God must also reveal the strategy for the military event. The ark of the covenant and the trumpets in the processions around Jericho emphasize the ritual dimensions of this warfare. The final step of the procedure is called the *kherem*, or ban or devotion to destruction. Everyone and everything taken in the battle is dedicated to YHWH (since the battle and victory belong to YHWH) and then destroyed and removed from human use, as if sacrificed to YHWH. These battles have at times been called wars of annihilation or complete destruction. These texts create ethical difficulties, especially in the canon of Christian Scriptures, which often articulate an ideal of peace. The difficulty is not one easily solved, but some of the following considerations may be helpful to readers.

- Some battles are taken to be defenses of YHWH and of the faith of the covenant community (Num. 21:1; Josh. 10:1–7; 11:1–5).
- The text understands some of the destruction of Canaanites in terms of judgment on their worship of idols, an important focus of Deuteronomic faith (Deut. 20:17–18).
- The covenant context is central to these texts. Ancient Israel demonstrates obedience to covenant instruction that makes possible the fulfillment of the promise of a future and a place to embody the covenant and its attendant blessing to all.
- This kind of warfare was part of the culture in which these texts arose. Divine revelation comes in that context and culture. The Stele of Mesha recounts a battle against ancient Israel on behalf of the Moabite deity Chemosh. The cultural setting is important in considering these texts.
- This kind of historical instruction on warfare was given to the covenant community of ancient Israel and does not apply to any other nation in the past or present.
- Interpreters will need to consider these texts along with other biblical texts that argue for an approach emphasizing peacemaking (Isa. 2:1–4; Pss. 85:8–13; 122).

One way to think about the book of Joshua is that it accounts for the emergence of Israel in the land of Canaan by saying that YHWH created this people and gave them a place to live out the covenant relationship. The book recounts Israel's memory of this pivotal moment in the life of the community.

The Book of Judges

The book of Judges portrays early Israel as a loose tribal confederation. The tribes lived in various parts of the land of Canaan and were essentially united for worship and for military needs. Beyond those needs, there was not a lot of unity. The social and historical contexts described above in reference to the opening of the book suggest the lack of stability.

The leaders of the people are labeled "judges." Their primary task is to deliver the people from oppression, though they may have provided some other leadership. Such leaders were part of the organization of community life broadly in the ancient Near East in this time period.

The Judges cycle. The bulk of the book narrates the stories of the major judges—Othniel, Ehud, Deborah, Gideon, Jephthah, and Samson. Minor judges are also included (Judg. 3:31; 10:1–5; 12:8–15). The means for narrating the stories is a cycle introduced in chapter 2 of the book.

- The Israelites do evil in the sight of YHWH.
- As a consequence, they suffer oppression.
- Israel cries out to YHWH.
- YHWH raises up a deliverer, a judge.

The beginning of the story of Othniel in Judges 3:7–9 succinctly illustrates the pattern. The story of Ehud follows with the darkly

Figure 3.2. The distribution of the land to the twelve tribes of Israel

humorous deliverance from the rotund Moabite king Eglon. Chapters 4–5 recount the story of Deborah and her general Barak, and the deliverance of the people from the Canaanite king Jabin and his general Sisera, an Israelite victory celebrated in the poem in Judges 5. Women are central characters in the book of Judges. Chapters 6–9 recount the story of the unlikely judge Gideon, whose weakness the presence of YHWH turns to strength. With surprise tactics, Gideon delivers Israel from Midianite oppression. Following Gideon's success, his son Abimelech makes an unfortunate and failed attempt at a monarchy in early Israel (Judg. 9). Jephthah also delivers Israel, from the Ammonites, but takes a rash vow that leads to the sacrifice of his daughter. The final major judge is Samson, a Nazirite who delivers the Israelites from the Philistines in between his womanizing activities and the breaking of his Nazirite vow.

The Deuteronomic theme. It will be clear from the very brief summary above that the narratives of the judges recount a history that is not simply a repeated cycle. The stories of the judges recount a fairly quick downward spiral. The covenant history of Israel in the period of the judges is not going well. The two stories that conclude the book of Judges (chapters 17–21) show that **idolatry**, internecine warfare, and shocking inhumanity to others characterize early Israel and its covenant infidelity. The cycle of these stories fits well the Deuteronomic theme of covenant faith. The judges were likely tribal leaders, and the Deuteronomic editors have shaped their narratives to portray a particular view of Israel's covenant faithlessness in this era. The cycle also demonstrates that repentance is the means of renewing the covenant relationship that YHWH seeks for Israel. Even in the low point at the end of the period of the judges, YHWH has not abandoned the covenant relationship with Israel. Very important in the narrative of the Former Prophets is the conclusion of the book of Judges: "In those days there was no king in Israel; all the people did what was right in their own eyes" (21:25).

Movement to Monarchy

The historical and social contexts articulated above suggest that the earliest time for Israel in the land of Canaan was a time of considerable transition. Martin Noth, using an analogy with Greek history, characterized the confederation as an **amphictyony** (a system of states organized around a religious center), but the confederation in Joshua and Judges appears to have been more loosely organized than the Greek system. Eventually, Israel emerged as a force in Canaanite life, often in conflict with the Philistines.

Major Characters in the Transition to Monarchy

Samuel was the last of the judges. He was also a prophetic and priestly figure and the one who anointed the first two kings. He marks the transition from the tribal league with charismatic leaders, those the divine presence called for particular tasks, to a kingdom with an established monarchy. The book of 1 Samuel begins with the story of Samuel's birth and dedication to divine service. God calls Samuel as a prophet, and he trains as a priest at the sanctuary at Shiloh. The picture of life in the tribal confederation is one in which corruption and inattentiveness to covenant with YHWH rule the day. Samuel rises to be the clear leader of the people. Part of the narrative in this section centers on the ark of the covenant and illustrates some of the dynamics of the era. The Philistines constantly press Israel, and the Israelites call for the ark to lead them into battle. In a disastrous battle at Aphek-Ebenezer, the Philistines capture the ark. The ark causes trouble in the Philistine camp and in the temple of their god Dagon (1 Sam. 5), showing with considerable humor the power of the divine presence of YHWH, and so the Philistines eventually return the ark to Israelite territory. These narratives suggest that YHWH is powerfully present but that the tribes of Israel do not know how to serve the covenant God faithfully.

Saul is a second transition figure in these texts. Although Samuel anoints him the first king in ancient Israel, the Israelites acclaim him as king after a military deliverance of the people in the manner of a judge. Beginning in chapter 9, 1 Samuel tells the story of the rise and fall of Saul, whose reign has more the feel of that of a tribal chieftain and has a tragic dimension to it. Saul garnered military success in the manner of the judges (1 Sam. 14:47–48) but is not treated kindly in the tradition. His time leads to the heroic David.

Because there had not been a king in Israel before this time, the question of succession is a live one. Saul's son Jonathan is a popular military hero, but David is the hero of the masses. He receives Saul's daughter Michal in marriage and so becomes part of the royal family. At the same time, Saul becomes extremely suspicious of the ambitious David, and the two men come to blows, with Saul eventually pursuing David out of panic and fear that the younger hero will take the throne. Saul, along with his son Jonathan, comes to a tragic end in battle. David has by then become something of an outlaw in the southern part of the kingdom and has worked with the outcasts who have joined him to protect Hebrews in that region. David is a kind of Robin Hood figure in the area, popular with women, and building a power base as a charismatic "man of the people." When Saul meets his demise, the leaders of the military eventually turn to David to unite the kingdom under his rule. Second Samuel 7 recounts the promise of the prophet Nathan that David and his sons will rule over the people in Jerusalem as the divinely chosen monarchs.

Kingship in Israel

First Samuel 8–9 recounts the story of the origin of kingship in Israel. Israel's life as a loose confederation of tribes has reached its limits. The aggressive Philistines press the people on every side. Geography, lack of communication, and lack of a central organizing authority divide the tribes. Since other nations around them are progressing with monarchies, the people ask their leader, Samuel, for a king. Samuel, in the place of YHWH, warns the people of dangers in a monarchical system. Kings could lead the people away from loyalty to their covenant with YHWH; the kingdom could become allied with other peoples and their idols. **Syncretism**, the mixing of religions, was a real threat as the Israelites often related to their Canaanite neighbors with their worship of the Baals. Another concern was the place of the king. In Egypt the pharaoh had divine qualities. That was not an option in Israel because they had only one God: the covenant God YHWH. So Israel comes to terms with the monarchy by establishing a king who is God's representative. Israel's kingship is a sacral kingship in which the monarch is a kind of intermediary who rules over the people in Jerusalem as God's representative and servant and who represents the people in interceding for the community before YHWH. This view is something of an uneasy compromise, as reflected in the text, especially in the conflicting connections between Samuel, Saul, and David and the covenant God YHWH. The prophetic theology of history these texts reflect trumpets the concern that a powerful monarch could lead to covenant disobedience, the avenue of death in the view of the Deuteronomic historians (Deut. 17:14–20). This concern about the future plays itself out in the context of a powerful era of ancient Israel's history: the time of the united kingdom of David and Solomon and then the time of the divided kingdoms of Israel and Judah.

David's Reign

The book of 1 Samuel tells the story of David's rise to power. In an unlikely move at the instruction of YHWH, Samuel anoints David as king. David, the shepherd boy and musician, then begins a public career first in the service of King Saul. He defeats the Philistine giant Goliath, and his fame begins to spread. He enters the Saulide family and is closely connected with Saul's son Jonathan. The fragile and tragic Saul comes to see David as a competitor for the throne and pursues him as a mortal enemy. David sets up a camp in the southern part of the kingdom and begins to curry favor with the local citizenry. After Saul and his sons die in battle with the Philistines, David is made king over Judah and, after considerable intrigue and infighting, over the united kingdom of Israel.

Central to David's reign is the move to make Jerusalem the capital city of the kingdom and the center of worship of the covenant God YHWH. David hearkens back to the traditions of the ark of the covenant as the central visible symbol of divine presence in the community and with considerable difficulty brings the ark into Jerusalem with great pomp and circumstance. Jerusalem is a city with no tribal loyalties in Israel. It has been a Jebusite stronghold. It is also easy to defend. The transfer of the monarchy to Jerusalem and the tie of the city to the Davidic line are among the brilliant moves of David. The moving of the ark of the covenant to the capital city powerfully symbolizes YHWH's choice of this place and of this monarchical line. David has now forcefully established his power as king politically, militarily, socially, and theologically as promised in the Nathan **prophecy** (2 Sam. 7). He then sets about shaping his kingdom with a royal bureaucracy. He establishes a cabinet with Joab as the chief of armed forces, Benaiah as chief of the royal guards, Zadok and Abiathar as chief priests, Jehoshaphat as recorder, and Seraiah as secretary of state.

The court history of King David in 2 Samuel 8–20 and 1 Kings 1–2 recounts the reign of David with attention to the question of who will succeed David. This intriguing set of narratives immediately follows the Nathan prophecy and sees the prophecy worked out in the life of the Davidic line. These chapters

PRIESTS

Priests were central to the life of ancient Israel during much of the story that the Old Testament tells. The Old Testament account of priesthood is multifaceted. Moses's brother, Aaron, is a defining character for the priesthood. The priestly role centers on worship and especially sacrifice; the books of Exodus, Leviticus, and Numbers give special attention to that role as well as the related role of Levites. Since the story of ancient Israel is at base a theological story, priests were also influential in the whole of life, including the political and social arenas, and thus the chief priests are listed as leaders in David's reign. The Old Testament often holds priests in high esteem, but there are also examples of corrupt priests, such as in the line of Eli or Amaziah, who opposes Amos the prophet. In Second Temple Judaism, priests took on considerable political power and often came to be associated with distant imperial figures who were viewed as oppressors. Some New Testament texts reflect this more negative view of priests.

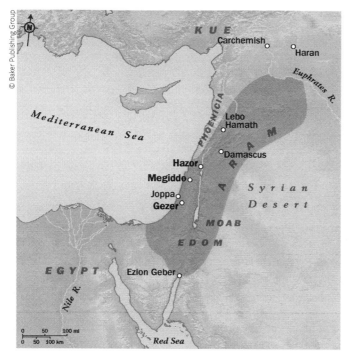

Figure 3.3. **Israel under the rule of David and Solomon**

form a novella in which the action takes place in conversations and in family contexts. In these narratives the reign of David and succession to the throne play out amid the normal occurrences of life. David rules as the chosen one with victories and with compassion. The public servant King David is successful. Yet the family portrait of David is not so positive. David indulges in the heinous affair with Bathsheba and seeks to cover it up. He loses the child of the affair, but Solomon is born shortly thereafter. David then survives various family intrigues and immoralities and rebellions. The narrative is fast paced and includes many conflicts. In due time and with much palace intrigue, Solomon—the first remaining son born subsequent to the Nathan prophecy—succeeds his father as king and establishes himself on the throne. David has passed the throne to his son. Rather than determining the outcome of such events by way of theophany, YHWH appears to be behind the scenes and trusting David to move ahead as the king who has the abilities and provisions for ruling in Jerusalem. The means of recounting history in this set of narratives are significant. The account has been called the first secular history, which may be an overstatement, but the historiography traces God's involvement through persons and everyday events; the narratives have the feel of normal life.

It is fair to characterize David as a "glorious rascal." He was the great king of Israel, but he went astray in many ways. The Old Testament portrays him as a flawed hero, but one of remarkable influence and popularity. David's contributions include the following:

- Uniting the kingdom
- Establishing Jerusalem as the capital

- Defeating competing armies
- Establishing a cabinet to rule
- Beginning worship in Jerusalem/Zion
- Leaving a legacy for the future

The books of Samuel and Kings, in line with the Deuteronomic view of history, have an uneasy response to monarchy and its power. The issue is not the success of the royal house or the popularity of the king but faithfulness to the covenant with YHWH. The Nathan prophecy raises that concern, which becomes embodied in the Davidic line. Biblical scholars sometimes describe the Nathan prophecy as the first articulation of the Davidic covenant. Some contrast this covenant with the Mosaic (or Sinaitic) covenant, because the covenant with David emphasizes promise rather than Torah. Some suggest that this "royal ideology" that became popular in ancient Israel led to a decline in faithfulness to the covenant relationship with YHWH.

Solomon's Reign

The reigns of the three kings of the united kingdom cover nearly a century.

- Saul, 1020–1000 BCE
- David, 1000–961 BCE
- Solomon, 961–922 BCE

The first chapters of 1 Kings recount the story of Solomon. From a governing perspective, the story begins well and declines over time. First Kings characterizes Solomon as a brilliant economist but not an expert at public relations. He ruthlessly establishes himself on the throne. Wisdom and culture thrive during his reign, and he pursues various foreign alliances as the ruler of an influential empire. Those alliances often include marriage to foreign princesses. Solomon takes over his father David's kingdom and organizes it in order to best exploit its resources. Both David and Solomon make efforts to overcome loyalties to the various tribes throughout the kingdom. Solomon seeks to foster loyalty to the central government in Jerusalem. In the process, his reign takes on an oppressive tone. Solomon establishes the corvée, in which families yield to subscription (or forced labor) in service of the throne one month out of three. He emphasizes mining and trade and undertakes major construction projects, including building cities and a fleet. The most important building project during Solomon's reign is the temple in Jerusalem; 1 Kings 8 recounts its dedication. All of this commerce and building brings attendant taxation and harsh service and a degeneration in Solomon's success.

The Division of the Kingdoms

First Kings 12 recounts the gathering of tribal leaders at the death of Solomon. Solomon's son **Rehoboam** expects the people to acclaim him as king, but the leaders of the northern tribes are very troubled by the oppressive nature of Solomon's reign. The conflict leads to a split of the kingdom into two: the Northern Kingdom of Israel with **Jeroboam I** as its first ruler and the Southern Kingdom of Judah with Rehoboam as king. The account of the Northern Kingdom in the books of Kings demonstrates that these historical texts are more commentary than chronicle. From the beginning, the northern state was outcast. Jeroboam establishes sanctuaries at Bethel and Dan so that worshipers will stay away from the Davidic ideology in Jerusalem at festival time and also support the northern economy. At these sanctuaries Jeroboam sets up golden calves, which the Deuteronomic historians see as idols. Only full commitment to the pure worship of YHWH in the Jerusalem temple is acceptable to them. This theme pervades the accounts of the kings of the Northern Kingdom.

King **Omri** establishes Samaria as the northern capital, and he and his son Ahab have successful reigns from economic and military perspectives. From the Deuteronomic perspective of covenant loyalty, however, these reigns are decidedly unsuccessful. Canaanite fertility religion influences the

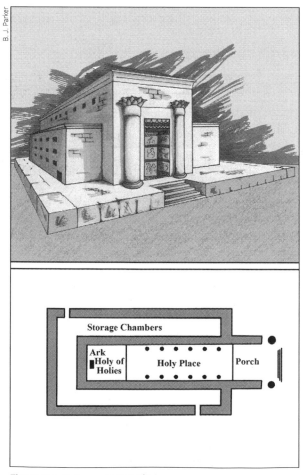

B. J. Parker

Storage Chambers

Ark
Holy of
Holies

Holy Place

Porch

Figure 3.4. **Solomon's temple**

people, and, judging from both the Former and Latter Prophets, syncretism becomes the order of the day. Ahab marries Jezebel, a worshiper of Baal Melqart, and difficulties ensue according to the covenant pattern of consequences for keeping and breaking covenant. The confrontation on Mount Carmel between the prophet Elijah and the prophets of Baal symbolizes the conflict (1 Kings 18). The story of the stealing of the vineyard and the "trumped up" execution of its owner, Naboth, symbolize corrupt royal power and the influence of idolatry. Prophets such as Elijah become the voice for loyalty to YHWH. Elijah's successor, Elisha, also participates in the political life of the kingdom by blessing Jehu's overthrow of the Omride dynasty. Jeroboam II succeeds Jehu and brings some stability to the north, but after his death the kingdom declines quickly. The Assyrian Empire from the north and its ally Syria begin to exert

Figure 3.5. Israel and Judah during the divided kingdom

pressure on Israel, and in the mid-730s BCE things come to a head with what is often labeled the **Syro-Ephraimite Crisis** (after Syria and Ephraim, the major tribe in the north). The kingdom survives that skirmish only to see its demise in the next decade. Its capital, Samaria, falls in 722/721 BCE. The kingdom had seen little royal stability in its two centuries; the task of many kings was simply to survive and remain on the throne.

Committed History

Our brief survey has indicated that the history recounted in 1–2 Kings is history committed to the covenant ideology articulated in Deuteronomy. In that context, these texts narrate the stories of the various kings. One of the literary devices the text uses to help readers follow the story line is the pattern that introduces and concludes the accounts of the reigns of the kings. Each account begins with the announcement that the king has taken the throne and dates the reign in line with the reigns of the other (northern or southern) kingdom, called **synchronistic dating**. Then the Deuteronomic historian gives the residence, length of reign, and comment on the religion of the king. For kings in the Southern Kingdom of Judah, the historian also states the age, mother (and home), and wife of the king. At the conclusion of the account of the reign, the historian indicates sources used to narrate the history (such as the royal archives of the Books of the Chronicles of the Kings of Israel and Judah), chronicles the death and burial of the king, and announces the successor to the throne. These notices help organize the accounts of the royal reigns. They also give the historian an opportunity to comment on the faith of the king. The criteria of faithfulness are always tied to loyalty to the pure worship of YHWH at the temple in Jerusalem and to covenant with YHWH. Those criteria indicate that all the kings of the Northern Kingdom were outcasts. This framework for understanding the accounts of the kings hearkens back to the Deuteronomic context of the Former Prophets. These narratives begin to make clear that it is the prophets who speak for that covenant loyalty (see Deut. 17:14–20).

The Latter Prophets

Our previous look at the Former Prophets provides the historical background for our look at the Latter Prophets. We will again be concerned about matters of history, literature, and theology as we examine the various books that carry the names of the prophets Isaiah, Jeremiah, Ezekiel, and the Twelve. We will come to see that these books are essentially collections of prophecies or the sayings of these prophetic figures. Their words come to us through the cultural codes of the various eras of ancient Israel's story. If we are to get the fullest portrait we can of the messages these prophets delivered, we need some sense of the prophets' historical backgrounds and the contexts in which they prophesied. So we begin with the phenomenon of prophecy in ancient Israel.

1. The classic expressions of prophecy were oral in nature. Amos and Hosea, for example, came preaching to crowds in the Northern Kingdom of Israel in the eighth century BCE.
2. The classic expressions of prophecy were spoken and written in poetic form, as evidenced in the opening words of the prophetic book of Amos:

> The LORD roars from Zion,
>> and utters his voice from Jerusalem;
> the pastures of the shepherds wither,
>> and the top of Carmel dries up. (Amos 1:2)

We will have a full look at Hebrew poetry in the section on the Writings, but this one verse with only a surface reading demonstrates the poetic qualities of parallel lines and poetic imagery. The poetic nature of the prophetic texts is a central component in understanding them; but not all prophetic texts are in poetic form, and the distinction between prose and poetry is not always obvious in Hebrew. Careful readers will need to consider the form of the prophetic text as part of the interpretive process.

3. The prophets spoke in short speeches. The book of Amos consists of several such prophetic speeches.

4. The prophets spoke in a historical setting. Amos and Hosea preached in the Northern Kingdom of Israel in the eighth century BCE.

5. The prophetic words came into written forms in the books carrying the names of the prophets. The prophets spoke, and their supporters remembered and preserved these words, which were often unpopular. Those who put together the prophetic corpus shaped the books to proclaim the prophetic message by linking prophetic sayings and then linking prophetic books. Those who shaped these books had a vision for the future of God's people and sought to proclaim the importance of the covenant relationship with YHWH for the community.

The short prophetic speeches are called **oracles**, prophetic words from God. Typically an oracle includes a proclamation from God, either of coming trouble or of hope, along with a reason for that proclamation often related to the loyalty of the people (or the lack thereof) or the loyalty of YHWH. These oracles reflect an experience of the prophet with God in which the prophet is gripped by a message to be proclaimed to the people of that day. The prophet reflects on the message and begins to put it into words and into poetic form that will communicate in a powerful way.

Prophecy in ancient Israel is a phenomenon from a culture very different from that of the twenty-first century in the West. In sum, it is speech often using shocking language to get the attention of a crowd. We read these oracles in the literary context of prophetic books, collections of words communicating a divine message. The words are meant to be heard and remembered. One way for contemporary readers to account for this background of Old

Testament prophecy and to perceive the impact of the words on an audience in the ancient Near East is to read the prophetic books aloud and in brief poetic segments.

The word *prophet* comes from the Greek *prophētēs*, meaning one who speaks for another, but the Hebrew Scriptures use a number of terms to identify these mediators between the divine and the human. The most common Hebrew term is *nabi'*, probably indicating one who has been called to a task. Today prophets are often thought of as predictors of the future. Part of the nature of prophecy is to speak about the future—the immediate future related to its ancient audience—and to indicate how God is getting ready to act. Only in that sense is prophecy foretelling. Prophecy is also forthtelling; it speaks forth the word of YHWH and in that sense is preaching of righteousness. Abraham Joshua Heschel speaks of prophecy in terms of the divine interpretation of the present. The prophets bring ancient Israel's faith traditions—Torah, cultic traditions, wisdom perspectives—to bear in interpreting life for the people of faith and apply these traditions to the present relationship of the community with YHWH. In that sense, the prophets are messengers of the covenant God; YHWH has called them out to deliver these oracles from the divine. Today the prophets are popularly known for their words of coming judgment because of the community's covenant failings, but they also at times speak words of powerful hope. The purpose of these oracles of judgment and salvation is to call the people to covenant faithfulness; therein is found wholeness of life. The prophets speak to the pivotal moments in ancient Israel's narrative and bring those moments into the arena of faith.

Most societies include figures that communicate between the spirit world and the human realm; anthropologists label them shamans. The ancient Near East was no different in seeking messages from the divine. Such figures could communicate a message from the heavens in ways that other methods of divination could not. The Hebrew Scriptures reflect the presence of a variety of such figures. That is to say that prophecy did not develop in a vacuum in ancient Israel; it has a history. We have already noted the example of Balaam in the book of Numbers. Ecstatic groups existed in the ancient Near East and were called prophets. Archaeologists have discovered examples of prophetic oracles from the Mesopotamian city of Mari similar in form to prophetic oracles in ancient Israel. In the discussion of the Former Prophets, we noted the figures of Samuel, Elijah, and Elisha, whom the text calls prophets and who spoke powerfully against syncretism and called the people to covenant faithfulness. These early or preclassical prophets gave way in the eighth century to the classical or canonical prophets, those whose words are preserved in canonical books bearing the name of the prophet. Prophets, together with kings, priests, and sages, are significant as leaders in the covenant community.

The first of these prophets was Amos, who uses the faith traditions of the clans, of worship, of covenant to communicate a message in his day. His message marks a departure from previous prophecies, for he addresses the whole of the people Israel and, given the current life of that community, speaks of a coming destruction of the covenant relationship with YHWH.

Amos and Hosea

Amos and Hosea, the first of the canonical prophets, preached in the Northern Kingdom. The setting is the middle of the eighth century BCE. Amos came first, probably in the decade of the 760s, when the ruler in Israel was Jeroboam II (786–746). Second Kings 14:23–29 describes the context. On the surface, this is a time of expansion and stability in the north, but the prophetic word makes clear that all is not well in this community. The gap between the rich and the poor is at the heart of the corruption of the time. Hosea, who comes a bit later (750–725), begins to see the major decline of the Northern Kingdom as it moves toward defeat at the hands of the Assyrians. The opening verses of these books (Amos 1:1; Hosea 1:1) serve as the superscriptions of the collections of prophetic proclamations and place their messages in the context of the reigns of the later kings of the north.

Amos. Amos was a sheep breeder from the Southern Kingdom of Judah and thus an outsider. He was a man of considerable rhetorical gifts and was painfully aware of the faith traditions of Israel and of the corruption lying at the center of life in the Northern Kingdom in the middle of the eighth century.

The opening prophetic oracle in Amos is a series of prophecies of coming judgment on the nations, beginning with Syria, Philistia, Tyre, Edom, Ammon, and Moab. Then the prophet turns to Judah and finally to Israel. In this gripping indictment of war crimes, the orator circles the map with harsh words for the enemies of Israel only then to lambast the community of the Northern Kingdom for their oppression of the poor and powerless. Further oracles lead to Amos's central emphasis on justice and righteousness (Amos 5:21–24):

> But let justice roll down like waters,
>   and righteousness like an ever-flowing stream. (5:24)

Amos also recounts visions of the coming end of the community because of its basic corruption. This message was not popular with the leaders of the community, and Amos 7:10–17 recounts an encounter between the prophet and Amaziah, a priestly figure tied to the rulers of the kingdom. The book continues with additional oracles of judgment, though its conclusion in chapter 9 suggests that there is hope for the community beyond the coming turmoil.

The message of Amos is that the **Day of YHWH**, a day of justice and reckoning for the community of Israel, is at hand. Destruction is coming for three reasons:

- Oppression of the poor
- Corruption in the legal system
- Decadence in the religious life of the community

The Day of YHWH becomes an important tradition in the Latter Prophets. It is the day of the victory and reign of YHWH over those who oppose the divine will. In Amos, Israel is among those who oppose YHWH. One way of thinking about the concerns the Latter Prophets express is that the prophets oppose two kinds of sin: social injustice and idolatry. The issue for Amos is social injustice, reflected in his key terms of justice and righteousness. A just society meets the needs of the people; righteousness has to do with divinely initiated right relationship with YHWH enacted in right human relationships. Israel, Amos declares, has forgotten that YHWH provides for all the members of the community. For the other prophet, in the north, the emphasis is idolatry.

Hosea. Hosea appears to be a native of the north who knows well the community's worship traditions. He eloquently calls the community to faithfulness in the relationship with YHWH in the latter years of the Northern Kingdom's existence. As with Amos's prophecies, Hosea's prophecies were preserved and made their way to the Southern Kingdom to be included in the Latter Prophets.

SOCIAL JUSTICE

Contemporary readers may bring their own notions of social justice to their hermeneutical work with the Latter Prophets, and those notions may emphasize retributive justice. For Amos, social justice is at heart an issue of faith. The covenant God YHWH delivers the community of ancient Israel and thus calls the community to live out this right relationship (righteousness) with YHWH in right relationships with each other, in just relationships with integrity. Because the covenant God provides life for the community, the prophetic understanding of justice begins with the need for the community to see that all its members have what is needed for wholeness of life. That is the basic sense of justice in the prophetic view: that all have what they need for a full life.

The opening of the book of Hosea is somewhat distinctive in the Latter Prophets in that it recounts the family biography of the prophet, a biography that becomes something of a parable of YHWH's experience with Israel. The opening verses and the third chapter recount the story of Hosea and his wife, Gomer. The second chapter applies the story to the relationship of YHWH and Israel. The traditional retelling of the story is that Hosea marries Gomer, "a wife of whoredom," who bears children named Jezreel, indicating a coming defeat of Israel at Jezreel; Lo-ruhamah, indicating no forgiveness for Israel; and Lo-ammi, meaning "not my people." Gomer leaves Hosea, and in chapter 3 Hosea buys back Gomer from a life of prostitution and gradually reestablishes a faithful relationship with her. This turbulent and difficult marriage becomes the image of the adulterous (read "idolatrous") relationship of Israel with YHWH. The people have gone after other gods and will see the consequences of their faithlessness, but there is hope beyond the coming trouble.

The poetic prophecies of Hosea focus on YHWH's indictment of Israel and lay out the case against the people, using the prophet's key words:

> Hear the word of the LORD, O people of Israel;
>> for the LORD has an indictment against the inhabitants of the land.
> There is no faithfulness or loyalty,
>> and no knowledge of God in the land. (Hosea 4:1)

The book continues by recounting the lessons of history from the relationship of YHWH and Israel. YHWH graciously created Israel as a covenant people, but the people continue to break covenant by going after other gods. The book concludes with a tone of hope based on the continuing grace of YHWH.

Hosea's message begins with the divine love for Israel, and marriage becomes the governing metaphor for the book. Because only YHWH can give life to Israel, the prophet employs a metaphor that suggests divine jealousy; YHWH is zealous for Israel to have fullness of life found only in faithful covenant relationship with YHWH. The prophet thus fervently opposes any syncretism. He charges the leaders of the kingdom with leading the people toward Baal's fertility religion, which offers empty promises of abundance. The prophet rails that Israel has gone after the idols in acts of adultery in their relationship with YHWH. Hosea calls for the community to go back to the wilderness and the beginning of the "marriage" relationship with YHWH and to renew a faithful relationship.

This brief sketch of Amos and Hosea suggests that the prophets' powerful rhetoric embodies a radical proclamation in their day. Amos and Hosea were in one sense ambassadors or advocates for the faithful covenant relationship with YHWH to which Israel was called. The messenger, the prophet, receives a word from the divine king ("Thus says the LORD") and as the ambassador delivers the message to the covenant community, a message calling for faithfulness and justice.

Isaiah and Micah

Isaiah. The major prophetic figure in the Southern Kingdom of Judah in the eighth century is Isaiah of Jerusalem. Isaiah is a significant personage in the capital of the Southern Kingdom who has access to the highest positions of power. His prophecies revolve around three crises in the life of the nation:

THE QUESTION OF AUTHORSHIP

Many scholars over the last two centuries have suggested that the book of Isaiah originated in stages. Chapters 1–39 relate primarily to Isaiah of Jerusalem (742–700 BCE). Chapters 40–55 come from an exilic prophet who carries the Isaianic tradition into the sixth century. Chapters 56–66 relate to the time after the return from exile. Scholars often label these parts of the book First (or Proto-) Isaiah, Second (or Deutero-) Isaiah, and Third (or Trito-) Isaiah. There are several reasons scholars suggest multiple authorship of the book:

1. Beginning in chapter 40, the clearly assumed setting is the sixth century, after the fall of Jerusalem.
2. The language, style, and concepts change with chapter 40.
3. Prophets spoke to the spiritual condition of their audience and to the issues of their day.

Some have responded that tradition only speaks of one Isaiah. Most scholars today, however, agree that the book contains a variety of prophecies from different times, all in the tradition of Isaiah of Jerusalem. The connection between the prophetic proclamation and the life of the prophet's audience is crucial in this debate. A number of scholars today would agree that the book originated by way of a process that included various prophetic voices and editors but would also suggest that the question of how the book came together as a whole is important and that readers need to think about how the various parts of the book fit together. In this volume, we will take seriously the historical setting in chapters 1–39 and the historical setting in chapters 40–66. We will consider Isaiah 40–66 in light of the exile and its aftermath.

- *The Syro-Ephraimite Crisis around 735 BCE*. The Northern Kingdom seeks to pressure Judah into a military alliance with Syria against the Assyrian Empire from Mesopotamia. Isaiah's view is that the leaders of the kingdom should put their trust in YHWH rather than in any alliances. Some of the famous texts from the prophet (e.g., Isa. 9:2–7; 11:1–6) come from this time.
- *The Assyrian threat around 711 BCE*. The threat is again loyalty to foreign alliances rather than to YHWH.
- *The Assyrian siege of Jerusalem in 701 BCE*. Isaiah's view is that God will deliver the city, and this prophecy comes to pass.

Isaiah 1 introduces the prophet's preaching and is followed by prophecies on Judah and Jerusalem (chaps. 2–12), followed by prophecies against other nations and cities (chaps. 13–23), before the prophet returns to the subject of Judah and Jerusalem (chaps. 28–33). Intervening chapters take an **apocalyptic** tone (chaps. 24–27 and 34–35). (We will explore the apocalyptic genre in chapter 4.) Narratives about Isaiah, Hezekiah, and Jerusalem conclude the first major section of the book. The account of Isaiah's call in chapter 6 provides a good summary of the prophet's message. In the temple, the prophet has a vision of the Holy One of Israel, who is present with the people in Zion and who receives praise from seraphs. Isaiah confesses his sin and responds to the call to proclaim a difficult message to a people who do not follow this holy YHWH. The prophet respects the traditions of the Davidic covenant and holds king and community accountable to the responsibilities of faithfulness in that covenant tradition. Israel's response to a holy God needs to be consistent faithfulness even in the face of crises. Isaiah pronounces judgment on

THE IMMANUEL PROPHECY

The Immanuel prophecy in Isaiah 7 clearly relates to the Syro-Ephraimite Crisis listed in the text and recounted earlier in relation to the books of Kings. Isaiah declares that YHWH will give King Ahaz a sign, a child born to a young woman. Before this child will come of age, the leaders of both the Northern Kingdom of Israel (and its major tribe Ephraim) and Syria will be no more. The child is a sign of divine presence, divine presence that holds Judah accountable for its faith in YHWH. Some interpreters understand the child as a royal child to be born, perhaps Hezekiah; others suggest that the child is a son of Isaiah. In the New Testament, Matthew applies this prophecy to Jesus as "Immanuel," who is born of a virgin. (The Septuagint's translation of Isa. 7:14 uses the term *virgin*.)

a community that has gone astray and holds out hope for a faithful remnant beyond the coming judgment.

Micah. The other prophet in Judah in the last half of the eighth century is Micah from Moresheth-Gath. He represents the rural communities and in that sense presents a striking contrast to the urbane Isaiah. Micah proclaims that a theophany is at hand and that it will bring judgment on false prophets, corrupt courts, and greedy leaders. Injustice characterizes the life of the community. The book of Micah follows a judgment-hope pattern; hope beyond this judgment will come for a remnant. Micah 6:1–8 articulates a brief and powerful summary of the preaching of the eighth-century prophets. The prophetic indictment of Israel is that the people want to offer empty sacrifices unrelated to the rest of their common life. What YHWH seeks from the people is expressed in 6:8: "to do justice, and to love kindness, and to walk humbly with your God."

Historical Developments of the Southern Kingdom of Judah

The kingdom of Judah experiences more stability on the throne than the Northern Kingdom, since the Davidic line is still in place in Jerusalem. Asa and Jehoshaphat have successful reigns. Athaliah is an aberration; she violently takes the throne in the tradition of her northern relatives but is eventually overthrown, and Judah puts Joash back on the Davidic throne. Uzziah as well as Jotham, Ahaz, Hezekiah, and Manasseh enjoy long reigns.

Hezekiah survives an invasion from Assyria at the end of the eighth century and is something of a reformer. Manasseh, on the other hand, seems to have supported syncretism and oppression in the land. In 640 BCE the young Josiah comes to the throne. In 621 his advisors find a scroll as workers are remodeling and reforming the temple. That Torah scroll shapes a powerful reform in Jerusalem. Because other empires surrounding Israel at that point are not strong, Josiah is able to pursue his own course.

The major elements of the reform follow:

- Covenant renewal and emphasis on Torah
- Destruction of worship in the temple influenced by Assyrian customs, including divination, magic, and sacred prostitution
- Renewal of the celebration of Passover
- Centralization of worship in the Jerusalem temple

These reforms bring destruction of other sanctuaries and the moving of sanctuary personnel to Jerusalem. We noted in the section on the Pentateuch that these reforms followed the heart of the Deuteronomic Torah. These moves

HISTORICAL TIME LINE FOR THE
KINGDOMS OF ISRAEL AND JUDAH

Date (BCE)	Israel	Judah	Hebrew Prophet
	Jeroboam I (922–901)	Rehoboam (922–915)	
		Abijah (915–913)	
	Nadab (901–900)	Asa (913–873)	
900	Baasha (900–877)		
	Elah (877–876)		
	Zimri (876)		
	Omri (876–869)	Jehoshaphat (873–849)	
	Ahab (869–850)		Elijah (Israel)
850	Ahaziah (850–849)	Jehoram (849–842)	
	Jehoram (849–842)	Ahaziah (842)	Elisha (Israel)
	Jehu's Revolt (842)		
	Jehu (842–815)	Athaliah (842–837)	
	Jehoahaz (815–801)	Joash (837–800)	
800	Jehoash (801–786)	Amaziah (800–783)	
	Jereboam II (786–746)	Uzziah (783–742)	Amos (Israel)
750	Zechariah (746–745)		Hosea (Israel)
	Shallum (745)		
	Menahem (745–738)	Jotham (742–735)	
	Pekahiah (738–737)		Isaiah (Judah)
	Pekah (737–732)	Ahaz (735–715)	
	Hoshea (732–724)		Micah (Judah)
722/721	Fall of Israel		
700		Hezekiah (715–687)	
650		Manasseh (687–642)	
		Amon (642–640)	
		Josiah (640–609)	Jeremiah
			Zephaniah
621		Deuteronomic reforms	
			Nahum
		Jehoahaz (609)	
600		Jehoiakim (609–598/597)	
598/597		First Babylonian sack of Jerusalem	
		Jehoiachin (598/597)	Habakkuk
		Zedekiah (597–587)	Ezekiel
587		Fall of Jerusalem	Jeremiah taken to Egypt
587–538		Babylonian captivity	

bring significant change in Jerusalem and win praise for Josiah from the Deuteronomic historians, but in the end the reforms deal with externals rather than internals in the life of the community and so are short-lived. Josiah dies at an early age in battle, and the decline of the Southern Kingdom is at hand.

Eventually, Jehoiakim is put on the throne as a puppet of the influential Egyptian Empire. At the other end of the Fertile Crescent, the Babylonians defeat the Assyrians at the Battle of Carchemish in 605, and they come to dominance in the region with the leader Nebuchadnezzar. Jehoiakim waffles between loyalty to these various imperial powers and to those in Judah who seek an independent course. In 598/597 BCE Babylonian armies lay siege to Jerusalem, and eventually the king dies. The royal son Jehoiachin takes the throne, and the city surrenders. The victors take a first group of deportees, including the king, as prisoners to Babylon. Jehoiachin's uncle Zedekiah is then put on the throne, but in 587/586 BCE the Babylonian armies return, leaving the Davidic capital of Jerusalem and its temple in ruins. The Babylonian exile has begun.

Many interpreters suggest that because Jerusalem had been spared in earlier crises, the people had come to believe in the inviolability of Zion—Zion/Jerusalem was the city of YHWH, and YHWH would not allow it to fall. As a result of this overconfidence, the people had not attended to issues of covenant faithfulness. The book of 2 Kings ends with Jerusalem in ruins and the Davidic king and the leaders of Israel in exile in Babylon. At the end of the book, the Babylonians release the Davidic king from prison, though he is still in exile. Was this a sign that YHWH was not finished with the Davidic promise?

The archaeological record of the ancient Israelite monarchy has occasioned great debate recently. There appears to be sufficient evidence to support the basics of the biblical history. It is also the case, however, that many readers likely imagine the united and divided kingdoms on a much grander scale than the material remains suggest. The account above makes it clear that the Former Prophets provide commentary on the move to monarchy in ancient Israel and on the history of covenant keeping and breaking during the times of the united and divided kingdoms of Israel and Judah. The expressions of covenant, both the Sinai covenant and the covenant with David, are central to understanding these texts and comprehending their import for the story of ancient Israel with their God YHWH. The emphasis of the Former Prophets is on the covenant implications of the history.

Jeremiah

The major prophetic figure in Jerusalem in the seventh century is Jeremiah (626–580 BCE). His work relates to three periods:

1. *The reign of Josiah*. Jeremiah speaks prophecies of judgment in the time prior to Josiah's Deuteronomic reform. Once reform begins, the prophet apparently hopes that the reform constitutes repentance, and thus he is silent in support of the movement.

2. *The reign of Jehoiakim*. Jehoiakim reverses the reform movement and draws Jeremiah's ire. Jeremiah 19, 20, 22, and 36 come from this period. The king and prophet have a stormy relationship. Jeremiah's message of coming trouble is not popular with the leaders of the kingdom.

3. *The reign of Zedekiah and beyond*. This period witnesses the fall of Jerusalem and the beginning of the Babylonian exile. As Judah falls, Jeremiah's prophecies become more hopeful (Jer. 29). Eventually, Jeremiah is kidnapped and taken to Egypt, where his life apparently comes to an end.

Questions about the composition and organization of the book of Jeremiah are complicated and very difficult to answer. There are two textual traditions. The Greek text has a different organization and is a good bit shorter than the Hebrew text; some scholars suggest that the Greek often represents an earlier tradition. The book includes poetic prophecies, prose sermons, and biographical information on the prophet. A number of critical scholars, such as Sigmund Mowinckel, suggest that the book originated by way of a lengthy process with prophetic oracles and narratives edited by Deuteronomists; these critical scholars understand Jeremiah's more hopeful prophecies as later additions. It is entirely possible that Jeremiah and his scribe, Baruch, began to collect the prophet's oracles. The prose sermons interpret those oracles in terms of covenant, and the biographical narratives provide the setting in which the prophecies arose. The book concludes with oracles against other nations, an indication of YHWH's sovereignty over all. A particular feature of the book of Jeremiah is a collection of Jeremiah's laments (11:18–23; 12:1–6; 15:10–12, 15–21; 17:12–18; 18:18–23; 20:7–18). The prophet makes use of the lament tradition featured in the Psalms as a way to complain to YHWH about the difficulty of his prophetic task. These prayers are remarkably honest and have the effect of humanizing the prophet in a way that marks a shift in the prophetic tradition; we have more biographical information about Jeremiah than we do for any other prophet. These prayers also imply that the people rejected Jeremiah's message through no fault of the prophet and suggest that the people still stand in need of repentance.

The book of Jeremiah begins with the call of this prophet, who comes from a priestly family. The prophet has a difficult ministry with a hard word initially for this people; he will proclaim that the familiar and overpowering enemy from the north will come and wreak havoc on Jerusalem. This poetic gathering of infinitives summarizes the prophet's task:

> to pluck up and to pull down,
> to destroy and to overthrow,
> to build and to plant. (1:10)

The first half of the book records prophecies against Judah and Jerusalem for their idolatry and their social injustice. Chapter 7 records Jeremiah's temple sermon in which the prophet makes the attitude of the people into a poetic tune to indicate that the people trust only in the presence of the temple and do not believe that YHWH will let the city fall. The sermon calls for a profound repentance and return to covenant faith; see chapter 26 for an account of the sermon. Jeremiah proclaims that the people are living covenant disobedience and thus will suffer the necessary consequences. Chapters 13–18 detail the consequences of this covenant disobedience. The covenant God YHWH has been faithful to Israel and asks for faithfulness from Israel in response.

When Judah begins to fall, Jeremiah's prophecies become more hopeful for life beyond the defeat. In chapter 31 Jeremiah proclaims the oracle of a new covenant, the promise of a new internal way to create a covenant community. The focus remains on the covenant relationship at divine initiative and centered on Torah, but in the days to come YHWH will write the Torah on the hearts of all people. Jeremiah's message centers on covenant faithfulness in all of life. He begins with words of judgment but moves to hope. Biblical scholars have aptly described him as the grieving prophet, for he grieves over

JEREMIAH AND HANANIAH

The book of Jeremiah presents narratives centered on prophetic conflict between Jeremiah and other prophets, especially Hananiah in chapters 27–29. Other prophets are in Jerusalem at the time, and they are painting a much more pleasant picture of the coming days than is the dour Jeremiah. The bases of prophetic authority in the Old Testament are the call of the prophet and the prophet's continuing access to the throne room of God to receive the revelatory message. Jeremiah describes the second basis of authority in chapter 23, beginning with verse 9. The difficulty is that the people are not really equipped to differentiate the true prophets from the false ones by way of these bases of authority. All prophets claimed such authority. Jeremiah stands on the side of a proclamation of judgment. In the end, Hananiah's demise authenticates Jeremiah's prophecy that Judah will serve Babylon, a message that is not only unpopular but also borders on treason.

PROPHETIC SIGN ACTS

Jeremiah acted out a number of prophecies as symbolic actions, or **sign acts**. He wore an ox yoke to symbolize Judah's coming servitude to Babylon (Jer. 27–28) and smashed a pot as a sign of coming destruction (Jer. 19). He also procured a field behind enemy lines as a sign of future hope (Jer. 32). In the previous century, Isaiah walked about naked to symbolize coming imprisonment (Isa. 20). Some would interpret Hosea's marriage to Gomer as a prophetic sign act (Hosea 1–3). Ezekiel, in the sixth century, acted out a number of his prophecies. He constructed a model of Jerusalem to demonstrate its destruction and cooked food over dung to indicate the difficulties of the siege against the city (Ezek. 4). He also shaved his beard and hair to symbolize the coming destruction and captivity (Ezek. 5). These acts are particularly intense ways to proclaim a prophetic message, and some would suggest that the acts begin the fulfillment of the prophecies.

the sin of the people and its consequences. His anguished prophecies reflect what Abraham Joshua Heschel has called the divine pathos, YHWH's empathy with the people as they build for themselves a future of trouble and death. The prophet calls for repentance of the individual and the community; therein lies hope.

Other Prophetic Voices in the Seventh Century

Zephaniah. Zephaniah prophesies around 626 BCE, in Josiah's reign prior to the reform. His message is analogous to Jeremiah's in that time, and scholars often suggest that the two prophets' oracles encouraged the much-needed move to reform. The book follows a common prophetic pattern of judgment on Judah and Jerusalem, followed by judgment on other nations, followed by prophecies of hope. Zephaniah's judgment oracles hearken back to the language of Amos and the coming Day of YHWH as a day of judgment brought by oppressive enemies. The judgment will be severe for stubborn Jerusalem. Judgment also comes upon the nations. The hope for restoration is in the form of a remnant, hearkening back to Isaiah. The reasons for judgment are standard for the prophets: idolatry and social injustice.

Nahum. Nahum prophesies at a similar time, around 625 BCE. The book begins with an **acrostic** hymn to YHWH as a God who brings justice upon the wicked. The wicked in this case are Assyria and its capital of Nineveh. The remainder of the brief book vividly recounts the fall of the Assyrian capital. This prophecy is rather different from Jeremiah's and Zephaniah's. It addresses Judah in saying that God is sovereign and will eventually bring the oppressive Assyrian capital to naught, a word of hope for the oppressed people of Judah.

Habakkuk. Habakkuk comes near the end of the seventh century, after Josiah's death and in a time when Babylon is conquering Assyria. The book uses the psalmic tradition of lament as a way to craft a dialogue between the prophet and YHWH, a dialogue on the justice of God. The book begins with a lament questioning how YHWH can allow injustice and evil to continue. The answer is that Assyria will mete out divine judgment. The prophet responds with the question of how YHWH can use Assyria for divine purposes when Assyria is even more wicked than Judah. The answer is that Assyria will see its demise from Babylon. The book's last chapter is another plea for YHWH to restore the fortunes of Judah. The answer is an account of a theophany in which YHWH brings a severe hope. The book's final word is an assurance of the justice and faithfulness of God. Thus Habakkuk uses the liturgical tradition of a prayer for help followed by a divine response to shape his message about divine justice.

Exile and Beyond

The move to monarchy resulted in a profound adjustment for ancient Israel, but the fall of Jerusalem to the Babylonian armies and the ensuing exile bring major trauma for this community. Life as this community has known it is at an end. Israel has no means of justice (the king) and no means of atonement (the temple). Babylon now controls the future for this people. In the course of time, the **Persians** succeed the Babylonian Empire in controlling Mesopotamia, and the Persians then take center stage. The Assyrians' policy of dealing with conquered peoples has been particularly harsh; it blunts the people's opposition to their overlords by moving and mixing the people. Babylon exiles conquered peoples. The Persians take the view that conquered peoples are more cooperative in their homelands as part of the broader empire. In 538 BCE the Persian ruler **Cyrus** issues an edict that allows the return of Israel to their land. With that move, we come to the beginnings of Judaism, the remnants of Judah. Some of the people return to the land. Ezra and Nehemiah come to positions of leadership in the restored community. Although it is difficult to reconstruct the history here, between 450 and 400 BCE, Ezra, a priest and scribe, leads the people in religious reform centered on renewal of the covenant and obedience to Torah. Nehemiah, who is governor for two terms, leads in rebuilding Jerusalem and the province. Some people never left the land and are suspicious of the returnees, as are others in the surrounding area. Still, the community works to rebuild its life.

TRANSITIONS IN THE JUDEAN REGION

The Judean region experienced numerous political and cultural transitions from the tenth to first centuries BCE:

1. The kingdom of Judah (tenth to sixth century BCE)
    Rehoboam (922–915)
    Asa (913–873)
    Jehoshaphat (873–849)
    Athaliah (842–837)
    Uzziah (783–742)
    Hezekiah (715–687)
    Manasseh (687–642)
    Josiah (640–609)
    Jehoiakim (609–598/597)
2. Babylonian period (sixth century BCE)
    Fall of Jerusalem (587/586)
    Exile in Babylon (586–538)
3. Persian period (sixth to fourth century BCE)
    Ezra (between 450 and 400)
    Nehemiah (445–433)
4. Greek period (fourth to first century BCE)
    Maccabean Revolt (167–142)

The exilic and postexilic periods greatly influenced Judaism. Among the impacts are the following:

- A radical emphasis on monotheism in the face of polytheism
- The centrality of Torah as defining Judaism
- An emphasis on family and the synagogue in place of the temple
- The flowering of the wisdom tradition
- Persian influence in the areas of cosmology and the personification of evil
- Questions about the future: Will it be in continuity or discontinuity with the present?
- Questions about the life of the people of YHWH: Do they live in continuity or discontinuity with other peoples?
- Beginning of the end of prophecy

These concerns continued into the subsequent Greek and Roman periods.

Prophets of the Exile

The trauma of the fall of Jerusalem and the beginning of the Babylonian exile brings the end of life as Judah has known it. The fall of the capital means there is no king to bring justice and no temple to make atonement possible. The center of the community's world does not hold, and community life is no more. What about the prophets? Many prophets in Jerusalem have proclaimed false hope, and so their credibility takes a nosedive. One prophetic voice, however, speaks a strange and intriguing word in this traumatic context, a word first of strong judgment and then of even stronger grace.

Ezekiel. Ezekiel's prophecies relate to three eras:

- 593–587 BCE. Ezekiel is among those taken to Babylon in the first deportation of 597. His task is to prepare the Hebrews for the coming fall of Jerusalem, so his prophecies emphasize strong judgment.
- 586 BCE. Around the fall of Jerusalem, the prophet's message begins to make a transition toward hope.
- 585–571 BCE. After the fall of Jerusalem, Ezekiel's message turns to hope.

The book preserving Ezekiel's prophetic messages seems to follow two organizational schemes. It generally follows the tripartite pattern we have seen in other prophetic books: judgment on Judah and Jerusalem, judgment on other nations, and hope for the future. It is also concerned to follow the chronological movement of Ezekiel's ministry, a concern not particularly present in the prophetic books we have seen previously. Ezekiel is a priest, and his book reflects that background and special concern for the **cult**, Jerusalem's organized worship primarily in the temple. The prophet is very concerned about the violation of the holiness of the Jerusalem temple by way of idolatry. Because of that violation, the divine glory or presence will leave the temple, which has become unclean, and Jerusalem will fall. Restoration will come only after the experience of defeat. Ezekiel's prophecies often reflect the great trauma of the exilic crisis and likely for that reason are often extreme prophecies—on several occasions acted out as prophetic signs—and may seem bizarre to contemporary readers. The book has a strong visionary tone; prophecies frequently come in the form of visions and articulate a vision of what is to come.

As one of the exiles in the first deportation of 597 BCE, Ezekiel has visions calling him to prophesy of the divine presence in Babylon and of the coming destruction of Jerusalem. The prophet uses symbolic acts and allegories to proclaim this message brought on by the idolatry of ancient Israel. For example, in chapter 4, God instructs Ezekiel to build a model of Jerusalem and of the coming siege against it. In chapter 12, the prophet is to enact the coming departure from Jerusalem and the march into the captivity of exile. In addition to the devastating fall of Jerusalem, the prophet also pronounces judgment on nations surrounding Israel, including Egypt. Jerusalem falls (Ezek. 33), and the prophetic word begins to move toward hope. The vision of the valley of dry bones (Ezek. 37) envisions a new life for Israel. The concluding section of the book (chapters 40–48) articulates the priestly reorganization of the restored community with the divine glory having returned to the restored temple: "And the name of the city from that time on shall be, The LORD is There" (48:35).

Isaiah 40–66. Chapters 40–66 of the book of Isaiah preserve important and eloquent prophetic proclamations in the context of exile. These chapters proclaim good news for exiles: there will be a second exodus. As YHWH brought Israel out of Egypt, so God will bring Israel out of Babylon. This section of the book begins with the call to comfort the people because the punishment of exile is at an end. The prophet declares that the Persian ruler Cyrus, who has now succeeded the Babylonians as the dominating empire in Mesopotamia, will act as the chosen one of YHWH and make it possible for the remnant of Judah to return to Jerusalem. This exilic prophetic voice in the tradition of Isaiah of Jerusalem combines the theological perspectives of YHWH as both redeemer and creator. The One who created will now bring the people out of exile. The prophet uses a variety of prophetic forms to convince the people of this message—debating with the people and putting their doubts on trial, and speaking salvation oracles (e.g., 41:8–13; 43:1–7).

These chapters also include four songs on the Servant of YHWH (42:1–4; 49:1–6; 50:4–9; 52:13–53:12). Scholars have often struggled over the identity of this Servant in the context of prophecy in the exile. At times the Servant appears to be Israel, especially in chapter 49, but at other times the Servant appears to be an individual, perhaps a prophetic or royal figure or a new Moses who will lead the exodus from exile. The Servant will endure much to accomplish the will of YHWH. Chapters 56–66 of Isaiah reflect a later time, after the return of exiles to Palestine, and the struggles that the return brought for the community as it sought to fulfill the divine promises of restoration. The massive prophetic tradition of Isaiah speaks to several historical instances and in the process shapes a message central to the Hebrew Scriptures and to Christian tradition. Seeing the book as a whole, with its various parts integrated, is a significant part of the interpretive task.

Obadiah. The brief book of Obadiah also reflects the experience of exile and follows the tripartite pattern we have seen in other prophets. Obadiah indicates that judgment has come upon Jerusalem and Judah and now will come upon the nations, especially Edom, which betrayed its brother Israel as Babylon was destroying Jerusalem. Edomites should act in a brotherly way, since they are the descendants of Esau, brother to Jacob/Israel. Judgment will come upon Edom, and hope will find Israel. The voice of Obadiah is among the several prophets who interpret the trauma of exile for ancient Israel and, in doing so, help the remnant of Judah begin to see a future.

The Chronicler's Work

The Writings preserve an additional account of the history of ancient Israel in the books of 1–2 Chronicles, Ezra, and Nehemiah. This distinctive account relates to the time after the exile. Martin Noth suggested that the **Chronicler** edited all of these books together since they exhibit similarities in language, style, movement, and thought. More recent critical studies suggest that 1–2 Chronicles are related to the books of Ezra and Nehemiah but contain some distinctions. These historical books come from Jerusalem after the restoration and reflect that setting and its concerns. Noth dated the works to the fourth century; some would place 1–2 Chronicles earlier than the other two books. In either case, the shapers of 1–2 Chronicles had access to source materials such as records and memoirs and the Former Prophets. These historians have definite views about history and about the history they recount. First Chronicles begins with a very long, holy genealogy, tracking history from Adam to David and seeing the divine promise pass through those generations. The remainder of the book recounts David's reign. Second Chronicles begins with the reign of Solomon and then, starting in chapter 10, recounts the narrative of the divided kingdoms.

The interests of the Chronicler's work include the following:

1. *The line of promise.* The legitimate leaders are always in the right place at the right time. That view also applies to the leaders of the people after the restoration.
2. *The glorification of Davidic kingship on Zion.* David is the great hero of history, followed by Moses. The telling of David's story does not emphasize his foibles. The appropriate line of kings and priests is in place to make a future possible after the exile.
3. *Judah as the only true Israel.* The remnants of Judah after the exile continue the covenant community.
4. *Worship in the **second temple** as the continuity of true Israel.* The people complete the rebuilding of the temple in 515 BCE, and they apparently expand its courtyards from time to time. Liturgical matters are central

to these books; proper worship with its proper organization, music, and Levitical leaders exemplifies the true Israel after the restoration.

5. *Contesters as false voices.* Those who oppose the Chronicler's view face retribution and are to be resisted. The Chronicler's view is the divine view.

These books recount the history of ancient Israel for the time of the second temple and look to a future restoration and covenant renewal. This theological historiography is itself part of the story of ancient Israel.

Esther and Ruth

Esther. The theological concerns the Chronicler's work reflects are part of the broader picture of the early Jewish community in the Second Temple period. The short story of Esther from around 300 BCE articulates a strong argument for divine providence for the Jewish community in the Persian Empire. Queen Esther, the faithful Jewish heroine, leads the people to resist the oppressors of the world. The book tends toward a particularist view or exclusive view of the faith community, as does the Chronicler's work. The concern here is that the Jewish community survives in the face of opposition and pressures toward assimilation. The idea that God will particularly preserve the Jews (as opposed to other peoples) leads the community to nurture its identity and attend to its distinctiveness. This view is not the only articulation of the nature of the faith community, but it is one of the responses to the trauma of exile and represents an important outlook in the period beyond the exile.

Ruth. The book of Ruth takes a somewhat different approach. This short story also articulates a view of divine providence, but it is a hidden providence revealed in the relationships in the story. Ruth and Naomi and Boaz demonstrate loyalty in relationships as they survive in the midst of desperate circumstances. The view here tends toward a universal or inclusive view. God is the God of all people. Even foreign Moabite women like Ruth are God's people, and in the world of the Persian Empire, the community needs to relate to them. Ruth is even part of the Davidic royal line. The book of Jonah takes a similar approach. The viewpoint in Jonah is in some tension with that in Esther, but both books are important in the Second Temple period as the community seeks to come to terms with questions of how to live as the people of YHWH in the Persian Empire—by emphasizing their identity articulated in Torah (Esther) or by emphasizing that all are created by YHWH (Jonah). The book of Ruth takes the latter stance. The date of the book is a matter of debate, though the book is found in the Writings, the last section of the Hebrew canon. Its language and style fit the era of the second temple, it clearly tells a story from an idyllic past, and its perspective fits the time after the exile. Perhaps it came from that period and is among the later Old Testament texts.

These concerns of the postexilic era continue beyond the time of the Old Testament. The account given here reflects some of the issues facing the covenant community as it continues to journey through history.

Prophets of the Return

Haggai. The brief prophetic book of Haggai deals with the community following the return from exile. Haggai seeks to encourage the people to move on with rebuilding the temple so that YHWH will be with the community as they worship in a rebuilt Jerusalem. With the political leadership of Zerubbabel and the priestly leadership of Joshua, the people work at the task of rebuilding. Haggai's prophecy is in the form of a prophetic disputation to encourage the restored community. The hope is that Zerubbabel will lead the community into a future that will not disappoint.

Zechariah. The first part of the book of Zechariah comes from the same time as the prophecies of Haggai. The first eight chapters of the book recount a variety of visions in apocalyptic guise—visions of the heavenly horsemen, the iron horns, Joshua on trial before YHWH, an angel, a lampstand, a flying scroll, a woman going into exile, and God's chariots. These visions function to encourage the community that their exile is at an end. The community needs to rebuild Jerusalem and the temple as a way to gather people in the faith of YHWH. Judgment will now come on the nations, and God will restore Israel. The victory and reign of YHWH will come from Zion. Chapters 9–14 move more toward the form of apocalyptic literature and the coming reign of God.

Malachi. The prophecy of Malachi comes from the Persian period not long after 500 BCE. The people completed the rebuilding of the temple in 515 BCE; Malachi appears to be set between that date and the work of Ezra and Nehemiah. The book preserves six oracles that articulate YHWH's love of Israel and concern that Israel respond to this divine initiative with covenant faithfulness. The prophet rails against inappropriate sacrifices in which the priests are leading the community and against the dissolution of marriages in order to better oneself economically. The prophet is concerned that the struggling community after the return from exile is losing any hope in divine justice. He calls the people to live faithfully while looking forward to the coming day in which God will bring about the justice that covenant implies.

Malachi operates from the tradition of covenant and emphasizes the institutions of cult and family, for it is in worship and in family that faith is passed through the generations. The form of Malachi's prophecy is one of prophetic dispute or dialogue in which the prophet begins with a statement in the voice of YHWH and then articulates a question from the people. The dialogue continues in that vein. The prophet is well versed in the worship traditions of the people and so perhaps has a background related to priestly groups. Malachi speaks to his setting, in which there is considerable discouragement and cynicism about YHWH's involvement in life. The prophet speaks of the divine pathos, the divine hope and work for the people to again enjoy the covenant blessings. In order for that to happen, the people must accept the prophetic words of judgment as calls to covenant faithfulness.

Late Prophetic Voices

Joel. Scholars often debate the date of the book of Joel. Some suggest it is the first prophetic book, and some suggest it is the last. The book uses a lot of traditional material and seems best placed late in the Old Testament period because of its language, relation to history, and description of worship. The book begins with a lament over a severe locust plague that is a harbinger of the coming Day of YHWH. The prophet calls for repentance, and the book turns to hope found in faithfulness. The Day in the end brings great joy. The prophet uses the worship language of prayers of lament as a means of calling the people to faith and hope. The book exhibits the tripartite scheme of judgment on Judah and Jerusalem, followed by judgment on the nations, followed by hope for the future, as seen in other prophetic collections.

Jonah. The book of Jonah is different from other prophetic books in that it preserves the story of the prophet rather than the prophet's sermons. Second Kings 14:25 mentions the prophet Jonah in the Northern Kingdom during the reign of Jeroboam II. The short story preserved in the book is somewhat vague about that history and recounts the story from a distance to articulate a prophetic message. YHWH calls the prophet Jonah to deliver to the city of Nineveh, capital of the legendarily harsh Assyrian Empire, a message calling for repentance. Jonah seeks to flee from this task. In a story told with delight and irony, Jonah ends up overboard in the sea but is delivered by a great fish that throws him up on the land, where he is given another opportunity to go to Nineveh. He goes and preaches but five words, and the whole of Nineveh, from king all the way down to the cattle, repents. Jonah responds with hostility, for he represents a Jewish attitude that God will care for the Jews (particularism) and wipe out all of their enemies. The message of the prophetic short story is that the sovereign creator God YHWH does not support exclusivist tendencies in early Judaism but is concerned about all of creation.

THE PROPHETS

Amos   ca. 760 BCE
Before the fall of the Northern Kingdom
Israel's election is at an end; there is no justice or righteousness

Hosea   750–725 BCE
Before the fall of the Northern Kingdom
Israel will receive judgment because they have forsaken YHWH for Baal

Isaiah   742–700 BCE
Deals with the Syro-Ephraimite and Assyrian crises
God is the "Holy One of Israel"
Chapters 40–66 relate to deliverance from exile

Micah   Eighth century BCE
Judgment on social injustice and hope for the future

Zephaniah   ca. 626 BCE
Strong judgment tempered by the idea of a remnant

Nahum   ca. 625 BCE
God will act for the people in the destruction of Nineveh

Habakkuk   ca. 600 BCE
Dialogue on the justice of God

Jeremiah   ca. 626–580 BCE
Oracles against Judah and the nations
Biographical information about the prophet
The new covenant

Ezekiel   ca. 593–571 BCE
Extensive use of visions and symbols
The departure of YHWH's glory and the future restoration of Israel

Obadiah   Early 6th century BCE
Judgment upon Edom, destroyer of Jerusalem

Haggai   520 BCE
Rebuilding the temple

Zechariah   ca. 520 BCE
Rebuilding the temple; God is still active after the exile
Chapters 9–14 apparently relate to later time periods

Malachi   ca. 500 BCE
Emphasis on right worship

Joel   ca. 400 BCE
Locust plague and the Day of YHWH

Jonah   ca. 400 BCE
God is the Lord of all nations

Ancient Israel's encounter with the phenomenon of prophecy saw a brief resurgence after the Babylonian exile. The prophets in this period helped the community understand their new context in the aftermath of death and dispersion. These books reflect a shift in the prophetic tradition that can be connected to the fall of Jerusalem in 587/586 BCE. This shift can especially be seen in the following:

1. The move from poetry to prose
2. The increased use of traditional material
3. A continued emphasis on the need for social justice
4. A concern with the question of how the community will live as people of YHWH—in inclusive ways relating positively to other peoples or in exclusive ways emphasizing the particular relationship of YHWH with the Jewish community
5. A concern with the question of how to view the future—as being in continuity with the present or as being in discontinuity with the present, in which case the divine kingdom will radically break into the world. This apocalyptic view of the future comes more to the fore.

In time, prophecy faded from the scene. The community came to deal with the issues of the day in a variety of ways centered on reflection on their faith in a new context.

The Book of the Twelve

Our look at the Latter Prophets has focused on the chronological order of the books and their tie to the historical materials in the Former Prophets. We considered the Major Prophets and those with particular significance in the movements of the history of ancient Israel and Judah. The prophetic books are, for the most part, collections of prophetic oracles spoken to the community in the time of the kings, the time of exile, and the time after return from Babylon. A number of Old Testament scholars today would suggest a slightly different emphasis, arguing that there are only four prophetic books: Isaiah, Jeremiah, Ezekiel, and the **Book of the Twelve**. Scribes have gathered the Twelve, often unfortunately called the Minor Prophets, together as one prophetic collection. The editors collected the prophecies in mostly chronological order and pieced the oracles together with catchwords and similar themes to bring the book together as a whole. There were precursors to the Book of the Twelve, such as the collection of Amos, Hosea, Micah, and Zephaniah and the collection of Haggai and Zechariah 1–8. In each case the editors have purposely linked the books together to compose a whole with its own message. This perspective suggests that readers take the Twelve as chapters in one book of prophetic collections rather than as twelve different books and that reading the Twelve as a whole was an ancient tradition. This view is one of the intriguing developments in contemporary biblical scholarship.

Theological Reflection: Crises of Monarchy and Exile

The Former and Latter Prophets narrate ancient Israel's experiment with monarchy. The move to such a form of society took time and shaped a new way of life for the Hebrews—from a loose tribal confederation to an expanding kingdom to a division into the Northern and Southern Kingdoms to the demise of each. The Former Prophets portray this shift with the charismatic David leading the way. Jerusalem, with its bureaucracy and its temple, became central to ancient Israel's cultural memory. The kings and their minions came to provide for the community. Part of the justification for this major societal shift is the message that YHWH, Israel's creator and redeemer, has chosen the kings to rule over the people. The Davidic line and other leaders of the kingdom become a means to routinize life for this community. The shift was no doubt traumatic in many ways, and the Former Prophets are clearly uneasy with the threat of royal corruption. The Latter Prophets are often front and center in their critique of monarchy. In their view, the provision of the central institution of the monarchy displaced the concern for faithfulness to the covenant with YHWH in the life of ancient Israel. The move to a more stratified, consumerist society led the people toward the idol worship of Canaanite culture, which promised fertility in all dimensions of life. It also led to the push to possess more and so to oppress those with little power or voice. Such social injustice and idolatry brought stinging pronouncements from the prophets against covenant breaking. Because most of the prophetic voices address the covenant people of YHWH, however, the prophecies maintain a creative tension between the announcement of judgment and the divine hope that initiated the covenant relationship: YHWH's steadfast love and faithfulness toward the people. Hosea and Jeremiah provide especially striking examples of this tension. In the end, the final prophetic word is one not of judgment but of hope for restoration beyond the consequences of Israel's corrupt life.

The view of history in the Former Prophets is that Israel struggled to make the shift to a monarchical society only to see that order fall in the sixth century BCE. The prose accounts of the fall of Jerusalem and the prophetic interpretations of those events communicate a sense of trauma for the community and its traditions. The hope of justice in the royal, Davidic ideal has crumbled. The priestly institution of atonement in the Jerusalem temple is literally left in ruins. The places and hopes of families and individuals are literally in the rubble. What has happened? What of the future for this people of YHWH? Where is YHWH? Chaos seems to rule the day. Ancient Israel's theologians struggled with these issues related to **theodicy**, as do theologians in the twenty-first century. The fall of Jerusalem to Babylon and its aftermath brought the greatest community trauma in the history of ancient Israel. The people's center did not hold, and life as they had known it disintegrated. What is to come of Israel and Israel's faith? And what about YHWH? The grief is palpable in Jeremiah and Ezekiel, and the struggle in the aftermath in Malachi. The poetry of Psalms 74, 79, 137, and the book of Lamentations articulates the crisis in profound ways. The crisis shapes the story of Judaism. The Pentateuch, Former Prophets, and Latter Prophets all seek to understand the narrative of the community called ancient Israel and its deity YHWH. The literature from the pivotal moments in that story shapes the community and helps readers and hearers to understand the story of faith. Future generations of readers can follow these paths and find their places in the narrative's pivotal moments and primary themes.

SUGGESTED READING

Fretheim, Terence E. *Deuteronomistic History*. Interpreting Biblical Texts. Nashville: Abingdon, 1983.

Heschel, Abraham J. *The Prophets*. New York: Perennial, 2001.

McKenzie, Steven L. *Introduction to the Historical Books: Strategies for Reading*. Grand Rapids: Eerdmans, 2010.

Nelson, Richard D. *The Historical Books*. Nashville: Abingdon, 1998.

Nogalski, James D. *Introduction to the Hebrew Prophets*. Nashville: Abingdon, 2018.

Petersen, David L. *The Prophetic Literature: An Introduction*. Louisville: Westminster John Knox, 2002.

Reddit, Paul L. *Introduction to the Prophets*. Grand Rapids: Eerdmans, 2008.

Writings

The third division of the Hebrew canon is the Writings, or *Ketuvim*. The last of the three divisions contains a great variety of types of literature, including the Psalms, Wisdom literature, and historical books. In various ways these books all continue to interpret YHWH's work of creation and of covenant relationship with Israel. The Writings add to the perspectives we have encountered in the Torah and Prophets, placing front and center poetic interpretations of the narrative.

The Context of the Writings

The third division of the Hebrew canon is, as its name suggests, a collection of various kinds of writings that hold authority for the faith community, ancient Israel. The collection includes worship literature, a variety of wisdom reflections, short stories, historical accounts, and the apocalyptic book of Daniel. We have already commented on the historical books of 1–2 Chronicles, Ezra, and Nehemiah as well as on Ruth and Esther, though some further comment on these last two books will be in order. The historical contexts from which these texts arose are the time of the united and divided kingdoms and the time of exile and its aftermath. We have described those settings in chapter 3. The more specific contexts that provide helpful background for these books are the institutions associated with worship and education in ancient Israel. We will consider those institutions when we come to relevant parts of the Writings.

Hebrew Poetry

Essential for constructive readings of the Psalms and Wisdom literature is an awareness of Hebrew poetry. Although Hebrew poetry has a kind of rhythm, scholars have not satisfactorily been able to recover the details of that dimension. What is clear about Hebrew poetry and can be seen in English translations is what has come to be called *parallelism*. The poets use parallel words, lines, and sections to communicate in a memorable way. One might say these parallel structures produce echo effects, in effect stating, "Yes, and what is more . . ." Traditionally, scholars have identified three types of parallelism:

1. *Synonymous parallelism*, in which the sense of the second line is similar to that of the first.

    The heavens are telling the glory of God;
    and the firmament proclaims his handiwork. (Ps. 19:1)

2. *Antithetic parallelism*, in which the second line articulates a contrast to the first.

    For the wicked shall be cut off,
    but those who wait for the Lord shall inherit the land. (Ps. 37:9)

3. *Stair-step parallelism*, in which the second line takes the thought a step further.

    For the Lord is a great God,
    and a great King above all gods. (Ps. 95:3)

It would be a mistake for readers to think that every verse of Hebrew poetry consists of two parallel lines or that all lines of the verses relate in one of these three ways. The poetry is more sophisticated than that. It is helpful, nonetheless, to note the various parallel structures in Hebrew poetry and to reflect on how they communicate content. Attending to how a poem constructs meaning is an astute strategy for the interpreter.

The fact that prophetic oracles, psalms, and wisdom texts are often in poetic form has further implications for interpretation. In contrast to many of the prose texts we have examined in the Pentateuch and Former Prophets, these poetic texts play on imagery, repetition, and other poetic devices, such as alliteration, assonance, and the use of the central vocabulary of ancient Israel's faith tradition. Such poetic form makes it possible to communicate a passionate faith. The poetry is at times deceptively simple. Readers need to take special care and sensitivity to see the implications and connections of the poetic language. The formal structures and rhythms of poetry demand a great deal from readers. The ordering of Hebrew poetry is also important for the interpreter. Poems often become more specific or more intense; there is movement between the lines toward a goal. How poetic texts use language and to what end will be central to our look at the Psalms and the Wisdom literature in the Writings.

The Psalms

Worship and the Psalms

The primary worship book in the Hebrew Bible or Old Testament is the book of Psalms. The name of the book comes from its Greek title meaning "songs." Another name for the book, the Psalter, is based on the Latin title, which reflects the name for the musical instrument ("stringed instrument") used to accompany the songs. The translation of the Hebrew title is "Book of Praises," reflecting the use of the **psalms** in worship. The Psalter consists of 150 psalms organized in five books or collections, perhaps in analogy to the five books of Moses, or Pentateuch. Each book concludes with a **benediction**, a brief word of blessing and thanksgiving to God (e.g., Ps. 41:13).

The Psalter is actually a collection of collections, as suggested in the superscriptions or headings above many of the psalms (116 of 150). These superscriptions often include the following:

1. The liturgical collection from which the psalm comes
2. Technical terms for use of the text in worship
3. Historical notes suggesting prose Old Testament texts to read along with the psalm

Psalm 57 carries a superscription that illustrates these various features: "To the leader: Do Not Destroy" (instruction to the worship leader on the tune to accompany the song); "Of David" (liturgical collection); "A Miktam, when he fled from Saul, in the cave" (an invitation to read the psalm in tandem with the narrative of Saul's pursuit of David as a realistic setting for the prayer; see 1 Sam. 22:1).

A good number of the superscriptions associate psalms with King David. Readers have often taken these superscriptions in terms of authorship, but the

> **THE FIVE BOOKS OF PSALMS**
>
> Psalms 1–41
> Psalms 42–72
> Psalms 73–89
> Psalms 90–106
> Psalms 107–150

```
PSALMS COLLECTIONS

Among the collections composing the Psalter
are the following:

Davidic Collections    Psalms 3–41; 51–72; 138–145
Korahite Collections   Psalms 42–49; 84–85; 87–88
Asaphite Collection    Psalms 73–83
Songs of Ascents       Psalms 120–134
```

Hebrew preposition used with the king's name can mean a variety of things, such as "for David," "to David," or "belonging to David." Given the use of similar superscriptions in the Psalms and elsewhere, the phrase likely indicates that the psalm comes from the Davidic (that is, royal) collection of psalms authorized for use in worship in Jerusalem. Elsewhere the Old Testament characterizes David as a singer of psalms. Perhaps the best conclusion to draw from the evidence is that David was the patron of worship in Jerusalem and of the use of psalms in worship.

Form Criticism and the Psalms

In the last century, scholars interpreted the Psalms primarily through the tool of **form criticism**. That is, central to the interpretive task has been classifying each psalm according to form and then asking where in ancient Israel's social and religious life these songs arose. Hermann Gunkel, working at the end of the nineteenth century and beginning of the twentieth, began this movement to put the study of the Psalms on a firm footing. By comparing the various psalms within the Hebrew Scriptures and comparing them with other ancient Near Eastern psalms, he categorized them by way of poetic structure, vocabulary, and religious feeling, just as we might categorize worship music today. Gunkel's work resulted in an organized way for modern interpreters to study the Psalms in light of other texts. Claus Westermann, working later in the twentieth century, emphasized that the major psalm types were the hymns of praise and the prayers for help (**lament psalms**). Gunkel's student Sigmund Mowinckel explored more seriously the institutional context from which the Psalms arose, arguing that the Psalms came from ancient Israel's cult, or organized worship, centered in the Jerusalem temple. In worship, the congregation articulated in word and deed its relationship to the deity. The implication of this view is that the language of the Psalms reflects actual acts of worship (e.g., Pss. 26:6–7; 95:2, 6). Still central to Psalms interpretation in the twenty-first century is the emphasis on the types of psalms and their background in the cult, the form-critical approach. This approach contrasts with the earlier personal/historical method, in which interpreters sought a context in a person's life or in the history of ancient Israel from which a psalm arose. The open poetic language of the Psalms makes it extraordinarily difficult to identify such specific contexts. The language of the Psalms is more representative than autobiographical.

A CLASSIFICATION OF THE PSALMS

I. Praise
  A. General hymns
       29, 33, 68, 100, 103, 105, 111, 113, 114, 115, 117, 134, 135, 139, 145, 146, 147, 149, 150
  B. Creation psalms
       8, 19, 65, 104, 148
  C. Enthronement psalms
       47, 93, 95, 96, 97, 98, 99
  D. Zion psalms
       46, 48, 76, 84, 87, 122
  E. Entrance liturgies
       15, 24
  F. Hymns with prophetic warnings
       50, 81, 82
  G. Trust psalms
       23, 91, 121, 125, 131
  H. Thanksgiving psalms
     1. Individual psalms
         30, 34, 41, 66, 92, 116, 118, 138
     2. Community psalms
         67, 75, 107, 124, 129, 136
II. Lament
  A. Individual psalms
       3, 4, 5, 6, 7, 9–10, 11, 13, 16, 17, 22, 25, 26, 27, 28, 31, 35, 36, 38, 39, 40, 42–43, 51, 52, 54, 55, 56, 57, 59, 61, 62, 63, 64, 69, 70, 71, 77, 86, 88, 94, 102, 109, 120, 130, 140, 141, 142, 143
  B. Community psalms
       12, 14, 44, 53, 58, 60, 74, 79, 80, 83, 85, 90, 106, 108, 123, 126, 137
III. Royal psalms
       2, 18, 20, 21, 45, 72, 89, 101, 110, 132, 144
IV. Wisdom psalms
       1, 32, 37, 49, 73, 78, 112, 119, 127, 128, 133

A couple of examples are in order. Although Psalm 117 consists of only two verses, it illustrates well a hymn of praise. It begins with a call to praise with the standard term *Hallelujah* (Praise YHWH). With the Hebrew particle meaning "because" or "for," the poem gives the reason for the praise of YHWH: the enduring divine steadfast love and trustworthiness.

> For great is his steadfast love toward us,
> and the faithfulness of the LORD endures forever.
> Praise the LORD! (117:2)

The psalm ends as it begins, with a renewed call to praise.

Psalm 13 illustrates well the **lament psalms**. This prayed poem addresses YHWH and, by way of four questions, characterizes a crisis.

> How long, O LORD? Will you forget me forever?
> How long will you hide your face from me?
> How long must I bear pain in my soul,
> and have sorrow in my heart all day long?
> How long shall my enemy be exalted over me? (13:1–2)

Verses 3–4 fervently plead for divine aid. The last two verses of the psalm suggest that a change in the perspective of the speaker has come to pass and divine assistance is now assured.

Psalms 13 and 117 illustrate the two major types of psalms: lament and praise. The link between these two types comes in the psalms of thanksgiving. Lament psalms often conclude with a vow to praise the God who comes to deliver (e.g., Ps. 13:6); thanksgiving psalms such as Psalm 30 fulfill the vow. The worshiper announces the purpose of offering praise and thanksgiving to God and then narrates the crisis, the prayer, and the deliverance by YHWH. The psalm concludes with a renewed vow of praise and thanksgiving. The royal psalms reflect the place of the monarchy in ancient Israel's cultic traditions. Psalm 2, for example, celebrates—perhaps as part of the coronation—the divine choice of the Davidic king to rule in Jerusalem.

The Psalms are ancient Israel's pilgrimage songs of faith, the songs they sang in the journey of faith and in their times of worship. These songs express their faith and help the community to come to terms with and confirm that faith. The Psalter is a central affirmation of the heart of Old Testament faith. In these texts the community honestly and passionately speaks to YHWH in prayer and praise. As a result, the Psalter is both the hymnbook and prayer book of the Hebrew Scriptures.

Contemporary Scholarship and the Psalms

Contemporary Psalms scholars are moving beyond the form-critical approach and giving fresh emphasis to the shape of the book of Psalms as a whole using canonical and **rhetorical criticism**. Previous generations of scholars have focused on individual psalm texts. Those who study the Psalter in the twenty-first century also consider the question of how each psalm relates to the texts surrounding it in the book. Greater attention to the poetic form and style of the Psalms is also important in contemporary Psalms interpretation. Repetition, poetic imagery, and the use of particular vocabulary—in addition to the use of parallel structures—all contribute to the way poems communicate meaning. How images of refuge, for example, function in various contexts in the Psalter can have profound impact on readers of the Psalms.

Scholars have made various proposals for the message of the Psalter as a whole. The sequence of the 150 psalms does appear to hold significance. Most scholars agree that the first two psalms introduce the book, and there is a growing consensus that Psalms 146–150 form a fivefold doxology to conclude the Psalter. The evidence suggests that Books I–III have a different editorial frame than do Books IV–V. Responding to the fall of the Davidic kingdom portrayed in Psalm 89, Books IV–V emphasize the reign of YHWH.

Books I–III. Perhaps it would be helpful to consider further the movement of the book of Psalms. The book begins with a wisdom psalm that contrasts the righteous and the wicked and urges readers to follow divine instruction (Torah) as the guide for the life of righteousness (Ps. 1:2). This suggests that the subsequent psalms are part of this divine instruction. Psalm 2 then introduces the Davidic kingdom with its divinely established ruler. This ruler

THE PSALMS AND TEXTUAL CRITICISM

The oldest available manuscripts of the Psalms in Hebrew are included in the Dead Sea Scrolls, noted in chapter 2 as a significant archaeological find in the twentieth century. There are a number of scrolls that include Psalms texts, though these scrolls are often fragmentary. These texts date from the second century BCE to the first century CE. Another important Psalms text from a similar time period is the Greek Septuagint Psalter. These manuscripts suggest to textual critics that the Psalms texts are stable but that the sequence of psalms followed in the Hebrew Masoretic Text was not set at this point in the historical process of the shaping of the book of Psalms in the Hebrew canon. Current scholars have not found a consensus about that process. This information about various versions of the Psalter provides helpful background when considering the organization of the book of Psalms.

faces conflict with enemies, and that reality leads to a series of psalms that reflect the conflicts and troubles of life. Most of the psalms in Book I (Pss. 1–41) are cries for help (laments) from individuals. These prayers portray a sojourn in the grip of deadly forces and articulate petitions for divine aid. These examples of the honest dialogue of faith instruct the community in the central faithful act of prayer, both urging the community to engage in this dialogue and encouraging worshipers to take refuge in YHWH.

Book II of the Psalter (Pss. 42–72) continues with the emphasis on prayers from individuals in the midst of difficulties. The opening psalm of the book calls on a moving image to articulate the speaker's need.

> As a deer longs for flowing streams,
>   so my soul longs for you, O God.
> My soul thirsts for God,
>   for the living God. (42:1–2)

An emphasis of a number of psalms in this section of the Psalter is the unrelenting presence of enemies. In the laments, three characters come to the fore: the speaker, who represents the righteous; the enemies; and God. The speaker seeks God's help in the face of the persistent and troubling onslaught of the enemies. Refuge in YHWH is the powerful hope of these worshipers at prayer. Psalms 46 and 48 celebrate the powerful divine presence with the community in Zion/Jerusalem and its temple.

Book I is dominated by an initial collection of Davidic psalms. Book II begins with a collection of Korahite psalms (Pss. 42–49) and continues with Davidic psalms. Book III begins with a collection of psalms of Asaph (Pss. 73–83) and

A FEMINIST INTERPRETATION OF PSALMS 42–43

Denise Dombkowski Hopkins has provided an intriguing feminist interpretation of Psalms 42–43. Most interpreters suggest that these texts were initially one psalm. Dombkowski Hopkins associates the text with the experiences of Miriam and Hannah as women in the Old Testament. She imagines alternative superscriptions: "A Psalm of Miriam, when she was shut out of the camp for seven days after challenging Moses' leadership (Num. 12:15)" or "A prayer of Hannah, when she made pilgrimage to Shiloh to pray for a son."[a] She connects the psalm's opening image of a thirsting doe and further imagery of tears and water with women's experience of exclusion. This feminist interpretation pushes readers to encounter this psalm in different ways than the standard commentary does.

[a] Denise Dombkowski Hopkins, *Psalms Books 2–3*, Wisdom Commentary (Collegeville, MN: Liturgical Press, 2016), 6, 14.

continues with Korahite psalms (Pss. 84–85; 87–88). These groups were likely psalm singers and collectors associated with the temple. Scholars sometimes designate Psalms 42–83 as the Elohistic Psalter, reflecting a preference for the divine name Elohim rather than YHWH. The presence of these overlapping collections also reflects the process by which the Psalter became the collection of collections we read in the Old Testament today. Book III is a bit different in that it seems to relate to the fall of Jerusalem in the sixth century BCE (see, e.g., Pss. 74; 79; 89) and the trouble that the defeat brings, all the while addressing the powerful God who delivers and blesses. The concluding psalms of Book III are striking laments. Psalm 88 is the most consistently anguished prayer in all of the Psalter, and Psalm 89 is a royal lament on the occasion of the fall of Jerusalem. The Davidic kingdom instituted in Psalm 2 has now collapsed.

> Lord, where is your steadfast love of old,
>   which by your faithfulness you swore to David? (89:49)

Books IV–V. Book IV (Pss. 90–106) begins with a prayer of Moses and so takes the community of readers back to the time before the Davidic kingdom and very quickly moves to a powerful celebration of the kingship of YHWH (Pss. 93–100). This praise of YHWH as creator and ruler of all calls for the worshiping community to sing a new song and thus be able to find its way in the pilgrimage of faith after the shattering destruction of the Davidic kingdom and its Jerusalem temple. Community psalms of praise assert a much greater presence in the latter part of the Hebrew Psalter, and yet those who collected the book of Psalms were also keenly aware of the needs of the worshiping community in the time after the fall of Jerusalem to the Babylonians.

AN EXERCISE: INTERPRETING PSALM 6

Read Psalm 6, a lament psalm, and answer the following questions.

- How does the psalm alternate between petition and complaint?
- How do you explain the sudden change of mood beginning with verse 8?
- How might the prayer fit in an ancient ritual of healing?
- How is Psalm 6 similar to and different from other laments in the beginning of the Psalter (Pss. 3–7)?
- Where is the divine name YHWH repeated in the psalm?
- What is the significance of weeping in the prayer?
- How do your answers shape your understanding of the psalm?

The final book of the Psalter (Pss. 107–150) also reflects the context of exile and its aftermath, as Psalm 107 suggests. Important in this section are the extensive meditation on God's instruction (Ps. 119) and the collection known as the Psalms of Ascents (Pss. 120–134). This collection of pilgrimage songs portrays a worshiping community yearning for the divine presence centered in the temple on Mount Zion. Psalm 137 articulates in striking ways the terrible grief over the destruction of the temple. Then with an additional collection of Davidic psalms—a reassertion of lament—the Psalter moves toward its conclusion with five psalms of praise culminating in the uninhibited call to praise in Psalm 150.

> Let everything that breathes praise the LORD!
> Praise the LORD! (150:6)

The Psalter has moved from its initial portrayal of the life of obedience through the honest dialogue of faith to the joyful praise of YHWH, who is present to bless.

The Wisdom Books

Biblical scholars traditionally designate the books of Proverbs, Job, and Ecclesiastes as the Wisdom books. The perspectives on Hebrew poetry discussed above in relation to the Psalms are also relevant to the Wisdom literature, but the context is different. Since these important books may not be very familiar to readers, we will begin with some background information on wisdom.

The Hebrew term for wisdom (*khokmah*) has a variety of connotations, such as describing someone who is skilled (Exod. 28:3) or clever (2 Sam. 13:3) at a task. The term can also suggest encyclopedic knowledge (1 Kings 10:6–7), moral discernment (1 Kings 3:9, 12), or reverence for God (Prov. 1:7). Proverbs 1–9 personifies wisdom as Woman Wisdom, through whom YHWH speaks. The heart is the seat of wisdom, and the opposite of wisdom is folly. Wisdom thus has a wide range of meanings as it relates to various parts of the Hebrew Scriptures. We will see below the particular ways in which the term characterizes the books of Proverbs, Job, and Ecclesiastes.

The Context of Wisdom

The background to these books is what scholars have come to call the "wisdom movement" in ancient Israel. These scholars often suggest that the movement became definable in Solomon's court with the need for sages or wise teachers to administer the developing empire. Some have also suggested there were schools associated with the Jerusalem court, just as there were schools in Egypt. In this setting, the sages would pass on the traditions of ancient Israel to the next generation. The heading that begins Proverbs 25 suggests that there were sages in the time of King Hezekiah who were concerned with preserving and passing on wisdom. This emphasis on wisdom was not without precedent, for no doubt Hebrew families had passed wisdom down through the generations. The wisdom movement took on some official status during the time of the monarchy. It seems to have flowered rather late in the history of ancient Israel. Prior to the fall of Jerusalem in the sixth century, kings and then priests and prophets and then the wise teachers or sages led the people. After the fall of Jerusalem, the influence of the types of leaders changed; priests led the way, followed by the wise. Prophets and kings lost influence. Wisdom became very important in the Second Temple period.

The book of 1 Kings associates Solomon with wisdom (1 Kings 4:29–34; 5:12; 10). Solomon's international relationships in commerce and diplomacy, especially with Egypt, also seem to tie the ruler to wisdom. Ancient Near Eastern cultures around Israel produced wisdom texts; Egypt produced a number of such texts. Perhaps it is fair to say that just as the Hebrew Scriptures associate Moses with Torah and David with Psalms, so the canon associates Solomon, the paradigmatic wise ruler, with wisdom. As wisdom's patron, Solomon is the one who supported it and gave it cultural legitimacy.

This background of terminology and context will be helpful to interpreters of the Wisdom books, though the exact understanding of wisdom in the Hebrew Scriptures has been something of an enigma. What follows is an attempt to provide a framework for reading Proverbs, Job, and Ecclesiastes. Readers should be aware, however, that one of the attractions of the Wisdom books is that they keep readers wondering and exploring. Interpretation of these texts is never really complete.

The Old Testament understanding of wisdom includes the following:

- Wisdom derives from observation or experience. It reflects on the business of daily living, such as eating and speaking.
- Wisdom is connected with morality and justice. It is about living the good, moral life as developed in practical affairs and relationships (see, e.g., Prov. 11:17). Social ethics are at the center of a lifestyle shaped by wisdom.
- God is the source of wisdom (Job 28).
- In a way analogous to Torah, wisdom instructs in the life of faith.

Wisdom is thus a way of seeing the relationship between God and humanity by seeking to understand and live by the orderly processes of life. One gains wisdom through observation. The sages are teachers who pass on this wisdom in the teacher/learner relationship.

Creation theology stands behind wisdom. God placed wisdom in the world in the process of creation and enables the sages to find that wisdom and pass it on to others as a way of commending it for living. That is part of the divine blessing in creation, part of the power to grow and thrive in the world; living in line with wisdom brings wholeness or integrity to persons and communities. The Hebrew Bible includes two types of Wisdom literature: pragmatic and speculative. The book of Proverbs is the prime example of pragmatic or practical wisdom; it articulates traditional generalizations about life. Readers might think of how they pass on wisdom to younger siblings, or to younger students about the transition from high school to college. In attractive poetic style, these sayings hand down basic wisdom for living as God intended. The books of Job and Ecclesiastes exemplify the second type of Wisdom literature, speculative wisdom. These books speculate about the meaning of life and question traditional perspectives. We will consider first Proverbs as pragmatic wisdom and then Job and Ecclesiastes as speculative wisdom.

Proverbs

In our look at the book of Proverbs, we begin with matters of form. A **proverb** is a compact, memorable, applicable teaching about life. Most cultures articulate proverbs such as "The apple does not fall far from the tree" or "Like mother, like daughter." A proverb provides practical instruction, a kind of how-to for living fully. The etymology of the Hebrew term for proverb, *mashal*, suggests that such sayings in ancient Israel include a comparative element. These sayings come in a variety of types:

1. Comparisons: Proverbs 15:16, 17; 16:8
2. Similitudes: Proverbs 25:11; 26:11
3. Observations: Proverbs 10:12; 16:18
4. Paradoxes: Proverbs 27:14; 29:5
5. Opposites: Proverbs 17:22; 27:7
6. Characteristic behavior: Proverbs 10:18; 20:4

The sages employ proverbs to pass on practical wisdom. The sayings are concrete, brief, pungent, and cogent, causing the reader/hearer to reflect on how to live in line with the created order. It is important for readers of the book of Proverbs to understand that these sayings are not intended to cover all the questions of life. Rather, the sayings articulate the tendencies or baselines for living and can be compared to warning signs. A speed-limit sign warns drivers to stay within a certain speed for basic safety. Some drivers may go faster and make a curve; other drivers may observe the speed limit but for some reason not make a curve. Still, the safest practice is for drivers to follow the warning. The sayings of the sages provide education for full living but not an explanation of all of life's challenges. Traditional wisdom encourages diligence in living (e.g., 6:10–11) but does not attempt to explain all the difficulties people encounter. The book of Proverbs provides encouragement for those who seek to learn practical wholeness and integrity in life.

The pragmatic wisdom contained in Proverbs provides a baseline for readers of the Wisdom books. The headings of Proverbs associate the book with Solomon, the patron of wisdom in ancient Israel (1:1; 10:1; 25:1), and with other sages (22:17; 24:23; 30:1; 31:1). The sayings collected in the book date from a variety of time periods and came to be associated with education in ancient Israel. The initial primary audience of the book was likely young people.

The book's educational purpose is on display in its opening poem, which concludes with a tie between wisdom and reverence for God.

> The fear of the LORD is the beginning of knowledge;
>   fools despise wisdom and instruction. (1:7)

Proverbs 1–9 calls readers and hearers to learn wisdom (e.g., 2:2; 8:32–36). The voice of wisdom in these chapters comes in the form of a personification of Woman Wisdom, who speaks in the first person and calls out to those who need to learn. The contrast to Woman Wisdom is Dame Folly, who seductively

ANCIENT NEAR EASTERN WISDOM

Cultures in Mesopotamia and Egypt produced a number of wisdom texts. For example, the **Wisdom of Amenemope** exhibits many points of comparison with Proverbs 22:17–24:22. It is likely that this section of Proverbs has a literary relationship with the Egyptian text. Wisdom was not limited to ancient Israel's experience. Examples include the Babylonian Theodicy (composed around 1000 BCE), the Words of Ahiqar (from Egypt, sixth to fifth century BCE), A Man and His God (from ancient Sumeria around 2000 BCE), and the Instruction of Merikare (an Egyptian text most likely dating to the mid-third millennium BCE).

leads to death. Following the call to wisdom, the book contains collections of practical observations and instructions for the young, as detailed above. Consider two examples:

> Whoever walks with the wise becomes wise,
>> but the companion of fools suffers harm. (13:20)

> Pride goes before destruction,
>> and a haughty spirit before a fall. (16:18)

The sayings articulate a moral order to life in terms of traditional generalizations about how to live fully and faithfully. One could call them observations for successful living, as structured by the Creator.

The book's opening section (chaps. 1–9) provides a theological base for the collections of proverbial sayings that follow. In the opening chapters, Woman Wisdom calls the young to learn wisdom; the book also concludes with a poetic portrayal of a woman who embodies wisdom as the fear of YHWH. Living in line with the wisdom articulated in the sayings is a means of incorporating the fear of YHWH into daily life. A number of the sayings take the form of folk wisdom without any explicit theological language, but as a canonical book Proverbs puts the sayings in the context of wisdom origi-nating from the Creator. For example, Proverbs 27:23–27 is a longer saying about flocks and grazing, agriculture common to the ancient setting. In the context of the book, the saying affirms the flocks as provision for life from the Creator and urges good stewardship of this gift.

The sages in Proverbs focus on the contrast between the wise (righteous) and foolish (wicked) and on the implications of the two lifestyles. The say-ings educate young people, especially young men, by warning of dangers and encouraging positive life decisions and self-control, especially when it comes to passions. The strange woman (Dame Folly) is seductive and dan-gerous. The sages single out adultery, drunkenness, laziness, and gossip for strong warnings, for these lead to death. Proverbs is also conscious of the influence of peer pressure.

> My child, if sinners entice you,
>> do not consent. (1:10)

All these dangers have a death-giving impact, but the goal of the wisdom teachers is fullness of life.

OUTLINE OF PROVERBS

Proverbs 1–9. Call to wisdom
Proverbs 10–22:16. Solomonic proverbs
Proverbs 22:17–24. Sayings of the wise
Proverbs 25–29. Solomonic proverbs
Proverbs 30. Sayings of Agur
Proverbs 31:1–9. Sayings of Lemuel
Proverbs 31:10–31. A wise woman

AN EXERCISE: INTERPRETING PROVERBS 11:1–11

Read Proverbs 11:1–11 and answer the following questions.

- What kind of parallelism characterizes these sayings?
- Sketch the characterization of the righteous and the wicked. Where do these two lifestyles lead?
- What is the connection between these lifestyles and the community?
- How do your answers shape the interpretation of this passage?

> In the path of righteousness there is life,
> in walking its path there is no death. (12:28)

Job

The book of Job articulates one of the great mysteries of life. The book tells the story of Job the sage, a "blameless and upright" man "who feared God and turned away from evil" (1:1). The text presents the character Job in a patriarchal setting, but it is important for readers to separate the question of the portrayal of the character Job and the date for the writing of the book. Most interpreters suggest that the book as a whole came together over time and likely is to be dated after the sixth-century fall of Jerusalem, when questions of suffering pressed on ancient Israel. As with the book of Proverbs, scholars often compare Job to other ancient Near Eastern wisdom literature, especially the Babylonian Theodicy, a text that takes the form of a dialogue between a sufferer and a comforter. The questions central to the book of Job are universal questions, though the resolution in Job is rather different from that of this Babylonian analogue.

The prose prologue in chapters 1–2 introduces the wise and righteous Job, who enjoys all the benefits of a wise lifestyle with family and wealth. Suddenly in verse 6, the scene shifts to the heavenly throne room of God, where the council of divine messengers has gathered. Among the council is the *satan*; the term in Hebrew is clearly a title with the definite article attached—the accuser. YHWH asks the prosecutor (the *satan*) if he has considered the wise and righteous Job in his journeys upon the earth. The accuser responds with the question, "Does Job fear God for nothing?" (1:9). The implication is that Job is wise and righteous because of all the benefits of family and wealth that result. And so YHWH and the accuser agree on a test of Job. Job's property and children are taken from him. Job grieves but maintains his wisdom and faith. In a second test, Job loses his health and contracts incredible sickness. At this point in the narrative, the earthly council convenes with "Job's three friends," Eliphaz, Bildad, and Zophar, who powerfully express their grief at Job's trouble and woe, sitting with him in silence. Job breaks the silence in chapter 3 with one of the most profound laments ever penned. Job curses the day on which he was born; he wishes that he had been stillborn.

Chapter 4 opens a poetic dialogue between Job and his three friends. The dialogue has three cycles; in each cycle Eliphaz, Bildad, and Zophar make speeches, and Job responds to each speech. Each of the cycles seems to have a theme. In chapters 4–14, the question is about God. Job's three interlocutors portray God as one who rewards righteous living and punishes evil. The implication is that Job is receiving punishment for evil. Job's response is that his experience contradicts their argument. In the second cycle of speeches, chapters 15–21, the three frenemies characterize the wicked person, with the implication that Job is that person. In the third cycle, chapters 22–31, the exchange becomes even more blunt, with the theme from the three that Job is sinful and thus the cause of his own suffering. Job's view is that his suffering actually provides a counter to their argument. He refutes the notion that there is always a one-to-one correspondence between righteousness and reward and between evil and woe. He rejects this orthodox doctrine of reward and retribution. As the "dialogue" continues, the speakers talk past each other and Job turns more and more away from Eliphaz, Bildad, and Zophar and toward God, whom he comes to see as both his real problem and his only hope:

> Even when I cry out, "Violence!" I am not answered;
>   I call aloud, but there is no justice.
> [God] has walled up my way so that I cannot pass,
>   and he has set darkness upon my paths. (19:7–8)

Job has mounted a powerful case against God in this dialogue. The conclusion of the third cycle of speeches is somewhat confused as to who is speaking. Chapter 28 interrupts with a hymn to wisdom. It is followed by Job's final plea, which concludes with his words of self-defense against the accusations that he has lived an unrighteous, unethical, and foolish life (Job 31). Chapters 32–37 present four uninterrupted speeches from a new character named Elihu, who angrily repeats some of the arguments of the "three friends" and prepares readers for what is to follow.

In chapter 38, we finally come to the speeches of YHWH out of the whirlwind. In elegant poetry, YHWH points to the wonders of creation that are in the care of YHWH and not Job. It is YHWH and not Job who reigns in the universe. Job's initial response (40:1–5) is silence. Yet shortly thereafter he confesses (42:1–6) that he has encountered the divine and his view has changed. The prose epilogue in chapter 42 confirms that it was Job and not the "three friends" who spoke rightly of YHWH, and the book concludes with the restoration of Job. The frame of the book suggests that there is an order to life—and that life poses many questions.

So what are readers to make of this remarkable and puzzling piece of literature? The book deals with the undeserved suffering of Job, who "was blameless and upright, one who feared God and turned away from evil" (1:1). The difficulty is that the book does not give a satisfying explanation of that suffering. Elihu suggests a disciplinary view of suffering, but that does not seem to fit Job's life or the book's message as a whole. The problem of theodicy, or the justice of God, is a central issue in contemporary theology. The traditional articulation of the issue is how one can claim an all-good and all-powerful God in the face of the evil and suffering in the world. Such theoretical issues are not at the core of the book of Job; rather, the book focuses on the troubles in the life of the character Job. With the contrary example of Job's undeserved suffering, the book rejects a necessary and consistent doctrine of reward and retribution that always explains both the benefits and the woes of life by way of one's behavior. Some have suggested that the key to the book's import is the question of the *satan* put in Job 1:9: "Does Job fear God for nothing?" That is, can people of faith serve God for the sake of righteousness alone rather than for any benefits in life? Scholars have come to call this question the issue of disinterested righteousness. A different approach to the book brings the focus to the speeches of YHWH as the culmination and suggests that the book is more about encounter with the divine in the midst of trouble than it is about theoretical explanations of suffering.

The history of the interpretation of Job rightly shows that a number of issues appear in the text: theodicy, undeserved suffering, the moral order of life, disinterested righteousness, and the encounter with the divine in the midst of suffering. To put these issues in context, it is important to consider the form of the book. The narrative frames a wisdom dialogue between the frenemies Eliphaz, Bildad, and Zophar, who articulate the traditional popular wisdom that life brings benefits to the righteous and trouble to the wicked, and Job, who questions this orthodox wisdom by way of his own undeserved suffering. Combining this insight with the canonical impulse of interpreting the book in the context of the wisdom movement, perhaps the best way to put the primary theme of the book is that it is a meditation on the limits of human wisdom. The book concludes with the view that there is a moral order to life, but the dialogue and the divine response also make it clear that there are many questions humans will not be able to answer in a satisfying way. To put the matter another way, the book of Job serves as a critical corrective to an overly simplistic interpretation of Proverbs that suggests that the human community has settled the explanations of life and its ambiguities.

Ecclesiastes

The third book in the traditional listing of the Wisdom literature is Ecclesiastes. The title comes from the Greek version and ties the book to the gathered assembly; the Hebrew title, *Qoheleth*, makes a similar connection. The title suggests that the book gathers the wisdom of the teacher of the assembled community. The first part of the book indicates a connection with Solomon as the patron of wisdom (1:1, 12, 16; 2), but the latter part of the book seems to move away from that association. Perhaps the connection with Solomon serves to legitimize the book's wisdom, which does not always take

---

A FRAMEWORK FOR READING THE WISDOM BOOKS

I. Proverbs
  A. Reverence for God underlies all maxims, even if it is not explicitly stated.
  B. The proverbs are understood as part of the instruction for honoring God and finding life.
  C. No premium is placed on failure, indolence, stupidity, mediocrity, tactlessness, and friendlessness. The wisdom teachers value the opposite.
  D. Wisdom is not automatic but needs to be learned. Proverbs are thus often pithy condensations of years of experience.
  E. Wisdom celebrates life. Wisdom speaks little of disease, suffering, or problems. It may seem simplistic (in Proverbs), but wisdom gives guidance that represents tendencies.
II. Job and Ecclesiastes are the complement to Proverbs
  A. Job is partly a reaction against a simplistic understanding of Proverbs. It is concerned with how persons will or should react if all they value is removed. How can life be worthwhile when that happens?
  B. Job protests against the wisdom of the day that claims humans can control life. It suggests that if life has any inner reason, it is known to God alone. The character Job is not the model of the patient sufferer, the stoic. His deep rage at the distresses that assail him comes across in a thundering majesty of rhetoric. His is a mighty rage. Job asks angry questions and waits for an answer. God responds, "None of your business!" Life is in God's hands, not ours, so we are to put our faith in God.
  C. Ecclesiastes asserts that life has order but that the control of that order does not lie with humans. Rather, glimpses of order are seen in the seasons and rhythms whose inner workings humanity cannot know.

the orthodox path on life's significance. The text suggests that the writer is one who has experienced a great deal in life and reflects on its significance. Most interpreters would date the book rather late in the Old Testament era. Although there is no consensus on the organization of this wisdom treatise, the text gives readers some clues. The book speaks of a series of tests to seek the meaning of life; the result is that the meaning is not found. While wisdom is better than folly, even it does not answer the riddles of life. The first half of the book speaks of "vanity and a chasing after wind" (1:14; 2:11, 17, 26; 4:4, 16; 6:9); the second half speaks of human inability to know the future (6:12; 8:17; 10:14). The book's conclusion suggests that, though humans do not know the shape of what is to come, the best option for living is reverence for God and God's instruction.

The book's opening poem uses a variety of images to announce the Teacher's (Qoheleth's) theme of vanity, that which is fleeting and futile. It is important for readers to remember that Ecclesiastes is a Wisdom book, and this context is important for interpreting the opening poem and the book's message. Qoheleth's concern seems to be not so much skepticism about all of life as a skepticism about human ability to control and manage life. A strict doctrine of reward and retribution that explains all the events of life is not true to the Teacher's experience. What is true to the observation of this wisdom teacher is the freedom of God. God is the one who gives and rules life. Under the primary theme of the freedom of God, Qoheleth advises to make the most of life and help one another while realizing that too much righteousness and too much folly are deadly (7:16–17; 8:15). The book is a wonder to read, for it cleverly and unexpectedly subverts readers' views and raises many questions about life, faith, and wisdom. Some interpreters have seen Ecclesiastes as a nihilistic treatise, but interpreting Ecclesiastes as part of the Old Testament's wisdom tradition suggests that it is a contrast to the view that the community has answered all the riddles of life and of God. Proverbs, Job, and Ecclesiastes give readers a full look at the various dimensions of life as God created it. The wisdom tradition develops further in the intertestamental period, especially in Sirach and the Wisdom of Solomon.

Daniel

Popular interpretations of the Hebrew Scriptures often lump apocalyptic literature with the Latter Prophets. The phenomenon of prophecy is certainly part of the background for apocalyptic literature, but the form is somewhat different. The term *apocalyptic* derives from the Greek heading of the New Testament book of Revelation (the Apocalypse) and suggests uncovering or revealing. Features of Jewish apocalyptic writings include the following:

1. Dreams, visions, and auditions
2. Angelology and demonology
3. Cosmic upheavals
4. An emphasis on messianism
5. Numerology (study of the significance of numbers)
6. Strong emphasis on judgment
7. Eschatology (study of the last things)

Apocalyptists tend to be visionaries and so find ways to communicate with the faithful in the midst of difficult times. Some interpreters have labeled these writings as tracts for bad times or as political cartoons with a surreal feel. The message of apocalyptic is that God is in control of history and that, because of that hope, the faithful can endure the evils of the current age. The emphasis is on the culmination of history and the justice it will bring. That emphasis encourages the community to stand with faithfulness to the one true God, who will bring history to its proper conclusion. Scholars have associated this literature with both wisdom texts and prophetic texts in that it reveals the coming kingdom of God and encourages righteous living. The form is somewhat different, however, with an emphasis on visions and symbols. Interpreters often take the imagery as a means of communicating with an oppressed people by way of images and symbols that the oppressed community will understand but the oppressors will not. Scholars often identify Isaiah 24–27, parts of Ezekiel, Zechariah 9–14, and Joel as examples of apocalyptic writing.

The book of Daniel is the primary example of apocalyptic literature in the Hebrew Bible. The book is located in the Writings section of the Hebrew canon. Chapters 1–6 narrate the experiences of Daniel and his compatriots set in the time of Babylonian exile (1:1–2). Central to these narratives are the dreams of the Babylonian ruler Nebuchadnezzar, first occurring in chapter 2. The dreams concentrate on the nations and the Most High God and typically portray four kingdoms of this world that will fall and be followed by the kingdom of God, which will last forever. Scholars usually identify the four corrupt kingdoms of this world as the kingdoms of Babylon, Media, Persia, and Greece (and all its evil successors). The highly symbolic portrayals suggest these identifications. The consistent import of the dreams is that these kingdoms will fall, but the kingdom of God will stand. Chapter 3 recounts the story of the rescue of Shadrach, Meshach, and Abednego—Daniel's friends and faithful servants of God—from the fiery furnace where the Babylonians put them when they resist Babylonian idolatry. Chapters 4 and 5 pronounce judgment on Nebuchadnezzar and Belshazzar, another Babylonian ruler. In chapter 6, God rescues Daniel from the lions' den as he faithfully resists idolatry. The second half of the book of Daniel features Daniel's apocalyptic visions, with an emphasis on the Medes and Persians in chapter 8. Chapter 9 recounts Daniel's prayer and the hopeful vision of Gabriel. The final chapters of the book recount further visions and revelations of the mysteries of the coming kingdom of God and the hope of an afterlife.

The book of Daniel provides a unified message as an apocalyptic writing. The message comes in its narratives and its vision accounts. The visions articulate the hope that history will come to its just culmination. With that hope the oppressed community can faithfully embrace the fullness of life in courageous obedience and resist idol worship and the lifestyle of the Babylonian overlords. The message is consonant with the prophetic proclamation, though it takes a different form for a different context. The prophets proclaimed "Thus says the Lord"; Daniel the seer recounts that he had a dream. The dream focuses on the fall of the corrupt and oppressive kingdoms of this age and the coming of the everlasting kingdom of God "that shall not pass away, . . . that shall never be destroyed" (7:14). The book exemplifies the features of apocalyptic listed above: cosmic upheavals, emphatic judgment, messianism, visions with traumatic effects on the seer, angels and demons, and significant numbers.

Most interpreters date the book of Daniel in the second century BCE as a reflection of the oppressive reign of **Antiochus IV Epiphanes**. Antiochus IV's persecution of the Jewish community and especially his disregard of their religious practices are pivotal in the history of Judaism. The book of Daniel is part of the Writings, the last section of the Hebrew canon, and some suggest that its theology and apocalyptic form fit that time. The languages of the book would also fit a later time period; the text of Daniel 2:4–7:28 is in Aramaic. Scholars often interpret the book as a pseudonymous writing, in the name of Daniel. If so, the authors were looking to Daniel and his Jewish compatriots in an earlier period of persecution (the Babylonian exile) for guidance during the persecution of their own day (second century BCE).

Some interpreters would argue for an exilic date for the book, citing tradition and inspiration as support for an earlier date and suggesting that the language and theology also fit the exilic era. They argue that the placement of the book in the Writings has more to do with the canonization process than with the date of writing. They also appeal to connections with wisdom for the canonical placement. The stories of the first part of Daniel could have originated in the exilic setting and been passed down until they were included in the book. The visions of the latter half of the book, however, lend much historical support for the second-century date. The **apocalypse** concludes with an openness looking toward the future. The community awaits the fulfillment of the hope of the everlasting kingdom of God and embraces full and faithful life in the already but not yet.

The Five Scrolls

The Writings also include the collection called the **Megilloth**, or brief scrolls. These are the five books of Ruth, Esther, Ecclesiastes, Song of Songs, and Lamentations. The books all have some connections with the wisdom and poetry of the Writings, and each book has an association with a Jewish festival. Their use in worship no doubt ensured their inclusion in the Hebrew canon.

Ruth

The book of Ruth narrates the survival of the Moabite Ruth and her mother-in-law, Naomi, with the help of Boaz. The story shows divine providence in the natural processes of life and models life-giving relationships between the characters. The narrative makes clear that the people of God include even non-Israelite women. The short story thus has a teaching or wisdom function and is told at Pentecost. We considered the book in the treatment of exile in chapter 3.

Esther

The book of Esther narrates the survival of the Jewish people in the face of the evil Haman and his henchmen. Queen Esther works to see that the divine care for the Jewish people comes to fruition in their defeat of the Persians. The story espouses a particularist view that God particularly cares for the Jewish community. The story is the basis for the Feast of Purim, during which it is dramatically recounted, serving a didactic function. We considered the book in the treatment of exile in chapter 3.

Ecclesiastes

The book of Ecclesiastes (Qoheleth) affirms the freedom of God to determine life and advises the community to make the most of life in that context. The treatise, written in the form of a royal testament or final instruction of wisdom from the teacher to the students, makes clear that there are limits to what the human community can control. The famous poem that begins chapter 3 affirms these limits: "For everything there is a season, and a time for every matter under heaven" (3:1). We considered this book above with the Wisdom literature. Ecclesiastes is read as part of the Feast of Tabernacles.

Song of Songs

Interpreters sometimes refer to the Song of Songs as the Song of Solomon or simply as the Song or the Canticle. The connection to Solomon ties the book to wisdom traditions. The book is a collection of love poems celebrating the gift of human love between a man and woman in rather explicit poetry. The imagery illustrates well the difference between the cultural setting of the book's origins and the setting of twenty-first-century readers. The history of interpretation includes a long tradition of reading the book as an allegory of the love of God for Israel or of Christ for the church, but the initial writing of the book reflects the wisdom practice of celebrating the basic joys of the life God created, including the love between a woman and a man. The Song of Songs is celebrated as part of the festival of Passover.

Lamentations

The book of Lamentations is part of the marking of the Ninth of Ab (the name of the month), which centers on mourning over the destruction of Jerusalem and the temple in the sixth century BCE by the Babylonians (and later in the first century CE by the Romans). The book is a series of acrostic poems that lament the fall of the city and the resulting devastation. The poems are akin to the laments in the book of Psalms, and scholars often compare them to other ancient Near Eastern laments related to the destruction of cities. The poetry articulates profound grief and functions as an important part of the community's memory of this troublesome part of its story. The poems thus shape the community's grief and teach the expression of such passionate concern in the context of relationship with the creator God, YHWH.

Theological Reflection: Faith and Culture

The Writings, as the third section of the Hebrew Scriptures, betray many links to the Hebrew traditions of wisdom. These (mostly) poetic texts interpret for readers and hearers the Primary History of ancient Israel (Genesis–2 Kings) and move the story beyond the Second Temple period. They connect cultural memory with lived experience and hope in a variety of ways. The traditional Wisdom books—Proverbs, Job, and Ecclesiastes—provide a good starting place to think about these issues. The goal and meaning of life in traditional wisdom is found in healthy community. The community can learn to live in line with God's created order and embrace justice. This hope has been entrusted to humans, who have been given life to celebrate and appreciate. Central to such a lifestyle are both the humanities and the sciences, the artifacts of culture. In this version of biblical humanism, life and the created order are good and to be fully enjoyed and sustained in a responsible way. People experience this life in the basic realities of sex and money, of government and family, of work and play, of table manners and cultural customs. Women and men are God's icons in celebrating and nurturing fullness of life in its integrity. Humans are God's trusted creatures to whom God gives life and who are responsible for it. The book of Proverbs passes on traditional wisdom for such life. The Song of Songs celebrates the sexual dimension of that life, and the short stories of Ruth and Esther remind the community of divine providence in the midst of troubles. These wisdom texts interact with culture, since wisdom is a universal phenomenon and its source is God. In that sense, these texts take a positive view of culture. That view of culture is rather different than the view of many texts in the Latter Prophets. The prophets often warn of the dangers of culture, especially cultural expressions of other peoples and faiths. Wisdom's openness to find divine revelation wherever it may be found, in a variety of contexts and texts, and its call for faithfulness in such a cosmopolitan setting complements the polemical quality of prophetic texts. The Prophets and the Writings provide two sides to the coin of the relationship between faith and culture.

Many of the psalms celebrate the creation theology that undergirds traditional wisdom. The psalms of praise celebrate YHWH as trustworthy creator and sovereign who gives life and continues to be present with the community to bless and teach. The royal psalms illustrate God's work in society to sustain faith and ethics while celebrating the Davidic kingdom. A number of other psalms have a didactic focus. This same God enables the sages to learn wisdom and teach it to others. This connection between Psalms and Proverbs suggests another connection between faith and culture—a community nurtures and sustains its cultural memory in worship. The use of the Psalms in worship and the use of the Megilloth in festival settings illustrate the staying power of faith as part of the culture that ancient Israel bequeathed to continuing communities. Such a faith is both robust and honest. The ever-present lament psalms and the book of Lamentations demonstrate the candor of ancient Israel's worship. Here the community in an uninhibited way processes the trouble and woe of life in moving prayer spoken to the One who is in a position to change oppression and injustice.

The traditional Wisdom books also partake of this honest dialogue of faith. The book of Job exhibits many connections with the lament psalms. Job cries out in severe pain and, as the book progresses, directs that pain primarily to God. Job is able to find a way forward in the profound and mysterious encounter with this God who answers, sometimes in enigmatic ways. Qoheleth continues the meditation on the limits of human ability to control life and its consequences. God is the one who gives life; the human task is to make the most of whatever is given. These texts suggest that faith and worship must include the most difficult questions of life; only then is some kind of way forward possible for the community of faith. The Writings bear witness to a faith that both gives life and entertains life's deepest questions.

The book of Daniel exhibits connections to wisdom, especially in the narratives that suggest important didactic purposes. At the same time, the book's apocalyptic vision sees a future determined by the sudden coming of the divine kingdom to bring a reality radically different from this age. Such a vision of the age to come is rather different from the historical books in the Writings (1–2 Chronicles, Ezra, and Nehemiah). These texts, treated in chapter 3 under the rubric of exile, see the future in continuity with the present, a future in which the ancient Israelite community continues to live out its covenant faith. This creative tension between different views of the future continues into the intertestamental period as the faith community lives between the memory of ancient Israel and the birth of the Christian church and the eschaton.

Contemporary Old Testament scholarship has begun to explore how these texts related to social settings in the lives of ancient people groups. The narratives of the Primary History likely came from active scribal communities. Songs and poetry lived in sanctuaries and in domestic rituals and eventually in synagogues. The scribes and theologians of this ancient faith community preserved and shaped a canon that reveals multiple facets of the story of YHWH and ancient Israel, and in so doing made it possible for future communities of faith to enter the story that brings life.

SUGGESTED READING

Bellinger, W. H., Jr. *Psalms: A Guide to Studying the Psalter*. 2nd ed. Grand Rapids: Baker Academic, 2012.

————. *Psalms as a Grammar for Faith: Prayer and Praise.* Waco: Baylor University Press, 2019.

Brown, William P. *Seeing the Psalms: A Theology of Metaphor.* Louisville: Westminster John Knox, 2002.

Clifford, Richard J. *The Wisdom Literature.* Interpreting Biblical Texts. Nashville: Abingdon, 1998.

Cook, Stephen L. *The Apocalyptic Literature.* Interpreting Biblical Texts. Nashville: Abingdon, 2003.

deClaissé-Walford, Nancy L. *Introduction to the Psalms: A Song from Ancient Israel.* St. Louis: Chalice, 2004.

Dell, Katharine. *Get Wisdom, Get Insight: An Introduction to Israel's Wisdom.* Macon, GA: Smyth & Helwys, 2000.

Nowell, Irene. *Song of Songs, Ruth, Lamentations, Ecclesiastes, Esther.* New Collegeville Bible Commentary 24. Collegeville, MN: Liturgical Press, 2013.

PART TWO

THE NEW TESTAMENT

Between the Testaments

As a collection, the books of the Old Testament largely chronicle the story of the Hebrew people up through the fifth century BCE. The books of the New Testament resume the story in the first century CE. Major transitions and developments took place, however, in the four centuries between the Testaments. In this chapter we will sketch a variety of historical, literary, and theological shifts that took place between the fourth century BCE and the first century CE.

Sociohistorical Developments

The Spread of Hellenism

Alexander the Great. The cultural landscape of the ancient Mediterranean world was radically transformed as a result of **Alexander the Great**'s victorious military campaign. Alexander, the son of King Philip of Macedonia, first used his military acumen and might to consolidate the Greek armies. Once he had the benefit of a united Greek force, he took on and eventually conquered the Persian Empire, despite being greatly outnumbered in numerous battles. In the process, Alexander gained control of the regions of Judea and Samaria in 332 BCE, when he defeated the Persians at the Battle of Issus. Ultimately, though, Alexander's grand plans for a worldwide kingdom were never fully realized. Shortly after conquering Greek, Egyptian, and Persian territories, Alexander developed a fever and died at the age of thirty-three in 323 BCE.

Alexander's conquest was no doubt motivated by a desire for power, but it was also driven by his desire to spread Greek culture and ideas (**Hellenism**) throughout the world. Because he believed that Hellenistic, or Greek, culture was superior to the ideas and customs found in other regions, Alexander reasoned that those whom he conquered would eventually come to appreciate the gift of Hellenism that he had brought to them. To some degree, Alexander succeeded in his desire to spread Greek culture. For example, in the regions of the world that Alexander conquered, Greek became a universal language.

Ptolemies. When Alexander realized his death was imminent, he determined that his generals would compete for control of the various territories he had conquered. After a decade of struggle, Alexander's kingdom was ultimately divided into four major regions. The Egyptian region to the south of Judea came under the control of General Ptolemy, whose descendants and subjects are known as the **Ptolemies**. Consequently, Alexandria, Egypt, served as the capital for the Ptolemaic kings. In addition to ruling Egypt, these Greeks served as the overlords of Palestine for most of the period between 323 and 198 BCE.

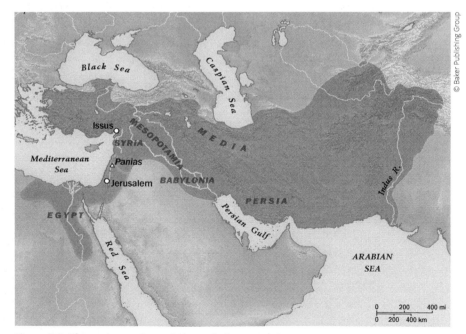

© Baker Publishing Group

Figure 5.1. The eastern extent of Alexander's conquest

Seleucids. General Seleucus, whose descendants and subjects were known as the Seleucids, acquired the Syrian region to the north of Judea. Antioch of Syria served as the capital for the Seleucid kings. While these Greeks had intermittent control of Palestine at points between 323 and 198 BCE, they gained definitive control over Judea and Samaria in a series of events that took place between 223 and 198 BCE. In particular, the Seleucid king Antiochus III took control of Jerusalem in 198 BCE, and the Seleucids became the established overlords of Palestine.

The lives of the Palestinian Jews took a turn for the worse, however, when Antiochus IV, who preferred the title Epiphanes ("god manifest"), became the Seleucid king in 175 BCE. Unlike Alexander, who hoped that non-Greeks would eventually adopt Hellenistic culture because they recognized its superiority, Antiochus IV forced Hellenism on the Jewish people. On the one hand, he outlawed many Jewish religious practices, such as temple sacrifices, circumcision, Sabbath observances, and food laws. On the other hand, he ordered the Jewish people to participate in Greek religious practices, such as offering sacrifices to Zeus. Perhaps most notoriously, Antiochus IV plundered and took control of the Jewish temple in Jerusalem. He entered the holy of holies, confiscated valuable ornaments, renamed the temple in honor of Zeus, placed a statue of Zeus on the altar, and ordered that swine (which the Jews considered to be unclean) be sacrificed on the altar. Furthermore, Antiochus IV severely punished, tortured, and killed numerous Jews who defied his decrees. (As discussed in chapter 4, the book of Daniel was almost certainly composed in the midst of this second-century-BCE context while the Jews looked to the heroes of the past to gain direction for their response to persecution in the present.)

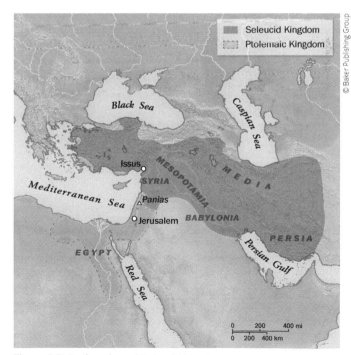

Figure 5.2. **Ptolemaic and Seleucid kingdoms**

Jewish Reaction

During the Hellenistic era (and extending into the Roman era), tremendous theological and cultural diversity developed within Judaism. Decisions were forced on the Jewish people, whose responses varied. Some Jews willingly embraced Hellenism and their foreign overlords, either because they valued Greek culture or because they thought embracing Hellenism was politically advantageous. Other Jews rejected Hellenism altogether. Most Jews, however, likely reacted in a manner that falls somewhere in between the two ends of the spectrum.

Adoption of Hellenism. There is little doubt that many Jews adopted aspects of Hellenism. For example, during the Ptolemaic and Seleucid eras, many Jews routinely dressed in Greek clothes and participated (without clothes) in the Greek gymnasium that was built in Jerusalem. Some even took steps to hide their circumcision, or reverse it through a painful surgical procedure, thereby allowing them to participate fully in the gymnasium. Moreover, as Greek became the dominant Mediterranean language, many Jews began to write out their theological reflections using Greek as opposed to Hebrew or Aramaic.

Importantly, beginning in the mid-third century BCE, Jewish scholars translated into Greek the various scrolls that made up the Hebrew Scriptures. These Greek translations became the standard form of the Jewish Scriptures that most Jews and early Christians used for the next few centuries. We refer to these Greek translations of the Hebrew Scriptures as the Septuagint, or **LXX**. The name derives from the Jewish legend that seventy or seventy-two translators, at the request of King Ptolemy II, translated the Pentateuch without error into Greek over a period of seventy days. Regardless of the legend, the Septuagint provides evidence that many devout Jews throughout the Mediterranean world adopted at least a measure of Hellenism when they began to rely heavily on Greek translations of their Scriptures.

Rejection of Hellenism. It is equally clear that many Jews throughout the Mediterranean world rejected the primary aspects of Hellenism. For example, many Judean Jews, in an attempt to remain faithful, resisted the mandates of the Seleucid king Antiochus IV. These Jewish martyrs chose to die rather than to worship the Greek gods or pay homage to the Seleucid kings. Despite being tortured and dismembered, they remained devoted to their belief in and their worship of the God of Abraham, Isaac, and Jacob.

Maccabean Revolt. The **Maccabean Revolt** may provide the most vivid illustration of Jewish resistance to Hellenism in the time between the Old and New Testaments. In 167 BCE, a priest in Modein named Mattathias refused to offer pagan sacrifices as Antiochus IV had decreed. While resisting,

THE GREEK ERA

332 BCE	Alexander the Great gains control of Judea
323 BCE	Alexander the Great dies and Ptolemy gains control of Judea
198 BCE	The Seleucids gain control of Judea
175 BCE	Antiochus IV becomes the Seleucid king
167 BCE	The Maccabean Revolt begins
164 BCE	Jews regain control of the Jerusalem temple
142 BCE	Jews gain political independence from the Seleucids

Mattathias killed a Jew who chose to offer pagan sacrifices and a Seleucid military officer who was implementing the king's orders. As a result, Mattathias and his five sons fled to the Palestinian hills and lived in caves. Many other Jews eventually joined them. From there, the Jewish rebels engaged in guerrilla warfare against their Seleucid overlords, whom the Jews envisioned as oppressors and as agents of religious contamination. Rather than line up for a frontal assault on a battlefield, these Jewish resistance fighters often attacked Seleucid convoys as they traveled in small numbers along rural roads.

These rebels are closely linked with a group known as the Hasideans, the "pious ones," who sought to separate themselves from religious and cultural pollution while faithfully adhering to the Mosaic law. The Maccabean Revolt, which lasted twenty-five years, apparently received its name from Mattathias's sons, especially Judas. Later writers suggested that Judas was so effective at planning and executing surprise attacks on the Seleucids that his followers gave him the nickname "Maccabee," which means "The Hammer."

In the midst of the Maccabean Revolt, King Antiochus IV and his Seleucid armies were forced to focus their attention on threats to their northern, Syrian border. As a result, the Seleucid defenses in Jerusalem were increasingly vulnerable. The Jewish freedom fighters won a series of battles and then took control of Jerusalem in 164 BCE. At that point, the Judean Jews rededicated the temple in Jerusalem as the center of their worship, taking steps to purify the temple from the "pollution" of the pagan Seleucids. The Jewish festival that celebrates the purification and rededication of the temple in 164 BCE is known as Hanukkah.

A Jewish State and the Hasmonean Dynasty

Even though their struggles with the Seleucids endured for several more years, Palestinian Jews secured a measure of freedom once they regained control of Jerusalem. In particular, from 142 to 63 BCE, Palestinian Jews were essentially free from the control of foreign rulers and were able to establish a Jewish state. Yet chaos and internal disputes characterized life in Palestine during this time period. In particular, what began as a Jewish resistance movement against the Seleucids primarily motivated by religious concerns devolved into ongoing internal battles for political power among the various Jewish groups. In essence, the Jews began by battling the Seleucids but ended up battling one another.

The gradual conflation of religious and political objectives is best illustrated in the titles used by the Jewish leaders in the years that followed the Maccabean Revolt. For example, Simon, one of Mattathias's sons, functioned as "high priest" and "commander and leader of the Jews" from 142 to 134 BCE (1 Maccabees 13:41–42). Next, John Hyrcanus, one of Mattathias's grandsons, led the Judean Jews from 134 to 104 BCE also under the title of "high priest." His son, Aristobulus I, however, increased his political power and prestige by taking on the titles of "king" and "high priest" from 104 to 103 BCE. Not surprisingly, separatist movements like the **Pharisees**, who focused on religious matters, often found themselves at odds with the Jewish "kings" of this time period. For example, Alexander Jannaeus, who ruled as "king" and "high priest" from 103 to 76 BCE, reportedly crucified more than eight hundred Pharisees after the Pharisees (among others) criticized the Jewish monarch for being corrupt.

The string of leaders who reigned over Judea between 142 and 63 BCE is known as the **Hasmonean dynasty**. Josephus, the late-first-century-CE Jewish historian, suggests (*Jewish Antiquities* 12.6.1) that the Hasmonean name likely derived from Mattathias's great-grandfather, Asamoneus. Regardless, the Hasmonean rulers, despite their frequent attempts to maintain control through violence, were politically weak. For example, after the death of their mother (Queen Alexandra), Alexander Jannaeus's sons, Hyrcanus II and Aristobulus II, vied for control of Judea, but neither was strong enough to grasp it firmly. In an ill-advised move, both would-be Judean rulers sent word to the Roman general Pompey requesting his help. Both brothers promised favors to Rome in exchange for Rome's friendship and military support. In essence, each brother asked Pompey to send Roman troops to Judea to help him overcome his sibling.

Interactions with Rome

Rather than electing to create a long-term, reciprocal partnership with either sibling, General Pompey eventually sent Roman troops into Palestine to take control. Beginning in 63 BCE, Rome officially took possession of the Jewish homelands, which were then divided into a variety of distinct districts.

THE ROMAN ERA

63 BCE	The Romans gain control of Judea
37–4 BCE	Herod the Great serves as king of Judea
ca. 7–4 BCE	Jesus is born, prior to the death of Herod the Great
ca. 30 CE	Pontius Pilate orders Jesus's crucifixion
66–73 CE	The Jewish War with Rome
70 CE	The Romans destroy the Jerusalem temple
132–35 CE	The Bar Kokhba Revolt

At times Rome governed the Jews through Jewish figureheads. For example, after overthrowing Aristobulus II, Pompey appointed John Hyrcanus II to serve as high priest. Pompey also appointed Antipater to serve as governor of Judea from 63 to 37 BCE, because Antipater had supported him during his overthrow of Palestine. Similarly, Antipater's son, **Herod the Great**, was appointed king of Judea from 37 to 4 BCE; and even though Herod's kingdom expanded beyond Judea, he remained subject to Roman authority. At other times, Rome appointed Roman emissaries to serve as governors of the region. For example, the Roman official **Pontius Pilate** served as the governor of Judea from 26 to 36 CE. Regardless of the precise arrangement, beginning in 63 BCE Rome was unquestionably in charge. Jewish leaders had no choice but to give priority to the interests of Rome in the region. Furthermore, Roman control of Palestine remained constant until the Roman Empire began to crumble in the fifth century CE.

The Roman Empire. In the meantime, Rome transformed from a republic into an empire. After Julius Caesar was assassinated in 44 BCE, civil war broke out as potential leaders vied for power. In 27 BCE Octavian prevailed, which brought an end to the civil war and ushered in peace throughout Roman lands. Consequently, Octavian was given the title of Augustus ("exalted one") and was commonly referred to as the "savior" of the Roman civilization. In part because of Octavian's military strength and popularity, he was able to move Rome from a representative form of government to the rule of a single, authoritative emperor.

The Jewish War with Rome. The relationship between the Jews and their Roman overlords was often strained. The tension between the two reached a crescendo in 66 CE. Jewish resistance grew to the point that it angered Rome, and Rome responded by sending additional troops to Palestine. A war between Rome and many Judean Jews lasted from 66 to 73 CE. In 70 CE the Romans conquered Jerusalem, tore down its walls, and destroyed the Jewish temple. The destruction of the temple by the

Romans topped off a humiliating defeat for the Judean Jews. The loss of the temple permanently altered the trajectory of Judaism. For example, animal sacrifices ceased at that point. In addition, discussions about the Hebrew Scriptures and involvement in Jewish synagogues took on an even greater importance, and many influential rabbis took up residence outside Jerusalem after 70 CE.

The Bar Kokhba Revolt. The last notable attempt by Judean Jews to oust their Roman overlords occurred when a group of Jews led by Simon bar Kosiba (later known as Simon bar Kokhba) rebelled against Rome in 132 CE. Within three years, the Roman armies completely squelched the uprising. Rome's response to the **Bar Kokhba Revolt** was even harsher than its decision to destroy the Jewish temple in 70 CE. This time the Romans leveled the entire city of Jerusalem and forbade all Jews from ever again living in Judea. Rome's drastic response meant that Jerusalem would not have a significant Jewish population again until the modern era.

Jewish Beliefs and Religious Practices in Antiquity

From the third century BCE through the first century CE, a significant degree of religious and cultural diversity developed among the Jewish peoples. Judaism essentially splintered into various branches that held distinct viewpoints regarding worship, the extent of the biblical canon, proper religious practices, God's will, and the nature of human existence.

The Diaspora

Perhaps the first distinction that needs to be drawn among Jews in antiquity is a geographical one. The Greek term *diaspora* was commonly applied to Jews who lived outside Palestine. The **Diaspora** literally refers to "the dispersion" or "the scattering" of the Jews. By the time of Jesus, large populations of Jews existed throughout the Mediterranean world, particularly in cities like Alexandria, Babylon, and Rome. Numerous theological and cultural differences arose between Jews in the Diaspora and Judean Jews. For many of the Jews in the Diaspora, temple worship, food laws, and at times even circumcision were debated practices. Jews in the Diaspora also had diverse reactions to Greco-Roman culture and practices. Regardless, these Mediterranean Jews were easily identified as Jews by their adherence to a monotheistic understanding of God and their reverence for the Hebrew Scriptures, in particular the Pentateuch.

Palestinian Jews

Even within the region of Palestine, religious and cultural diversity characterized Judaism from the third century BCE to the first century CE. For instance, Josephus, the ancient Jewish historian, highlights three religious sects among the Judean Jews: Pharisees, **Sadducees**, and **Essenes**. According to Josephus (*Jewish Antiquities* 13.5.9; 18.1.2–6; *Jewish War* 2.8.2–14), the Essenes believed that God determines all of life, the Sadducees believed that God refrains from affecting human affairs, and the Pharisees believed that both God and humans contribute to the final outcome of human affairs. Ultimately, though, while ancient writers provide us with some information about a few variations of Palestinian Judaism in the first century CE, our knowledge remains limited. Below we will sketch some of the religious diversity among first-century-CE Jews. It should be noted, however, that many Jews may not have exclusively identified with any particular religious sect.

Pharisees. The Pharisees strove to embody virtuous living as the Mosaic law prescribed. Maintaining ritual purity was highly important to them. In part these concerns arose out of their emphasis on the existence of the human soul after death. The Pharisees taught that in the afterlife humans would either be punished for unfaithfulness to the covenant relationship that God graciously provided or be rewarded for their faithfulness with bodily resurrection. Consequently, they strove to be skillful interpreters and faithful practitioners of the law. In addition to the Hebrew Scriptures, the Pharisees highly revered the oral traditions that their Jewish ancestors had handed down.

MESSIAH

Messiah is the Hebrew word for "anointed one." In the Old Testament, the term most commonly refers to kings and high priests who have been anointed by God to serve in leadership roles. When the Hebrew Scriptures were translated into Greek, the translators used the word *christos* ("christ") to describe an anointed one. Between the writing of the Old and New Testaments, the term *messiah* begins to appear in some Jewish texts to refer to a (usually royal) figure who would act on behalf of or in tandem with God's decisive, end-time action. Not all Jews had an expectation for such a figure, and for those who did, the figure's mission or task varied: to rule over God's restored, peaceable kingdom; to administer God's end-time judgment; or to conquer the oppressing enemy of God's people. Curiously, the Dead Sea Scrolls contain a few references to two messiahs—a royal messiah and a priestly messiah. Thus, messianic expectations (or lack thereof) represent another point of diversity that characterized this period of Judaism.

Scholars generally contend that the Pharisees descended from the Hasideans, the resistance movement that originated during the Maccabean Revolt, and that the Pharisees morphed into **rabbinic Judaism** after the destruction of the Jewish temple in 70 CE.

Sadducees. The Sadducees likely dated back to the time of the Maccabeans (second century BCE). Because they did not believe in the resurrection of the dead or in an afterlife of any kind, they did not believe in postmortem rewards for faithfulness or punishment for unfaithfulness. Instead, they held that each person must choose what is good and prudent in this life. In addition, they did not consider the oral traditions about the law to be authoritative, only the Scriptures themselves. The Sadducees were often associated with the Jewish temple in Jerusalem, and many of the high priests who oversaw temple worship in the first century CE were affiliated with the Sadducees. It appears that many Sadducees were associated with the upper class and often supported the social and political status quo.

Essenes. The Essenes believed that in the afterlife a person's soul would experience either a reward for righteousness or a punishment for evil. Consequently, they strove for righteous lives, pure worship, and the denial of human passions and pleasures. The Essenes criticized the temple establishment in Jerusalem because they felt the temple fostered impure worship practices. Similarly, they criticized other religious sects, like the Sadducees and the Pharisees, for not achieving true righteousness. The Essenes often separated themselves from others, lived in communal settings, and established a routine of daily prayer and religious washings. Josephus indicates that the Essenes shared their possessions, avoided wealth and luxury, ate meals together, strictly observed the Sabbath, emphasized the equitable treatment of all the members, and severely punished members who sinned. Moreover, in an effort to avoid quarrels, many Essenes abstained from marriage.

Revolutionaries. A variety of Jewish revolutionary movements grew up among Palestinian Jews during the first centuries BCE and CE. For example, many Jews highly valued Jewish independence and refused to acknowledge any leader as ruler or lord besides the God of Abraham, Isaac, and Jacob. At times these Jewish revolutionaries refused to pay taxes, spoke of revolt, and knowingly accepted the possibility of personal suffering in an attempt to serve God rather than pagan leaders or idols. Among others, groups like the **Zealots**, the Sicarii, and a group that Josephus describes as the "Fourth Philosophy" (*Jewish Antiquities* 18.1.6) fit within this revolutionary stream of Judaism. In particular, the Zealots are widely known for their active participation in the Jewish War with Rome (66–73 CE).

Samaritans. The Samaritans constituted an important branch of Judaism that developed during or soon after the Assyrian and Babylonian exiles. This group of Israelite descendants has a long history that extends even into the modern era. Their sacred temple stood on Mount Gerizim in the hill country between Galilee and Judea. The Samaritans looked to the Pentateuch as authoritative Scripture and greatly revered Moses. Yet for a variety of reasons, the Samaritans often found themselves at odds with other Jews from Galilee and Judea. At times this cultural and religious tension boiled over into violent encounters.

Christians. There is little doubt that people who lived in Mediterranean territories in the first century CE considered Christianity to be a branch of Judaism. The earliest followers of Jesus were Jewish. These Jews held the conviction that Jesus was the long-awaited Jewish Messiah. In addition, they revered the Hebrew Scriptures; worshiped the God of Abraham, Isaac, and Jacob; and even worshiped in the Jerusalem temple prior to its destruction. Most significant, the Jesus followers were dedicated monotheists, whereas adherents of other Mediterranean religions were not. As a result, even though an increasing number of **Gentiles** embraced Christianity over time, and even though Christianity and Judaism evolved into separate worldwide religions, in the first century CE Christianity is best described from a historical perspective as one form of Judaism among many.

Rabbinic Judaism. Scholars think that just as Christianity changed dramatically after the fall of the Jerusalem temple in 70 CE, Pharisaic Judaism did as well. Whereas other religious sects faded away after the Jewish War with the Romans (66–73 CE), the sect of the Pharisees apparently survived by morphing into what became known as rabbinic Judaism, the predecessor of modern forms of Judaism. Jews within this stream of Judaism gathered in the synagogues, revered the Hebrew Scriptures, and received guidance from their teachers or rabbis. Within twenty years after the fall of the temple, these rabbinic teachers began to cluster in Jamnia on the Judean coastline. Over time, they compiled a variety of additional religious texts that either interpreted or supplemented the Hebrew Scriptures. For example, the Mishnah was likely composed around 200 CE, though many of its teachings and ideas probably existed in an oral form long before then. The Mishnah purportedly captures the oral teachings of Moses that were handed down along with the written Scriptures.

The Apocrypha

In addition to the Old and New Testaments, we have access to a variety of ancient religious writings that illuminate thought patterns from the time period between the Testaments. The assorted texts have been grouped into collections known as the Old Testament Apocrypha and the Old Testament

Pseudepigrapha (Jewish writings that never attained canonical status). These texts were largely written by Jewish authors prior to the time of Jesus. Some of the texts, however, may have been written or edited by Christians shortly after the death of Jesus. Other important collections of Jewish literature from between the time of Alexander the Great and the period shortly after Jesus include the works of the Jewish philosopher Philo and the Jewish historian Josephus, the Dead Sea Scrolls, and the earliest rabbinic texts. As we did in chapter 1, we will briefly elaborate on the Apocrypha because of its relationship with the Christian Scriptures.

The Old Testament Apocrypha played a prominent role in the Greek and Latin translations of the Old Testament. What sets these Jewish religious texts apart from others is that at some point in time, especially from the fifth century CE onward, some Christians have regarded these texts as part of the canon of Christian Scriptures. For example, both Roman Catholic and Eastern Orthodox Christians deem many of these books to be Scripture (see chapter 1). Catholics label them "deuterocanonical" because they became canonical later than other writings. On the other hand, neither Jews nor Protestant Christians consider the books to be Scripture, and therefore neither group includes them in the canon of the Hebrew Bible or Old Testament. Moreover, when Protestants do include them in the printing of contemporary Bibles, they generally follow the example of Martin Luther's 1534 translation of the Bible and place them in an appendix under the title of Apocrypha (as opposed to placing them in the Old Testament). Although it is not clear what the fourth-century scholar Jerome meant by calling these texts *apocrypha* ("hidden" or "obscure"), for Protestants it implies a lower level of legitimacy and usefulness.

There is also no consensus on the best way to organize these books when printing them or even on the proper way to count them. For example, some of the books were composed as later additions to the Old Testament books of Esther, Psalms, and Daniel. As a result, some have thought of the Apocrypha as consisting of as few as seven books, while others envision the Apocrypha as consisting of fourteen separate books.

The Apocrypha includes numerous literary styles (or genres). Some of the narrative texts are best described as historiography or ancient history writing. The books of 1, 2, and 3 Maccabees and 1 Esdras fall into this category. For example, both 1 and 2 Maccabees describe the spread of Hellenism, the ruthless persecution of the Jews by Antiochus IV, and the Jewish resistance movement led by Judas Maccabeus and members of his family. Other narratives take the form of novels. Judith, Tobit, Additions to Daniel (Susanna, and Bel and the Dragon), and Additions to Esther fall in this category. Other books belong to the genre of philosophical or wisdom writings; Wisdom of

Solomon and Wisdom of Ben Sira (or Sirach) are representative of this philosophical style. Finally, 2 Esdras 3–14 (also known as 4 Ezra) is an apocalyptic text possibly written by Christians around the end of the first century CE.

Greek and Roman Beliefs and Religious Practices in Antiquity

Polytheism

Beliefs about the **Olympian gods**, also known as classical mythology or paganism, provided a framework for religious thought in the ancient Greek and Roman societies up through the second century CE. In fact, throughout the period in which the authors of the New Testament were writing, the majority of people living in the Mediterranean basin would have honored multiple deities through sacrifices, ritual gifts, and festivals. The gods were worshiped not only in public temples but also in voluntary associations and private households.

In addition to multiple gods, Greek and Roman polytheism envisioned a hierarchy of those divine beings. Zeus (or Jupiter) was thought of as the king of the gods, but all of the gods who resided on Mount Olympus—for example, Poseidon (or Neptune)—were deemed to be powerful. Other lesser gods were associated with specific regions or unusual origins, but it was important to offer sacrifices to them nonetheless. Civil governments often supported paganism because of the belief that the actions or reactions of the gods had a direct, corporate impact on the entire region. Moreover, those who worshiped the Olympian gods primarily strove to identify and carry out proper sacrifices as distinct from proper beliefs and proper actions. In large part because of the fundamental nature of polytheism, tolerance of others' religious practices was valued highly. In fact, Greeks and Romans strove to incorporate newly identified gods into their preexisting ritual practices.

Philosophy

In many ways Greek and Roman philosophical schools provided critiques of traditional religion. Philosophers often redirected the adherents of paganism by questioning common religious assumptions. This dynamic was especially prevalent in the time period between the Testaments. For example, the **Epicureans** aimed to free humans from the fear of death and the fear of the gods by arguing that the gods do not really exist. Instead, humans should realize they are free to pursue the best possible life. Similarly, the **Stoics** sought the inner peace that comes from living in accordance with reason and the divinely ordered universe as opposed to the fear of the gods or other fearful aspects of life beyond one's control. Thus, in many ways Greek and Roman philosophy opened the door for alternative belief systems in the ancient Mediterranean world.

Emperor Cult

In addition to traditional religious activities, worship of the Roman emperor became an important development in the religious and political landscape of the Roman Empire. Following Julius Caesar's death (44 BCE), belief in the divine status of the emperor increasingly permeated the cities of the empire, particularly in the eastern part of the Mediterranean world. Over time, coins and inscriptions publicly proclaimed the emperors as "divine," "lord," "savior," and "son of a god." Temples were erected for the veneration of the emperors. Initially, particularly in Rome and the western part of the empire, it was believed that emperors became gods at death. But in the eastern regions of the empire, where there was a tradition of deified rulers, the worship of living emperors began to emerge. In the first century CE, emperors did not require their subjects to worship them, and they generally abstained from self-promotion of any divine status (the exceptions being Caligula [37–41 CE], Nero [54–68 CE], and Domitian [81–96 CE]). Consequently, the worship of the Roman emperors, which was closely associated with showing loyalty to the Roman Empire, presented Christians in antiquity with a particularly stark decision.

Mystery Religions

The Roman civil wars left many Romans looking for religious alternatives to traditional religion. Greeks and Romans grew increasingly interested in the possibility of an afterlife as well as the idea of a personal relationship with a god. A group of Eastern religions offered answers to these questions and helped to fill the void left by traditional religion. These Eastern religions, many of which were new to the Roman Empire, were practiced largely within secret associations that required membership fees and oaths of secrecy. Contemporary scholars have adopted the umbrella term *mystery religions* to refer to them. The cults of Cybele, Isis, Demeter, Dionysus, and Mithras were especially popular religious movements (or "mystery religions") in the first to third century CE.

Christianity

After the death of Jesus, Christianity slowly gained acceptance among Greeks and Romans (or Gentiles) over the next four centuries. Early on, Christianity faced many challenges largely because of its monotheistic convictions in a predominantly polytheistic society. The situation changed drastically, however, when the Roman emperor Constantine identified himself as a Christian in 313 CE. Shortly thereafter, Christianity became the official religion of the Roman Empire and received favored status. Eventually, all other forms of worship were forbidden.

SUGGESTED READING

Boccaccini, Gabriele. *Middle Judaism: Jewish Thought, 300 BCE to 200 CE*. Minneapolis: Fortress, 1991.

Brown, Raymond E. *An Introduction to the New Testament*. The Anchor Bible Reference Library. New York: Doubleday, 1997.

Cohen, Shaye J. D. *From the Maccabees to the Mishnah*. 3rd ed. Louisville: Westminster John Knox, 2014.

deSilva, David A. *Introducing the Apocrypha: Messages, Context, and Significance*. 2nd ed. Grand Rapids: Baker Academic, 2018.

Klauck, Hans-Josef. *The Religious Context of Early Christianity: A Guide to Graeco-Roman Religions*. Translated by Brian McNeil. Minneapolis: Fortress, 2003.

VanderKam, James C. *An Introduction to Early Judaism*. Grand Rapids: Eerdmans, 2001.

6

The Gospels and the Acts of the Apostles

The New Testament begins with four distinct narratives about the life and ministry of Jesus. They are the Gospel according to Matthew, the Gospel according to Mark, the Gospel according to Luke, and the Gospel according to John. Following the Gospels is a narrative about the ministry of the earliest followers of Jesus called the Acts of the Apostles. Most scholars think that Acts was written by the same author as the Gospel of Luke and serves as a sequel to that Gospel.

Even though the Gospels and Acts are located at the beginning of the New Testament, these texts are not the earliest New Testament texts; that distinc tion goes to Paul's letters, which were written in the 50s and 60s CE. The four Gospels were written between the years 65 and 100 CE by anonymous, second-generation Christians. The names of Matthew, Mark, Luke, and John are secondary attributions that originated in the early to mid-second century CE, though these names probably had some basis in tradition.

In this chapter, we will first consider the historical settings of the Gospels and Acts. Next, we will examine the literary features and themes of each of the five books. Finally, we will give some thought to both the common convictions and the diverse perspectives that are found in the Gospels and Acts.

The World of the Gospels

Elements of two distinct historical contexts are evident within the Gospels: the Palestinian world of Jesus and the world of the evangelists (the authors of the Gospels). Writing decades after the death of Jesus, the evangelists received traditions about Jesus from others and shaped those traditions to address their own religious and social settings as well as their theological and literary interests. Though the two worlds share much in common (e.g., Roman rule, an agrarian economy, a kinship society, and the influence of Hellenism), they also have differences, and knowledge of these differences can provide a more informed reading of the Gospels.

The Palestinian World of Jesus

Roman Palestine included the areas of Idumea, Judea, Samaria, Galilee, Syria, Gaulanitis, Decapolis, and Perea. Jesus grew up in the small Galilean

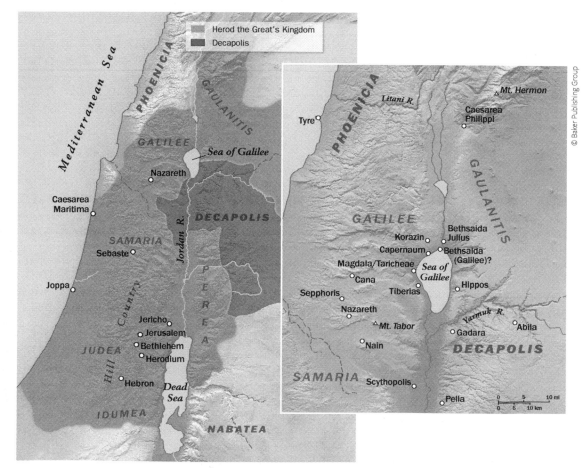

Figure 6.1. Roman Palestine with Galilee

village of Nazareth but was executed by crucifixion in Jerusalem, the capital city of Judea. In Matthew, Mark, and Luke (which are called the **Synoptic Gospels**), Jesus's ministry is based in Galilee with movement to surrounding areas; his only visit to Jerusalem is for the Passover festival when he is arrested and put to death. In the Gospel of John, however, Jesus traverses back and forth from Jerusalem to Galilee and celebrates three Passover festivals in Jerusalem.

During the time of Jesus's ministry, **Herod Antipas**, the son of Herod the Great, ruled Galilee (and Perea). Herod Antipas was a client ruler of Rome, meaning that he was appointed by Rome and ruled in loyalty to and under the expectation of Rome. Herod Antipas had his own army, which consisted of Jewish troops and foreign mercenaries. He also paid tribute to Rome, which he acquired from the Galilean population, many of whom understood it as Roman taxation. It is important to note, then, that Roman rule in Galilee was a mediated rule, not an occupation.

The population and culture in the region of Galilee were predominantly Jewish, although there were non-Jews (who were called Gentiles) in the neighboring cities of Scythopolis and Caesarea Philippi and the adjacent regions of Decapolis and Gaulanitis. Herod Antipas utilized Jewish officials in his administration, and he respected Jewish customs and sensibilities, at least in the public domain. He did not imprint his image or the image of the emperor on his coins, nor did he introduce pagan symbols or temples into Galilean cities, even in the cities of Sepphoris and Tiberias, which he reconstructed (the former) or built (the latter) according to Roman architecture. Furthermore, archaeology has revealed a Jewish culture in Galilee quite similar to that in Judea: the ubiquitous use of stone vessels and stepped, plastered pools both reflecting concerns for purity; and the practice of secondary burials, in which the corpse was laid in a tomb until after decay, when the bones were repositioned beside the bones of deceased relatives in the same tomb. Thus, though Jesus encountered Gentiles in his occasional excursions to neighboring regions (e.g., Mark 5:1–20; 7:24–8:9), he was shaped by his Jewish heritage and he ministered within a Jewish context.

Unlike the political situation in Galilee, a Roman governor ruled Judea. The Roman governor resided in the coastal city of Caesarea with approximately three thousand Roman troops. He traveled to Jerusalem several times a year for religious festivals, such as Passover, when the population of Jerusalem may have increased up to tenfold. Because of his usual absence, the Roman governor relied on the Jewish high priest and priestly aristocracy for the day-to-day administration of Jerusalem and its surrounding vicinities. The high priest was appointed by and accountable to the Roman governor, but he had some liberties to govern according to Jewish traditions, including within the courts, as long as it did not undermine Roman rule. The Roman governor also invited counsel from the Jewish high priest on special matters pertaining to the Jewish people—not necessarily because he was sympathetic toward the Jewish people but to avoid situations that might cause a riot. This arrangement is evident in the Gospel accounts of Jesus's arrest and execution (e.g., Mark 14:43–15:39). Thus, in the first century CE, the Jewish high priest was as much a political figure as a religious one.

Guarding against potential revolts, the Romans were vigilant in their efforts to maintain the stability of the *Pax Romana* ("peace of Rome"). As mentioned in chapter 5, the first Jewish revolt against the Romans broke out in Palestine in 66 CE. It ended in a crushing defeat of the Jewish rebels and the destruction of the Jewish temple in Jerusalem (70 CE). It is difficult to assess how much of this revolutionary spirit existed during the time of Jesus, some thirty to forty years before the revolt.

There were violent uprisings during times of political transition, such as after the death of Herod the Great in 4 BCE and when a Roman governor was first appointed over Judea in 6 CE. In 26 CE the Roman governor, Pontius Pilate, ordered Roman standards, which included an image of the emperor, to be brought into Jerusalem. This action offended Jewish sensibilities concerning images, especially in the holy city. But in this case, the Jewish response was not violent; it was just the opposite. A large delegation of Jews went to Pilate and contested this course of action. When Pilate refused their request and ordered soldiers to draw their swords, the Jews offered their necks, indicating that they would rather die than have their law violated. Pilate was affected by their conviction, removed the standards from Jerusalem, and returned to Caesarea. Thus, during the time of Jesus, any controversial incident had the potential to cause a local riot in Roman Palestine, and local rulers (e.g., Herod Antipas, the Roman governor, and the Jewish high priest) consistently acted to avoid and curtail any such disturbances. At the same time, we should not envision a widespread revolutionary movement among the populace during Jesus's lifetime that was ready and willing to go to war against the Romans.

The World of the Evangelists

As one would expect, the Gospels reflect the Palestinian world of Jesus, but they also reflect the world of their authors. Jesus spoke in Aramaic; the Gospels were written in Greek. Jesus's ministry was rural; the Gospels likely originated in urban settings. Jesus taught in oral forms; the Gospels are literary productions (though certainly they were read aloud and experienced aurally). In addition, the Gospels contain glimpses of each evangelist's community situation. As a result, scholars usually reconstruct the world of the evangelists in two ways: (1) the broader context of the Greco-Roman world (see "Greek and Roman Beliefs and Religious Practices in Antiquity" in chap. 5), and (2) the specific communities from which or to which the evangelists wrote. We will now turn our attention to a discussion of the evangelists and their respective communities.

The Gospel of Mark was probably written in Rome during a time when Christians experienced various kinds of persecution and affliction, either under the emperor Nero (64 CE) or as a backlash from the Jewish revolt in Judea (66–73 CE). According to Mark, Jesus dies a dark, forsaken death and summons, "If any want to become my followers, let them deny themselves and take up their cross and follow me" (8:34). Jesus's prediction about trials and tribulations (Mark 13) seems especially applicable to Mark's audience. Moreover, the Gospel of Mark portrays the disciples as misunderstanding Jesus and failing in their loyalty to him, thus providing empathetic models for those in the Markan community who have failed Jesus in their own times of trial. Mark's proclivities for translating Aramaic terms (3:17; 7:34; 10:46; 15:22, 34), explaining Jewish ritual practices (7:3–4), and using Latinisms (3:5, 9; 6:37; 15:19) suggest that Mark was writing for a Gentile Christian audience.

The Gospel of Matthew most likely originated from Antioch in Syria and alludes to a bitter local separation between the Christian community (mostly Jewish Christians) and the Jewish community, likely in the 80s CE. This estrangement is evident in Matthew's reference to a story "still told among the Jews to this day" (Matthew's day, of course) that Jesus was not raised from the dead but that his disciples stole his body from the burial tomb (28:11–15). The tension is also evident in Jesus's unrelenting "woes" (or prophetic curses) that are leveled against the Pharisees in 23:1–36 and in the self-imposed responsibility by "the [Jewish] people as a whole" (27:25) for the death of Jesus. Though later interpreters have used Matthew's text, particularly 27:25, to support anti-Semitic actions and perspectives, informed readers should understand the Gospel in its historical context reflecting an *intra*-Jewish polemic: a conflict between Christian Jews and non-Christian Jews who formulated theological and communal self-definitions over against one another.

Discerning the community situation of the Gospel of John is more complex. First, the Gospel of John is closely associated with the three New Testament letters 1, 2, and 3 John. Although these four texts (the Gospel of John and the Johannine letters) probably do not come from the same author, they were likely written in and for the same community. Thus, the Johannine letters by nature of their genre help us sketch a clearer picture of the community within which and for which the Gospel of John was written. Second, the Gospel of John does not simply reflect this community at one moment in time. Rather, it alludes to problematic issues that arose at different stages of the Johannine community's history. So criticisms against "the Jews" in the Gospel of John most likely originate from the community's early history when a conflict arose between Jewish Christians and other Jews over the divine status of Jesus (5:18). This type of separation would have naturally led the Johannine community to reach out to Gentiles (12:20–23). Subsequently, theological disputes developed between the Johannine Christians and other Christian groups (6:60–69). Eventually, the Johannine community experienced its own schism (1 John 2:18–19; 3 John): some Johannine Christians had begun to exalt Jesus's divinity to the extent of denying his humanity (1 John 4:2–3; 2 John 7; cf. John 1:14). Consequently, the emphasis on Jesus's call to unity and love became the Johannine community's strategy for group cohesion in the face of conflict and faction (John 15; 1 John 4:7–21).

The Gospel of Luke also presents a challenge in terms of identifying a community behind the text. Most scholars recognize that the Gospel of Luke, along with the Acts of the Apostles, is a more sophisticated literary composition than the other Gospels. Such a literary accomplishment seems to presume a more general Christian audience rather than a specific, local community. Moreover, Luke and Acts are both addressed to a certain Theophilus (Luke 1:3; Acts 1:1), who was perhaps Luke's patron. This practice suggests that Luke and Acts constitute a literary production that is intended for a more public audience. Thus, it is difficult to discern a local situation driving and shaping the narratives of Luke and Acts as in Matthew and Mark. Instead, the Gospel of Luke was likely intended for a wider Christian, mostly Gentile readership addressing larger issues of the Christian movement as a whole.

The Genre and Literary Tradition of the Gospels

The Genre of the Gospels

The term *gospel* (Greek, *euangelion*) means "good news." It initially referred to an oral announcement or proclamation, both in the Jewish Scriptures and in Greco-Roman writings. In the Christian tradition, it is first associated with Jesus, who proclaimed "the good news of God" (Mark 1:14) and "the good news of the kingdom" (Matt. 4:23). The earliest Christians also preached "the gospel of God" (Rom. 1:1), but by that point "gospel" (or "good news") also encompassed the person of Jesus: "the gospel concerning his Son" (Rom. 1:3; cf. Rom. 15:19; 2 Cor. 2:12; 1 Thess. 3:1–2). It is not until the second century CE that the term *gospel* becomes a designation for literary texts that narrate the life and ministry of Jesus, a designation perhaps influenced by the Gospel of Mark's introductory statement: "The beginning of the good news [gospel] of Jesus Christ, the Son of God" (Mark 1:1). This development of the term *gospel* raises questions about the type of literature the Gospels represent. Are there other ancient texts comparable to the Gospels?

Though some interpreters have argued that the Gospels represent a unique literary type, most modern scholars now recognize that the Gospels belong to the genre of **ancient biography**, referred to as a "life" (Greek, *bios*; Latin, *vita*). Examples of other ancient biographies include Tacitus's *Agricola*, Lucian's *Demonax*, Diogenes Laertius's *Lives of Eminent Philosophers*, and Philo's *Life of Moses*. It is important to recognize the differences between ancient biographies and modern biographies. Authors of modern biographies attempt to provide an objective and comprehensive account of a person's life by giving attention to the subject's early psychological development, demonstrating how the subject was a product of his or her own time and culture, and carefully documenting the facts by citing sources. Ancient biographies, however, were not written to be objective. Instead, the authors of ancient biographies hoped readers would adopt a particular perception of the subject and imitate the subject's life. They sought to portray the essence of a person by composing a selective narrative of sayings and deeds that culminated with the subject's death. In particular, it was thought that the subject's death most clearly illuminated the subject's essential character or core self.

While writing their ancient biographies about Jesus, the authors of the Gospels selected, arranged, and shaped traditions and sources with the hope of persuading their readers to adopt specific viewpoints about Jesus. Consequently, scholars commonly compare the Gospels to artistic portraits. There is

THE "HISTORICAL JESUS"

While all scholars recognize the portrait-like character of Jesus in the Gospels, some are more interested in discovering the "Jesus of history" behind the interpretative narratives of the Gospels. Using a variety of methods and criteria, these scholars strip the Gospels of their interpretative elements in order to get back to the "historical Jesus." Scholars have offered various reconstructions of the "historical Jesus," and ironically these scholarly constructs differ from one another as much as the Gospels themselves differ. This variety stems from the criteria used to compile the reconstructions and from the prior assumptions held by scholars regarding the degree of continuity that exists between the depiction of Jesus in the Gospels and the actual Jesus of history. Some stress a radical discontinuity; others emphasize a realistic continuity.

an interpretative element in each composition. Just as an artist seeks to create an impression of her subject by selecting a particular setting or pose, choosing the appropriate medium, and highlighting certain features, the Gospel writers use a variety of literary and rhetorical strategies to create a narrative depiction of Jesus. The Gospels are artistic portraits of Jesus (ancient biographies); they are not impartial photographs (as many envision modern biographies). And yet, while emphasizing this interpretative nature of the Gospels, it is also important to note that the Gospels are the primary sources for what is called the "search for the **historical Jesus**."

The Literary Tradition of the Gospels

We have noted that the Gospels were written thirty-five to seventy years after the death of Jesus by anonymous, second-generation Christians. Add to this the fact that Jesus was a traveling teacher-prophet who proclaimed his message in villages and the countryside, leaving no known writings. Furthermore, we have no evidence that Jesus's disciples ever took written notes during his ministry. So, we must ask, what sources did the authors of the Gospels rely on to compose their "lives" of Jesus?

Almost certainly, the memories of the life and ministry of Jesus were preserved in oral tradition, particularly in the worshiping, missionary, and teaching ministries of the early Christian communities. As the oral memories moved beyond their Aramaic origins to Greek-speaking communities and from Jewish settings to non-Jewish environs, the narrations of those memories were adapted and shaped for new audiences and situations.

In addition to oral traditions, the evangelists depended on written sources when composing their narratives. This use of written sources is most evident with the Gospels of Matthew, Mark, and Luke. Because they have such striking verbal similarities, there must be a literary relationship among these Gospels. In other words, one or two of these Gospels almost certainly served as a source for the others. The ambiguous literary relationship of Matthew, Mark, and Luke is known as the "**synoptic problem**." The word *synoptic* means "see together" and refers here to the fact that Matthew, Mark, and Luke share similar structure, content, and wording. Thus, the Gospels of Matthew, Mark, and Luke are known as the Synoptic Gospels.

So what is the literary relationship among the Synoptic Gospels? Which evangelists used which Gospels as sources for their narratives about Jesus? The proposed solutions to these questions are complex, yet any solution to the synoptic problem begins with determining which Gospel was written first.

Matthean priority. Following tradition and the canonical order of the Gospels, the fourth-century bishop Augustine held that the Gospel of Matthew was the earliest Gospel written. He believed that Mark was an abbreviation of Matthew's Gospel and that Luke used both Matthew and Mark as sources. The idea that Matthew was first and used by Mark and Luke has found limited scholarly support. A nineteenth-century scholar named J. J. Griesbach modified Augustine's theory by positing that Mark's Gospel was the last to be written. He argued that Mark drew on both Matthew and Luke to create a sort of truncated digest of these two Gospels.

Both Augustine's and Griesbach's solutions to the synoptic problem are referred to as the **"Two-Gospel Hypothesis,"** because in each case two Gospels serve as sources for the last Gospel written. But the Two-Gospel Hypothesis with its Matthean priority (the idea that Matthew was written first) faces a major obstacle: Why would Mark omit significant portions of Matthew's Gospel, like the infancy narrative (Matt. 1–2), the Sermon on the Mount (Matt. 5–7), and resurrection appearances (Matt. 28)? This obstacle, among others, has led most scholars to different conclusions.

Markan priority. The scholarly consensus today is that the Gospel of Mark is the earliest Gospel and that it served as a source document for Matthew

Figure 6.2. **Solutions to the synoptic problem with Matthean priority**

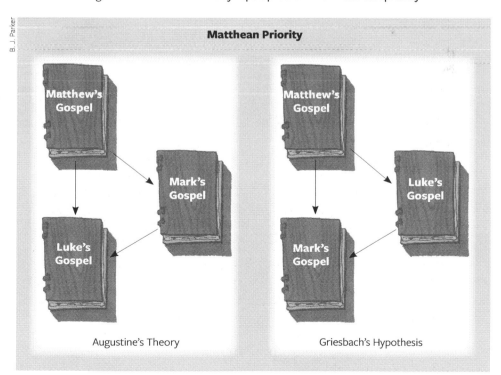

B. J. Parker

and Luke. The basic reason is that Matthew and Luke seem to "improve" on Mark. Mark's beginning and ending seem incomplete. Mark does not include Jesus's birth and post-resurrection appearances, whereas Matthew and Luke do. Matthew and Luke also correct Mark's sometimes awkward Greek and smooth out places where Mark's narrative seems clumsy. It is more logical to envision Matthew and Luke making improvements to their source (Mark) than to envision Mark creating a less polished and less complete narrative from his more polished and more complete sources (Matthew and Luke).

There are two solutions to the synoptic problem that begin with Markan priority. The first solution, called the **"Two-Source Hypothesis,"** is the dominant theory in Gospel studies. As the designation suggests, this theory posits two sources for Matthew and Luke. The first source, as already indicated, is Mark's Gospel. According to the Two-Source Hypothesis, both Matthew and Luke used Mark as a source, but they did not have knowledge of one another. This suggestion grows partly from a comparison of the beginnings and endings of Matthew and Luke. While Matthew and Luke both provide an infancy narrative, their infancy narratives differ significantly. The same is

Figure 6.3. **Solutions to the synoptic problem with Markan priority**

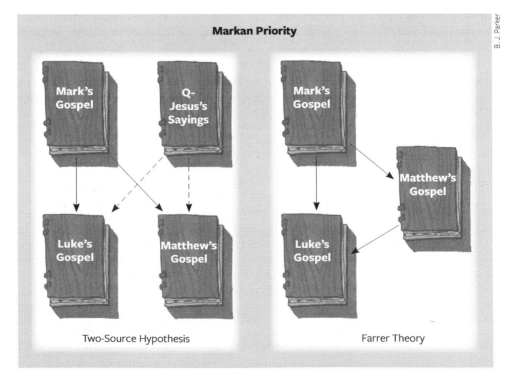

true for the resurrection appearances in both Gospels. The differences make sense if Matthew and Luke wrote independently of one another.

But if Matthew and Luke are composed without knowledge of the other, how can they share over two hundred verses of non-Markan material? This led scholars to suspect they drew from another, unknown source, which is called **Q** (based on the German word for "source," *Quelle*). Q is a hypothetical source reconstructed from the approximately 220–230 verses shared by Matthew and Luke but not shared by Mark. Thus, the Two-Source Hypothesis posits that Matthew and Luke independently used Mark and Q as written sources of information while composing their Gospels.

The other solution to the synoptic problem with Markan priority is called the "**Farrer Theory**," named after a twentieth-century scholar named Austin Farrer who first proposed the argument. The Farrer Theory seeks to provide an explanation to the synoptic problem by embracing the idea of Markan priority while eliminating dependence on a hypothetical document like Q. Dismissing Q means, however, that in order to account for the approximately 220 to 230 verses that Matthew and Luke share in common, one must affirm that either Matthew or Luke depended on the other. The Farrer Theory postulates that Matthew used Mark and that Luke used both Mark and Matthew. But how does one account for the significant differences between Matthew and Luke? The Farrer Theory envisions the Gospel writers more as authors than as mere collectors or editors of sources. Thus, Matthew and Luke are not slaves to their sources, but use them for their own purposes and audiences.

The Gospel of John. The literary relationship between the Gospel of John and the Synoptic Gospels is debated. In the last century, most interpreters thought that John was composed independently of the Synoptic Gospels, noting how John's account of Jesus is remarkably distinct from that of the Synoptics. Whereas the Synoptic Gospels show Jesus casting out evil spirits from possessed persons, John lacks any exorcisms. The main forms of Jesus's teaching in the Synoptic Gospels are **parables** and aphorisms, yet these types of instruction are missing in John's Gospel; instead, Jesus teaches by means of long speeches. In the Synoptic Gospels, Jesus's disruptive actions in the temple take place in the last week of his life (Mark 11); in John's Gospel, however, the disruptive actions take place at the beginning of Jesus's ministry (John 2). John and the Synoptics share some basic contours of the life of Jesus, and even some of the same stories, but these similarities are attributed to John's knowledge of traditions that predated Mark's Gospel as well as ongoing oral traditions that were shaped by the Synoptic Gospels. More recently, however, some scholars have argued that the Gospel of John was composed with knowledge of the Synoptic Gospels, particularly Mark and Luke. In relation to Luke, John contains some striking similarities in features and phrasing (e.g., Luke 22:3 // John 13:27; Luke 22:50 // John 18:10; Luke 24:15–16 // John 20:14). In relation to Mark, John shares a macrostructure and specific episode sequences that are best explained by John's knowledge of Mark's narrative, not just common traditions.

Summary. This source-critical discussion of the Gospels may seem a bit pedantic, but these studies serve as the basis for a number of other studies. For example, knowing that Mark is the earliest Gospel and that Matthew and Luke used it as a source allows scholars to discern better Matthew's and Luke's theological emphases and literary tendencies based on how they edited and adapted Mark's Gospel (redaction criticism). This discussion also aids historians in their reconstruction of early Christianity. If Mark was the first Gospel written and Matthew and Luke came later, historians may have a better sense of the development of Christian thought and communities. These questions about sources, traditions, and Gospel communities contribute to our knowledge of the history of early Christianity.

The Gospel according to Mark

The Prologue (1:1–15)

The beginning. The opening verse articulates the primary message of Mark's Gospel. In 1:1 the author (traditionally referred to as Mark) announces the good news that Jesus is the "Christ" (or "Messiah") and the "Son of God" (according to many ancient manuscripts). These twin themes guide the rhetorical argument of the rest of the book. In particular, Mark hopes to convince his readers in the first half of the book that Jesus is the Son of God (1:16–8:26) and in the last half of the book that Jesus is the long-expected Jewish Messiah, though a Messiah who will suffer (8:27–16:8).

Preparation for ministry. At Jesus's baptism (1:4–11) and in Jesus's temptation by Satan in the wilderness (1:12–13), we see the dramatic presence of God's Spirit both upon and around Jesus. For instance, at the baptism, the Spirit of God descends on Jesus, and the heavenly voice applies the title "Son of God" to Jesus (cf. 1:1). Thus, from the very beginning Mark shows his readers that God is guiding Jesus through God's Spirit and empowering Jesus to accomplish God's will. Mark's first readers would have likely recalled the manner in which God guided and sustained the Hebrews in the Sinai wilderness years earlier. Now, the same God is guiding and sustaining Jesus.

Mark concludes the prologue in 1:14–15 by combining seemingly opposite ideas. Mark informs us that John the Baptizer, despite receiving a warm welcome from the people of Judea (1:5), has already been arrested by the authorities. John's arrest foreshadows the far greater opposition that both John and Jesus will later encounter. Simultaneously, Mark emphasizes that the events surrounding Jesus's ministry are to be considered "good news," because Jesus's ministry is linked to the in-breaking of the kingdom of God. Jesus's arrival signals the beginning of an age when God's rule, as opposed to the rule of others, will be most fully realized in the world.

Jesus's Ministry in and around Galilee (1:16–8:26)

Beginning with 1:16, the author narrates Jesus's ministry in the northern region of Galilee. During this period Jesus moves quickly, recruits followers, performs numerous miracles, teaches his followers about God's ways, encounters opposition, and keeps his messianic identity a secret.

Calling disciples. As his first public action, Jesus calls people to follow him. From the beginning, one can immediately detect the importance of discipleship in this book. For example, in 1:16–20 Jesus asks Simon (later known as Peter), along with Andrew, James, and John, to follow him. In 3:13–19 Jesus again calls people to follow him. Then, from among his many followers, Jesus appoints twelve to be his apostles whom he designates to proclaim his message and perform deeds similar to those that he performs (6:6b–13). The selection of twelve apostles likely correlates to the twelve tribes of Israel in the Hebrew Scriptures. Mark's readers should again notice that through Jesus and his disciples, God is somehow restoring or reconstituting God's people as the kingdom of God.

Miracles. Jesus's numerous miracles ultimately verify that Jesus has a special relationship with God and that "Son of God" is an appropriate title for Jesus. For example, Jesus exorcises many demons from people (1:21–28, 32–34, 39; 3:11–12; 5:1–20; 7:24–30). In these passages, we see Jesus battle the demons while demonstrating his superior power and authority. In

---

SON OF GOD

The title "Son of God" may have evoked numerous images among those living in the first century CE. For those heavily shaped by Greek and Roman cultures, the phrase may have recalled legendary figures who were purportedly the biological descendants of a human parent and a god. For those shaped more by the Jewish Scriptures, the phrase may have recalled God's favored servants. For instance, Israel's kings were occasionally referred to as sons of God (e.g., 2 Sam. 7:1–17). Regardless, Mark's first readers would have had to read Mark's Gospel to understand the full significance of this title.

addition, Jesus heals the sick, paralyzed, deaf, and blind and even raises the dead (1:29–34, 40–45; 2:1–12; 3:1–6, 7–10; 5:21–43; 7:31–37; 8:22–26). Jesus exerts control over nature when he calms the storm (4:35–41), walks on water (6:47–52), and multiplies food for large crowds of people (6:30–44; 8:1–10). Thus, readers should conclude from Mark 1–8 that Jesus has authority over all creation, including demons, diseases, and nature.

Teachings. Jesus repeatedly teaches his disciples about the characteristics of the kingdom of God. For instance, in 4:1–20 Jesus tells the parable of the sower, which focuses on the miraculous, though often hidden, growth of the kingdom of God that occurs despite the conflicts and trials encountered by God's servants.

Opposition. In Mark 1–8 the scribes, the Pharisees, Jesus's family, and those from Jesus's hometown all oppose him. For example, the Pharisees believe that it is improper for Jesus to eat with sinners and tax collectors (2:13–22), and they think Jesus violates the Sabbath when he plucks grain from the fields (2:23–28) and again when he heals a man with a withered hand (3:1–6). The scribes accuse Jesus of blasphemy when he forgives sins (2:6–7), and they accuse him of drawing on the powers of Satan when Jesus casts out demons (3:22). Those in Jesus's hometown, and perhaps even his own family members, believe Jesus is out of his mind (3:19b–35). Moreover, those in the synagogue in Jesus's hometown do not honor Jesus (6:1–6).

In short, in Mark 1–8 the author narrates Jesus's words and deeds while showing readers that Jesus is the Son of God. Also, while Jesus ushers in the kingdom of God, he simultaneously encounters opposition. Clearly, Jesus's enemies do not have the power to stop Jesus, but the foreshadowing of a tragic resolution to this story continues to build.

Moreover, in the last unit of the first half of this Gospel (8:14–26), readers should notice a couple of peculiar passages. First, in 8:14–21 Jesus makes

"MESSIANIC SECRET"

Despite the fact that Mark informs his readers of Jesus's messianic identity in 1:1, Jesus himself shields his followers from that same conclusion throughout the first half of Mark's Gospel. In fact, Jesus commands both the demons (1:24–25, 34; 3:11–12) and his disciples (8:29–30; 9:7–9) not to share their knowledge of his identity with others until after the resurrection. Scholars refer to this secretive impulse, which is primarily found in Mark's Gospel, as the **"messianic secret."**

exceedingly negative comments about his disciples. Up to this point, the disciples have failed to see, hear, or remember properly when it comes to Jesus's words and deeds. Second, in 8:22–26 Jesus heals a blind man in a peculiar manner the blind man's sight arrives in two stages. Whereas Mark highlights Jesus's power and authority in other passages, here Mark seemingly emphasizes the blind man's condition. Many interpreters contend that the blind man in this passage metaphorically depicts the condition of the disciples in Mark's Gospel. At this point in the story, the disciples have moved from complete blindness to partial blindness when it comes to understanding Jesus's identity. Yet the disciples remain half blind and in need of additional insight that only Jesus can provide.

Jesus's Journey to Jerusalem (8:27–10:52)

Beginning at 8:27, Jesus journeys from the northern region of Galilee toward Jerusalem in the southern region of Judea. Jesus's travels then continue until he arrives in Jerusalem in 10:52.

The pivot point in Mark's Gospel occurs in 8:29 when Peter becomes the first person in the narrative to apply the title of "Messiah" (or "Christ") to Jesus. When Peter utters these words, the entire narrative shifts. Whereas 1:16–8.26 focuses on Jesus as the "Son of God," Peter's confession of Jesus as the "Christ" charts the course for 8:27–15:39. In the second half of his Gospel, Mark primarily demonstrates how Jesus fulfills the role of the Jewish Messiah.

For many first-century Jews, however, Jesus's actions and experiences as described in Mark 8–15 would hardly prove that Jesus is the chosen harbinger of God's kingdom. Instead, Jesus's behavior and experiences more closely resemble those of a martyr than of the long-awaited Jewish Messiah. Consequently, Mark constructs a two-pronged argument in the second half of the Gospel. First, Jesus is identified as the Messiah. Second, Jesus teaches his disciples that the true calling of the Messiah is to function as a suffering servant as opposed to a typical ruler who gains power through the use of military might.

Opposition. Surprisingly, during this journey Jesus's own disciples provide the primary obstacle for Jesus and his stated mission. The conflict revolves around differing understandings of the title "Messiah" and already reaches its most critical point in 8:30. As soon as Peter proclaims Jesus as the Messiah, Jesus orders his disciples not to relay that information to others. Next, Jesus offers the first of three passion (or suffering and death) predictions. Jesus teaches his disciples that he must suffer, be rejected by the religious leaders, be killed, and rise again (8:27–32). This prediction shocks Peter so much that he rebukes Jesus. In response, Jesus rebukes Peter. Subsequently, Jesus again predicts his suffering and death in 9:30–31 and 10:33–34. In essence, he does not deny that the title of Messiah applies to him, but he insists that the term *Messiah* must be defined properly.

Teachings and discipleship. The journey to Jerusalem provides Jesus with an opportunity to explain his identity and mission to the disciples while simultaneously defining the role of a disciple. Jesus repeatedly indicates that both he and his disciples will suffer. In 8:34–38 Jesus says that his disciples must be willing to sacrifice their lives if they vow allegiance to him. Moreover, Jesus prohibits his disciples from seeking earthly power. Whereas the disciples argue about who is the greatest (9:33–34), Jesus teaches them to be like powerless servants and children (9:35–37).

Two events affirm the validity of Jesus's radical teachings. First, when Jesus climbs a mountain with Peter, James, and John, his body is transfigured such that Jesus becomes dazzling white (9:2–8). Moses and Elijah, notable servants of God from the past who likewise experienced rejection while carrying out the will of God, join Jesus. Most important, the voice of God comes from heaven proclaiming Jesus as God's Son and directing the disciples to listen to him. Thus, the voice from heaven verifies that the disciples should submit to Jesus's radical teachings about a suffering Messiah and suffering disciples.

Finally, Jesus's journey from Galilee in the north to Jerusalem in the south concludes with Jesus's healing a second blind man, named Bartimaeus (10:46–52). Not only does Jesus heal this man instantaneously, but Bartimaeus seems to have a robust understanding of Jesus's identity. If the blind man in 8:22–26 illustrates the disciples' need for additional insight, the healing of Bartimaeus provides a foretaste of the greater clarity that is to come.

The Markan Passion Narrative (11:1–16:8)

Triumphal entry. When Jesus first arrives in Jerusalem, many people greet him and proclaim that Israel's kingdom, as it existed under King David, is returning to power (11:1–11). The tone of the crowd's initial reception of Jesus is celebrative and optimistic.

Temple. Jesus's actions on his second day in Jerusalem lead to sharp conflict. As is often the case in this Gospel, Mark 11:12–25 unfolds in a 1–2–1 sandwich format (known as an **intercalation**). The author begins one story, switches to a second story, and then returns to the first story. The two stories help to interpret each other. So Jesus's cursing of the fig tree for its lack of fruit (11:12–14 and 11:20–25) seems to provide commentary on Jesus's sharp criticisms and disruptive actions in the temple (11:15–19).

Not surprisingly, the Jewish religious leaders are angered by Jesus's actions in the temple. When Jesus arrives in Jerusalem, his relationship with the

Jewish religious leaders deteriorates quickly. The opposition to Jesus, which has been building throughout this Gospel, reaches its zenith in Mark 11–15. Jesus's actions in the temple lead to his eventual arrest and death (11:18).

Teachings. In Mark 13, which is often referred to as "the Little Apocalypse," Jesus responds to the disciples' questions about the timing of the destruction of the temple and the suffering that the disciples will endure. Rather than providing a precise timetable, Jesus cautions his disciples to stay awake and alert during such ominous times.

As the time of Passover nears, Jesus asks his disciples to prepare a meal in an upper room (14:12–16). During Jesus's last meal with his disciples, he predicts the betrayal of Judas, one of the twelve apostles, and he speaks of the wine and bread as representations of his own body and blood, which will be sacrificed in his upcoming death (14:17–31). In particular, Jesus links his blood to the covenant that God has forged with his people. In some way Jesus's death appears to function as a sacrifice that ratifies or restores Israel's covenant with God.

Arrest and trials. Later that same night, Judas guides a delegation from the Jewish religious leaders to Jesus, who is arrested by the mob (14:43–49). All of Jesus's disciples abandon him out of fear (14:50–52). Thereafter, a court of Jewish religious leaders tries Jesus (14:53). At one point the high priest asks whether Jesus is "the Messiah, the Son of the Blessed One" (14:61). Mark's readers should recognize that the high priest essentially employs the same two titles featured in 1:1—Christ and Son of God. When Jesus affirms these titles, the religious leaders condemn him for religious blasphemy (14:62–65) and take him to Pontius Pilate, the Roman governor of Judea (15:1).

Rather than inquiring about Jewish religious matters, Pilate quizzes Jesus about political matters, asking whether Jesus considers himself to be the "King of the Jews" (15:2–5). As a Roman governor, Pilate guards against all forms of rebellion against Caesar and Rome. He finds no fault in Jesus, however, and attempts to release him. But when the angry crowd demands crucifixion, Pilate appeases them (15:6–15). Thus, Roman officials and soldiers have now joined in the opposition to Jesus.

Crucifixion. Ironically, even as the Roman soldiers mock Jesus by saluting him as "King of the Jews" and placing a placard reading "The King of the Jews" above him on the cross, Mark's readers know the soldiers' derisive words actually articulate a truth that has been taught throughout this Gospel (15:16–20, 25–32). The Roman soldiers unknowingly proclaim Jesus's rightful status.

While on the cross, Jesus experiences a sense of extreme abandonment. His only words from the cross form a probing question. Quoting Psalm 22:1, Jesus cries out, "My God, my God, why have you forsaken me?" (15:34). Not only have the disciples abandoned him, but Jesus asks whether God has as well. Then he dies (15:37).

Then, surprisingly, a Roman soldier who watches Jesus's crucifixion says, "Truly this man was God's Son!" (15:39). Thus, an unsuspecting Gentile who serves the Roman government utters one of the two titles that have guided this Gospel. As a result, Mark's portrayal of the Messiah's identity is most clearly identified in his suffering and death.

Resurrection. Despite the emphasis on Jesus's suffering, Mark concludes on a victorious note. Signs of hope appear when the women faithfully stand near Jesus during the crucifixion and a council member boldly asks to bury Jesus's body (15:40–47). Finally, we read that Jesus is raised from the dead just as he had predicted (16:6). Strangely though, the disciples continue to struggle. Even though a messenger directs the women to go and tell the other disciples about Jesus's resurrection, they flee in fear and tell no one (16:7–8). Consequently, the Gospel of Mark ends on a triumphant note for Jesus and another dramatic failure for the disciples.

Additions. The earliest manuscripts of the Gospel of Mark do not include 16:9–20. These verses were most likely added to later copies of this Gospel. Much of this material apparently derives from Matthew, Luke, John, and Acts.

The Gospel according to Matthew

Matthew's Gospel is structured around five major sections, alternating between narrative and discourse materials, with a narrative introduction (1:1–2:23) and conclusion (26:1–28:20).

The Origin of Jesus (1:1–2:23)

The author (traditionally referred to as Matthew) begins the story of Jesus with topics that are common in ancient biographies (e.g., ancestors, homeland and native city, and circumstances surrounding the birth, especially divine signs), but he shapes these topics in a manner that serves his theological interests.

A providential origin. Matthew demonstrates that the origin of Jesus is initiated, guided, and ordained by God. Not only is the conception of Jesus "from the Holy Spirit" (1:18, 20), but the time of Jesus's birth is divinely appointed (1:17). Dreams function as divine interventions that ensure Jesus's and Mary's safety (1:20–25; 2:12, 13–14, 19–20, 22). Fulfilled prophecies signify that God's will is being accomplished in the events surrounding Jesus's birth (1:22–23; 2:5, 15, 17–18, 23). And the star serves as a divine sign for the **magi** (or "wise men") that the "king of the Jews" is born (2:2, 9). Jesus is "God with us" (1:23), because at every turn divine providence is at work in the events surrounding the origin of Jesus.

Anchored in the traditions of Israel. Matthew asserts from the very beginning that Jesus is the Messiah, the son of David, and the son of Abraham (1:1). The subsequent genealogy substantiates these claims, especially the connection with David. The genealogy is structured around the number fourteen (1:17). Interestingly, the number fourteen is also the numerical value of David's name in Hebrew (*dwd, d* = 4, *w* = 6, *d* = 4). The name David also is the fourteenth name listed in the genealogy. Moreover, only David and Jesus have titles in the genealogy; David is called king in 1:6, and Jesus is called Messiah in 1:17. This connection with David functions to legitimize Jesus's identity as Messiah, a title sometimes associated with an ideal, Davidic ruler (cf. 2 Sam. 7; Isa. 11:1–10).

Matthew uses the literary device of typology to connect Jesus with Moses. He writes his narrative about Jesus in a way that evokes the memory of Moses. Consider the following parallels between Jesus in Matthew 1–2 and traditions about Moses around the time Matthew wrote his Gospel.

Traditions about Moses	Matthew 1–2
In a dream, God announces to Moses's father that the child will deliver the Hebrews from their distress (Josephus, *Jewish Antiquities* 2.210–16).	In a dream, an angel of the Lord announces to Joseph that the child will "save his people from their sins" (Matt. 1:21).
Pharaoh orders the death of Hebrew male babies (Exod. 1:16) because sacred scribes informed him about the birth of a future deliverer (Josephus, *Jewish Antiquities* 2.205–9).	Herod orders the death of infants in Bethlehem because the chief priests and scribes informed him that Bethlehem is the birthplace of the Messiah, and Herod fears a rival to his reign (Matt. 2:3–6, 16).
After Moses has fled from Egypt to avoid death, the Lord tells Moses, "Go to Egypt, for the ones seeking your life are dead" (Exod. 4:19 LXX).	After Joseph has fled to Egypt to protect Jesus from death, an angel of the Lord tells Joseph, "Get up, take the child and his mother, and go to the land of Israel, for those who were seeking the child's life are dead" (Matt. 2:20).

Matthew continues this Moses typology beyond Matthew 1–2. The typology functions to portray Jesus as a "new Moses," the authoritative prophet-teacher who delivers his people and instructs them in the way of righteousness.

Finally, Matthew demonstrates how Jesus's life fulfills Israel's prophecies (1:22–23; 2:5, 15, 17–18, 23). Not only do these fulfillment statements communicate divine providence, but these statements also connect Jesus's story with the story of Israel.

WOMEN IN JESUS'S GENEALOGY

Matthew's inclusion of women in Jesus's genealogy is highly unusual, and the women he names are even more surprising. Tamar, Rahab, Ruth, and "the wife of Uriah" (or Bathsheba) were all non-Israelites. These women also share stories that feature sexual encounters, whether suggestively or overtly (Gen. 38; Josh. 2; Ruth 3; 2 Sam. 11). And yet, despite the scandalous nature of these stories, each woman is remembered for her positive actions and subsequent role in carrying out God's plan. Of course, Mary is also named in Jesus's genealogy (1:16). Mary was not a Gentile, but her pregnancy prior to marriage would be scandalous, perhaps even engendering contempt among some in Matthew's day. Matthew unequivocally explains that Mary's pregnancy is a result of divine intervention (1:18, 20), but he also cleverly reminds his readers that God has accomplished the divine plan through heroic women whom others have questioned.

Foreshadowing Gentile inclusion. Matthew 1–2 also subtly anticipates the inclusion of Gentiles for salvation, which is explicitly realized at the end of the Gospel (28:19). This anticipation begins with the introductory statement that Jesus is the son of Abraham (1:1). God's covenant with Abraham was not limited to the people of Israel but included promises that Abraham would be the father of nations (Gen. 17:6, 16) and that through him "all the families of the earth" would be blessed (Gen. 12:3).

This theme of Gentile inclusion is also present in Jesus's genealogy, which includes non-Israelite women: Tamar the Canaanite (1:3; cf. Gen. 38:1–6), Rahab the Canaanite (1:5; cf. Josh. 2), Ruth the Moabite (1:5; cf. Ruth 1:1–5), and Bathsheba, the wife of Uriah the Hittite (1:6; cf. 2 Sam. 11). As a result, Gentiles are part of the lineage of Jesus the Messiah, and the salvation the Messiah provides will extend to Gentiles (28:19).

Lastly, the motif of Gentile inclusion appears in the account of the magi, the "wise men." When these Gentile astrologers interpret a star as signifying the birth of a Jewish king, they journey to Judea to offer gifts and pay homage (2:1–11). This reverent act by these Gentiles stands in stark contrast to Herod and the Jerusalem leaders, who respond with fear and conspire to kill the Messiah (2:3–8, 16).

Jesus's Public Ministry Commences (3:1–7:29)

Matthew 3:1–4:17 (narrative)—Fulfilling righteousness. Beginning with chapter 3, the narrative depicts the adult Jesus's public ministry. Matthew follows the outline of Mark's Gospel, but elaborates on the preaching of

John the Baptist, Jesus's baptism, and the temptations of Jesus. This textual unit is bracketed by the proclamation "Repent, for the kingdom of heaven has come near" (a device known as an **inclusio**), first by John the Baptist (3:2) and then by Jesus (4:17). In the process, John functions as an Elijah figure who demands repentance and prepares Israel for the Messiah (2 Kings 2:1, 11; Mal. 4:5–6; cf. Matt. 11:11–15).

In contrast to Mark's Gospel, in Matthew's Gospel Jesus provides a reason for his baptism: "to fulfill all righteousness" (3:15). Righteousness is an important theme in Matthew's Gospel (1:19; 5:6, 10, 20; 6:1, 33; 21:32). In most cases, the term *righteousness* refers to doing what is right in relation to God's covenant requirements; it is the human obligation of the covenant relationship. The human obligation may be what Jesus means in 3:15; his baptism fulfills what God requires of him. But "righteousness" can also refer to God's saving activity; it is the divine responsibility of the covenant relationship. If Jesus's words in 3:15 refer to God fulfilling all righteousness, then Jesus means that the event of his baptism inaugurates God's saving action (cf. 21:31b–32).

Matthew expands Mark's terse description of Jesus's temptation (Mark 1:12–13). Matthew describes three separate occasions when the devil tempts Jesus. In each instance Jesus rebuffs the devil by quoting Scripture. The temptations are reminiscent of Israel's testing in the wilderness, particularly issues of sustenance and idolatry (Exod. 16; 32; cf. Deut. 8:2). Unlike Israel's failures, though, Jesus is faithful and fulfills Israel's righteousness.

Matthew 4:18–7:29 (discourse)—A greater righteousness. The first major teaching unit in Matthew's Gospel, traditionally called "the Sermon on the Mount," is introduced by the call of Jesus's first disciples (4:18–22) and healings that attract crowds (4:23–25). As a result, the disciples constitute the audience for Jesus's teaching (5:1), but crowds overhear (7:28–29).

Just as Moses received Torah on Mount Sinai in order to teach the Israelites how to be the people of God, Jesus now teaches his disciples on a mountain how to be the people of God. This new instruction does not "abolish the law or the prophets" (5:17) but represents an advancement of covenant righteousness given this new juncture in God's salvation history (cf. 1:17; 4:17). Jesus "fulfills" (5:17), or brings to completion, what God ultimately envisions for his people. The reality of this vision is called the "kingdom of heaven," and it calls for a greater righteousness. The theme of righteousness is present in each of the major sections of the Sermon on the Mount (5:6, 10, 20; 6:1, 33).

- *Introductory announcement (5:1–16).* The kingdom of heaven requires certain spiritual dispositions, and Jesus congratulates those who have such character, like being poor in spirit and hungry for righteousness.

- *Intensification of the law and prophets (5:17–48).* Jesus provides the authoritative interpretation of Torah by explicating the divine intent behind Torah and intensifying God's demand for Torah righteousness.
- *Proper practice of righteousness (6:1–18).* Jesus addresses proper practice of the three traditional Jewish acts of piety or righteousness: almsgiving, prayer, and fasting. Each should be done without fanfare and in secret, so that only God sees and rewards.
- *God or material wealth (6:19–34).* Jesus describes the incompatibility between a life oriented toward possessions and a life oriented toward God.
- *Concluding sayings (7:1–27).* Jesus ends with miscellaneous teachings and an exhortation to put his instructions into action.

Miracles and the Twelve (8:1–11:1)

Matthew 8:1–9:37 (narrative)—Ministry of miracles. Next, Matthew narrates miraculous deeds as a series of three triads with each triad concluding with the issue of discipleship.

- Three miracles (8:1–17) + would-be disciples (8:18–22)
- Three miracles (8:23–9:8) + the call of Matthew and a question about disciples' fasting (9:9–17)
- Three miracles (9:18–34) + the need for "laborers" (9:35–38)

The concluding text unit also functions as a transition to the discourse. The request in 9:38—"Ask the Lord of the harvest to send out laborers into his harvest"—is answered by Jesus's "sending out" the Twelve (10:5, 16).

Matthew 10:1–11:1 (discourse)—Instructions for the Twelve. In the second major discourse Jesus instructs and commissions the twelve disciples. The ministry of the Twelve is an extension of Jesus's own ministry. Just as Jesus proclaims "the good news of the kingdom" (9:35; cf. 4:17, 23), the Twelve should also "proclaim the good news" (10:7). Just as Jesus "[cured] every disease and sickness" (9:35; cf. 4:23), the Twelve also receive authority to "cure every disease and every sickness" (10:1; cf. 10:8). Matthew likely intended for his readers to "overhear" these instructions as their own, both those traveling prophets who proclaimed the gospel and those who supported and welcomed these proclaimers.

Controversy and the Kingdom of Heaven (11:2–13:53)

Matthew 11:2–12:50 (narrative)—Questions, conflict, and rejection. The third section of Matthew's Gospel describes the developing controversy and rejection of the Messiah by "this generation" of Israel (11:16; 12:39, 41, 42, 45). This rejection was prefigured by Israel's rejection of John the Baptist (11:7–19). Despite Jesus's deeds of power that manifest the presence of the kingdom, many have not repented and so will be judged. The Pharisees appear in chapter 12 as conspicuous opponents of Jesus. They raise questions about his activities on the Sabbath day; accuse him of acting on behalf of Beelzebub, the ruler of the demons; and ask for a sign. Their decisive response is to find a way "to destroy him" (12:14). Matthew characterizes these unrepentant Pharisees as a part of this "evil and adulterous generation" (12:39), who will be judged and condemned (12:33–45).

Matthew 13:1–53 (discourse)—Kingdom parables. For the third major discourse, Matthew utilizes Mark's parable chapter (Mark 4) and expands it from four parables to seven parables. In Matthew's Gospel, the parables explain why Jesus and his proclamation of the kingdom of heaven are met with diverse responses, especially negative ones. The first two parables, along with their interpretations, reveal that the devil is at work in the hearts of people. The experience of persecution, the cares of this world, and the lure of wealth also contribute to a rejection of the kingdom of heaven. On the other hand, the Twelve represent the twelve tribes of Israel, and they have left everything to follow Jesus (4:18–22; 9:9); they know the treasure that is the kingdom of heaven. So, for now, there exists simultaneously the righteous and the unrighteous, and not until the end-time judgment will God separate the two groups and condemn the wicked (13:24–30, 36–43, 47–50).

Ministry and the Church (13:53–18:35)

Matthew 13:53–17:27 (narrative)—Ministry to the church. This narrative section brings together and carries forward a variety of themes from the previous two narrative sections, especially those of rejection and opposition. In addition, this narrative section begins to focus on a ministry to the community of disciples. Matthew's Gospel is the only Gospel that uses the term *church*—and Matthew uses it twice in this fourth major division, once in the narrative (16:18) and once in the discourse (18:17). Moreover, in Matthew, Jesus facilitates his ministry to the church through Peter, once again in both the narrative and the discourse. In essence, Peter functions as the representative of the community of disciples or church. For example, when

Peter confesses that Jesus is "the Messiah, the Son of the living God," Jesus responds by stating that he will build his church on this "rock" and will grant to Peter the keys to the kingdom of heaven (16:13–20). (Interpreters debate whether the emphasis falls on Peter himself or the act and content of Peter's confession.) Only Matthew includes this response (see also 14:28–33; 17:1–8, 24–27 for episodes involving Peter).

Matthew 18:1–35 (discourse)—Instructions for the church. The fourth major discourse addresses the community's life together. The disciples should not cause one another to sin; the "little ones" in 18:6, 10 refers either to other believers, missionaries, or new converts. If one member sins against another, there is a formal procedure to follow, with forgiveness and restoration always being the objective.

Ministry Finale (19:1–25:46)

Matthew 19:1–23:39 (narrative)—Arriving in Jerusalem. With this narrative section, Jesus's earthly ministry comes to its final destination. The first part features Jesus on the way to Jerusalem and continues themes from earlier sections. The second part shows Jesus entering Jerusalem as a humble, royal Messiah (21:1–11) and making a symbolic gesture of judgment on the temple (21:12–17). The narrative concludes with Jesus leveling a series of prophetic curses or woes against the Pharisees (23:1–36) and offering a lament over Jerusalem (23:37–39). The prophetic curses are unique to Matthew's Gospel and may reflect the Matthean community's polemics against non-Christian Jews of their day.

Matthew 24:1–25:46 (discourse)—Final judgment. The final discourse in Matthew's Gospel presents Jesus speaking to his disciples about the end time, with the coming of the Son of Man and the last judgment. Before the coming of the Son of Man, false messiahs will arrive and the righteous will suffer (24:1–31). Scholars debate whether these events reflect the situation of the Matthean community or are traditional apocalyptic scenarios. Jesus then teaches about the necessity of being found faithful when the end comes and the final judgment commences (24:36–25:46).

Death and Resurrection (26:1–28:20)

The death of Jesus. Matthew's passion narrative closely follows the sequence in Mark's Gospel, but it contains elaborations and additions that result in a distinctly Matthean portrayal of the death of Jesus. First, Matthew connects the infancy narrative and the passion narrative, creating a consistent and coherent story about Jesus.

- At the Passover meal, Jesus announces that the cup represents the "blood of the covenant, which is poured out for many for the forgiveness of sins" (26:28). The phrase "for the forgiveness of sins" rejoins the proclamation at Jesus's birth, that "he will save his people from their sins" (1:21).

- At the beginning and end of Matthew's Gospel, Gentiles (the magi and Pilate's wife) act positively on behalf of Jesus because of dreams (2:12; 27:19). These Gentiles stand in contrast to Roman rulers (Herod the Great and Pilate) and the chief priests (2:1–5, 16–17; 27:1–2, 15–26).

- The infancy narrative contains five statements about the fulfillment of scriptural prophecy (1:22–23; 2:5, 15, 17–18, 23). A high convergence of scriptural fulfillments (26:24, 31, 54, 56; 27:9–10) and allusions (26:15, 24, 63; 27:14, 30–31, 33–34, 43, 46, 51–53, 57) returns in the passion narrative. These allusions and fulfillments ensure confidence that Jesus's birth and death are in accordance with God's providence.

Second, Matthew includes an account of Judas's death (27:3–10), which contributes to Matthew's passion narrative in two ways.

- It juxtaposes two different responses by Peter and Judas in the wake of their forsaking Jesus. Jesus foretold both failings at the Passover meal (26:20–25, 31–35); both Peter and Judas refute Jesus's assertions (26:25, 33); and both Peter and Judas have remorse (26:75; 27:3). Their responses, however, differ. Judas hangs himself (27:3–10), exacting upon himself the penalty for shedding "innocent blood" (27:4)—a life for a life (Lev. 24:21). Yet according to Matthew, Jesus gives his life as a "ransom" (20:28), and thus Peter experiences restoration and is still counted among Jesus's disciples (28:16).

- It introduces the theme of responsibility for Jesus's "innocent blood." Judas confesses his guilt for "betraying innocent blood" (27:4), attempts to absolve himself by returning the "blood money" (27:6), and hangs himself. The chief priests fear ritual impurity from the returned blood money and take steps to avoid guilt. Pilate too tries to escape guilt by washing his hands and declaring, "I am innocent of this man's blood" (27:24); but his words and action only confirm his guilt. In response, the "people as a whole" accept responsibility: "His blood be on us and on our children" (27:25). From Matthew's perspective, the people represent "this generation" whose ancestors murdered the prophets (25:29–36) and now take responsibility for the death of the

Messiah. (Matthew does not view this as an indictment on all Jews but likely connects it to the destruction of the temple in 70 CE.)

Finally, in addition to Mark's daytime darkness and the tearing of the temple veil, Matthew adds a powerful earthquake that ruptures rocks and opens tombs, from which many people are raised (27:52). The constellation of these events (i.e., the failing of the sun, the earthquake, and the resurrection of the righteous) reflects common apocalyptic motifs associated with the "day of the Lord," with its accompanying judgment and salvation. In Matthew, Jesus's death and resurrection initiate the apocalyptic act of God, that decisive end-time intervention by God to set aright all creation.

The resurrection of Jesus. Matthew abandons Mark's ending of the empty tomb and the silence of fearful women for a conclusion more informed by early Christian tradition. Matthew includes unique features like the guarding of the tomb (27:62–66; 28:11–15), the descending angel and earthquake (28:2), and Jesus's appearance to the women and their response of worship (28:9; cf. 2:11; 14:33; 17:6; 28:17). In addition, the commissioning scene (28:16–20), traditionally called "the Great Commission," portrays Jesus as the divinely appointed, authoritative prophet-teacher. The commission emphasizes making disciples among both Jews and Gentiles and teaching them all that Jesus instructed.

The Gospel according to Luke

Jesus's Origins and Preparation for Ministry (1:1–4:13)

Prologue. The author (traditionally referred to as Luke) begins the Gospel of Luke with a sophisticated sentence that resembles prefaces found in Greek histories from the classical period (1:1–4). In the process the author shows awareness of other ancient writings about Jesus and expresses his desire to relay the truth about Jesus in an orderly fashion (1:3). It is not completely clear, however, whether "orderly" refers to the narrative's chronology, theological trajectory, or flow of argumentation.

Jesus's conception, birth, and boyhood. In 1:5–2:52 Luke narrates the origins of both John the Baptist and Jesus in an interwoven, parallel fashion. Luke repeatedly links the lives of John and Jesus together, yet he consistently demonstrates that Jesus is the superior member of the tandem. For example, the angel says that John will come "with the spirit and power of Elijah" (1:17), but the angel says that Jesus "will be called the Son of the Most High" and "will reign over the house of Jacob" and that "of his kingdom there will be no end" (1:32–33). Similar dynamics exist between the births (1:57–58; 2:1–20), naming (1:59–79; 2:21–28), and maturation (1:80; 2:39–52) of John and Jesus. The interwoven parallelism between John and Jesus in 1:5–2:52 likely illustrates the continuity with and compatibility between God's work in the past and the present while simultaneously showing that God's work in and through Jesus is superior.

In addition, Luke greatly emphasizes the humble circumstances that surround Jesus's birth. For example, he narrates Jesus's origins through the eyes of Mary. This seemingly insignificant young woman has the honor of providing the introductory testimony about Jesus's conception (1:26–56). Similarly, an angel selects working-class shepherds to function as the earthly heralds of Jesus's birth (2:8–20). And these unnamed shepherds find the baby lying in an animal's feeding trough. The roles played by Mary and the shepherds foreshadow the prominent roles that women and the poor will play throughout this book, and the manger sets the tone for Jesus's humble life of service.

From the outset, Luke indicates that Jesus's life and ministry will lead to reversal throughout the cosmos. In particular, Mary's song in 1:46–55, often referred to as "the **Magnificat**," solidifies this idea. Mary breaks out in victorious praise about the conception of Jesus in her womb. She begins by praising God for showing mercy to her, a lowly servant, and reversing her fortune. She ends by praising God for showing mercy to "his servant Israel" (1:54). In her song she describes God as a savior who reverses the fate of the proud, the powerful, the rich, the lowly, and the hungry. Shortly thereafter, an angel proclaims Jesus as "Savior" (2:11), thereby highlighting the idea that God's salvific intervention in the world will come about through Jesus (2:30; 19:9; cf. Acts 4:12; 16:31).

Genealogy. Luke provides Jesus's genealogy, but he places it at the end of Luke 3 when Jesus is already a grown man (3:23–38). In effect, Luke delays the discussion of Jesus's human ancestry until after the heavenly voice has already declared Jesus to be God's Son (3:22). Then Luke works backward

---

SAVIOR

For many of Luke's readers, the term *savior* would have been associated primarily with concepts that derive from Greco-Roman culture. For example, Greek and Roman gods (like Zeus and Asclepius), military leaders, and emperors (especially Caesar Augustus) were often described as "saviors." With the exception of John 4:42, Luke is the only evangelist who includes this terminology with regard to God (1:47) and Jesus (2:11). As a result, Luke's first readers may have perceived an implied contrast between Jesus and the Roman rulers of their day.

in time, tracing Jesus's ancestry all the way back to Adam, the ancestor of all humanity (Gen. 2–3). In doing so Luke sets up the universal significance of Jesus. Jesus has come not only from and for the descendants of Abraham (the Jews) but also from and for the descendants of Adam (all humanity).

Temptation. The devil tempts Jesus using God's words from the baptism (4:1–13). Twice the devil starts by saying, "If you are the Son of God" (Luke 4:3, 9). In both instances, the devil tempts Jesus to use his authority in ways that God does not intend. Furthermore, the devil distorts the Scriptures and presents his final temptation in the temple area. Thus, the misuse of religious authority for personal profit or power is linked to the work of the devil early on in Luke's Gospel. Perhaps Luke also wants his readers to observe that Jesus resists temptations in the wilderness that are similar to those that Israel failed to withstand when they similarly wandered in the wilderness.

Ministry in and around Galilee (4:14–9:50)

Sermon at Nazareth. Unlike Mark, Luke introduces Jesus's ministry in Galilee by relaying the story of Jesus's rejection in his hometown synagogue (4:14–30; cf. Mark 6:1–6). In the process, Luke incorporates a variety of literary themes that guide the rest of the book.

First, the theme of reversal resurfaces in the first words that Jesus speaks during his public ministry. Jesus reads Isaiah 61:1–2b and announces its fulfillment. The quotation, however, describes God's redemptive promises to assist those who are in need—the poor, the captives, and the blind. In essence, Jesus proclaims that his life and ministry are now fulfilling God's promises of dramatic reversal.

Second, Jesus's sermon at Nazareth introduces the idea that Jesus is a great prophet. For instance, the Isaiah passage that Jesus applies to himself appears to describe the call of a prophet. Additionally, Jesus refers to himself as a prophet in 4:24, and he references the experiences of the Old Testament prophets Elijah and Elisha in 4:25–30. Hereafter, Luke interprets Jesus's miraculous deeds, bold words, and eventual rejection as the by-products of Jesus's identity as a prophet of God.

Finally, those present in the Nazareth synagogue initially praise Jesus for his words. Yet their praise turns to rage after Jesus refers to two instances in which God selectively shows mercy to Gentiles rather than Israelites. This passage foreshadows God's future mercy toward Gentiles as well as the future anger that some first-century Jews show in response to God's kindness toward the Gentiles.

Sermon on the Plain. Jesus's teachings in 6:17–49 are often labeled "the Sermon on the Plain" in contrast to "the Sermon on the Mount" (Matt. 5–7). The two sermons have many similarities—so many similarities that most scholars believe the sermons derive from a common source or collection of Jesus's sayings (e.g., Q). Yet there are startling differences amid the dramatic similarities.

For example, Luke's version of this material is much briefer than Matthew's, and it accentuates Jesus's humility. Beginning in 6:17, Jesus descends from a mountain to a flat place or plain where he stands among "a great multitude of people" and teaches. Jesus concludes his teaching in 6:49, a mere thirty-three verses later. Here, Jesus is not on the mountain, but he is with and among the crowds. The humble infant has become a humble teacher who remains with the people.

Also, in Luke "the **beatitudes**" (cf. Matt. 5:3–12) exhibit prophetic themes and accentuate the idea of reversal. Jesus declares blessings on some and woes on others. He announces that God will soon bless the poor, hungry, mournful, and persecuted. Conversely, he announces that the rich, well fed, content, and well liked will soon experience a reversal of fortune. Thus, Luke again highlights Jesus's concern for the physical needs of his disciples (6:17–26) and Jesus's desire that his disciples act generously and mercifully toward their enemies (6:27–36).

Disciples' failures. Even though Luke provides a portrait of the disciples that is more positive than Mark's (cf. Mark 4:40; 8:27–33; Luke 8:24; 9:18–22), Luke makes it clear that Jesus's disciples are still in need of growth at the end of Jesus's Galilean ministry. In particular, Luke connects four passages that show the shortcomings of the disciples. Jesus's disciples are unable to help a demon-possessed boy (9:37–43a), and they cannot understand Jesus's prediction about his future suffering (9:43b–45). Next, the disciples argue about who among them is the greatest, despite Jesus's emphasis on service (9:46–48); and finally, the disciples misidentify a friend as a foe (9:49–50).

The Journey to Jerusalem (9:51–19:28)

Journey. Jesus's journey to Jerusalem takes on structural and thematic importance in Luke's Gospel. Compared to the journey narrative in Mark's Gospel, Jesus's journey to Jerusalem in Luke's Gospel is lengthy; it accounts for more than one-third of the text. Most of the material in this section is either unique to Luke or shared with Matthew.

When Jesus begins his journey to Jerusalem, Luke accentuates the gravity of Jesus's actions. In 9:51 Luke writes, "When the days drew near for him to be taken up, he set his face to go to Jerusalem." The phrase "to be taken up" most clearly refers to Jesus's ascension (24:50–53). Yet the phrase may carry a secondary allusion to Jesus's suffering on the cross. Regardless, Jesus "sets his face," which connotes intentional resolve, "to go to Jerusalem," which Jesus later describes as "the city that kills the prophets" (13:34). Thus, 9:51 marks a transition and also demonstrates Jesus's resolve to fulfill the role that has been given to him.

Jesus immediately experiences rejection on his journey (9:52–53). Just as he was initially rejected in Galilee (4:14–30), so now he is rejected in Samaria. In response, James and John want to call down fire to destroy the Samaritans who reject Jesus (9:54). The prophet Elijah did something similar in 2 Kings 1:1–16. Jesus, however, rebukes his disciples for proposing retribution and merely moves on (9:55–56). Jesus opts for mercy rather than vengeance, thereby showing that he is a compassionate prophet.

Discipleship. Jesus most clearly defines what it means to be a disciple during the journey narrative. In fact, the journey itself seems to shape the disciples in a positive manner. For example, a lawyer near the beginning and a rich man near the end of the journey ask Jesus, "What must I do to inherit eternal life?" (10:25; 18:18). Consequently, Luke's readers must be mindful of that question throughout the journey. Most of the material that lies between the two bookended questions contributes to an overarching answer for Luke's readers.

Further illustrating the contours of discipleship, Jesus commissions the twelve apostles in 9:1–6. Jesus commissions seventy-two other disciples in 10:1–24, a passage that appears only in Luke's Gospel and to which Luke dedicates far more space than the commissioning of the Twelve. Hence, discipleship is in no way limited exclusively to the twelve apostles. Instead, Jesus has many followers in Luke's Gospel (e.g., 8:1–3; 19:37–38). Moreover, these additional disciples have been empowered to perform actions similar to those of Jesus (10:9, 17–20) and the Twelve (9:1–6). Yet, as is the case with Jesus and the Twelve (9:5), even these seventy-two unnamed disciples should anticipate rejection (10:3–16).

Teachings. Humility, compassion, and generosity dominate Jesus's teachings as he travels to Jerusalem. In response to a badgering lawyer, Jesus explains in the parable of the good Samaritan (10:29–37) the importance of showing mercy to "outsiders." In contrast to the dominant culture of his day, Jesus teaches his disciples to invite guests to their banquets who are too poor to reciprocate (14:12–14); and in response to the sneers of the Pharisees and scribes, Jesus uses three parables in 15:1–24 to illustrate the manner in which God welcomes repentant sinners.

Similarly, in 16:19–31, Jesus narrates the parable of the rich man and Lazarus to illustrate the proper use of possessions. In the spirit of reversal, the

PARABLES

The parables of Jesus have literary affinities with the Old Testament *mashal* (e.g., Judg. 9:7–20; 2 Sam. 12:1–4; Isa. 5:1–6), Jewish rabbinic material, and the fable tradition of the Greco-Roman world. Parables are short, fictional narratives that draw on real-life scenarios for the purpose of metaphorical meaning. This metaphorical lesson can be theological or moral or both, depending on its literary context. And although they reflect common, everyday occurrences, parables often contain a surprising or provocative element that challenges the audience's values and perceptions.

Scholars often distinguish between the earliest form of Jesus's parables and the representation of those parables given by the Gospel writers in their respective narratives. Jesus's telling of a parable most likely concerned the kingdom of God and was open-ended, inviting a response and interpretation from the hearers. As such, the parables could elicit more than one meaning or interpretation. But the Gospel writers have shaped the parables for their narrative purposes and often provide a particular meaning of a parable for their readers. For example, read the parable of the lost sheep found in both Matthew (18:12–14) and Luke (15:4–7), and answer the following questions:

- Read the narrative context for the parable in each Gospel (Matt. 18 and Luke 15). What is the purpose or lesson of the parable for each Gospel writer?
- Can you identify Matthew's and Luke's respective interpretative comments (the "moral of the story") for the parable?
- How would you reconstruct the original form of the parable based on a comparison of Matthew's and Luke's versions of the parable?

rich man, who failed to show mercy when he was alive, receives no mercy when he is dead. Alternatively, in the afterlife God blesses the poor man, who experienced severe poverty when he was alive. Altogether, Jesus suggests that God has great concern for those in need and great contempt for those who fail to aid those in need.

Ministry in Jerusalem (19:28–24:53)

Even after Jesus enters Jerusalem, Luke continues to portray Jesus as a great prophet. In fact, Jesus's words frequently establish a prophecy-fulfillment pattern. Jesus knows what the immediate future holds, and the events unfold as he predicts. For example, Jesus foretells the presence of the colt (19:30, 32), the destruction of Jerusalem (19:41–44; 21:20–24), the setting of the Last Supper (22:10–13), his own suffering (22:15–16; 24:6–8), Judas's betrayal

(22:21–22), Peter's denial (22:34), and Peter's repentance (22:31–32). Nothing that happens in Jerusalem catches Jesus off guard. Rather, he knowingly and willingly follows the plan of God.

Arrival. Upon his arrival in Jerusalem, Jesus is clearly identified as a king. In fact, "the whole multitude of the disciples" boldly welcomes Jesus as "the king who comes in the name of the Lord!" They proclaim, "Peace in heaven, and glory in the highest heaven!" (19:37–38). At Jesus's birth, a multitude of angels proclaim, "Glory to God in the highest heaven, and on earth peace among those whom he favors!" (2:13–14). Now, the multitude of disciples takes over that duty.

Almost certainly, Luke's first readers would have perceived an underlying comparison in 19:28–44. In contrast to the *Pax Romana* ("peace of Rome") that Caesar Augustus was famous for establishing (cf. 2:1), "King" Jesus's "peace" extends throughout the entire cosmos. As a result, the Pharisees immediately ask Jesus to stop these bold and perhaps politically charged statements of the disciples (19:39–40).

Arrest. When the crowd arrives to arrest Jesus (22:47–53), the disciples do not flee or abandon Jesus; rather, they are prepared to fight. In fact, the disciples appear to misinterpret Jesus's instructions about buying swords (22:35–38). One of the disciples even cuts off the ear of the high priest's slave. Jesus, however, does not wish to battle with swords. Instead, he stops his disciples and heals the slave's ear. In essence, Jesus brings peace even as he is confronted by "the power of darkness" (22:53).

Trials and crucifixion. In Luke's passion narrative (23:1–49), he repeatedly depicts Jesus as an innocent martyr. For instance, the Jewish religious leaders accuse Jesus of corrupting the nation, discouraging Jews from paying Roman taxes, and claiming to be "a king" (23:2). Yet on three occasions Pilate concludes that Jesus is innocent of all charges (23:4, 13–16, 22). Herod also finds no guilt and takes no action (23:11, 15). Even at the crucifixion a criminal points out that Jesus "has done nothing wrong" (23:41). Finally,

---

PRAYER

Luke greatly emphasizes the practice of prayer in his Gospel. Notably, Jesus prays prior to his baptism (3:21), his healing of a paralyzed man (5:16), his call of disciples (6:12–13), his transfiguration (9:28–29), and his arrest (22:40–46). Jesus even prays from the cross in 23:34 and 23:46. Moreover, Jesus teaches his disciples to pray in 11:1–2; 18:1–11; 21:34–36; and 22:40–46. Consequently, prayer appears to be an important means through which God reveals God's guidance to both Jesus and Jesus's disciples.

upon Jesus's death, a Roman centurion exclaims, "Certainly this man was innocent" (23:47). In short, Luke wants his readers to know that Jesus does not die for crimes against Rome. He is innocent of all wrongdoing, yet he willingly dies as God's faithful servant (22:42).

Even on the cross, Jesus focuses on the needs of others and the will of God. For instance, according to many manuscripts, Jesus asks the Father to forgive those who crucify him (23:34). In addition, in 23:43 Jesus issues forgiveness to the criminal next to him. Finally, unlike in Mark and Matthew, Jesus does not cry out to God with a sense of abandonment. Rather, he places his trust in God. Jesus concludes his life by saying, "Father, into your hands I commend my spirit" (23:46). As an innocent martyr, Jesus knows he rests within God's overarching plan for redemption.

Post-resurrection events. Geographically, Luke concludes his Gospel with stories about Jesus's post-resurrection appearances in and around Jerusalem (24:13–53). Theologically, Luke concludes with an emphasis on the history of God's redemptive work in the world. Jesus explains that his role as the Messiah was to suffer, die, and rise from the dead (24:46). Moreover, he teaches his disciples to proclaim "repentance and forgiveness of sins . . . to all nations" (24:47). The salvation of God now extends to all who respond positively to the disciples' proclamation about Jesus. Finally, only Luke among the Gospel writers narrates Jesus's ascension "into heaven" (24:50–52).

The Gospel according to John

The Prologue (1:1–18)

In 1:1–18 the author (traditionally referred to as John) provides a highly poetic and theologically rich introduction to Jesus. John begins the story long before Jesus's birth. In fact, John claims that God's *logos* ("the Word") existed prior to creation and was used by God "in the beginning" as God created the world (1:1–5). The *logos* is the source of all life and light in the world. Moreover, God has repeatedly worked in the world through the *logos* to guide and rescue God's people. Yet humans have repeatedly failed to recognize or follow God's redemptive guidance in the past (1:10–13).

As a result, God's preexistent *logos* has become incarnate as Jesus (1:14). God's "grace and truth" can now be best comprehended through Jesus as opposed to other means like Moses or the law (1:17). Even though "no one has ever seen God," Jesus, the embodied *logos*, now makes God known to the world (1:18; cf. 6:46).

LOGOS

The Greek term *logos* carried a variety of meanings in antiquity (e.g., word, statement, thought). Philosophical conversations about *logos* were widespread. For example, Stoic philosophers often spoke of the *logos* as the unifying agent or logic of the universe. Similarly, some Jewish writers (e.g., Philo) used the terms *logos* and *sophia* (wisdom) interchangeably as they described God's creative and redemptive work in the world. When John employs the term *logos* in 1:1 and 1:14, he appears to build on these preexisting conversations.

Later, John shows how Jesus's ascension returns Jesus to his rightful place with the Father (16:5, 28; 20:17). Thus, John articulates a three-stage **Christology** consisting of Jesus's preexistence, incarnation, and heavenly ascension. John shows that Jesus has an exceedingly close and unique relationship with God (10:30, 38; 14:11). From the beginning, Jesus functions as God's Word, carries out God's work, and reveals God's nature to the world. Furthermore, those who welcome Jesus as God's "only Son" (1:18) in turn become the "children of God" (1:12–13).

The Book of Signs (1:19–12:50)

Scholars commonly describe John 1:19–12:50 as the "Book of Signs." Here, Jesus performs seven signs or miraculous deeds that display his power and reveal his true identity. In response to these signs, many believe while others immediately oppose Jesus. In fact, in John 5–12, both belief in and opposition to Jesus grow increasingly strong with each subsequent sign.

The witness of John (the Baptist). John (the Baptist) plays a prominent role throughout the first chapter of this Gospel. Importantly, though, while John's baptizing ministry is mentioned (1:19–42), John's primary task involves testifying about Jesus's true identity. For example, when John sees Jesus, he says, "Here is the Lamb of God who takes away the sin of the world!" (1:29). In addition, John claims that Jesus is the Son of God, and he testifies to having seen the Spirit descend on Jesus (1:32–34).

John's testimony provides the impetus for two of John's own disciples to begin following Jesus (1:35–40). We see a pattern in the Gospel whereby truthful testimonies about Jesus lead others to believe in him. For example, John's testimony causes Andrew to follow Jesus (1:35–40), Andrew's testimony brings Peter along (1:41–42), and Philip's witness persuades Nathanael to follow (1:45–51). Consequently, readers should immediately recognize that faithful discipleship in John's Gospel includes providing a witness about Jesus.

Jesus's identity is never hidden in this Gospel; rather, many understand Jesus's importance from the start.

Turning water into wine. Jesus performs the first of his miraculous signs in 2:1–11 at a private wedding at Cana. In keeping with the pattern that re-surfaces in each of Jesus's signs, someone (in this case Jesus's mother) first petitions Jesus to rectify an undesirable situation. Yet no human directs Jesus; only God does. Nevertheless, Jesus eventually intervenes and turns water into wine, which in turn leads many to believe in him.

The way that Jesus carries out the miracle is as startling and as theologically significant as the miracle itself. In particular, Jesus first asks servants to place water inside the "stone water jars" that were used "for the Jewish rites of purification" (2:6). In noting this John's Gospel contrasts the limited power of the Jewish rites of purification with the unlimited power of Jesus. In essence, rather than using the pots to remove defilement, Jesus uses them to re-create water into an entirely new substance. The dialogue in this unit about the superiority of the "new wine" provides commentary on the superiority of Jesus's work (2:9–10).

Critique of the temple. Whereas the authors of the Synoptic Gospels all place Jesus's critique of the Jewish temple at the end of his ministry, John places it at the beginning. In fact, Jesus's actions in the temple on his first of three trips to Jerusalem constitute his first public actions in John's Gospel (2:13–22). As a result, Jesus's critique of the temple provides a prism through which John's readers must look as they interpret the rest of the Gospel. Notice, however, that Jesus does more than critique the existing temple. He also speaks of his body as a temple in 2:19, 21–22, perhaps suggesting that Jesus himself replaces the existing temple.

Samaritan woman. In 4:1–42 Jesus converses with a woman at a well in Samaria. She asks him to weigh in on a preexisting debate about where faithful worship should occur, Mount Gerizim in Samaria or the temple in Jerusalem. Instead of siding with either location, Jesus speaks of worshiping "the Father in spirit and truth," which Jesus himself establishes (4:23). In short, Jesus ushers in a new type of worship that surpasses the preexisting temple practices in Samaria and Judea alike.

Opposition. The idea that Jesus's power surpasses the religious rituals and institutions of his day continues throughout this Gospel. For example, Jesus performs five signs in the context of Jewish water rituals, festivals, or holy days (5:2–9; 6:1–14, 16–21; 9:1–12; 11:38–44). In each instance, John demonstrates that Jesus's power and ministry now surpass the benefit of the religious practices that preceded him. Consequently, John's readers should not be surprised when the opposition from the Jewish religious leaders toward Jesus grows increasingly strong.

Feeding of the five thousand. John narrates the feeding of the five thousand in a distinct manner (6:1–71). First, a large crowd flocks to Jesus in Galilee instead of traveling to Jerusalem for the Passover as one might expect. Thus, Jesus is portrayed as being greater than the Passover just as he was shown to be greater than the water rituals and the temple. Jesus is also portrayed as being similar to and yet greater than the manna that God provided for the Hebrews in the wilderness. Jesus is the "true bread from heaven" that the Father provides (6:32–51). Yet, unlike the manna that perished, this new bread from heaven "endures for eternal life" (6:27, 58). Hence, in John 6 Jesus shows that he himself is ultimately the sustenance that the multitude needs.

Furthermore, John does not include an account of the "Last Supper" as we see in the Synoptic Gospels. Rather, eucharistic images and language are present in John 6. For example, at the feeding of the five thousand, Jesus takes the loaves, gives thanks, and personally distributes the food to the people. Even more, Jesus creates a direct link between the "bread" and his body (6:51). Jesus says, "Those who eat my flesh and drink my blood have eternal life, and I will raise them up on the last day" (6:54). Thus, in John the passage that sets up later Christian conversations about the Eucharist or Lord's Supper takes place while Jesus is still ministering in Galilee as opposed to during the last week in Jerusalem. In essence, John associates the ingesting of the body and blood of Jesus primarily with Jesus's incarnation, life, and ministry rather than with his death.

Healing the man born blind. In 9:1–7 Jesus gives sight to a blind man. Jesus's actions illuminate the manner in which Jesus is "the light of the world" (8:12; 9:5). The bulk of John 9, however, chronicles the various responses to the miracle. The neighbors and the Pharisees do not believe a miracle has

---

"I AM" STATEMENTS

In John 6, Jesus issues his first of seven "I am" statements that are combined with a predicate nominative: "I am the bread of life" (6:35, 48, 51). The other statements are "I am the light of the world" (8:12; 9:5); "I am the gate" (10:7, 9); "I am the good shepherd" (10:11, 14); "I am the resurrection and the life" (11:25); "I am the way, and the truth, and the life" (14:6); and "I am the true vine" (15:1, 5). Interpreters often contend that Jesus uses the "I am" formula (Greek, *egō eimi*) in these seven statements in order to mimic God's response of "I AM WHO I AM" in Exodus 3:14 (LXX, *egō eimi*). Regardless, these statements directly build on the miracles that Jesus performs, and they greatly advance the theological understanding of Jesus in John's Gospel.

taken place, so they question both the parents and the man repeatedly. The man's parents are afraid to testify regarding the miracle, fearing they will be expelled from the Jewish synagogue. The blind man, however, functions as an ideal disciple. He repeatedly provides a faithful and courageous witness about Jesus. Moreover, his understanding of Jesus's identity grows throughout the story (9:11, 17, 33, 38). The Pharisees, however, grow increasingly blind about spiritual matters (9:16, 24, 30–33). In the end, the Pharisees are depicted as sinful because they refuse to believe in Jesus's power and identity.

Raising Lazarus. In 11:38–44 Jesus raises Lazarus from the dead. In the process, John illuminates the manner in which Jesus is indeed "the resurrection and the life" (11:25). Lazarus's experiences likewise foreshadow Jesus's own death and resurrection. For example, when the high priest reacts to the miracle, he unknowingly voices the explanation in this Gospel for Jesus's eventual death: Jesus is the one who will die in order to rescue "the dispersed children of God" (11:49–52).

Literarily, the raising of Lazarus functions as the pivot point in John's Gospel. Jesus performs his final and climactic sign when he raises Lazarus (12:18). In addition, the raising of Lazarus is the event in John that ultimately leads to the arrest and crucifixion of Jesus (11:53, 57). But when Jesus predicts his impending death in 12:23–26, he employs the language of glorification; for example, he says, "The hour has come for the Son of Man to be glorified." Similarly, in 12:27–29 Jesus raises the rhetorical question with his disciples about whether he should ask the Father to save him from "this hour." Yet Jesus declines even to ask, because "it is for this reason" that he has come. Instead, Jesus prays simply that the Father will glorify his name, and the Father verbally responds by saying, "I have glorified it, and I will glorify it again." In essence, John portrays Jesus's crucifixion and death as Jesus's triumphant glorification.

"THE JEWS"

John frequently refers to "the Jews" in this Gospel. Tragically, careless interpretations of this terminology have at times led to violence against Jews by Christians. For example, John often speaks negatively about "the Jews" who contribute to Jesus's death (e.g., 5:18; 7:1; 9:22; 10:31; 18:31; 19:7, 38). Yet at other times John uses the designation "the Jews" in a neutral manner (e.g., 2:13; 10:19; 11:19; 19:40) or even a positive manner (e.g., 8:31; 11:45; 12:11). In essence, John refers to more than one group of people with the same terminology. Therefore, each time one encounters the words "the Jews" in this Gospel, it is best to ask, "To whom specifically is John referring?"

The Book of Glory (13:1–20:31)

The last third of John's Gospel has often been described as the "Book of Glory," in large part because of John's depiction of Jesus's crucifixion as a glorification (13:31–33; 17:1–5). This large unit can be subdivided into Jesus's farewell speech to his disciples in John 13–17 and Jesus's arrest, trial, death, and resurrection in John 18–20.

Farewell speech. Jesus interacts exclusively with his disciples for a final time in John 13–17. At Jesus's last meal with the disciples, he washes their feet (13:1–20) and warns them of Judas's impending betrayal (13:21–30). In the process, Jesus leaves his disciples with a new command, repeatedly instructing them to love one another (13:34–35; 14:21–24; 15:12–17). Finally, in John 17, Jesus prays at length for his followers.

Eschatology. Scholars debate John's theological understanding of the climactic moment in human history. For instance, in John 14, Jesus encourages his disciples by describing a future heavenly experience. He says, "If I go and prepare a place for you, I will come again and will take you to myself" (14:3). Many contend that those comments represent a "future eschatology" (cf. 6:39–40, 44, 54; 12:25, 48; 14:1–4). At other points, however, John articulates a "realized eschatology." Jesus's own life and ministry carry out God's judgment (3:19; 5:22, 27, 30; 9:39–40; 12:31), give eternal life (3:36; 5:21–24; 6:47), inaugurate God's blessing on those who believe (5:24–25; 14:12–14), and defeat the forces of evil (12:31; 16:7–11). From this angle of vision, Jesus's life is the climactic moment in human history. Judgment, eternal life, and God's blessings are already present realities for the believers reading John's Gospel.

The Advocate. Jesus also promises that he will send an "Advocate" (14:16–17, 25–26; 15:26–27; 16:7–11). The Advocate, or Holy Spirit, will teach, remind, and comfort the disciples in Jesus's absence. Because Satan, the "ruler of this world," has no power over Jesus (14:30), the believers who are strengthened by the Advocate will likewise receive the necessary fortitude to withstand Satan's attacks and persecution from "the world" (14:27–30; 16:7–11, 33; 17:11–12, 15–16). Yet the future is already present for John's readers. For example, in John 20, when Jesus appears to his disciples shortly after the resurrection, he commissions them and breathes the Holy Spirit on them (20:21–22). He gives the Holy Spirit even before he departs, thereby fully equipping the disciples to carry out their commission.

Arrest. John includes many unique details in his narration of the arrest of Jesus. First, only John mentions that Roman soldiers join the Jewish religious leaders when Jesus is arrested (18:1–3). Thus, from the beginning, John holds both Jews and Gentiles responsible for the events that unfold in Jerusalem.

Furthermore, an entire detachment of Roman soldiers (approximately six hundred men) arrives to incarcerate Jesus. Despite this massive military force, Jesus initiates and guides the action. Most notably, when Jesus says, "I am he" (Greek, *egō eimi*), the entire mob steps back and falls to the ground (18:5 6). John's readers should realize that Jesus has more than enough power to thwart his opponents. Nevertheless, Jesus yields himself to arrest and his God-ordained fate (18:7–11).

Trials. Annas (18:13), Caiaphas (18:24), and Pilate (18:28) all interrogate Jesus. Interspersed between these trial scenes, Peter is likewise questioned by a woman (18:16). The responses of Jesus and Peter to these interrogations, however, are profoundly different. Whereas Jesus boldly identifies himself and his purposes (18:20–21, 23, 34, 36, 37; 19:11), Peter denies that he even knows Jesus (18:17, 25, 27). Contrary to what would be expected of an ideal disciple, Peter refuses to testify about Jesus; yet Jesus courageously testifies about himself even in the face of death (18:37).

King. Throughout chapters 18–19, John overwhelmingly portrays Jesus as a king. For example, John uses the word *king* (Greek, *basileus*) twelve times in these two chapters. In response to Pilate, Jesus points out that his "kingdom" is not of this world (18:36). Jesus is clothed with a crown of thorns and a purple robe, saluted as a king, and heralded as a king. As a result, Jesus's crucifixion, which has already been described as Jesus's glorification, now takes on the connotations of a coronation. The clearest proclamation of Jesus's kingship in John's Gospel takes place while Jesus is on the cross.

Crucifixion and Passover. John indicates that Jesus's crucifixion takes place on "the day of Preparation for the Passover," the first day of celebrations commemorating the Hebrews' liberation from Egypt (19:14, 31). In essence, in John's Gospel Jesus is crucified on the same day that the Passover lambs are slaughtered, rather than after the Passover meal has been eaten as the Synoptic Gospels have it. Thus, John appears to compare Jesus with the Passover lambs (cf. 1:29, 36). Yet in keeping with John's theological perspective, Jesus surpasses that which precedes him—even the traditional Passover meal.

Belief. John ends his Gospel by focusing on the need to believe in Jesus. For example, after the resurrection, the disciple "whom Jesus loved" believes (20:2, 8). In addition, Thomas, after initially hesitating, believes when Jesus says, "Do not doubt but believe" (20:25–28). Finally, the author indicates that he has narrated Jesus's miraculous signs so that the readers would either come to believe or continue to "believe that Jesus is the Messiah, the Son of God" (20:31). Belief and witness are the proper responses to Jesus and to this Gospel.

The Acts of the Apostles

Authorship, Date, and Genre

Authorship. Debates about the authorship of Acts often revolve around whether the same person wrote both Luke and Acts. At numerous points, the two books share similar thought patterns, vocabulary, writing styles, and rhetorical structures. In addition, both books are dedicated to the same person, Theophilus (Luke 1:3; Acts 1:1). Consequently, most scholars believe the same author wrote both Luke and Acts. At the very least, we can say that the author of Acts wanted readers to think that the author of Luke also wrote Acts.

A second debate about the authorship of Acts pertains to a possible relationship between the author and the apostle Paul. For instance, Acts 9 and 13–28 focus primarily on Paul, demonstrating a significant awareness of Paul's life and work. Also, when narrating events from Paul's ministry, the author at times uses the pronoun *we*, seemingly suggesting that the author is traveling alongside Paul. Evidence against an actual relationship between the author and Paul includes problematic timelines, the absence of any reference to Paul's letters, differing versions of some events (e.g., the **Jerusalem Council** in Acts 15 and Gal. 2), and differences in some theological viewpoints. As a result, scholarly opinions vary. Some argue that the author of Acts knew and traveled with Paul, but perhaps only for limited amounts of time. Many others do not believe the author of Acts had any firsthand knowledge of the apostle.

Date. The time period in which Acts was written is heavily debated and is intimately connected to scholars' conclusions about the identity of the author and the relationship between the books of Luke and Acts. Opinions about the date of Acts range from shortly after Luke was written (ca. 80–85 CE), to approximately ten to fifteen years after Luke was written (ca. 95–100 CE), and even to more than thirty years after Luke was written (ca. 110–30 CE).

Genre. Even less consensus exists among scholars regarding the literary genre of Acts. Acts possesses elements that resemble a variety of ancient literary genres, but it does not entirely fit with any of them. Some interpreters describe Acts as a type of Greek historiography. Here, interpreters describe Acts as a foundation document that narrates the formation and growth of a community (the church) while relying on speeches (e.g., 22:3–21), eyewitness reports (e.g., 15:7–9), and letters (e.g., 23:26–30) as corroborating evidence. Others contend that Acts, like Luke, conforms to the genre of ancient biography. This idea gains more strength if one sees Luke and Acts as a continuous story, with the believers in Acts functioning as the outgrowth of the life and ministry of Jesus. In essence, these interpreters see Acts as the second half of the story of Jesus's life. Some others notice similarities between Acts and ancient Greek novels. Scholars in this camp argue that the author hoped simultaneously to edify and to entertain readers by including suspenseful, miraculous, and humorous episodes, all of which are prominent in Greek novels. Finally, some argue that the author created an entirely new genre when writing Acts.

Introduction (1:1–26)

In the opening chapter, the author conveys a profound sense of continuity with the events that take place beforehand in Luke's Gospel. For example, in 1:1–26 the author (hereafter referred to as Luke) mentions an earlier book, Theophilus (cf. Luke 1:3), Jesus's post-resurrection appearances, the kingdom of God, John the Baptist, the Holy Spirit (cf. Luke 1:35; 3:22; 4:1, 14, 18), Jesus's ascension (cf. Luke 24:50–53), the Mount of Olives, an upper room, a list of apostles, references to female disciples (cf. Luke 8:1–3), comments about disciples "devoting themselves to prayer" (Acts 1:14), and the effort to secure a twelfth apostle as a replacement for Judas. Thus, Acts begins by establishing continuity with the Gospel of Luke. While the transition is not seamless, the opening verses appear to characterize Acts as a continuation of or sequel to Luke.

Acts 1:8 functions as the prophecy that outlines the rest of the book. Jesus tells his disciples that once they are baptized with the Holy Spirit, they will provide a witness to Jesus in Jerusalem, Judea, and Samaria and even to the ends of the earth. The narrative in chapters 2–28 follows that same geographical expansion. Just as Jesus's journey from Galilee to Jerusalem constitutes the major movement in Luke, so also the witness about Jesus moves outward from Jerusalem in Acts.

Witnesses in Jerusalem (2:1–8:3)

Holy Spirit. Jesus and the Holy Spirit are intimately linked from the beginning of Acts (e.g., 1:8; 2:33, 38; 7:55; 9:17; 10:38). Luke goes as far as saying that Jesus instructs his disciples "through the Holy Spirit" prior to his ascension (1:2) and that "the Spirit of Jesus" guides Paul and Timothy well after (16:7). Not surprisingly, some have suggested that the Holy Spirit is the main character in Acts. It is through the Spirit that Jesus's work on earth continues after his ascension. In particular, the Holy Spirit empowers Jesus's disciples to serve as witnesses to Jesus's resurrection and to produce words and deeds that are similar to those of Jesus.

Pentecost. During the festival of Pentecost, the Holy Spirit descends on Jesus's followers (2:1–13). Luke says that the disciples are filled with the Spirit and begin to speak in other languages, and that "devout Jews from every nation under heaven" (2:5) hear the speech in their native languages. Notice, however, that the Spirit's arrival is marked not only by miraculous signs that point to a revelation of God but by triumph over potential hindrances to a worldwide witness. In essence, by miraculously overcoming the language barrier, the witness about Jesus and the plot of Acts are free to advance.

At numerous points, the collective experience of the Christians in Acts mirrors the experience of Jesus in Luke. For example, just as the Spirit descends on, fills, and guides Jesus (Luke 3:21–22; 4:1, 14; Acts 10:38), so the Spirit descends on, baptizes, fills, and guides the believers in Acts (1:5; 2:3–4; cf. 7:55; 8:29; 9:31; 10:19; 11:12; 13:2; 16:6). Also, just as we encounter summary statements about Jesus's growth in Luke (Luke 2:39–40, 52), so also we encounter summary statements in Acts that chronicle the growth and maturation of the community of believers (e.g., 2:41–47).

Peter. On an individual level, Peter's words and deeds in Acts 1–12 greatly resemble those of Jesus. Much like Jesus and the prophets, Peter authoritatively interprets Scripture and narrates God's redemptive work throughout time (2:14–40; 3:12–26; 4:8–12; 5:29–32; 10:34–43). In addition, he heals people who are sick and lame "in the name of Jesus" (3:1–10, 16; 4:7–10, 18, 30; 9:32–35; cf. 5:15–16), raises a woman from the dead (9:36–43), pronounces God's judgment on those interested in personal gain (5:1–11; 8:20–23), and is arrested and tried by the religious and political authorities (4:1–22; 5:17–28; 12:1–19). In essence, Peter provides a faithful extension of the prophetic ministry of Jesus in Acts because of the empowering work of the Holy Spirit among the believers (4:8).

Internal and external threats. Luke draws attention to the internal and external challenges that threaten the community of believers. For example, in 5:1–11 Ananias and Sapphira attempt to deceive their fellow believers. Similarly, in 6:1–7 rapid growth and cultural differences threaten to cripple the expansion and unity of the believers in Jerusalem. On the other hand, Stephen's arrest and trial serve as a prime example of persecution by those outside the Christian community. The Jewish religious leaders accuse Stephen of committing blasphemy and opposing the temple (6:8–15), much as they accused Jesus. They go on to stone Stephen, who responds as an innocent martyr in much the same way that Jesus did in Luke. Stephen asks Jesus not to hold this sin against his attackers, and he asks Jesus to receive his spirit (7:58–60; cf. Luke 23:34, 46).

Despite challenges, the growth of the believing community remains steady. In fact, Luke routinely redirects his readers' attention away from specific hardships and toward the overarching work of God throughout history (often called "salvation history"). In Acts 7, for example, Luke accomplishes this goal primarily by means of Stephen's lengthy speech. Here, Stephen provides a macro-level view by tracing God's redemptive work throughout the times of Abraham, Moses, David, and Jesus.

Similarly, Luke shifts his readers' focus away from specific congregational crises and conflicts to salvation history by means of summary statements interspersed throughout the narrative (e.g., 5:12–16; 6:7; cf. 1:12–14; 2:41–46). As a result, the reader should realize that "the word of God" (4:31; 6:7; cf. 8:14; 12:24) continues to spread and to triumph despite occasional problems. In essence, human deception and internal quarrels do not derail the work of the Holy Spirit or the expansion of the witness about Jesus.

Despite Stephen's tragic death (Acts 6–7), the reader quickly realizes that persecution actually aids the growth of the believing community. When persecution scatters the believers beyond Jerusalem (8:1), it simultaneously scatters "the word" about Jesus to new regions (8:4; 11:19). Consequently, from a literary and theological perspective, the violence of the opponents unintentionally furthers the plan of God and the plot of Acts as first outlined in 1:8. The witness of the believers moves from Jerusalem into Judea, Samaria, and beyond (8:1, 5, 14, 25; 9:31, 42; 11:19).

Witnesses in Judea and Samaria (8:4–11:18)

Saul's conversion and call. In Acts 9:1–31, Luke describes the conversion of Saul, a rabid persecutor of "the Way" who becomes a devout adherent of it. Saul (later known as Paul) does not transition from being irreligious to religious. Rather, he is portrayed as a devout Jew who experiences a theophany (or vision of God). What startles him, however, is that the one he addresses as "Lord" turns out to be the exalted Jesus, and those he persecutes turn out to be intimately linked with "the Lord Jesus." Thus, Saul's conversion pertains to his stance toward Jesus and Jesus's disciples. Moreover, by narrating this event three times in Acts (9:1–31; 22:4–16; 26:9–18), Luke suggests that Saul's conversion is of paramount importance.

In the midst of Saul's conversion, Luke embeds and accentuates Saul's divine commission in 9:15–16 (22:14–16; 26:16–18). Here, Saul is instructed by God to testify about Jesus "before Gentiles and kings and before the people of Israel." Luke's repetitious attention to this call reminds his readers that God is the one who ordains and initiates the Gentile mission—not Peter, Saul, or any other human.

Cornelius's conversion. Luke likewise narrates Cornelius's conversion three times (10:1–48; 11:1–18; 15:7–9), thereby highlighting its importance and creating a natural comparison with Saul's conversion. Cornelius is also a pious person who responds in a dramatic way to the witness about Jesus. In this instance, however, the one converted is not a Jewish opponent but a pagan soldier. This first public conversion of a Gentile functions as the main pivot point in Acts. Afterward, the book largely, though not exclusively, focuses on the growth of Christianity among the Gentiles. Thus, the universal aspect of the witness about Jesus as foreshadowed in 1:8 finds fruition in Acts 10–28.

Peter's transformation. In Acts 10, Peter also experiences a dramatic transition. He sees a vision and hears a heavenly voice command him three times to eat unclean animals (cf. Lev. 11); but each time Peter refuses, thereby displaying his devotion to God and his faithfulness to Torah. Eventually, however, Peter realizes that the unclean animals in his vision represent "unclean" people. He concludes that "God shows no partiality but in every nation anyone who fears him and does what is right is acceptable to him" (10:34–35).

Shortly thereafter, the Holy Spirit falls on those in Cornelius's household (10:44–48). Some have referred to this event as "the Gentile Pentecost," drawing a comparison with the Spirit's arrival among the Jewish believers in Acts 2. Thus, Luke demonstrates once again that the Holy Spirit, as God's agent, is the one propelling the action forward. Similar to his role in Acts 2, Peter functions primarily as a witness to and as an interpreter of these dramatic events.

Witnesses to the Rest of the World (11:19–19:20)

When persecution spreads the witness about Jesus to Antioch in Syria, both Jews and Gentiles respond positively to the testimony about Jesus (11:19–21). More than simply the message about Jesus spreads outward, however; the geographical center of influence for the Christian movement also spreads outward. Clearly, Christians in Jerusalem remain highly influential; but with the expansion of Christianity into Gentile territories, multiple "centers" of early Christianity develop—Antioch being one of them.

Paul's first missionary journey. The Holy Spirit again guides the action by instructing the congregation at Antioch to send out Barnabas and Paul to spread the word about Jesus farther into Gentile territory (13:1–4). This send-off initiates what interpreters traditionally describe as Paul's "first missionary journey." Barnabas and Paul depart from Antioch, travel to Cyprus and Asia Minor, and then return to Antioch (13:1–14:28). It would be a mistake, however, to think that Paul follows a well-planned travel itinerary. Rather, forces beyond Paul's control—namely, the Spirit and persecution—propel his movements. In the meantime, Paul provides a witness.

Similar to Peter's, Paul's words and deeds in Acts also greatly resemble the words and deeds of Jesus. Paul heals the sick and lame (14:8–10; 19:11–12; 28:7–10), casts out demons in "the name of Jesus" (16:16–18; 19:12–13), raises the dead (20:7–12), is arrested and tried by the authorities (16:19–24;

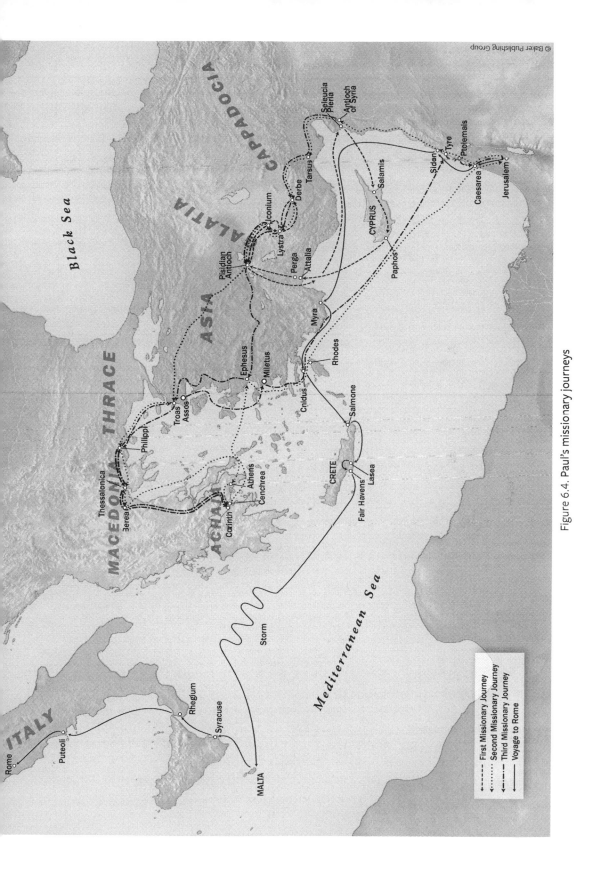

Figure 6.4. Paul's missionary journeys

18:12–13; 21:27–36; 22:24–28; 24:1–21; 25:6–12; 26:1–23), and is portrayed as being dutiful in regard to Roman law (16:35–40; 18:14–17; 23:29; 25:13–22, 25–27; 26:30–32; 28:17–22). In other words, Paul's ministry, empowered by the Holy Spirit, is another faithful extension of Jesus's ministry.

Moreover, Paul provides the pivotal speeches in the latter half of Acts. While speaking to Jews, Paul primarily declares that Jesus represents the climactic moment in God's redemptive work throughout time (13:16–41). In these Jewish settings, Paul cites events from Israel's history, the Jewish Scriptures, and Jesus's ministry as evidence to support his claims. Yet when speaking to Gentiles, Paul primarily proclaims that God is the creator and sustainer of the world (14:15–17; 17:22–31). In these Gentile contexts, Paul, as Luke portrays him, resembles a Greek philosopher and cites Greek religious practices (17:22–23) and Greek poets (17:28) as sources of authority to support his teachings about the man who was resurrected. In essence, Paul adapts his speeches to his context; his theological and rhetorical argument shifts with his audience.

As Paul begins his travels, a repetitive pattern develops. When he arrives in a new location, Paul proclaims the resurrection of Jesus first among the Jewish residents (13:5, 14–15; 14:1; 17:1–3, 10, 17; 18:4–5, 8, 19; 19:8; 28:17–23). Some respond and some do not (13:42–45; 17:1–9, 11–13; 19:9; 28:24). When rejection intensifies, however, Paul turns to the Gentiles of that region (13:46–47; 17:17; 18:6–7; 19:9; 28:28), many of whom believe (13:48–49; 17:32–34; 18:8). Yet the growth of the believing community eventually angers the Jewish or Gentile leaders of each region, who in turn persecute Paul and his coworkers (13:50–52; 14:2; 17:13) and force them to move on to the next city (14:2–7, 19–20; 17:14–15).

Jerusalem Council. In Acts 15, a new debate arises among the Jewish Christians gathered in Jerusalem. Rather than debate *whether* Gentiles can become followers of "the Way," they now debate *how* Gentiles are to receive God's salvation. Some, like the believing Pharisees, contend that the Gentiles must participate fully in Jewish religious practices like circumcision, food laws, and the Mosaic law in order to become followers of Jesus (15:1, 5).

In the end, however, through testimonies, the guidance of the Spirit, and the Scriptures, the assembly of Christians in Jerusalem concludes that the Gentiles are not required to keep the Jewish ritual laws (15:6–21). Rather, Jews and Gentiles are "saved through the grace of the Lord Jesus" (15:11). Consequently, from this point forward in Acts, Gentile converts are asked only to abstain from things associated with idols, sexual immorality, strangled food, and blood (15:19–21, 28–29; 21:25). Interpreters debate whether these instructions derive from the core ideals of the Jewish law that should apply to all humans or whether they enable Jewish Christians to interact fully with their new Gentile counterparts. Regardless, even in the midst of freeing the Gentile mission from the constraints of Jewish rituals and religious practices, the Hebrew Scriptures remain authoritative for interpreting God's will and guiding God's people.

Paul's second missionary journey. In 15:36–18:21, Paul, Silas, and Timothy set out from Antioch in Syria to visit and to strengthen the Christians in the regions where Paul has previously journeyed. Once again, though, the Holy Spirit guides them to travel to new areas and spread Christianity even farther into traditionally Gentile territories. In particular, on this second trip, the Holy Spirit guides Paul to spread the good news about Jesus in Macedonia, the Aegean peninsula, including cities like Athens (16:6–10; 17:15–16) and Corinth (18:1–11), as well as Ephesus (18:19), before returning to Antioch.

Notably, in Acts 16:12–16 we see a continued emphasis on the role of female disciples in Luke's writings. For example, when Lydia, a "dealer in purple cloth" in Philippi, hears the gospel, she and her household convert. Then, as the head of her household, Lydia extends hospitality to Paul, Silas, and Timothy. Thus, Luke portrays Lydia as both a cultural and spiritual leader (16:40). Luke also mentions other "leading women" (17:4; cf. 17:12, 34). Most notably, Priscilla serves as one of Paul's coworkers and trains other disciples, including Apollos (18:2–3, 18, 24–26). Finally, Luke mentions that Philip's four daughters all have "the gift of prophecy" (21:9).

Paul's Final Journeys (19:21–28:31)

Paul's third missionary journey. In 18:23 Paul departs again from Antioch for a third journey. While on this trip (18:23–19:19), Paul initially travels to Ephesus, where once again the Holy Spirit falls on a group of people. Yet Paul's third trip does not end in Antioch, as was the case with his previous

---

THE "WE" PASSAGES

Whereas the author primarily narrates Acts using a third-person narrator's perspective, in four sections of Acts the author employs the first-person plural pronoun (i.e., *we*) when narrating Paul's missionary travels (16:10–17; 20:5–15; 21:1–8; 27:1–28:16). Explanations for the author's use of *we* vary widely. For example, the use of *we* may derive from the author's comments about his own firsthand experiences, the author's use of an earlier source document written by someone else who had firsthand experiences, or the author's use of a literary device of the day that sought to enliven the narrative.

trips. Instead, much like Jesus, who "set his face to go to Jerusalem" (Luke 9:51), Paul now resolves "in the Spirit to go through Macedonia and Achaia, and then to go on to Jerusalem" (19:21).

Paul's decision to go to Jerusalem introduces an ominous tone into the narrative. For example, when speaking to the Ephesian elders (20:18–35), Paul anticipates that imprisonment and persecution await him in Jerusalem. Similarly, the Christians in Tyre warn Paul not to go to Jerusalem (21:4), and Agabus in Caesarea prophesies that Paul will be bound and arrested (21:10–11). Yet, echoing Jesus's prayer in Gethsemane in Luke 22:41–42, Paul merely says, "The Lord's will be done" (21:12–14).

Upon arriving in Jerusalem, Paul initially receives a warm welcome (21:17–20). As was the case with Jesus, the turning point comes when Paul enters the temple. The Jews in the temple seize, beat, accuse, and attempt to kill him (21:27–32). In addition, both the Roman and Jewish authorities interrogate and incarcerate him (22:24–23:10). A shift in the narrative occurs when the Lord speaks to Paul. Rather than being put to death in Jerusalem, the Lord informs Paul that he "must bear witness also in Rome" (23:11).

Paul's journey to Rome. Shortly thereafter, a Roman commander sends Paul to Caesarea, and thus the first stage of Paul's journey to Rome begins (23:23–33). After two years in Caesarea, Paul requests a hearing before the Roman emperor (25:6–12). Subsequently, even though both Agrippa and Festus declare Paul innocent under Roman law (25:25–27; 26:30–32), Paul's previous request mandates that he must present his defense before the emperor. Finally, after an arduous journey, Paul arrives in Rome as a prisoner (28:14). Yet even with Paul under house arrest, Acts concludes with Paul once again providing a witness about Jesus to Jews and Gentiles alike.

Theological Reflection: Unity and Diversity

For those who are new to the scholarly study of the Gospels and Acts, observations about the diverse perspectives and viewpoints among the canonical accounts of Jesus's life can be unsettling. In particular, those who have previously held a monolithic view of the Bible often struggle when they realize that the Gospel writers provide distinct details and articulate varied viewpoints about Jesus. Most early Christians, however, did not possess a monolithic view of the Scriptures and were therefore able to acknowledge and perhaps celebrate both the unifying elements and the diverse perspectives among the Gospels.

Four Witnesses, One Gospel

In the mid- to late second century CE, Irenaeus, the bishop of Lyons, addressed the topic of the four Gospels in *Against Heresies* 3.11.8–9. There he criticizes those who want more than or fewer than the four canonical Gospels found in the New Testament.

Unity. On the one hand, Irenaeus sees an overarching unity among the four canonical Gospels. He speaks of the one *Gospel*, which has four parts to it. He describes the four canonical texts as contributors to the singular good news about Jesus. Moreover, he claims that the four Gospels are all bound together by only one Spirit and that the four Gospels function as four pillars for the church. Importantly, he knows of other noncanonical gospels, but he does not believe that they participate in the one *Gospel* handed down by the apostles.

Diversity. On the other hand, Irenaeus celebrates the diversity of the four canonical Gospels. Rather than seeing it as a problem, Irenaeus believes the fourfold diversity is God-ordained. He argues both on the basis of ancient cosmological assumptions (e.g., the four corners of the world and the four winds that blow) and on the basis of scriptural logic (e.g., the four ancient covenants between God and humans) to claim that it is only right for the church to have four canonical Gospels about Jesus.

Furthermore, Irenaeus cites biblical visions that feature the images of a human face, a lion, an ox, and an eagle. For example, in Ezekiel 1:10 the creatures that guard the throne of God have four faces, one resembling each of the four images just mentioned. In Revelation 4:6–7 four different creatures, each having a face resembling one of the four images just mentioned, worship around God's throne. Irenaeus and many other Christians, as evidenced by centuries of Christian artwork and architecture, associated the unique theological viewpoints found in the four canonical Gospels with the four images found in Ezekiel and Revelation. Most often, Christians associated Matthew with the human face, Mark with the lion, Luke with the ox, and John with the eagle. In essence, many early Christians celebrated the diversity they encountered among the Gospels. At the very least, they concluded that the diversity in the Gospels matches the diversity of those worshiping and serving God. Also, some early Christians apparently thought of the four Gospels as a prophetic fulfillment of scriptural texts (namely, Ezekiel and Revelation).

Today, many scholars employ the terminology of "portraits of Jesus" when describing the four Gospels. Here, scholars acknowledge the distinct theological and literary elements in the various Gospels much as one would discuss four different portraits of the same person perhaps by different artists. Rather than conflating the four portraits into one harmonized picture as some of Irenaeus's "heretical" opponents desired to do, readers of the Gospels can learn to appreciate the theological richness and literary mastery of each of the four witnesses about Jesus.

Christology

Precisely because the Gospels and Acts are theologically diverse, their distinct portraits of Jesus can enrich our contemporary theological discussions. For example, notice the primary depictions of Jesus in the various Gospels. Mark sketches Jesus as the miracle-working Son of God and the long-expected Jewish Messiah. Yet Jesus is misunderstood and abandoned by everyone as he teaches that the true calling of the Messiah is to suffer and die. Jesus fulfills the role of the Suffering Servant about whom Isaiah wrote. In the meantime, Jesus's experiences are dark, and his sense of abandonment is profound.

Matthew focuses heavily on Jesus's Jewish heritage. Jesus can be understood best by comparing him with Abraham, Moses, and David. For example, like Moses, Jesus authoritatively proclaims God's word to the people during the Sermon on the Mount. Moreover, as the reader quickly discovers when the magi visit, Jesus is the great king who will surpass even what David accomplished. From Jesus's birth to his death, Matthew wants his readers to know that Jesus fulfills Scripture. Consequently, the Old Testament is the lens through which Jesus must be interpreted.

Luke shows his readers that Jesus is a humble and merciful Savior, even from birth. Jesus ushers in God's great reversal on behalf of God's servants. Like the prophets of old and yet far greater, he proclaims good news to the poor, the downtrodden, and the disenfranchised. Whereas Jesus is innocent of all wrongdoing, he nevertheless chooses to die as a martyr, thereby enabling all people to participate in the long history of God's salvation. On the other hand, in Acts, after Jesus's resurrection and ascension, God proclaims Jesus as Lord and Messiah (2:36). Moreover, the exalted Jesus continues to guide and care for his disciples from his position at the right hand of God (7:55) by means of the Holy Spirit.

Finally, John delves into the theological richness of Jesus's preexistence, incarnation, and ascension. From the outset, John reveals Jesus's exalted identity, and in the process Jesus reveals God to the readers. After describing Jesus's miraculous signs with the purpose of fostering belief in Jesus, John focuses on Jesus's death as the coronation of the all-powerful king. Jesus victoriously overcomes both Satan and the world, and all those who receive the Spirit that Jesus breathes on them will likewise experience the same kind of victory and eternal life beginning in the present and extending into the future.

Discipleship

The various authors of the Gospels and Acts also sketch different portraits of what it means to be an ideal disciple. Mark repeatedly clarifies that Jesus's disciples must be willing to suffer just as Jesus himself suffered. Until one grasps that idea, one misunderstands what it means to follow Jesus. Matthew accentuates Jesus's teachings, which show that ethical purity is as important as ritual purity. Jesus requires his disciples to live with a righteousness that far surpasses that of the Pharisees. Luke highlights many unnamed disciples in addition to the twelve apostles, thereby clarifying that Jesus's commission pertains to all who follow him. Moreover, prayer and the absence of greed must mark the life of a faithful disciple. In Acts, faithful believers provide a bold and courageous witness to Jesus's resurrection while the Holy Spirit empowers them to live and speak like Jesus. Also like Jesus, disciples must be willing to suffer for the gospel despite being innocent of wrongdoing. Finally, John repeatedly shows that those who believe in Jesus will provide a bold and courageous witness. Even in the face of persecution, as the man born blind experiences in John 9, Jesus's disciples must testify concerning the things they know to be true about Jesus. Moreover, love for one another must characterize all of Jesus's disciples.

Conclusion

If contemporary readers celebrate both the unity and the diversity of the four canonical Gospels and Acts as ancient Christians did, they may well discover a deeper sense of theological richness within each individual Gospel and within the biblical canon as a whole. Rather than posing either-or questions and demanding a singular answer when differences are encountered, readers should learn to appreciate a multidimensional picture of Jesus. Likewise, if readers can celebrate the unity and the diversity in the Gospels and Acts, they will be better equipped with a broader understanding of what Jesus required from his followers in the past, and perhaps requires today as well.

SUGGESTED READING

Bond, Helen. *The Historical Jesus: A Guide for the Perplexed*. London: T&T Clark, 2012.

Burridge, Richard A. *Four Gospels, One Jesus? A Symbolic Reading*. 2nd ed. Grand Rapids: Eerdmans, 2005.

Carroll, John T. *Jesus and the Gospels: An Introduction*. Louisville: Westminster John Knox, 2016.

Freyne, Seán. "The Galilean World of Jesus." In *The Early Christian World*, edited by Phillip F. Esler, 1:113–35. New York: Routledge, 2000.

Goodacre, Mark. *The Synoptic Problem: A Way through the Maze*. New York: T&T Clark, 2001.

Matthews, Shelly. *The Acts of the Apostles: An Introduction and Study Guide*. New York: Bloomsbury T&T Clark, 2017.

Powell, Mark Allan. *Fortress Introduction to the Gospels*. 2nd ed. Minneapolis: Fortress, 2019.

Sanders, E. P. "Jesus in Historical Context." *Theology Today* 50 (1993): 429–48.

7

Paul and the
Pauline Tradition

The apostle Paul is among the most influential figures in the history of Christianity. Up to a third of the New Testament has been attributed to Paul. He is often described as the first great Christian missionary among the Gentiles, and he made significant contributions to Christian theology, especially in regard to the soteriological (or salvific) significance of Jesus.

In this chapter we will first consider some historical questions that pertain to Paul's life, ministry, and letters. Second, we will discuss both the undisputed and disputed letters of Paul. Finally, we will consider some aspects of Paul's theology that appear throughout his writings.

Paul's Life, Ministry, and Letters

Paul's Life and Ministry

Sources. When piecing together Paul's biography, scholars prefer to rely on Paul's own writings (primary sources) for information. Yet of the thirteen letters attributed to Paul, scholars debate whether someone other than Paul wrote six of the thirteen (see "The Pauline Tradition" below). As a result, scholars generally look to Paul's seven "undisputed letters" as primary sources for biographical information about Paul. Those letters are Romans, 1–2 Corinthians, Galatians, Philippians, 1 Thessalonians, and Philemon.

Unfortunately, though, Paul tells us very little about his origins, his formative years, or his later travels in those letters.

Consequently, we rely significantly on secondary sources written by someone other than Paul to piece together Paul's biography. The Acts of the Apostles has a great deal to say about Paul. Yet Acts and Paul's letters do not always agree on specific details, and Acts was almost certainly written at least two decades after Paul's death, and possibly more. The six letters attributed to Paul that may have been written by someone else (or "the disputed letters")—Ephesians, Colossians, 2 Thessalonians, 1–2 Timothy, and Titus—are routinely consulted as secondary sources, but they add little biographical information about Paul. Finally, a variety of noncanonical texts discuss Paul at length (e.g., *The Acts of Paul*), but those texts were likely written long after Paul died and are therefore far less likely to have reliable information about Paul's life and ministry.

Origins. Paul was likely born between 5 and 10 CE to a Jewish family in Tarsus, a city in the Roman province of Cilicia in Asia Minor (Rom. 11:1; Phil. 3:5; Acts 9:11; 21:39; 22:3). Therefore, Paul (who is initially referred to in Acts by his Jewish name, Saul) may well have been a Roman citizen from birth as Luke, the author of Acts, contends (e.g., Acts 16:37–38; 22:25–29; 23:27; 25:8–12, 21). In addition, Paul and his family were practicing Jews. For example, Paul was circumcised on the eighth day of his life (Phil. 3:5; Acts 21:39; cf. Gen. 17:12).

Education and training. At some point, Paul relocated from Tarsus to Jerusalem, where Luke says Paul studied with Rabbi Gamaliel (Acts 22:3; 26:4). Moreover, both Paul and Acts indicate that Paul became a devout Pharisee and was well acquainted with Jewish theology (Gal. 1:13–14; Phil. 3:4–6; Acts 23:6–10). Paul's letters (e.g., 2 Cor. 11:6), and perhaps even his speeches in Acts, demonstrate that Paul also knew basic rhetorical techniques, which were standard components of a Greco-Roman education. In addition, Paul routinely drew on Hellenistic imagery in his letters; for example, notice his use of boxing and racing metaphors (1 Cor. 9:24–27; Phil. 3:12–15). Furthermore, Paul wrote in Greek and routinely quoted from the Septuagint, the Greek translation of the Hebrew Scriptures. In sum, whereas Acts highlights Paul's early Jewish training and his membership among the Pharisees, Paul's letters suggest that Paul was also heavily shaped by his native Hellenistic culture. Consequently, it is best to think of Paul as a Hellenistic Jew who was heavily shaped by both Greco-Roman and Judean cultures.

Conversion and call. Both Paul and Acts indicate that while traveling to Damascus to persecute Christians in that region, Paul experienced a dramatic vision of Jesus (1 Cor. 15:8–11; Gal. 1:11–23; Acts 9:1–8; 22:6–11; 26:12–20). Approximations regarding the date of this event generally fall between 32 and

35 CE. Even though the accounts vary as to what those traveling with Paul saw or heard, they agree that the resurrected Jesus spoke directly to Paul during the vision (see also Rom. 1:5; 1 Cor. 9:1). Thereafter, Paul championed the message that Jesus was the Jewish Messiah. Many have since referred to this experience as Paul's "conversion." Yet it is important to note that Paul was a practicing Jew who desired to serve God both before and after his Damascus road experience. His conversion pertained to his stance toward Jesus and Jesus's followers.

When recounting the Damascus road vision, however, both Paul and Acts primarily emphasize Paul's divine calling or commission to serve as an apostle to the Gentiles (Gal. 2:7–8). Because Paul was sanctioned directly by Jesus, he therefore argued that he was an apostle, one commissioned by Jesus. In keeping with this divine mandate, Paul consistently traveled to Hellenistic regions, started Christian congregations, and then provided guidance to those congregations. Paul was intent on speaking about Jesus to both Hellenistic Jews and pagan Gentiles. Paul, like many early Christians, believed that God welcomed both groups into a covenant relationship. Yet Paul was also quite progressive in his stance that Gentiles who become Christians should not be required to practice the ritual aspects of the Mosaic law.

IMPORTANT FIRST-CENTURY-BCE AND FIRST-CENTURY-CE DATES

63 BCE	The Romans gain control of Judea.
44 BCE	Julius Caesar is assassinated.
37–4 BCE	Herod the Great serves as king of Judea.
27 BCE	Octavian (or Augustus) becomes the first Roman emperor.
ca. 7–4 BCE	Jesus is born prior to the death of Herod the Great.
ca. 5–10 CE	Saul (later known as Paul) is born.
26–36 CE	Pontius Pilate serves as governor of Judea.
ca. 30 CE	Pontius Pilate orders Jesus's crucifixion.
ca. 32–35 CE	Saul (or Paul) has a vision of Jesus while traveling to Damascus.
ca. 46–49 CE	Christian leaders gather in Jerusalem to discuss Gentile conversion.
49 CE	Emperor Claudius expels all Jews from Rome.
50–52 CE	Paul spreads Christianity in Corinth.
50s–60s CE	Paul writes numerous letters to Christian congregations.
64 CE	Nero persecutes Christians in Rome (Peter and Paul are possibly martyred).
ca. 65–100 CE	The Gospels are written.
66–73 CE	The Jewish War with Rome erupts.
70 CE	The Romans sack Jerusalem and destroy the temple.

Jerusalem and the council. Paul's relationship with the Christians in Jerusalem is a topic of debate within the New Testament. While Acts portrays Paul as being continuously connected to the Christians in Jerusalem, Paul proclaims his theological independence from them. For example, in Acts, Paul makes five trips to Jerusalem after his vision of Jesus. Yet in his letters Paul refers to only three. Moreover, Paul contends that after his Damascus road experience he spent time in Arabia, not Jerusalem as Acts has it (Gal. 1:17; Acts 9:26–30). Then, Paul indicates that after three years he made a brief, private visit to Jerusalem to see Peter and James (Gal. 1:18–20). Next, Paul boasts that he waited fourteen years after his conversion before traveling to Jerusalem for his first public visit. Even then, he traveled to Jerusalem in order to provide a report on his missionary successes, not for theological tutoring (Gal. 2:1–10; Acts 15:1–29). Finally, Paul speaks of his plan to visit the church in Jerusalem so that he can deliver financial resources, which the Gentile congregations provided (Rom. 15:25–28; 1 Cor. 16:1–4).

It was during the second trip to Jerusalem that Paul and the leaders of the Jerusalem congregation took up the debate of whether Gentile converts needed to practice the ritualistic customs prescribed in the Torah. Yet whereas Acts describes a public debate and a widely circulated verdict, Paul describes a private meeting and possibly a private verdict. In addition, whereas Luke mentions four stipulations that likely coincide with Leviticus 18–20, Paul reports that the majority of those present agreed that Gentile converts did not need to practice the Torah rituals, affirmed his message and ministry, and only asked the Gentile converts "to remember the poor." Most scholars think this "Jerusalem Council" took place around 46–49 CE.

Travels. Both Paul and Acts agree that Paul spent time in Damascus and Syria (e.g., Antioch of Syria) in the years shortly after his Damascus road vision (Gal. 1:17–24). Then, according to Acts 13–14, when Paul initially set out to fulfill his calling, he first traveled to Cyprus and Asia Minor before returning to Antioch. (Paul, however, does not refer to those locations in Gal. 1:21.) Next, after the Jerusalem Council, Paul journeyed to Asia Minor and then on to Macedonia (e.g., Philippi and Thessalonica) and the Aegean peninsula (e.g., Athens and Corinth) (see 1 Thess. 2:2; 3:1; Acts 16:12–18:18).

Paul's year-and-a-half stay in Corinth provides us with our most concrete dates for Paul's life. While in Corinth, Paul stood for questioning before Gallio, who served as proconsul for one year in Achaia during 51–52 CE (Acts 18:11–17). So Paul's ministry in Corinth likely occurred between 50 and 52 CE. Acts then indicates that Paul departed from Antioch on another journey in order to visit many of the congregations that he previously founded (18:23–20:38). In the process, Paul spent two and a half years in Ephesus. Therefore, he likely wrote his letters in the 50s and perhaps the early 60s CE. Finally, in Romans 15:23–29

Paul speaks of his future plans to visit Jerusalem, Rome, and Spain in that order. Acts likewise narrates Paul's trip to Jerusalem and Rome, but not Spain.

The collection. In accordance with the outcome of the Jerusalem Council, Paul took up a monetary collection for the poor Christians in Jerusalem while traveling among the Gentile congregations (Rom. 15:25–29; 1 Cor. 16:1–4; 2 Cor. 8–9; Gal. 2:10). Paul evidently envisioned the collection as an opportunity to meet physical needs (2 Cor. 8:14; 9:12) and to strengthen the relationship between Gentile Christians and Jewish Christians (Rom. 15:27). In particular, even though Gentile Christians were not required to practice the ritual elements of the Mosaic law, the collection demonstrated that Gentile Christians maintained the ethical ideals found in the law. Moreover, the collection complied with the mandates of the Jerusalem Council (Gal. 2:10).

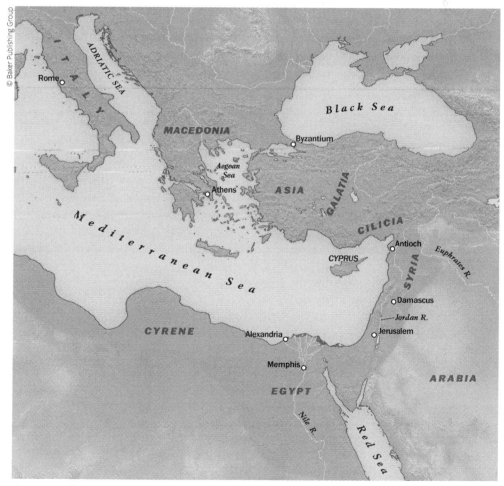

Figure 7.1. The Mediterranean basin

Imprisonment. Both Paul and Acts agree that Paul spent considerable time in prison as a result of his missionary work among the Gentiles and his volatile relationships with his fellow Jews. Moreover, Paul wrote letters while he was in prison. The "prison epistles" include the undisputed letters of Philippians and Philemon and the disputed letters of Ephesians, Colossians, 1–2 Timothy, and Titus. Acts mentions that Paul was imprisoned in Caesarea for two years after his arrest in Jerusalem (Acts 23:23; 24:27). In addition, Acts ends with Paul in house arrest in Rome (28:14, 30–31). Scholars wonder, however, whether there was at least a third imprisonment, possibly in Ephesus, where Paul spent two and a half years. In part, incarceration in a location like Ephesus would better explain Paul's ability to provide timely responses to ongoing matters that are addressed in the prison epistles.

Possible martyrdom. Acts does not narrate Paul's death. Yet writers from the beginning of the second century CE and beyond often speak of Paul's martyrdom in Rome (e.g., 1 Clement 5.5–7; Acts of Paul 11.1–7). We do not, however, have any earlier accounts that definitively corroborate this story, though some have viewed Colossians 1:24 and Ephesians 3:13 as veiled references to Paul's martyrdom by Paul's disciples. If Paul did die in Rome, he may well have been a victim of Nero's persecution in 64 CE.

The Form of Paul's Letters

As is true in any culture, verbal and written communications generally conform to socially recognized patterns. Such patterns of communication are easy to detect in ancient Greek and Roman letters. Not surprisingly, Paul wrote in the accepted literary patterns of his day. As a result, it is helpful to study ancient letter writing as a precursor to studying Paul's letters. In general, ancient Greco-Roman letters consisted of four main parts: the greeting, the prayer or thanksgiving, the body, and the closing.

Greeting. Letter greetings were often brief, and they routinely followed a standard sequence. The author first identified himself or herself. Next, the author identified the intended recipient of the letter. Finally, the author issued some type of introductory salutation to the recipient.

The greetings in Paul's letters follow the same sequence. First, Paul identifies himself and his coauthors (e.g., Timothy, Silvanus, and Titus) if there were any. Next, he identifies those to whom he writes (e.g., a Christian congregation). Finally, he issues an initial salutation to his recipients. Here, he often elongates his self-identification and his salutation. In particular, he often uses his self-identification to reassert his status as an apostle and uses the salutation to introduce the major themes of his letters. In essence, Paul's greetings establish a spiritual or ecclesiastical context for the rest of his comments.

Examples of Paul's greetings include Romans 1:1–7; 1 Corinthians 1:1–3; 2 Corinthians 1:1–2; Galatians 1:1–5; Philippians 1:1–2; 1 Thessalonians 1:1; and Philemon 1–3.

Prayer or thanksgiving. Next, ancient letter writers frequently recounted past prayers or voiced new prayers for their recipients. Most Greco-Roman prayer wishes were addressed to a god whom the author revered. Sometimes authors added or substituted a statement of thanksgiving for something the recipient of the letter previously said or did. On other occasions authors merged the two ideas by thanking the gods for the recipients.

Likewise, Paul routinely includes a statement of thanksgiving for his recipients. Here again, Paul often expands this section with theologically and thematically enriched comments. At times he thanks God for what the recipients have already done. At other times he thanks God for what he believes the recipients will soon do, like adopt the teachings that he provides in the remaining portions of his letter. Examples of Paul's thanksgivings include Romans 1:8–17; 1 Corinthians 1:4–9; 2 Corinthians 1:3–11; Philippians 1:3–11; 1 Thessalonians 1:2–5; and Philemon 4–7.

Body. Ancient authors used the body of the letter to articulate their primary reason for writing. For example, ancient authors routinely provided their recipients with new information or presented a request to their recipients.

Paul seeks to accomplish a variety of objectives in the body of his letters. (1) At times he reestablishes his credentials as an apostle. His apostolic status provides an authoritative foundation for the rest of his comments. (2) At other points, Paul attempts to persuade his recipients to affirm or to accept a theological teaching. (3) He provides pastoral advice, which he hopes will resolve a congregational crisis. (4) He gives moral or ethical directives to his readers. Here, Paul seeks to instruct the recipients about the behavioral fruits that are produced when a person is "in Christ." This *paraenetic* (ethical) material often takes the form of brief moral exhortations or lists of virtues and vices. (5) Paul also informs his recipients of his upcoming travel plans.

Closing. Ancient Greco-Roman letters generally concluded in a predictable manner. At times the author voiced a wish of well-being for the recipients. At other times the author asked the recipients to pass along greetings to others. At the end, the author generally offered a "farewell" statement.

Paul similarly makes great use of the closing section in his letters. His wishes for well-being often take the form of a prayer wish. In addition, Paul routinely greets many in the congregation he is addressing, and his final statements often take on the characteristics of a theologically enriched benediction. Examples of closing statements in Paul's letters include Romans 16:1–21; 1 Corinthians 16:19–24; 2 Corinthians 13:11–13; Galatians 6:16–18; Philippians 4:21–23; 1 Thessalonians 5:23–28; and Philemon 23–25.

The Nature and Collection of Paul's Letters

Occasional. First and foremost, Paul's letters are occasional in nature. Rather than writing a comprehensive overview of early Christian beliefs, Paul wrote to address specific situations. He wrote variously to correct theological misunderstandings and resolve congregational conflicts and counter flawed opinions about his apostolic authority. As a result, Paul provided pastoral guidance to congregations through his letters.

It is important to remember that Paul's letters provide a snapshot of an ongoing conversation between Paul and a particular congregation. With the exception of the church in Rome, Paul founded the congregations to which he wrote. An ongoing relationship between Paul and the congregations thus predated the letters. Consequently, Paul's letters present modern-day interpreters with a significant challenge. Interpreters must strive to discern the context and the content of the ongoing conversation between Paul and the congregations without getting lost in speculative and fanciful theories. Therefore, we look for clues within Paul's letters about the background conversation while cautiously drawing our conclusions.

Collected. Shortly after Paul wrote his letters, Christian congregations began to preserve and to collect them. These actions took place even among those who were not the original recipients of Paul's letters. As a result, Paul's occasional letters soon took on a general importance for all Christians living in the Mediterranean world. Evidence for this development is present even within the New Testament. For example, the author of Colossians (perhaps Paul himself) instructs the Christians at Colossae to exchange letters with the Laodiceans. Similarly, James seems to be aware of Paul's letters to the Romans and Galatians (2:14–26; cf. Rom. 4:1–13; Gal. 3:6–9). Finally, in 2 Peter, the author not only suggests that Paul's letters have been collected to some extent, but, startlingly, the author goes on to refer to Paul's letters as Scripture at a very early date (3:15–17).

Further evidence for the collection of Paul's letters among Christians to whom those letters were not originally addressed can be found in the Greek manuscripts of Paul's letters. For example, some manuscripts of Romans do not have Romans 16:1–24, which includes the names of those in Rome to whom Paul extends greetings. The dominant theory is that Christians reading Romans in worship settings outside Rome may have intentionally removed the verses. With the removal of the names of the Roman Christians, the letter could function as an address to all those who read it. Similarly, some manuscripts of Ephesians do not contain the reference to Ephesus in Ephesians 1:1. Again, many theorize that Christians outside Ephesus removed the name "Ephesus" so that the letter would more readily apply to them.

Additional letters. We do not have all the letters that Paul wrote. The best evidence for this conclusion is found in Paul's correspondence with the Corinthian Christians. In 1 Corinthians 5:9 Paul refers to a previous letter that we do not possess. Also, in 2 Corinthians 7:8 Paul refers to a previous letter that grieved the Corinthians. Since the content in 1 Corinthians does not match Paul's description of this "tearful letter," Paul most likely refers to another letter to the Corinthians that we do not possess. (Some have claimed that 2 Cor. 10–13 is the "tearful letter," because of its harsh tone.) Consequently, Paul sent at least four letters to the Corinthians, even though we possess only two. Along similar lines, we do not have Paul's letter to the Laodiceans to which Colossians 4:16 alludes. Thus, we know Paul wrote letters that did not become part of the New Testament. Perhaps that fact accentuates the importance of the letters that we do possess.

The First Letter of Paul to the Thessalonians

Occasion and Date

Among the extant letters of Paul, 1 Thessalonians is likely the oldest. If so, 1 Thessalonians would be the earliest Christian document in existence. Our ability to piece together the backstory behind Paul's letter to the Thessalonian Christians is limited. Paul first traveled to Thessalonica after leaving Philippi (2:2). Although many Gentiles in Thessalonica responded favorably to Paul's proclamation about Jesus (1:9; 2:14), Paul was forced to leave the place earlier than he desired because of persecution (2:13–17; cf. Acts 17:1–10).

Paul indicates that he wanted to return to Thessalonica but that Satan prevented him from doing so (2:18). As a result, he sent Timothy on his behalf. When Timothy rejoined Paul, most likely in Corinth, he reported that the Thessalonian Christians had experienced continued persecution (1:6; 2:14; 3:3–4) and were grappling with important theological questions as a result of the unexpected death of some of their fellow believers. In response, Paul writes this letter of encouragement and instruction to the Christians in Thessalonica. Because we are able to date Paul's stay in Corinth to approximately 50–52 CE, scholars commonly believe that Paul wrote 1 Thessalonians during that time frame.

Thanksgiving (1:2–10)

After a brief greeting (1:1), Paul begins the thanksgiving in 1:2. It is difficult, however, to discern where the thanksgiving ends and the body of the letter begins. Most commonly, scholars suggest that the thanksgiving runs from 1:2 through either 1:5 or 1:10. In part, this blurring of the lines between the thanksgiving and the body of the letter points to the overarching tone of encouragement that pervades the letter. Notice that Paul expresses his thankfulness for the Thessalonians again in 2:13–16 and 3:6–10.

Paul foreshadows his main ideas early in this letter. He begins the thanksgiving by outlining the identity and work of God, Jesus, and the Thessalonian Christians. For example, Paul contends that God, in contrast to the pagan gods, is the one "true God" (1:9), who has chosen, or elected, these Gentiles to be among God's covenant people (1:4). Jesus, whom God raised from the dead, is the Lord and the source of Christian hope (1:3, 10). When he returns, Jesus will rescue those who have faith in him from judgment and wrath, which are the natural outcomes for those who choose to worship idols rather than the one true God (1:10). In the meantime, Paul praises the Thessalonians for appropriately imitating Jesus and Paul in their actions while simultaneously providing an example for other Greek believers to emulate (1:6–10). In particular, this praiseworthy imitation is characterized by Christian faith, love, and hope (1:3).

Paul and the Thessalonians (2:1–3:13)

The body of the letter has two major sections. First, Paul recounts the positive interaction and good relationship that he has previously had with the Thessalonians. He begins by recalling his initial arrival and proclamation in Thessalonica. Paul points out that a desire to please God motivated him, not selfish gain like many itinerant teachers (2:1–7a). Instead, Paul interacted with the Thessalonians as a caring family member (2:7b–12). Even now, Paul stresses that his separation from the Thessalonian Christians and his inability to return to Thessalonica remain out of his control. His absence, however, does not mean that his affection for the Thessalonians has waned (2:17–20). Instead, his decision to send Timothy to Thessalonica is evidence of his continuous love for them (3:1–5). In addition, now that Timothy has returned from Thessalonica, Paul delights in Timothy's positive report that the Thessalonians' faith and love remain strong (3:5–13; cf. 1:3).

A Life Worthy of God (4:1–5:24)

Holy living. Paul's unselfish motives in the past now function as the trustworthy foundation on which his call for them to "lead a life worthy of God" (2:12) is based. Scholars often refer to this section as the "Great **Paraenesis**" because of its lengthy emphasis on Christian ethics. Here, Paul expounds on his earlier oral and written comments about how these recently converted

Gentile Christians in Thessalonica should live (4:1–2). For example, he begins by exhorting his readers to control their sexual behavior (4:3–5), to excel even more in their love for one another (4:6–10), and to support themselves by working (4:11–12).

Jesus's return. In 4:13–18 Paul elaborates on the nature of Christian hope, which was first introduced in 1:3. Timothy has apparently reported to Paul that the Thessalonians are grieving the recent death of their fellow believers and are fearing that their dead friends will be robbed of the wonderful benefits of Jesus's return (3:6; 4:13). Paul, however, informs the Thessalonians that the believers who have died will be raised up from the dead simultaneously with the Lord's return. Therefore, living Christians have no advantage over Christians who have already died. Both will fully experience Jesus's return and live with Jesus forever (4:15–18).

Vigilant waiting. In 5:1–11 Paul then takes up the question of when the ascended Jesus will descend, thereby reuniting all believers, both the living and the dead, and ushering in God's wrath for those who resist God (1:10; 5:3, 9). While Paul apparently expects Jesus to return during his lifetime (4:17), he instructs the Thessalonians to avoid speculation about the exact timing of the *parousia*. It could happen at any moment. As a result, the Thessalonians should live in a state of readiness while cultivating faith, love, and hope (5:8, 12–24).

In light of 4:13–5:11, scholars frequently point to the imminent eschatology (or the nearness of Jesus's return) that undergirds the entirety of 1 Thessalonians. Notably, in his later letters Paul seldom refers to the nearness of the *parousia*. Many explanations have been offered for Paul's change of tone.

THE *PAROUSIA*

In antiquity, the Greek word *parousia* generally referred to the "presence" or "arrival" of an individual. In Hellenistic contexts people often used the term more narrowly to describe the arrival of a royal official or ruler. In the New Testament, the term frequently refers to Jesus's expected return. For example, Paul refers to Jesus's coming or *parousia* as a source of hope in 1 Thessalonians 2:19; 3:13; 4:15; 5:23 (cf. 1 Cor. 15:23; 2 Thess. 2:1, 8). As a result, given that the Thessalonian church primarily consisted of Gentile converts, and given that emperor worship was prevalent in Thessalonica at the time of Paul's ministry, some have suggested that Paul implicitly contrasts Jesus and the Roman emperors through his use of the term *parousia* in 1 Thessalonians. For example, Paul contrasts proclamations of "peace and security" in 5:3, which were common Roman imperial claims, with the proclamation of Jesus's *parousia*.

Perhaps in his later letters Paul assumed his recipients already knew about the *parousia*; perhaps an emphasis on Jesus's coming was leading to communal problems (e.g., some electing not to work, 2 Thess. 3:6, 11); or perhaps Paul had grown to accept the idea that Jesus would not return as quickly as he had once expected.

The Letter of Paul to the Galatians

Paul's letter to the Galatians has greatly influenced Christian understandings of the significance of Jesus's death, a law-free gospel, and the equal status of Gentile and Jewish Christians. Each of those concepts contributed to the startling growth of Christianity among non-Jewish peoples. Much later, near the onset of the Protestant Reformation, Martin Luther also drew heavily from Galatians when calling for reform within the Roman Catholic Church. Thus, Galatians has had an enormous influence over the direction of Christian theology and praxis throughout the past twenty centuries.

Location, Date, and Occasion

Paul writes this letter to a group of "Galatian" congregations, but the exact location of those churches is unclear. A people identified as Galatians, who were of Celtic descent, had lived in the northern Galatia territory for approximately three centuries at the time that Paul wrote this letter. Yet in 25 BCE, Emperor Augustus also gave the name Galatia to a larger Roman province that extended much farther south into Asia Minor and included cities like Lystra and Derbe. As a result, during Paul's lifetime the term *Galatia* was associated with both the ethnic Galatians in the northern territory and a Roman province that extended much farther south. Paul could easily have been writing to congregations in either territory. Those who advocate for the north-Galatia hypothesis have often outnumbered those who hold the south-Galatia hypothesis, but scholars remain divided.

This debate about location has implications for the dating of Galatians. If the letter addressed the southern territory, Paul likely wrote around 50–51 CE. If it addressed the northern territory, Paul may have written as late as 55–56 CE. The significance of the date of Galatians pertains to its relationship with Paul's Letter to the Romans. In both letters Paul deals with the human predicament, the importance of Jesus's death and resurrection, Abraham's example, baptism, and the relationship between Jewish and Gentile Christians. Yet in Romans, Paul has seemingly refined some of the viewpoints that first appeared in Galatians. For example, Paul speaks more positively about the Mosaic law in Romans. It is easier to explain the developments in Paul's thought if a significant period of time elapsed between the two letters. Ultimately, though, scholarly opinions about the date of Galatians generally range between 50 and 56 CE.

Most scholars, though not all, agree that a group of Jewish Christian missionaries arrived in Galatia after Paul departed and instructed the Galatian Christians to practice the ritual aspects of Judaism (e.g., circumcision) as a by-product of their newly declared allegiance to Jesus, the Jewish Messiah. Scholars have often referred to these missionaries as "Judaizers" or "agitators." The strongest evidence for this hypothesis derives from the letter itself. For example, Galatians contains numerous references to circumcision (2:3–9; 5:2–3; 6:12–13), mealtime concerns (2:11–13), and possibly Jewish holy days and festivals (4:10). Additionally, Paul's scriptural quotations and his references to Abraham have led many to conclude that the missionaries supported their teachings by quoting the Jewish Scriptures and pointing to Abraham as the quintessential pagan convert, whom God instructed to be circumcised (3:6–18; 4:22). Also, some have pointed to Paul's comments about Jerusalem (1:17–18; 2:1–10; 4:25–26) and have suggested that the missionaries possibly originated from Jerusalem, may have attended the Jerusalem Council (e.g., 2:4–5), and may have been commissioned by the leaders of the Jerusalem congregation.

The Greeting (1:1–5)

Paul's defensive tone is apparent as he identifies himself in the greeting of the letter (1:1–2). Here, Paul definitively asserts his status as an apostle and establishes a contrast between human authorities and God. Believing that he stands with God and Jesus, Paul implies that his opponents stand with human authorities against God. Also, when Paul issues his salutation, he foreshadows two ideas about the work of Jesus, which he treats later in the letter: Jesus "gave himself for our sins," and Jesus's actions "set us free" (1:4).

The Rebuke (1:6–10)

In a move that would have startled his readers, Paul chooses not to include a thanksgiving in this letter. If the recipients failed to detect Paul's angry tone in the greeting, they almost certainly recognized Paul's ire in 1:6–10. Paul not only forgoes the thanksgiving but replaces it with condemnation and a curse. He accuses the Galatians of exchanging the true gospel for a perverted message about Jesus (1:6–7), and he pronounces a curse on anyone who teaches the false message that the Galatians have currently adopted (1:8–9).

Defense of Paul's Apostleship (1:11–2:14)

Moving into the body of his letter (1:11–6:10), Paul first seeks to reestablish the authority of his apostleship. He begins by reminding the Galatians of Jesus's revelation to him. In the process, Paul recalls his former life as a zealous Pharisee who opposed the Christian movement. Yet God, through Jesus, intervened and called Paul to proclaim to the Gentiles the grace that was manifest through Jesus (1:12–17). Importantly, this calling came directly from Jesus, not from human authorities and especially not from those in Jerusalem (1:1–2, 11–12, 17–20). Instead, except for a brief visit with Peter and James (1:18–19), Paul began fulfilling his God-given calling without any assistance from the authorities in Jerusalem (1:21–24).

At the same time, Paul recalls that fourteen years after Jesus first appeared to him, he traveled to Jerusalem to describe his ministry among the Gentiles to the Christian leaders in Jerusalem (2:1–2). At that time, the Jerusalem leaders affirmed Paul's work (2:3–10). Paul also recounts a later instance when Peter visited the Gentile believers in Antioch. When Peter began making distinctions between Jewish and Gentile Christians based on Old Testament holiness concerns, Paul rebuked Peter for his hypocrisy (2:11–14).

Defense of Paul's Gospel (2:15–4:31)

The gospel according to Paul. As a counterexample to Peter's waffling hypocrisy in Antioch, Paul unwaveringly and succinctly articulates what he considers to be the authentic gospel, the one he received directly from Jesus. Here, Paul sets up a second significant contrast. He argues that a great divide exists between the power of the Old Testament law and the power of Jesus (2:15–16). Paul argues that a person is "justified" (put into a proper covenant relationship with God) only because of Jesus's death. Justification cannot happen through the law, for the law is powerless to perform such an action. Human sinfulness (or "the flesh") overrides the benefits of the law. Instead, true justification happens only through "the faith of Jesus Christ."

Translators generally render the phrase "the faith of Jesus Christ" (2:16) in one of two ways, both of which represent valid translations of the Greek. The phrase could refer to human "faith in Jesus Christ," as Martin Luther translated it, or it could refer to "Jesus Christ's faithfulness." Scholars are increasingly opting for the latter possibility. Regardless, the fundamental contrast remains the same. Christ enables justification (or being made righteous) with God in a way that the law cannot (2:21).

Consequently, Paul also locates human enablement for proper Christian relationships and conduct in Christ as opposed to the law (2:19–20). In essence,

Peter's actions were hypocritical because he based his decision not to eat with Gentiles on distinctions that derived from Torah rituals, not Christ. Paul says that cannot be. Instead, proper understandings of justification, Christian relationships, and faithful living are based exclusively on Christ's enablement. Otherwise "Christ died for nothing" (2:21).

Evidence for Paul's gospel. After laying out his fundamental convictions about justification through Jesus, Paul then validates his message with various proofs. In each instance, Paul's argument supports the gospel he proclaims while simultaneously contradicting the version of the gospel that his opponents (likely Jewish Christian missionaries) proclaim.

First, in 3:1–5 Paul reminds the Galatians of their own conversion. In response to their belief in the crucified Messiah, God gave them the Spirit long before the Jewish Christian missionaries taught them to observe the customs found in the Torah. Paul asks whether God would have given the Spirit to the Galatians if they were misinformed about the true nature of the gospel.

Second, in 3:6–25 Paul turns to the scriptural example of Abraham. Most likely, the missionaries taught the Galatians to imitate Abraham's circumcision. Paul, however, quotes Genesis 15:6 and insists that Abraham was justified by his belief and not by the ritual of circumcision (3:6). Moreover, Paul argues that through Jesus, God's promise to Abraham has now been fulfilled (3:8, 14). In addition, the law, which God gave as a temporary aid while God's people were waiting for the fulfillment of the Abrahamic promises, no longer needs to serve as a disciplinarian (3:17–25).

Third, in 3:26–4:11 Paul stresses that since Jesus became Abraham's true offspring, those who are "in Christ" are all equal recipients of God's promises. Thus, there is no longer any distinction among those who have been

---

JUSTIFICATION

Paul uses a cluster of words that are related in Greek but not in English. The Greek root *dikai-* is present in Galatians as a verb (2:16–17; 3:8), a noun (2:21; 3:6, 21; 5:5), and an adjective (3:11). The adjective and noun are often respectively translated into English as "righteous" and "righteousness," but the verb is routinely translated as "to justify." Greek readers, however, would have recognized the close kinship among these words. Other possible renderings of the verb are "to make righteous" or perhaps "to grant righteousness." Paul uses *dikai-* terminology to speak primarily about how God "rectifies" a problematic situation. In essence, God creates a proper covenant relationship between God and humans where none exists. Therefore, we may envision justification as a declaration of change, an empowerment for partial change in the present, and perhaps the promise of complete change in the future.

"baptized into Christ" (3:26–28). All those "in Christ" have been equally set free from slavery to "the elemental spirits of the world" and fully adopted as God's children (4:1–11).

Fourth, in 4:12–20 Paul recalls the time when the Galatians first welcomed him and his message hospitably. He wonders where that goodwill has gone, since he has done nothing more than speak truthfully about the gospel to the Galatians (4:15–16).

Finally, in 4:21–31 Paul returns to the Jewish Scriptures for more evidence regarding the truth of his message. He sees an allegory in the persons of Sarah and Hagar (Gen. 15–21) that fits with his previous comments about spiritual enslavement versus spiritual liberation. Sarah gave birth to a free son, and Hagar gave birth to an enslaved son. Moreover, Paul compares the free son (Isaac) to the covenant (or promises) that God made with Abraham and to a heavenly Jerusalem. Alternatively, Paul compares the enslaved son (Ishmael) to the covenant that God made with Moses (the law) and to Jerusalem in Paul's day. Ultimately, as Sarah drove out Hagar, so Paul calls the Galatians to drive out those who are teaching slavery to the law and to the human authorities in Jerusalem.

The Life of Freedom in Christ (5:1–6:18)

In 5:13–15 Paul argues that living in freedom as a Christian ultimately comes with obligations that are characterized by love as opposed to the ritual practices of the law. Consequently, Paul exhorts the Galatian Christians to "live by the Spirit" (5:16). If they do so, the Spirit will guide them away from the urges to gratify the desires of the flesh (human indulgence and selfishness) (5:16–21) and toward the things of God (5:22–26). Even here, Christ's crucifixion is the act that frees believers from the flesh and frees them for the Spirit's work in and through them.

The First Letter of Paul to the Corinthians

In 1 Corinthians Paul addresses a series of problems that crept up in the lives and worship of the Corinthian Christians. As he responds to the ethical dilemmas facing the Corinthians, Paul relies heavily on Jesus's crucifixion and resurrection as the theological foundation and example from which to build. Christians throughout the centuries have often turned to Paul's theological application and appropriation of the gospel in 1 Corinthians as a model for how Christians can respond to ethical dilemmas in their own day.

Location, Date, and Occasion

Corinth was a renowned Greek city and cultural center located near two thriving seaports and a major trade route. In 146 BCE the Romans completely destroyed Corinth. In 44 BCE, less than one hundred years before Paul arrived in Corinth, the city was reconstituted as a Roman colony. Lower-class citizens and soldiers began to populate the city at Rome's request. On the one hand, these previously lower-class citizens discovered opportunities for making fortunes and raising their social status. On the other hand, ancient authors frequently refer to a great divide that existed between the rich and the poor in Corinth during the first and second centuries CE.

Paul likely introduced Christianity to those in Corinth around 50–52 CE (cf. Acts 18:1–17). Yet by the time Paul writes 1 Corinthians, he is in Ephesus (16:8) and he and the Corinthian Christians have engaged in an ongoing dialogue. For example, Paul has already written a previous letter to the Corinthians (5:9), received a letter from them (7:1), and heard an oral report about them (1:11). As a result, many scholars suggest 55–56 CE as the likely date of this letter.

As noted above, two specific events prompted this letter. First, Paul received an oral report from "Chloe's people" (perhaps her servants) describing

© Baker Publishing Group

Figure 7.2. **Location of Corinth of Achaia**

factions and quarrels that existed among the Christians in Corinth (1:11). At numerous points in 1 Corinthians (e.g., 1:10; 4:18; 5:1; 11:18; 15:12), he refers to and addresses this unsettling report. Second, Paul apparently received a letter from the Corinthian Christians seeking his input and advice on a variety of topics (7:1). Similarly, throughout 1 Corinthians (e.g., 7:1; 8:1; 12:1), Paul refers to this letter, perhaps at times even quoting the letter directly before supplying his responses.

Interpreters have offered numerous theories about the source of the divisions among the Christians in Corinth. In the past, many suggested that competing theological understandings of Christianity arose within a network of house churches. Today, more scholars believe the problems derived from a clash between Christianity and the prevailing culture. Many of these Gentile converts in Corinth apparently relied on their Roman values and customs for guidance on important matters such as sexual ethics, interactions among the different socioeconomic classes, decorum in worship settings, and evaluations of what is truly praiseworthy.

Paul, however, wants the example of Christ to take precedence over the cultural norms of the Roman Empire. Jesus's sacrificial death for the sake of others becomes the new model for Christians. Moreover, Jesus's resurrection necessitates that Christians keep God's future intervention into human history in the forefront of their minds. Perhaps Paul hoped that this eschatological emphasis on the future would correct the Corinthians' bad behavior in the present. Regardless, throughout this letter, Paul reminds the Corinthians of the gospel message with the hope of unifying these unrestrained Gentile Christians who are divided by wealth and status.

Greeting and Thanksgiving (1:1–9)

Paul begins with a customary greeting and thanksgiving. Here, he praises the Corinthian Christians for excelling in speech, knowledge, and spiritual gifts (1:5–7). Yet we later discover that the improper use of these same virtues is contributing to the divisions among the Corinthians. From the beginning, Paul therefore pairs these virtues with an eschatological reference to Jesus's return (1:7–8) and a theological perspective on the call to imitate Jesus (1:9; cf. 4:16). In essence, he reframes the three virtues he mentions in light of the gospel as opposed to Roman culture.

Corinthian Factions (1:10–4:21)

As Paul moves into the body of the letter, he immediately appeals to the Corinthian Christians to end the divisions that have fractured their relationships

(1:11–17). His clearest appeal for unity is in 1:10–11, which serves as the thesis statement for chapters 1–4 and perhaps the whole letter. Most likely, the Corinthians had formed cliques huddled around a person whom the group deemed to be especially praiseworthy based on Roman virtues like eloquence, wisdom, and societal influence. Notice, for example, that Paul warns against developing extreme loyalties to individual leaders (1:12–17; 3:4–11, 21–23; 4:6–7) and boasting in human wisdom, power, and knowledge (1:29–30; 2:5; 3:19–23). Instead, Paul argues that God's wisdom, as opposed to Greek wisdom (1:22), was manifest in Jesus's crucifixion (1:18–31; 2:7).

Improper Behavior (5:1–6:20)

In 1 Corinthians 5–6 Paul addresses two examples of bad behavior among the Corinthians that have been reported to him and that jeopardize the unity of the Corinthian Christians. First, in 5:1–13 he refers to a man who is living with his stepmother, an action that may have been equated with incest in antiquity. Paul condemns the sinful man (5:1, 3–5), yet he simultaneously chastises the Corinthian Christians for failing to reprimand the man themselves (5:2, 4–13). Perhaps the Christians in Corinth deemed the sinful man to be too important by Roman standards to take such prophetic action.

Second, Paul is deeply troubled to hear that the Corinthian Christians are taking legal disputes between Christians to the civil courts for resolution rather than working them out among themselves. From an eschatological perspective, Paul points out that Christians will one day judge the entire world; therefore, Christians are better equipped to resolve such conflicts (6:2–4). Furthermore, their Christian identity ought to overshadow their civic identity, and their primary loyalty should be to one another (6:5–6). Even then, Paul says that for the sake of unity it would be better for the Corinthians to allow themselves to be "wronged" than to take their complaints against their fellow Christians to non-Christians for resolution (6:7–8). Once again, Paul wants Jesus's sacrificial example to guide the Corinthians' behavior and decisions (6:7–20).

Sex and Marriage (7:1–40)

Beginning in 7:1 Paul answers questions raised by the Corinthians in their letter to him. For example, he says, "Now concerning the matters about which you wrote: 'It is well for a man not to touch a woman.'" Here, Paul apparently quotes the Corinthians' position before he provides his response to their inquiry. He first discusses the topic of sexual relations as it pertains to those who are already married (7:1–24), and then he addresses those who have never married (7:25–38).

For those who are married, Paul affirms that sexual relations are proper (7:1–7). For those who have never married, he recommends that they stay single (7:25–35). Notice, however, that Paul's viewpoint is decidedly eschatological. Because he expects Jesus to return quickly (7:26–29), Paul primarily advises the Corinthian Christians to remain in their present state. Whether a person is married (7:10–16), widowed (7:8–9, 39–40), or single, Paul suggests that they remain in their present condition and fulfill the obligations that pertain to that status (7:20, 24). Yet Paul stresses that these comments represent his own preferences. The Corinthians are free to make decisions that contribute most to their faithfulness toward God (7:28–40).

Food Sacrificed to Idols (8:1–11:1)

In 8:1–11:1 Paul provides his response to another Corinthian question—namely, whether it is proper for Christians to eat "food sacrificed to idols" (8:1a). At least some Corinthians apparently relied on the adage that "all of us possess knowledge" to guide them as they navigated this ethical dilemma (8:1b). Perhaps these same Christians reasoned that "no idol in the world really exists" and therefore felt free to participate in the traditional celebrations of the pagan temples (8:4, 10; 10:14, 21). This behavior in turn greatly unsettled other Christians in Corinth (8:9–11).

Paul counters the Corinthian adage about knowledge with his own adage: "Knowledge puffs up, but love builds up" (8:1c). He says that Christian love is to be valued more highly than philosophical wisdom (8:1–2). To illustrate his comments better, Paul uses his own life as an example in 1 Corinthians 9. He argues that he has the right to receive compensation as a minister of the gospel (9:1–14) but that he willingly forfeits that privilege so that the gospel might prosper (9:12–27). In the same way, he wants these "knowledgeable" Corinthians to forgo their rights and freedoms for the sake of their fellow Christians. Although Paul is willing to concede that the "knowledgeable ones"

"NOW CONCERNING"

Paul uses the phrase "now concerning" (Greek, *peri de*) in 1 Corinthians 7:1, 25; 8:1; 12:1; 16:1, 12. Each occurrence of this phrase in 1 Corinthians may refer to or perhaps even quote from the letter that the Corinthians previously sent to Paul (7:1). Interpreters must be cautious, however, because "now concerning" was also a common introductory phrase in antiquity (e.g., 1 Thess. 5:1). Regardless, the majority of scholars agree that throughout chapters 7–16 Paul is answering questions the Corinthian Christians initially raised.

are correct at points (e.g., that all meat sold in the marketplace is spiritually harmless), he argues that, for Christians, love and the desire to glorify God must outweigh "knowledge" and individual freedoms (10:23–33).

Disturbances in Worship (11:2–14:40)

In 1 Corinthians 11 Paul responds to reports about disturbances in worship at Corinth. Here, he cites three major problems. First, whereas it was appropriate that both men and women prayed and prophesied during worship (11:4–5), the physical appearance of the women was creating controversy. We are again uncertain of the exact problem. The women may have been letting their hair down during worship, or they may have been neglecting to wear veils that covered their heads. Regardless, Paul argues for proper decorum in worship (11:2–16).

Second, the practice of the Lord's Supper in Corinth was leading to divisions rather than unity (11:17–34). The failure to observe the Lord's Supper properly is another example of Roman values derailing Christian unity. In particular, the upper-class Christians were inconsiderate of the lower-class Christians with the result that the poor were left out of the meal altogether (11:21–22). Paul seeks to remedy the situation by reminding the Corinthians of Jesus's example (11:23–25) and the eschatological judgment (11:26–32). Each member of the church in Corinth should therefore examine himself or herself, making sure that worship practices strengthen Christian fellowship rather than weaken it.

The third worship problem, and another source of division among the Christians in Corinth, related to the improper use of spiritual gifts (1 Cor. 12–14). Again, Roman cultural values may well have been the root cause of the problem. Evidently, some Christians in Corinth bestowed higher praise or status on those Christians who possessed the gifts and skills most revered in the broader Roman society. In particular, some exaggerated the importance of the gift of tongues (or heavenly utterances) to the neglect of other spiritual gifts.

In response, in 1 Corinthians 12 Paul compares spiritual gifts to the various members of the human body (12:4–31). Each limb carries out a small role that contributes to the overall function of the body. Similarly, in chapter 14 Paul argues that the gift of tongues in particular is not greater than the gift of prophecy, and that the ultimate purpose of all spiritual gifts is to build up the community of Christians (14:12, 26). In the midst of his discussion about spiritual gifts (1 Cor. 12–14), however, Paul inserts his famous discourse on love in chapter 13. Paul argues that love is the mandatory motivation that makes all spiritual gifts valuable. Without love, all spiritual gifts are useless.

In the latter portions of 1 Corinthians 14, Paul again teaches the Corinthians to strive for decorum in worship settings (14:33, 40). Because of his concern for outsiders (14:22–25), he wants the Corinthian Christians to use the gifts of both tongues and prophecy in an orderly manner. In addition, Paul apparently restricts the behavior of women in worship (14:33b–36). Perhaps he was again worried about the reaction of non-Christian outsiders, who may have been repulsed by the apparent disregard for Roman cultural norms shown by the Christian wives in Corinth. Some, however, doubt that Paul wrote 1 Corinthians 14:33b–36. Instead, they argue that a later editor added these verses, as evidenced by a disruption in the flow of Paul's logic and the displacement of these verses in some of our ancient manuscripts. Still others argue that the Corinthians were the ones restricting women in worship and that Paul was overturning that practice much like he overturned other Corinthian practices.

The Resurrection (15:1–58)

Paul also learned that some of the Christians in Corinth did not believe in the resurrection of the body (15:12). Perhaps once again, thought patterns that were prevalent in Roman society led these Christians to conclude that a soul lives on after the body dies; therefore, the resurrection of the body and Christian eschatology are unnecessary.

Regardless of the exact Corinthian position, Paul argues that when the Corinthians deny the future resurrection of the dead, they are also denying Christ's resurrection (15:13–19), which is the foundation of all Christian hope (15:3–11, 20–28, 57; cf. 6:14). Moreover, when the complete and final resurrection occurs, each person's "physical body" must be transformed into a "spiritual body" (15:35–57). Paul's comments on the hope of the resurrection also serve as the climax of Paul's call for unity in Corinth. A robust recollection of Jesus's ministry (15:1–11) and a robust understanding of Jesus's future intervention in history (15:20–28) should provide the foundation on which the Corinthian Christians can move toward unity and away from the issues that divide them.

The Second Letter of Paul to the Corinthians

A Composite Document?

The current structure of 2 Corinthians presents significant challenges for readers, so much so that we are forced to rely heavily on reasonable theories while discussing both the literary structure and the likely historical contexts for this document. Most scholars consider 2 Corinthians to be a **composite document** rather than one unified letter. Because of radical changes in tone between chapters 1–7 and 10–13, interpreters routinely suggest that 2 Corinthians consists of at least two and perhaps four or more Pauline letters or letter fragments that originally circulated separately but early Christians eventually edited together into one unified text.

A common reconstruction of the history of 2 Corinthians unfolds as follows. At some point after the Christians in Corinth received 1 Corinthians, Timothy reported to Paul that a group of Jewish Christian missionaries had arrived in Corinth and persuaded the congregation to adopt unhelpful perspectives. As a result, Paul himself traveled to Corinth to correct those misconceptions. He refers to this trip as a "painful visit" in which an individual greatly offended him (2 Cor. 2:1, 5–6; 7:12). In addition, somewhere along the way, Paul's relationship with the Corinthian congregation became severely strained. Rather than making a second "painful visit," Paul opted to write a "painful letter," evidently rebuking the Corinthians for their decisions and viewpoints (2 Cor. 2:1–4; 7:8). After reading Paul's "painful letter," the Corinthians changed course and renewed their allegiance to Paul. Titus, who may have delivered Paul's letter of rebuke, reported to Paul the Corinthians' change of heart, and the relationship between Paul and most of the Christians in Corinth was restored (2 Cor. 7:5–13).

Theories regarding the teachings of the opponents and the exact sequence of the ups and downs in Paul's relationship with the Corinthians are especially diverse. Many scholars, however, think that the group of opponents, whom Paul pejoratively labels "super-apostles" in 2 Corinthians 11:5 and 12:11, temporarily persuaded the Christians in Corinth to disregard or to undervalue Paul's authority, ministry, and teachings (see also 11:13, 15). These attitudes likely surfaced during Paul's "painful visit" to Corinth. For all of these reasons, a common approach to interpreting 2 Corinthians envisions chapters 10–13, with their harsh tone, as being written prior to chapters 1–7, with their conciliatory tone. If so, then chapters 10–13 may well be the "painful letter" that provoked the reconciliation that is evident in chapters 1–7.

Three Distinct Conversations

In keeping with this particular theoretical reconstruction, we describe 2 Corinthians as having three major sections: chapters 10–13, chapters 1–7, and chapters 8–9.

In chapters 10–13 Paul directly addresses his opponents' criticisms. For example, someone evidently criticized him for being bold and impressive in his letters but not when he was face-to-face with the Corinthians (10:1, 10; cf. 11:6; 12:11). In response, rather than boasting in his credentials, Paul boasts in his weakness (11:21b–12:10; 13:9). He characterizes himself using the countercultural values of "meekness and gentleness" that the crucified Christ embodied (10:1–6; cf. 12:9–10; 13:4). In the process, he employs sarcasm (11:21, 23) while giving voice to the logic of "a fool" who boasts in things other than Christ (11:1–12:10). Ultimately, he believes the "super-apostles" fall into this foolish trap (10:12, 18; 11:13–15).

In chapters 1–7 Paul reaffirms his love for the Corinthian congregation after the two parties have resolved their substantial dispute. He acknowledges that his rebuke of the straying Corinthians was harsh, but he remains thankful that his "tearful" or "painful" letter accomplished its goal by correcting the Corinthian Christians' errant course (2:3–4). Moreover, he is grateful that they once again esteem him highly (7:2–16).

Although chapters 1–9 may have originally constituted a single coherent letter, it is equally logical to envision chapters 8 and 9 as independent Pauline correspondences, one addressed to Corinth (8:1) and another addressed to the broader region of Achaia (9:2). These chapters describe the monetary collection (discussed above in the section "Paul's Life, Ministry, and Letters") that Paul gathered among the Gentile Christians in order to aid the poor Christians or "saints" in Jerusalem (8:4; 9:1). Paul calls for the Gentile Christians in Corinth and Achaia to set aside money in the present so that they will have sufficient funds in the future when he arrives (9:3–5). He likely hoped that through the sharing of financial resources, the Corinthians would be able to meet physical needs in Jerusalem, solidify a partnership of ministry with the Jewish Christians, and acknowledge their own spiritual indebtedness to those whose ancestors had been part of God's covenant people for generations.

The Letter of Paul to the Romans

Paul's letter to the Christians in Rome provides us with Paul's lengthiest and most refined comments about the human need for salvation, the nature of salvation, the resulting relationship between Jewish and Gentile Christians, and the manner in which God's righteousness should be reflected in the lives of Christians. As a result, throughout the past twenty centuries, Christians including Augustine, Aquinas, Luther, Calvin, Wesley, and Barth have often relied most heavily on Romans when seeking to understand the main tenets of the Christian faith.

Occasion and Date

Traditionally, Romans has been read as Paul's comprehensive overview of the Christian gospel. For many years, rather than thinking of Romans as Paul's pastoral response to specific concerns, interpreters saw Romans as Paul's systematic summary of the importance of Jesus that was compiled for a group of Christians about whom Paul knew very little. Without a doubt, Paul does indeed provide an overarching presentation of the gospel in his letter to the Roman Christians.

Yet scholars have increasingly argued that Romans is also a pastoral letter designed to address a specific situation. If so, the occasion is twofold. First, Paul plans to visit Rome in the near future before heading off to spread the gospel in Spain. He hopes the Christians in Rome will extend hospitality to him when he arrives and then provide him with financial resources as he departs (15:22–33). As a result, Paul provides the Roman Christians with a clear example of his message and ministry prior to his arrival so that they can begin to partner with him before he even arrives.

Second, the extensive list of greetings in Romans 16:1–16 strongly suggests that Paul already knew many of the Christians at Rome. It is therefore possible that Paul also knew something about the dynamics at work among the Christians in Rome. At the very least, Paul would have known that in 49 CE Emperor Claudius expelled all the Jews from Rome (including the Jewish Christians) because of an internal Jewish conflict. One ancient author, Suetonius, indicates that the Jews in Rome were repeatedly divided over a person named "Chrestos," which is likely a misspelling of the Greek word for "Christ" (*Christos*). Moreover, Luke informs us that Paul met Priscilla (or Prisca) and Aquila after they left Rome and traveled to Corinth because of Claudius's edict

Figure 7.3. **Location of Rome, capital city of the Roman Empire**

(Acts 18:1–3). Five years later, when Nero came to power in 54 CE, the ban was lifted, and Jews began returning to Rome. By the time Paul writes this letter, Prisca and Aquila have returned to Rome, and a church is meeting in their house (16:3–5). Consequently, Paul likely wrote Romans around 56–57 CE while residing in Corinth (Rom. 16:23; 1 Cor. 1:14).

Paul's pronounced emphasis in Romans on the relations between Jewish and Gentile Christians suggests that the various house churches in Rome (1:7; 16:5) were struggling with strained relationships between the two ethnic groups. A strong Jewish presence had existed in Rome for centuries. Nevertheless, at numerous points the Roman officials and Gentile citizenry had treated the Jews living in Rome harshly. In addition, some have theorized that Jewish Christians were likely the first leaders of the churches in Rome. Yet the sociological dynamics almost certainly shifted between 49 and 54 CE, when the Jews (including the Jewish Christians) were exiled from Rome. At that point, the situation would have forced the Gentile Christians to take up the mantle of leadership. When the Jewish Christians then returned to Rome, it may have been difficult to reintegrate the groups fully.

At the very least, Paul seems to be well aware of an ethnic, religious, and cultural divide when he writes his letter to the Christians at Rome. For example, a call for proper relations between Jewish and Gentile Christians implicitly undergirds all of Romans 1–8 and then moves to the forefront in Romans 9–11. In addition, Romans 14–15 takes up the debate of the weak and the strong, which seems to revolve around the question of Jewish food laws. Finally, Romans 16 includes Paul's greetings both to those who possess Jewish names and to those who possess Greek names.

At present, the majority of scholars assume that Emperor Claudius's edict in 49 CE likely exacerbated inherent cultural struggles between Christians in Rome. In fact, it is reasonable to surmise that Jewish and Gentile Christians needed to overcome cultural prejudices in almost any Mediterranean context where both groups were present. Yet after the emperor had shamed the Jewish Christians by expelling them from Rome for a time, the divide between Jewish and Gentile Christians likely reached its zenith when the Jewish Christians began to return. Consequently, in this letter Paul articulates a theological common ground that should allow the Jewish and Gentile Christians to overcome their differences.

Greeting, Thanksgiving, and the Gospel (1:1–17)

Paul begins with a typical, though lengthy, greeting and thanksgiving. He greets "all God's beloved in Rome," leaving open the strong possibility that numerous house churches existed in the large city of Rome. In addition,

Paul foreshadows the contours of his lengthy argument, which runs from 1:16–15:13. In particular, in Romans 1:16–17 Paul provides the overarching thesis statement for his argument and summarizes his understanding of the gospel before he proceeds to unpack the various implications of this statement. In short, God's righteousness and faithfulness were revealed through Jesus Christ, resulting in salvation for both Jews and Gentiles who respond with faith. Throughout the letter, Paul shows that, regardless of their heritage or status, neither Jewish Christians nor Gentile Christians have any grounds for arrogance or boasting. God is the sole source of righteousness and salvation.

God's Wrath (1:18–3:20)

In the first phase of his argument, Paul demonstrates that God's wrath is righteous and merited. Creation has revealed the truthfulness and reality of God from the beginning of time. Yet throughout history, humans—the Gentiles in particular—have opted to revere idols and to worship the creation rather than the Creator (1:18–23). As a result, God's condemnation of the Gentiles is merited. The Jews, however, are in an equally precarious situation. They have had the law, which provided them with truthful and reliable insight about God. Yet they have failed to keep the law (2:12–29), which means they too are subject to "God's righteous judgment" (2:5–11). Consequently, all humans, both Jews and Gentiles, are "under the power of sin" (3:9), and "the whole world" will "be held accountable to God" (3:19). God shows no partiality whatsoever, regardless of whether one is a Jew or a Gentile. Both Jews and Gentiles are equally sinful, equally worthy of God's wrath, and therefore equally in need of divine rescue (2:5–12; 3:9–20).

God's Gift of Justification (3:21–4:25)

Next, Paul argues that just as all people are under the power of sin, so also through Jesus all people, Jews and Gentiles alike, can benefit from God's grace and mercy. In particular, as a result of Jesus's sacrificial death, God is willing to pass over the sin of humans and grant them justification, a proper covenant relationship between God and humans (3:21–26). This act of unmerited graciousness further reveals God's righteousness. Importantly, though, God's mercy and righteousness are appropriated to humans through trust in Jesus's faithfulness, not through the law. Thus, Jewish and Gentile Christians now equally benefit from and are dependent on the righteousness of God that was revealed through Jesus Christ.

Paul turns to Abraham as an illustration of justification through faith as opposed to justification through the law. Abraham was indeed circumcised, but he practiced circumcision only after God deemed him to be righteous. He was declared righteous, or in right covenant relationship with God, at the point that he believed God and expressed faith in God (4:3, 9, 22). Consequently, Abraham now serves as the ancestor of all those who express a similar trust in God regardless of whether they practice circumcision (4:11–12). The promises that God first made to Abraham now extend to all those who believe (4:16–25).

The Effects of God's Salvation (5:1–8:39)

God has now infused peace into the covenant relationship between God and humans through the death and resurrection of Jesus Christ (5:1–5). The results are salvific on two levels. First, those who trust in Jesus's faithfulness have already been placed in a peaceful relationship with God in the present. Second, this act of justification also rescues believers from the future wrath of God (5:6–11). As a result, if Jews or Gentiles want to boast, they should boast in God's gifts of peace, love, and rescue (5:1, 8, 11).

Paul then gives voice to a series of questions that those who object to his law-free gospel could theoretically raise. This practice of voicing a theoretical opponent's position before stating one's own opinion was a common literary technique in antiquity known as a *diatribe*. In particular, Paul's opponents may have argued that Paul's teachings actually lead to sin and disdain for the Mosaic law (6:1, 15; 7:7, 13).

In response, Paul turns to the common experiences of baptism, slavery, and marriage to illustrate the permanent effects of faith in Christ and the goodness of the Mosaic law. For example, like a woman whose husband's death has freed her from the bonds of marriage, so also believers have been released from previous obligations to keep the law, even though the law served a good function. Like a woman who has remarried, those who trust in Jesus's faithfulness are now bound by a new obligation to live "the new life of the Spirit" (7:1–6).

In Romans 7–8 Paul continues to describe the permanent, life-altering impact that faith in Christ has on humans. In Romans 7 he uses the first-person pronoun "I." Many interpreters conclude that rather than speaking autobiographically, Paul here employs "I" to create a dramatic effect while giving voice to universal human experiences. In the process, Paul likely alludes to Adam (Gen. 3) and possibly Israel as examples of these universal human experiences. For example, he refers to the challenging experience of life under the authority of the Mosaic law (7:7–25). Even though the law beneficially provided valuable knowledge about God to humans, ultimately sin overpowered the good function of the law, with the result that "the very commandment that promised life proved death to me" (7:10). The universal plight of slavery to sin prevents humans from doing what they know to do and even what they want to do (7:14–20).

In Romans 8 Paul contrasts life under the power of sin with life under the power of the Spirit. Here, he describes the general experience of life after Christ has intervened and rescued those who trust in him (7:25). Because Jesus has conquered sin and introduced freedom in the Spirit (8:1–2), the Spirit (as opposed to sin) now dwells within the believer (8:9–11) and empowers the believer to live faithfully, the way God always intended (8:26–34).

Jewish and Gentile Christians (9:1–11:36)

Romans 1–8 contains an implicit message that the Jewish Christians in Rome should not display arrogance toward their Gentile counterparts, because Jewish Christians have no advantage over them. Even the benefit of the Mosaic law has been nullified by the power of sin. In Romans 9–11, however, Paul redirects his focus and prevents the Gentile Christians from arguing that God now favors the Gentiles more than the Jews.

Paul begins by identifying the Jews as his own kinsmen and chronicling the blessings that God has bestowed on the chosen people for centuries (9:1–5). At the same time, he acknowledges the difficulty of trying to explain why so many Jews have not responded with trust in Jesus, whom Paul proclaims as the Jewish Messiah. He first argues that the true members of Israel and the children of God are recognized not by bloodlines but by a proper covenant relationship with God. This answer requires him to address a second question. If God now chooses his people using a different standard than in the past, what does that say about God's righteousness? In essence, Paul's hypothetical opponent asks if the change in criteria makes God a promise breaker.

In response, rather than faulting God, Paul places the blame squarely on Israel for being slow to recognize and respond to God's work in Jesus. Even so, God has preserved a remnant of Jewish believers (9:19–29) and is utilizing the sluggish response of the Jews to open the door wider for the Gentiles (11:7–12, 25). Regardless, Paul directly forbids his Gentile readers from boasting in their present status as Christians (11:13, 17–18, 20). Moreover, he confidently states that "all Israel will be saved," though he does not explain when or how that will happen. Whenever the unbelieving Jews return to God and believe, despite their temporary unbelief, God will be merciful (11:25–36). In the meantime, Gentile Christians have no grounds for braggadocio against their Jewish counterparts.

God's Righteousness Manifest through Christians (12:1–15:13)

Paul goes on to argue that all Christians should be living examples of God's righteousness. In response to God's mercy, believers should give their lives back to God as an offering, allowing God to work in and through them (12:1–8). Paul exhorts his readers to foster loving and peaceful relationships both within the Christian community and throughout the broader society (12:9–13:12). Similarly, he instructs them to avoid self-indulgent behaviors and desires (13:11–14) and to defer to the wishes and the consciences of their fellow believers in regard to debated matters like food laws and holy days. Ultimately, since "Christ did not please himself," the strong (most likely the Gentile Christians) should likewise give up their preferences if those preferences hinder the weak (most likely the Jewish Christians) (14:1–15:13).

Greetings and Final Comments (15:14–16:27)

Finally, after discussing his travel plans, Paul issues numerous greetings to the Christians in Rome. In the process, he refers to Phoebe (who may be delivering this letter) as a deacon (16:1–2), Prisca as a coworker (16:3–4), and Junia as an apostle (16:7). All three of these greetings suggest that Paul held a high view of the role of women within the church.

The Letter of Paul to the Philippians

Despite the fact that Paul writes from prison (1:12–26) and expresses some concern about theological adversaries (1:15–18, 28–30; 3:2, 18–19), his letter to the Christians in Philippi is mostly characterized by joy and gratitude.

Location, Date, and Occasion

Paul founded the Philippian congregation (Acts 16:11–40), which was the first Christian church in Europe, and he seems to possess an especially close relationship with them (1:1–11). For instance, whereas Paul adamantly refused to accept financial assistance from other congregations (e.g., 2 Cor. 12:14), in this letter he thanks the Philippian Christians for their monetary aid (4:15–16). The assistance that the Philippians provide helps to sustain Paul during his incarceration (4:10–19). We are uncertain of the exact dates or location of Paul's imprisonment, though many scholars theorize that Paul corresponded with the Philippians while jailed in Ephesus between 56 and 58 CE. This theory accounts for the numerous trips that Epaphroditus and the Philippians made while providing assistance to Paul (2:19–30), given that a journey from Philippi to Ephesus would take significantly less time than journeys from either Rome or Caesarea, where we know Paul spent time in prison (Acts 23–25; 28).

Gratitude and Joy

Given his incarceration, the joy and thankfulness that Paul expresses in this letter are profound. Paul claims that his gratitude and optimistic disposition despite his circumstances derive from the example of Jesus, who showed humility and a willingness to endure hardships while obeying the Father's will. Many interpreters believe Paul quotes an early Christian hymn in Philippians 2:6–11 that predated this letter. If so, Paul would be recalling words that the Philippian Christians already knew and celebrated as they worshiped together, perhaps highlighting the contrast between the humble obedience of Jesus and the arrogant disobedience of Adam. As a result of Jesus's humility and obedience (2:6–8), God exalted Jesus as Lord of the entire cosmos in the wake of his death on a cross (2:9–11).

Paul desires to emulate Jesus's self-sacrificial disposition, and he exhorts the Philippians to do the same (2:5). Paul most clearly demonstrates disregard for his personal circumstances and ultimate regard for the good news about Jesus when he vows that he is ready and willing to face any circumstance (even prison) because he receives his strength from Christ (4:11–13). In a parallel fashion, Paul exhorts the Philippians to follow Jesus's example of humility and obedience to God's will. Following Jesus's example will help the congregation to maintain unity and faithfulness (2:1–4, 12–18; 4:2–3).

The Letter of Paul to Philemon

Among the undisputed letters of Paul, Philemon is the only letter addressed to an individual Christian rather than a congregation (v. 1). Paul does, however, greet other Christians in the vicinity (perhaps Colossae). For example, at the beginning of the letter Paul greets Apphia, Archippus, and the church that meets in Philemon's house (v. 2). So while it is clear that Paul directly addresses Philemon, it is equally clear that he expects an entire church to hear his comments, thereby creating some degree of accountability for Philemon as he considers his response to Paul's requests.

The context behind this correspondence is difficult to reconstruct. Paul is confined in prison (vv. 1, 9–10, 13). As with Philippians, many scholars theorize that Paul was jailed in Ephesus when he wrote this letter, but Rome and Caesarea remain viable options. Philemon owns a slave named Onesimus who has recently become a Christian after spending time with Paul while Paul was in prison (vv. 10, 16). Utilizing a pun, Paul claims that Onesimus, whose name in Greek means "useful," was formerly "useless" to Philemon but now has become "useful" (v. 11). Interpreters commonly conclude that Onesimus was a runaway slave who perhaps stole something as he departed (vv. 11, 15, 18). Regardless, Paul now sends Onesimus, along with this letter, back to Philemon (v. 12). He asks Philemon to welcome Onesimus back as if Philemon were welcoming Paul (v. 17).

What precisely Paul hopes Philemon will do when Onesimus returns is less clear. Most interpreters believe Paul wants Philemon to employ restraint, show love, and perhaps offer forgiveness to Onesimus. Notice, for instance, that Paul thanks God for Philemon's "love for all the saints" at the beginning of the letter (vv. 4–7). Beyond that, some think Paul wants Philemon to send Onesimus back to assist Paul as he remains in prison and in need of essential provisions (vv. 11, 13–14). Others argue that Paul ultimately wants Philemon to free Onesimus from his obligations as a slave because Paul hopes that Philemon will do more than Paul has even asked (v. 21).

Regardless of his exact thought process, Paul composes a powerfully persuasive letter. His most passionate comments derive from the fact that Onesimus recently converted to Christianity. Paul appeals to Philemon to treat Onesimus as a fellow believer rather than simply as a Roman slave. He wants Philemon to prioritize Christian kinship over all other legal and cultural protocols and norms.

The Pauline Tradition

As stated at the beginning of this chapter, scholars debate whether someone other than Paul wrote six of the thirteen letters attributed to him. These disputed letters are 2 Thessalonians, Colossians, Ephesians, and the **Pastoral Letters** (1 Timothy, 2 Timothy, and Titus). In general, the reasons for questioning the Pauline authorship of these letters revolve around issues of writing style and language, theology, and historical perspective. These issues will be noted below when discussing the letters themselves.

At this point, it is important to explain the term *disputed*. Varying degrees of scholarly consensus exist regarding Paul's authorship of these letters.

Some scholars argue that Paul is the author of one or more of these letters; other scholars conclude that Paul is not the author of some or all of the six letters. Therefore, we use the term *disputed*. This broad conversation tries to make sense of the evidence and account for the significant differences that appear between the so-called undisputed and disputed letters of Paul. Regardless, the academic question of Pauline authorship does not diminish the authority that these letters have for the faith and practice of Christianity. Whether Paul authored these letters or not, they are part of the Christian canon of Scripture and therefore function authoritatively for the Christian tradition.

Authorship in the Ancient World

Debates about Pauline authorship build on a more foundational consideration: authorship in the ancient world. The modern conception of authorship is quite narrow and precise, and it is formulated almost exclusively in terms of intellectual property. In antiquity the notion of authorship was more nebulous and expansive. Two ancient practices related to the authorship of texts illustrate this point.

First, Paul did not physically write the letters that he sent to his churches; he dictated them to a "secretary," or more technically an **amanuensis**. The use of a secretary in the production of texts was common in the Greco-Roman world and is evidenced in Paul's letters. So when one reads in Romans 16:22 that "I Tertius, the writer of this letter, greet you in the Lord," it is not in conflict with Paul as the authorial sender in Romans 1:1. Tertius is Paul's amanuensis, who simply adds his own greeting. In a similar though reverse fashion, Paul indicates at times that he himself is writing a personal greeting: "I, Paul, write this greeting with my own hand" (1 Cor. 16:21; cf. Gal. 6:11; Col. 4:18; 2 Thess. 3:17; Philem. 19). An amanuensis has been physically writing the letter, but Paul now takes the writing instrument for himself to make the greeting more personal.

One should not imagine that the task of an ancient secretary was solely to take dictation. Rather, a reliable amanuensis could be given considerable flexibility and freedom in the production of letters, such as providing drafts, editing, collecting, and sometimes even composing parts of or entire letters for his or her employer/master. Differences of language and style in some of the disputed Pauline letters, like Colossians, may reflect this last aspect. Paul may have directed a trustworthy amanuensis to compose a letter on his behalf. In that case, a secretary may have authored a letter, but Paul authorized it. Consequently, debates about the authorship of the Pauline letters become more complex in light of ancient secretarial practices.

A second and equally important practice related to the authorship of ancient texts is **pseudonymity**, or writing under a "false name." To modern sensitivities, the term itself has negative connotations, including the intent to deceive or to produce forgeries. And certainly in antiquity there are instances of people writing in the name of a well-known person in order to deceive others. But ancient pseudonymity was not an exclusively deceptive practice; it was a common practice in the Greco-Roman world, especially in philosophical traditions. In those cases, a disciple wrote in the name of the philosophical founder. For example, the ancient Greek philosopher Pythagoras left no writings, yet his philosophical teachings were passed down and circulated by subsequent disciples who wrote in his name. Why? Because the teachings originated with Pythagoras, and it was a way to honor their teacher. This sort of scenario is very probable for some of the disputed Pauline letters, particularly Ephesians and the Pastoral Letters. The differences in theology and historical perspective may be explained by a Pauline disciple writing in Paul's name who intended to pass on and apply faithfully Paul's teachings to a new situation. There is no intent to deceive, only to appropriate anew the Pauline tradition and acknowledge its apostolic origin. Perhaps modern readers can view this practice as an ancient form of citation. By writing in Paul's name, the disciple credited Paul with the teachings being communicated. In any case, modern readers should not evaluate ancient pseudonymity according to modern standards of intellectual or literary propriety.

Below, we discuss the six disputed letters attributed to Paul, focusing primarily on Ephesians and the Pastoral Letters.

Ephesians

Questions of authorship. The reasons for questioning the Pauline authorship of Ephesians include issues of writing style and language, historical perspective, and theology. We will address these three categories in order. First, Ephesians contains several long, complex sentences that reveal a rhetorical and grammatical flair that is distinct from Paul's other letters. For example, the opening blessing of 1:3–14 is one extended sentence in Greek, which in turn is followed by a one-sentence thanksgiving/prayer section in 1:15–23. In addition to these intricate sentences, other grammatical constructions contribute to a style that is slower paced and more ornate than Paul's usual direct style. Ephesians also contains phrases that reflect a new development of Pauline usage, and it includes vocabulary that reflects a post-Pauline period.

Second, in Paul's lifetime the questions of Gentile inclusion in the church and the relationship between Jewish and Gentile Christians were burning issues still being debated and worked out. Ephesians, however, presents these

Gentile issues as settled and resolved (2:11–22; 3:6), a situation realized after the life and ministry of Paul. Moreover, Ephesians portrays the apostles in a nostalgic, commemorative manner (2:20; 3:5). Therefore, the author may well be a second-generation Christian who looks back to the time of the apostles with admiration and respect.

Third, the theological perspective of Ephesians represents a development or shift of traditional Pauline theology. In 1 Thessalonians, Paul espouses an "imminent eschatology," the expectation that Christ's return was in the near future. As a consequence, Paul operates with an "already but not yet" view of salvation in 1 Thessalonians; Christ's return will bring to completion the redemption and salvation of believers. Alternatively, while Ephesians contains references to the future aspect of Christian redemption (1:14; 2:7; 4:30), it articulates an overwhelming emphasis on the present reality of salvation (2:4–10). Moreover, whereas Paul envisioned a future resurrection for believers at Christ's coming, Ephesians presents believers as already experiencing the benefits of the resurrection event—as already being raised up with Christ and seated with him in the heavenly sphere (2:6). Thus, some characterize Ephesians as having a "realized eschatology."

Theme. Unlike the occasional character of the undisputed letters of Paul, Ephesians is not responding to a particular problem or issue within a specific congregation. The perspective and tone of Ephesians are more reflective, contemplating the implications of the Pauline tradition for the church universal rather than an individual congregation. Even the reference to "Ephesus" in 1:1 is missing in some important, early manuscripts, leading some interpreters to argue that the reference to Ephesus was a later addition. The major theme of the letter is the significant, even cosmic, role of the church universal in God's plan. Not only is the church the recipient of God's grace and redemption, but it is also now the agent of God's design to gather all things together in Christ (1:22–23; 3:9–10) and the medium of God's revelation (3:10).

Introductory blessing (1:1–14). After a customary salutation (1:1–2), Ephesians begins with an extended blessing to God. This blessing is similar in form to the Jewish prayer-blessing, the *berakah*, and may be influenced by material used in early Christian worship. God is praised for graciously bestowing "every spiritual blessing" on the church (1:3). These spiritual benefits, which God has accomplished "in Christ" (1:3, 4, 7, 9, 10, 11, 13), are elegantly recounted throughout the blessing (1:5–14). Some interpreters have noted a trinitarian structure to this blessing: God the Father (1:3–6), Christ (1:7–12), and the Holy Spirit (1:13–14).

The church's divine vocation (1:15–3:21). The first half of the letter, framed by two prayers (1:15–23; 3:14–21), reflects on the church's role in God's plan. God plans "to gather up all things in [Christ], things in heaven and things on earth" (1:10), and the church is the agent by which this reconciling mission is accomplished in Christ. How so? First, the church is the body of Christ (1:22–23), and just as God raised Christ from the dead and seated him in heaven (1:20), so also God has raised and seated the church with Christ (2:1–10). This action demonstrates God's power, grace, and love (1:19–20; 2:4–5, 8). Second, the church is the example par excellence of God's reconciling mission. Through Christ's death, God has brought together Jews and Gentiles (2:11–22), which results in a "new humanity" (2:15), the church. This reconciliation of Jews and Gentiles was God's secret plan, a "mystery" (3:3–5, 9; cf. 1:3); but now God has revealed it and has chosen Paul to proclaim it (3:1–13). Because of this reconciling work of God, the church in its life together reveals the wisdom of God (3:10) and manifests the fullness of God's love (3:19).

Living a worthy life (4:1–6:24). The second half of the letter contains ethical exhortations designed to help readers "lead a life worthy of the calling to which you have been called" (4:1). First, although a diversity of ministries ("gifts") exists among believers, the church must preserve its unity by abiding in love (4:3–16). Second, readers receive practical instructions on Christian living (4:17–6:9). They are warned about the vices of their "former way of life" (4:22; 5:6; cf. 4:18) and exhorted to embody the virtues that go along with being "imitators of God" (5:1) and living as "children of light" (5:8). The implications of these Christian virtues (4:20–24) are then applied to household relations: husbands/wives (5:22–33), parents/children (6:1–4), and masters/slaves (6:5–9). Although the instructions to the less powerful (wives, children, slaves) are traditional and conform to the patriarchal culture of the Greco-Roman world, the Christian-laden directives to the husband/father/master potentially undermine the authority premise on which the Greco-Roman household was based. Third, as it seeks to live out its calling, the church faces a battle "against the spiritual forces of evil" (6:12). The author charges the readers to "be strong in the Lord" (6:10) and "put on the whole armor of God" (6:11, 14–17). This spiritual battle also requires the spiritual practice of prayer (6:18–20).

The Pastoral Letters—1 Timothy, 2 Timothy, and Titus

First Timothy, 2 Timothy, and Titus are referred to as the "Pastoral Letters," because the author gives instruction to Timothy and Titus so that they may serve as effective pastors for their respective churches. In particular, the author instructs the recipients about the organization, structure, and guidance of their respective churches. Because of similar language, content, and situation, it is conceivable that these letters originated as a literary corpus and

HOUSEHOLD CODES

Ephesians 5:22–6:9 addresses relationships within the Greco-Roman household. This type of instructive material is referred to as "**household codes**." Household codes are also found in Colossians 3:18–4:1 and 1 Peter 2:18–3:7, and they probably inform material in 1 Timothy (3:1–8; 5:1–6:2) and Titus (2:1–10). Household codes, however, were not unique to Christian writings. Instructions for households were common in Greco-Roman and Jewish political and moral writings. For example, the philosopher Aristotle (fourth century BCE) writes about "household management" and identifies the primary parts of the household as "master and slave, husband and wife, father and children" (*On Politics* 1.1252b)—the same relationships addressed in Ephesians. The various household codes in the New Testament function differently depending on their context. For example, the household codes in Ephesians and Colossians are notable for their insistence that the master/father/husband relate according to Christian virtues instead of the conventional authority and power exercised in the Greco-Roman world. Some interpreters argue that this Christian reconfiguration effectively undermines the authority structure promoted and assumed in secular Greco-Roman household codes. On the other hand, the household codes in 1 Peter give very little attention to the master/father/husband. First Peter emphasizes the traditional, submissive roles for slaves and wives, though the motivation for these roles is grounded in their Christian identity. This difference in balance arises from the context of 1 Peter, which directs readers to conform to the social expectations in order to dispel suspicion and contempt from their pagan neighbors or family members.

were intended to be read together. We will proceed with this assumption and treat the letters together.

Questions of authorship. Although there are a few proponents for Pauline authorship, most scholars consider the Pastoral Letters to be pseudonymous for a variety of reasons. First, all three letters share the same characteristic language and style, which supports the idea that these letters were produced together. This language and style, however, is strikingly different from that of the undisputed Pauline letters. For example, the Pastoral Letters include a high ratio of words and phrases that are not present in Paul's undisputed letters. Some scholars have even noted that the vocabulary and language of the Pastoral Letters have more in common with Acts than with Paul's letters.

Second, in Paul's letters, ministry is conducted and church leadership is exercised according to the Spirit-giftedness of all believers (Rom. 12:3–8; 1 Cor. 12:12–31; 14:26–33). The Pastoral Letters, however, envision and prescribe a hierarchal structure in which the authoritative roles of overseers/bishops, elders, and deacons dominate the concept of church leadership. This structure likely reflects an institutional development of the church near the end of the first century or early second century CE rather than in the time period of Paul's ministry.

Third, a vestige of traditional Pauline theology is evident in the Pastoral Letters (2 Tim. 1:9; Titus 2:11; 3:5), but the overall theology of the Pastorals is presented and expressed in a different manner than in the undisputed Pauline letters. For example, Paul's letters are generally structured with overt theological reflections constituting the first part of the letter and straightforward ethical instructions constituting the second part. In the Pastoral Letters, however, ethical material permeates the letters, supported occasionally by theological statements (e.g., 1 Tim. 2:1–6; 3:14–16). Furthermore, the Pastorals possess theological perspectives that are rarely seen in Paul's undisputed letters. The ethical material emphasizes "godliness" (1 Tim. 2:2; 3:16; 4:7–8; 6:3, 5, 6, 11; 2 Tim. 3:5, 12; Titus 1:1; 2:12) and "good works" (1 Tim. 2:10; 5:10, 25; 6:18; Titus 2:7, 14; 3:8, 14), common virtues in the Greco-Roman world, though certainly cast with Christian meaning here. In addition, the Pastorals predominantly refer to God and Christ as "Savior" (1 Tim. 1:1; 2:3; 4:10; 2 Tim. 1:10; Titus 1:3–4), which appears only once in Paul's undisputed letters (Phil. 3:20, and only in reference to Christ); and the Pastorals exhibit a distinctive use of the term "epiphany/appearing," which appears regularly to describe both Jesus's earthly ministry and future coming (1 Tim. 6:14; 2 Tim. 1:10; 4:1, 8; Titus 2:11, 13; 3:4).

Occasion and purpose. In the literary context of the Pastoral Letters, Timothy is in Ephesus and Titus is on the island of Crete. Both Timothy and Titus are tasked with the responsibility of establishing an organization of leadership (overseers/bishops, elders, and deacons) for their respective churches. Moreover, the churches of both Ephesus and Crete face the threat of false teaching. The two issues then coalesce to provide the purpose of the Pastoral Letters: to thwart the spread of false teaching by establishing a hierarchal leadership.

The nature of the false teaching. All three letters contain significant material related to false teaching (1 Tim. 1:3–7; 4:1–3; 6:3–5, 20–21; 2 Tim. 2:1–18, 23–26; 3:1–9, 13; 4:3–4; Titus 1:10–16; 3:9–11), thus indicating the importance of this issue for understanding the intent of the Pastoral Letters. In fact, 1 Timothy and Titus lack the customary thanksgiving section. Instead, the author immediately addresses the problem of false teachers (1 Tim. 1:3–7; Titus 1:10–16). This alternative teaching seems to be Jewish in nature (1 Tim. 1:7, 8; Titus 1:10, 14), but it is unclear whether the false teachers are non-Christian Jews, Jewish Christians, or Gentiles who have converted to Judaism. Though specifics are lacking, the false teaching contains "myths and endless genealogies" (1 Tim. 1:4; cf. 2 Tim. 4:4; Titus 1:14) and promotes itself as "knowledge" (Greek, *gnosis*), which may indicate an early form of Jewish **gnosticism** (1 Tim. 6:20). (Christian gnosticism was a significant threat to "orthodox" Christianity in the second century CE.) The false teachers also advocated for ascetic practices, such as forbidding marriage and demanding abstinence from foods (1 Tim. 4:3; cf. Titus 1:15). The false teachers are described as deceivers who themselves have been deceived by Satan (1 Tim. 4:1; 2 Tim. 2:26; 3:13; Titus 1:10). Their deception has found its way into individual households—probably meaning house churches—and has taken hold among a group of young women (2 Tim. 3:6–7; cf. 1 Tim. 5:11–15; Titus 2:3–4; 3:11). Given this situation, the directive in 1 Timothy 2:11–12 for women to be silent and not to teach appears to be a specific response to certain women disseminating this false teaching. This interpretation makes sense of the example of Eve as the deceived one in 1 Timothy 2:14, and it connects with the command for false teachers to be silenced in Titus 1:11.

Managing the household of God. In an attempt to suppress this false teaching, the author strategically implements the authoritative, hierarchal structure of the household into congregational contexts. Just as the husband/father/master exercised authority over the Greco-Roman household, the overseer/bishop is given authority to manage the "household of God" (1 Tim. 3:15; cf. 1 Tim. 3:3; Titus 1:7). Qualifications for an overseer/bishop are given in 1 Timothy 3:1–7 and Titus 1:5–9 ("elders" and "bishops" seem to be synonymous in Titus). Deacons (3:8–13), which may include women (3:11), fall below the overseer/bishop in the church structure. Equal to or perhaps included with the deacons are "the widows" (5:3–16), which seems to be a distinct ministry group with its own qualifications. Other groups within the "household of God" receive instructions about their conduct: elders (1 Tim. 5:17–22; Titus 2:2), older women (Titus 2:3–5), young men (Titus 2:6–8), and slaves (1 Tim. 6:1–2; Titus 2:9–10). Unlike the false teachers and their supporters, the members of the household of God are to show the truth of the gospel by their "good works" (1 Tim. 2:10; 5:10, 25; 6:18; Titus 1:16; 2:7, 14; 3:1, 8, 14).

Second Timothy. Although structured like a letter, 2 Timothy is similar to the literary form of a "last testament," in which a well-known person near death gives final instructions to his disciples or family. These last testaments, such as *The Testaments of the Twelve Patriarchs*, are almost exclusively pseudonymous writings. In the case of 2 Timothy, Paul faces death (4:6–8) and provides final guidance and wisdom for his "loyal child" Timothy (1:2). The final instructions still reflect the context of the false teaching (2:14–3:9); Timothy must be diligent against this threat. Paul offers himself as an example for Timothy, both in faithfully proclaiming the gospel (4:1–5) and in enduring subsequent suffering (1:8–14; 2:1–13).

Other Disputed Letters of Paul

We want to touch briefly on the two other disputed letters of Paul, 2 Thessalonians and Colossians.

Second Thessalonians. This letter has an uncanny resemblance to the structure of 1 Thessalonians, especially the double thanksgivings (1:3–12; 2:13–15; cf. 1 Thess. 1:2–10; 2:13–16), the double benedictions (2:16; 3:16; cf. 1 Thess. 3:11–13; 5:23–24), and the use of "finally" to introduce the section of ethical exhortations (3:1; cf. 1 Thess. 4:1). The two letters also share near verbatim parallels (3:16 // 1 Thess. 5:23; 3:8 // 1 Thess. 2:9; 3:5 // 1 Thess. 3:11; 2:13 // 1 Thess. 1:4), though 2 Thessalonians prefers the term *Lord*—a reference to Christ—in places where 1 Thessalonians uses "God" (see previous references). And yet the two letters are notably different in their eschatologies (views of the end time). In 1 Thessalonians, Paul says that "the day of the Lord will come like a thief in the night" (5:2; cf. 5:1–3), emphasizing the suddenness and unpredictability of Christ's coming. In 2 Thessalonians, however, the author refers to events—traditional apocalyptic scenarios—that must take place before "the coming of our Lord Jesus Christ" (2:1–17), in effect providing circumstances that will signal Christ's coming.

Many scholars argue that 2 Thessalonians is pseudonymous. If so, the writer imitated the structure and phraseology of 1 Thessalonians in order to address a post-Pauline audience that believes the coming of Christ "is already here" (2:2), which in turn has led to idleness (3:6–15). Further evidence for pseudonymous authorship includes the author's overly explicit claim for the letter's authenticity (3:17; cf. 2:2). On the other hand, if Paul wrote 2 Thessalonians it likely means that the Thessalonians misunderstood Paul's first letter, resulting in an "over-realized" eschatology. If so, Paul may have instructed his secretary to compose another letter (2 Thessalonians) based on 1 Thessalonians to correct this misinterpretation.

Colossians. Scholars often question Pauline authorship of Colossians for reasons similar to those we mentioned when discussing Ephesians: long, complex sentences (1:3–8; 2:6–15) and distinct theological perspectives. Similar to Ephesians, Colossians presents a "realized" eschatology (2:12–13; 3:1, 10), which emphasizes the present benefits of the resurrection event for believers. Colossians also refers to Christ as the "head" of the church (1:18; 2:19; cf. Eph. 1:22–23; 4:15; 5:23), a concept that is not found in the undisputed letters but likely represents a further development of Paul's image of the church as the body of Christ (cf. 1 Cor. 12:12–27). These similarities with Ephesians, along with the household codes (3:18–4:1; Eph. 5:22–6:9), suggest a possible literary relationship between the two letters. Most scholars argue that Colossians served as a basis for the composition of Ephesians.

On the other hand, if Paul authored Colossians, he wrote the letter from prison (4:3, 10, 18) to a church that he did not establish (1:7–8; 2:1). These circumstances may account for the differences that we see in Colossians as compared to Paul's undisputed letters. Paul may have tasked a trusted secretary with composing the letter with the help of Epaphras (1:7; 4:12), who had personal insight into the situation at Colossae. Thus, the theology of Colossians may be shaped more by its occasion and Epaphras's response than by Paul's traditional theology. In this scenario, Paul may have authorized rather than dictated the letter.

False teaching that promoted a philosophical and syncretic form of the Christian faith provides the occasion for this letter; that is, Colossians seeks to correct a brand of Christian faith that has merged with other religious traditions (2:8, 16–18, 20–23). Those who fostered this false teaching likely implied that something was lacking in the Colossians' salvation. In response, the author of Colossians describes a Christian faith that flows from a robust Christology. Central to the message of Colossians is the Christ-hymn (1:15–20), which concludes, "For in [Christ] all the fullness of God was pleased to dwell, and through him God was pleased to reconcile to himself all things, whether on earth or in heaven, by making peace through the blood of his cross" (1:19–20). Colossians assures its readers that nothing is lacking in Christ; Christ is all sufficient for the spiritual life of the Colossians (2:6–7; 3:1–17).

Theological Reflection: The Contours of Paul's Theology

Throughout this unit we have emphasized the occasional nature of Paul's letters. The letters are pastoral dispatches intended to address specific issues within specific congregations. But what informs Paul's instructions, advice, and directives? Is there a coherent thought world or belief system from which Paul addresses the contingent situations of his churches? Most scholars affirm that Paul's ministry was shaped and informed by a theological framework. Although disagreement continues as to what constitutes the center or foundation of that theological framework, there is a growing consensus about its contours.

Jewish Symbolic World

Past scholarship on Paul, particularly in the Protestant tradition, unfortunately constructed a Christian Paul who abandoned his Jewish heritage. But

Paul was a Christian Jew (or Jewish Christian) whose convictions, values, and perspectives were formed by a Jewish symbolic world. Certainly, this symbolic world was radically reconfigured by Christ's death and resurrection, but the Christ event itself was fundamentally understood according to a Jewish worldview and history. For Paul, the God of Israel accomplished the divine plan through the death and resurrection of Jesus, a plan that began with creation and the Abrahamic covenant. The God of Abraham, Isaac, and Jacob is the same God and Father of Jesus Christ. The God who delivered the Hebrew people from Egypt is the same God who raised Jesus from the dead and exalted him to a position of sovereignty. Paul believed that the death, resurrection, and future coming of Christ accomplish God's purposes for Israel and all the nations, as set forth in the Jewish Scriptures. How Paul understood God's work in and for the world certainly changed after his encounter with the risen Christ, but he still understood it as a divine work inextricably connected with Israel's story. To sever Paul's gospel from its Jewish moorings is to distort drastically its meaning and message.

Apocalyptic Perspective

Paul embraced a decisively apocalyptic theological framework. In our discussion of 1 Thessalonians, we introduced Paul's "imminent eschatology," the idea that Paul expected Christ to return soon. But this imminent eschatology constitutes only part of a larger end-time perspective called "apocalyptic." This early Jewish (and Christian) perspective saw reality in terms of two ages: (1) the present evil age, which is characterized by sin and death, and (2) the age to come, with a new heaven and new earth in which there will be no more sin or death, only eternal life and righteousness. It was believed that the transition from the present evil age to the age to come will come about by God's decisive intervention, which includes a universal resurrection of all the dead and a subsequent judgment. The resurrected righteous will be granted a place in the new heaven and new earth; the resurrected wicked will be consigned to a place of torment.

For Paul and those who embraced his teachings, the Christ event provided a distinct plot to this apocalyptic scenario. The death and resurrection of Jesus functioned as a sign that God's end-time action had begun—the beginning of the end. Resurrection itself is an end-time event. Yet the individual resurrection of Jesus occurred in the middle of time, and so it initiated the shifting of the ages. The present evil age is passing away, and a new creation is dawning (Rom. 13:11–12a; 1 Cor. 7:29–31). Accordingly, Paul refers to Jesus as the "first fruits of those who have died" (1 Cor. 15:20, 23). God's decisive intervention has begun, and it will be completed at Christ's coming (1 Cor.

15:23–24; 1 Thess. 4:12–18). This Christian version of the apocalyptic scenario creates a unique situation for Paul and his fellow Christians. They now live between the ages (e.g., 1 Cor. 10:11).

Paul's Apocalyptic Gospel

This apocalyptic perspective provides the framework for Paul's gospel: Christ "gave himself for our sins *to set us free from the present evil age*" (Gal. 1:4; emphasis added). Paul understands God's salvation as a cosmic event that undoes the enslaving power of sin and the present evil age (Rom. 6:1–23). As articulated in Colossians 1:13, God "has rescued us from the power of darkness and transferred us into the kingdom of his beloved Son." Paul contends that believers no longer live according to this age but are empowered by the Holy Spirit to live according to the age to come, the "new creation" (2 Cor. 5:17; cf. Gal. 5:22–26). Consequently, he describes this Christian existence as being "in Christ." Christian baptism initiates this spiritual participation "in Christ," as believers are buried into Christ's death and raised into "newness of life" (Rom. 6:1–11; cf. Gal. 3:27). Moreover, being "in Christ" has a communal dimension: "There is no longer Jew or Greek, there is no longer slave or free, there is no longer male and female; for all of you are one *in Christ Jesus*" (Gal. 3:28; emphasis added). This inclusive, communal existence "in Christ" further signifies that God's long-awaited, apocalyptic saving action has commenced.

....

SUGGESTED READING

Bassler, Jouette M. *Navigating Paul: An Introduction to Key Theological Concepts.* Louisville: Westminster John Knox, 2007.

Gaventa, Beverly Roberts. *Our Mother Saint Paul.* Louisville: Westminster John Knox, 2007.

Longenecker, Bruce W., and Todd D. Still. *Thinking through Paul: A Survey of His Life, Letters, and Theology.* Grand Rapids: Zondervan, 2014.

Roetzel, Calvin J. *The Letters of Paul: Conversations in Context.* 6th ed. Louisville: Westminster John Knox, 2015.

Schnelle, Udo. *Apostle Paul: His Life and Theology.* Translated by M. Eugene Boring. Grand Rapids: Baker Academic, 2005.

Thompson, James W. *Apostle of Persuasion: Theology and Rhetoric in the Pauline Letters.* Grand Rapids: Baker Academic, 2020.

8

The General Letters and Revelation

"**General Letters**" is a modern designation for a group of New Testament writings comprising Hebrews, James, 1–2 Peter, 1–3 John, and Jude. From a historical perspective, this designation can be misleading and confusing. The following points seek to clarify some issues.

- The designation "General Letters" intends to communicate that these "letters" address a "general" Christian audience, in contrast to Paul's letters, which address specific congregations. But, in fact, not all "General Letters" are general in their addresses, nor are they all letters.

- The title "General Letters" is based on the ancient, canonical collection known as the "**Catholic Epistles**." The term "catholic" is a transliteration of the Greek word *katholikos*, which means "universal" or "general." This canonical collection emerged in the late third century and included James, 1–2 Peter, 1–3 John, and Jude. It did not include Hebrews.

- Hebrews came into the New Testament canon by way of the Pauline Letters. Some ancient churches and leaders believed Paul wrote Hebrews and therefore included it in their Pauline collection. Others did not. The overwhelming consensus of modern scholarship is that Paul did not write Hebrews. As a consequence, Hebrews is usually treated with and counted among the "General Letters."

Revelation, which concludes the New Testament structurally, emerged as part of the New Testament canon apart from any collection (e.g., Pauline collection, four-Gospel collection, or the catholic collection). The history of Revelation's inclusion in the canon is complicated. Though widely accepted early, subsequent controversy over interpretation generated questions about its canonical status. Most Christian communities finally accepted Revelation as authoritative by the sixth century CE.

The World of Early Christians

Several of the General Letters and (partially) Revelation address the issue of Christian persecution. It is important to understand the nature of Christian persecution when reading these texts. Some imagine that early Christians lived an underground existence as a result of official Roman persecution. It is true that Christians were officially persecuted, but empire-wide persecution, decreed by the emperor, did not take place until 250 CE—and then it was only intermittent until 313 CE. Prior to that, in 64 CE the emperor Nero unleashed a cruel campaign against Christians, but his persecution was limited to Christians living in Rome. Nero used Roman Christians as scapegoats for the great fire of Rome. Also, some earlier historians believed that the emperor Domitian (81–96 CE) targeted Christians for persecution, but the evidence is simply lacking for any concerted, governmental persecution of Christians during this time.

Therefore, the best descriptors of Christian persecution in the first century CE are *local* and *sporadic*. Most Christians lived in relative peace, but at times some Christians in some places experienced outbreaks of persecution at the hands of local citizens or local civic leaders. Two examples demonstrate this local and sporadic persecution of Christians. The first example comes from Acts 19:21–41, which gives an account of a mob action against two Christian missionaries in the city of Ephesus. Local artisans, who crafted silver shrines of the goddess Artemis, stir up a riot because they perceive that the Christian message might (1) hurt their business and (2) deprive the goddess Artemis of her due worship. The mob drags two Christians to the town's theater, likely with the intent to inflict harm. The apostle Paul wants to join the two Christians, but "officials of the province of Asia" (19:31) urge him not to enter the theater. Eventually the town clerk arrives and calms the crowd, warning them about proper procedures for carrying out a charge against the two Christians. As a result, the mob disperses without incident. The following points should be observed. First, Christians already lived in Ephesus (19:1) presumably without being the object of persecution. This mob action was a spontaneous response to new Christian activity in the city. Second, the intended suffering came from local citizens, not the government. In fact, in this case local officials actually protected Christians, both Paul and his missionary companions. Third, this riot was motivated by both economic and religious factors. We will return to this issue of motivation below, but for now it is important to emphasize that this episode in Ephesus illustrates the local and sporadic nature of Christian persecution in the first century.

The second example comes from a non-Christian source, a correspondence between Pliny the Younger and the emperor Trajan (Pliny the Younger, *Epistles* 10.96–97). Pliny, who was the Roman governor of the region of Bithynia-Pontus in 110–12 CE (cf. 1 Pet. 1:1), writes to Emperor Trajan in order to receive counsel about how to examine Christians. Christians are being brought to Pliny, and in one case an anonymous pamphlet was sent with names of alleged Christians. Pliny states that he has never witnessed a trial of a Christian, and he is uncertain what to do. He then describes what he has done in the meantime. To those brought before him as Christians, he asked them if they were indeed Christians. If they answered yes, he asked two more times with warnings. Those who were consistent in their confession, Pliny ordered to be "led away" (presumably for execution). Those who were Roman citizens, however, he sent to Rome for trial (cf. Acts 23:26–30). Other accused persons denied that they were Christians; Pliny had them prove it by offering incense to the gods and the emperor and by cursing Christ. He further describes his attempt to find out the truth about Christianity by torturing "two women slaves, who were called deaconesses." The torture did not turn up any substantial wrongdoings, only a "disgusting, fanatical superstition."

Emperor Trajan responds that Pliny has followed a reasonable process, but the emperor insists on three things: (1) those who deny being Christians and demonstrate it by supplicating to the gods must be pardoned; (2) Christians are not to be searched for; and (3) anonymous accusations are absolutely prohibited as a basis for examining Christians. It is important to note the following. First, Christians were being brought to Pliny; as governor he did not seek them out, and Trajan explicitly forbade searching for Christians. Any charges against Christians came from local inhabitants and civic leaders. Second, despite Pliny's previous governmental roles in Rome, he had never seen a Christian on trial. The examination of Christians at high levels of government was not a common occurrence. In fact, Pliny's letter to Trajan is written late in his role as governor (112 CE), suggesting that for two years as governor in this region he had very little, if any, involvement with accusations against Christians.

Christians were harassed and at times maltreated primarily because of their refusal to worship any god except their own. The social and religious aspects of the Roman world were inseparable. Worshiping local and traditional deities accompanied both public and private events. People engaged in these religious activities hoping to garner the goodwill of the gods for all levels of society: families, cities, and empire. If the gods were not honored properly, disaster and calamity were sure results. Moreover, ancient religion included an economic dimension. In the example from Acts 19, we noted that local artisans believed their profits would suffer if the Christian message gained widespread acceptance. In essence, when Christians did not participate in the religious life of society, their neighbors viewed them with much suspicion, if not general contempt; Christians did not, in the eyes of their neighbors, seek the well-being of humanity. This suspicion and dislike created an environment of verbal and social harassment, which in turn resulted in random acts of violence.

One should not imagine a universal situation for all Christians. For one thing, Christians responded in different ways to this social tension. Some Christians may have tried to accommodate as much as possible without "crossing the line" of pagan worship. These Christians may have attended pagan festivals without legitimizing the sacrifices in their own consciences. Other Christians may have been more proactive in their dismissal of the gods. Instead of simply not participating, they may have spoken openly against the existence of the gods and the futility of worshiping them. Also, not all Christians were of equal social status, which resulted in different forms and levels of affliction. For example, the prospect for abuse would be greater for a Christian slave, whose refusal to worship his master's god could lead to abuse.

So the suffering of Christians during the time of the New Testament was erratic and "from below"—from the inhabitants of cities and rural areas. Most Christians lived in tension with their social surroundings, perhaps victimized more by prejudice than physical abuse. Many Christians lived out their lives with no persecution. Some Christians lived in an area for years with no problems, only to find themselves unexpectedly the target of harassment and maltreatment. The Christian experience of social harassment varied not only in kind and degree but from one place to another, from one household to another, and from one time to another.

The Letter to the Hebrews

Author and Audience

Hebrews is an anonymous work. It lacks the conventional salutation found in ancient letters. Neither the author nor the recipients are identified. The title "To the Hebrews" was likely added to the text in the second century CE and likely derives from the author's pervasive engagement with Jewish traditions within the text. Because Gentile converts were taught the Christian message as part and parcel of Israel's story (cf. Romans and Galatians), the heritage of this decisively Christian audience may have been Jewish, Gentile, or a mixture of the two. The concluding remarks include greetings from "those from Italy" (13:24), which may indicate an audience in Rome.

Occasion

Hebrews addresses a situation in which its readers have become sluggish in their Christian commitment and may be in danger of abandoning the Christian faith (5:11–6:12; 10:23–39; 11:12–29). This wearied faith and possible apostasy have come about because of the community's experiences of suffering (12:3–13; 13:3, 13). At first, the audience "endured a hard struggle with sufferings" and "cheerfully accepted the plundering of [their] properties" (10:32–34). But the continued hardships have taken their toll on the readers, threatening to undo their faith and hope. Hebrews exhorts its readers to endure and remain faithful.

Genre

Although Hebrews concludes like a letter (12:22–24), it does not begin with an introductory salutation; nor do the structure and content of Hebrews conform to what one would expect in the body of an ancient letter. The author refers to his writing as a "word of exhortation" (13:22), which is the same phrase describing Paul's speech in the setting of a synagogue (Acts 13:15). Most scholars identify the genre of Hebrews as a **homily** (or sermon), which is characterized primarily by an interplay between exposition of Scripture and exhortation. In the case of Hebrews, the exposition of Scripture supports the author's claims about Jesus. These christological interpretations provide the basis for subsequent exhortations. For example, the author argues that Jesus as Son of God is superior to angels by citing and commenting on a series of scriptural passages (1:5–14). This exposition is followed by an exhortation to "pay greater attention to what we have heard [= the Son's message], so that we do not drift away from it" (2:1–4, esp. 2:1).

Content

Hebrews is a sustained argument about the supremacy of Jesus and his salvation, which provides the basis for endurance and faithfulness on the part of the audience. A series of christological expositions and practical exhortations support the book's argument and mirror the macrostructure of Hebrews: exposition delineating the supremacy of Jesus (1:1–10:18) and exhortation to faithfulness and endurance (10:19–13:19). Hebrews can be outlined as follows:

1:4–4:13—Superiority of Jesus's word/message, with exhortations (2:1–4; 3:12–4:13)

    1:5–2:18—Superior to the angels

    3:1–4:13—Superior to Moses and Joshua

4:14–10:18—Superiority of Jesus's high priestly service/ministry, with exhortation (5:11–6:12)

    4:14–7:28—Superior priesthood

    8:1–10:18—Superior covenant (8:1–10:18), which includes a superior sanctuary (9:1–24) and a superior sacrifice (9:25–10:18)

10:19–13:19—Climactic exhortation to endurance and faithfulness

    10:19–39—Call to faithful endurance

    11:1–12:13—Examples of those who have been faithful

    12:14–29—Warning against being unfaithful

    13:1–19—Concluding communal, ethical instructions

The rhetorical argument of Hebrews develops in two ways. First, the supremacy of Jesus in relation to Israel's traditions is presented in terms of continuity rather than discontinuity, advancement rather than replacement. The author works with a rhetorical device called "comparison" (Greek, *synkrisis*), which compares the subject matter with something already perceived as honorable or positive. For example, to claim that Jesus is greater than the angels begins with a positive perception of angels. If the divine message of angels is valid (2:2), then how much more reliable is the message of God's Son (2:3–4)? Through the rhetoric of comparison, Hebrews argues that the message and ministry of Jesus constitute an advancement in the way that the God of Israel now acts; it is not a polemic against Judaism. Second, one must read the christological expositions in concert with the exhortations. In fact, the expositions set up the exhortations. So the exposition that Jesus is superior to angels has the intended goal of engendering confidence and assurance among the readers. Hebrews is not a christological essay; it is a "word of exhortation" (13:22).

The Letter of James

Authorship

The Letter of James begins like an ancient letter with a salutation indicating the sender and recipients. The sender/author is identified simply as "James, a servant of God and of the Lord Jesus Christ" (1:1). Many people in the

New Testament are named James, but tradition and modern scholarship have consistently identified only one person with the status and reputation to be a candidate for the James of this text: James the brother of Jesus. It seems that this James was not a disciple during Jesus's earthly ministry (Mark 3:21, 31–35; 6:1–6) but became a believer and apostle when the resurrected Jesus appeared to him (1 Cor. 15:7). He subsequently became the leader of the Jerusalem church, and his authority became equal to, if not greater than, Peter's (Gal. 1:18–19; 2:9; Acts 15).

Even though James the brother of Jesus may be identified as the putative author of this text, a number of scholars argue that the work is pseudonymous (written in the name of James by someone else). The reasons given for pseudonymity include the letter's sophisticated and polished Greek style (which would be unusual for a common Jew from Galilee), its use of the Septuagint instead of Hebrew texts, and the late acceptance of its canonical status in the church. Others affirm James as author by pointing to the text's thoroughly Jewish character (e.g., the readers' assembly is called a "synagogue" in 2:2), its reliance on the oral form of the Jesus tradition (see the text box below), and its knowledge of Palestinian climate ("the early and the late rains," 5:7)—all

THE JESUS TRADITION IN JAMES

James contains teaching material that is comparable to teachings present in Matthew's "Sermon on the Mount" (Matt. 5–7). James and Matthew most likely drew on similar traditions of Jesus's teachings. Consider the following examples:

On swearing

"But I say to you, Do not swear at all, either by heaven . . . or by the earth. . . . Let your word be 'Yes, Yes' or 'No, No'; anything more than this comes from the evil one" (Matt. 5:34–35, 37).

"Above all, my beloved, do not swear, either by heaven or by earth or by any other oath, but let your 'Yes' be yes and your 'No' be no, so that you may not fall under condemnation" (James 5:12).

On riches

"Do not store up for yourselves treasures on earth, where moth and rust consume and where thieves break in and steal; but store up for yourselves treasures in heaven, where neither moth nor rust consumes and where thieves do not break in and steal" (Matt. 6:19–20).

"Your riches have rotted, and your clothes are moth-eaten. Your gold and silver have rusted, and their rust will be evidence against you, and it will eat your flesh like fire. You have laid up treasure for the last days" (James 5:2–3).

Note: See also James 1:12 // Matt. 5:10; James 1:4 // Matt. 5:48; James 1:5 // Matt. 7:7; James 1:22 // Matt. 7:24; James 2:5 // Matt. 5:3; James 2:10 // Matt. 5:19; James 2:13 // Matt. 5:7; James 3:18 // Matt. 5:9; James 5:9 // Matt. 7:1.

of which point to an early Palestinian origin. Given the conflicting evidence, most scholars propose an editing process whereby someone later has selected and heavily edited early, authentic material from James.

Audience

The recipients are addressed as "the twelve tribes in the Dispersion" (1:1). The Jewish understanding of "Dispersion" meant those Jews living outside Palestine. Yet because many deemed early Christians, even Gentile Christians, to be the "true Israel" (see 1 Pet. 1:1), the recipients of this letter may have been either Jewish or Gentile Christians. Some interpreters have suggested that the book specifically addresses churches established by missionary activity from Jerusalem, where James was the leader.

Genre

Even though James begins like a letter (1:1), it does not conclude like a letter; and the body of the text does not have features associated with letters. The text of James most resembles what scholars call "paraenesis." Paraenesis is a form of moral exhortation that emphasizes traditional instructions in the mode of imperatives. Paraenesis also utilizes memory and imitation as ways of inculcating traditional moral instructions. Given this literary character, many interpreters compare James with the Wisdom literature of the Old Testament. As a form of paraenesis, then, the Letter of James seeks to remind its readers of their fundamental values and morals as they face internal challenges, especially conflict and favoritism (2:1–17; 4:1–12; 5:19–20; cf. 5:1–6).

Content

The structure of James is elusive, and interpreters have proposed a multitude of outlines. One feature, however, has gained wide consent. Chapter 1, with its proverb-like material, introduces themes that are developed later in the text:

Theme	Introduced	Developed
Enduring trials	1:2–4, 12–15	5:7–11
Nature of true wisdom	1:5–8, 16–18	3:13–4:10
Prayer of faith	1:6–7	5:13–18
Contrast of rich and poor	1:9–11	4:13–5:6
Controlling one's speech	1:19–21	3:1–12
Being doers of the word	1:22–26	2:14–26

James vs. Paul?

One of the more interesting interpretative issues in James is the author's apparent opposition to Paul. Paul states in Galatians 2:16, "We know that a person is justified not by works of the law but through faith in Jesus Christ." He goes on to present Abraham as an example and quotes Genesis 15:6 in support (Gal. 3:6). James states in 2:24, "You see that a person is justified by works and not by faith alone." James also refers to Abraham as an example and quotes Genesis 15:6 (2:21–23). Such parallels and similarities are not likely coincidence. So are Paul and James in conflict? Most likely one is responding to a distortion of the other's teaching. Either James is responding to persons who have distorted Paul's teaching of justification by faith, resulting in a libertine lifestyle (cf. 2 Pet. 3:15b–16), or Paul is responding to a misrepresentation of James's teaching (e.g., Gal. 2:12). Some interpreters maintain that Paul and James would be in agreement with each other. Notice that Paul uses the phrase "works of the law," specific acts prescribed by the law. James, on the other hand, simply uses the term "works," meaning those deeds that accompany faith. Paul actually praises the Thessalonians for their "work of faith and labor of love" (1 Thess. 1:3). Also, some scholars have noted the conceptual parallels between Paul's "fruit of the Spirit" (Gal. 5:22–26) and James's "wisdom from above" (3:17).

The First Letter of Peter

Authorship

This letter purports to come from "Peter, an apostle of Jesus Christ" (1:1a), the disciple of Jesus and prominent leader in the early church (Matt. 16:13–19; Acts 1–15; Gal. 1:18; 2:9). The text, however, lends itself to questions about Peter's authorship. In 1 Peter 5:13 the author refers to "Babylon," which is a common designation for Rome in Jewish and Christian writings after the destruction of the Jerusalem temple in 70 CE. However, tradition and evidence suggest that Peter was martyred in Rome around 65–67 CE, before Rome was commonly referred to as "Babylon." Moreover, the author refers to himself in the letter as an "elder" (5:1), which (1) is not a designation associated with the apostle Peter and (2) represents a development in church organization that best fits the latter part of the first century CE (cf. 5:2–5). Consequently, many interpreters consider 1 Peter to be a pseudonymous letter written after Peter died. Most likely, one or more of Peter's disciples wrote this letter by the authority of Peter's name and his apostolic tradition to address the situation of the letter's recipients.

Recipients

The salutation identifies the addressees as "the exiles of the Dispersion in Pontus, Galatia, Cappadocia, Asia, and Bithynia" (1:1b). These geographical locations were Roman regions that collectively made up Asia Minor (modern-day Turkey). Given the configuration of these regions in the first century, however, many scholars suggest that the intended recipients lived in the northern arc of Asia Minor and that the letter perhaps addressed Christian communities that were not founded by Paul (cf. Acts 16:6–10).

The recipients are primarily, if not exclusively, Gentile Christians (1:14, 18; 2:10; 4:1–4). Their designation as "exiles" and "resident aliens" (1:1b; 2:11; cf. 1:17) has been a point of debate among interpreters. Some scholars suggest that these are legal, social terms referring to Christians whose actual political and social status was marginal. Most scholars, however, understand the terms to be metaphorical, drawn from the Jewish Scriptures to indicate the Christians' new identity as a chosen people and to make sense of their difficult situation.

Occasion

Even though it addresses several churches in different regions, the letter assumes that these churches share a common situation. They are "suffering" on account of their Christian faithfulness (1:6; 2:12, 18–25; 3:13–18a; 4:12–19). Though the exact details of this maltreatment are lacking, much of

Figure 8.1. **Roman provinces of Asia Minor (modern-day Turkey)**

it is connected with verbal slander; they are "maligned" (2:12; 3:16), "blasphemed" (4:4; cf. 3:9), and "reviled" (4:14). The circumstances are similar to those of any minority group who experiences the rhetoric of stereotyping from the dominant culture. Such slander and prejudice fueled a situation that may have resulted in random acts of violence against Christians. Whether or not incidents of physical persecution occurred (2:18–25 may imply the abuse of Christian slaves), these Christians almost certainly experienced the negative economic and social consequences of such discrimination.

Genre

First Peter is an ancient letter with the customary salutation (1:1–2) and concluding remarks (5:12–14). Instead of a thanksgiving/prayer section, 1 Peter contains an extended blessing to God (1:3–12; cf. 2 Cor. 1:3–7) that moves seamlessly into the body of the letter (1:13–5:11). The body of the letter has two major divisions: 1:13–2:10, the new identity as the people of God; and 2:11–5:11, proper conduct in society and in suffering.

Message

In addressing these Gentile Christians in their trying situation, the author adopts a twofold approach. On the one hand, the letter articulates and reinforces the readers' communal identity as Christian believers. This emphasis on identity is communicated in several ways. First, the author stresses the readers' conversion: "Once you were not a people, but now you are the people of God" (2:10; see also 1:3–9, 14–21, 23; 2:1–3, 10, 25; 4:2–3). Second, as the people of God, the readers have now been granted the privileges and identity markers of Israel: "But you are a chosen race, a royal priesthood, a holy nation, God's own people" (2:9; see also 2:4). And as with Israel, this new identity redefines their earthly status as "exiles" and "aliens" (1:1; 2:11); their new identity leads to estrangement in this world. Third, as the estranged people of God, the readers now constitute the "household of God" (4:17; cf. 2:5, "spiritual house") and must love and care for one another (1:22; 3:8; 4:7–11; 5:1–5). Fourth, the author consistently anchors the readers' identity in Jesus Christ, especially in relation to Christ's own suffering and his coming glory. If the readers suffer for what is right, they "are sharing Christ's sufferings" (4:12–13; cf. 2:21–25; 3:18; 4:1–2). And though Christ suffered on earth, his subsequent revealing from heaven will be glorious, a glory that the suffering readers will also share (1:7, 11; 4:13; 5:1, 10).

On the other hand, the letter encourages the readers to adapt as much as possible to their social environment in order to avoid unnecessary slander and harassment. This policy of adaptation is found particularly in relation to the governing authorities (2:13–17) and household relations (2:18–3:7). The author exhorts the readers to "accept the authority of every human institution" (2:13) and to "honor the emperor" (2:17). Slaves and wives are instructed to conform to the traditional norms and values of their roles within the Greco-Roman household. Such conformity functions to counter accusations and suspicions of domestic and social sedition. Overall, the readers are to "conduct [themselves] honorably" among their unbelieving neighbors (2:12; cf. 3:15–16) and to provide no justification for the smear campaign waged against them. Perhaps their unbelieving neighbors will see their "honorable deeds and glorify God when he comes to judge" (2:12).

The Second Letter of Peter and the Letter of Jude

Literary Relationship

Scholars usually treat the letters of Jude and 2 Peter together because a literary relationship appears to exist between the two texts and because the situations they address are very similar, even though the time and place of their respective situations differ. For example, a close reading of Jude 4–18 and 2 Peter 2:1–3:4 reveals that rare Greek terms are replicated in both texts:

Term	Jude	2 Peter
"Blemishes"	12	2:13
"Waterless"	12	2:17
"Bombastic"	16	2:1
"Scoffers"	18	3:3

As a result, many scholars theorize that the author of 2 Peter relied on the text of Jude as a literary resource while composing his letter.

Jude

Jude is an ancient letter with an introductory salutation (1–2), body (3–23), and concluding doxology (24–25). The author identifies himself as "Jude, a servant of Jesus Christ and brother of James" (1). In English the name "Jude" is intended to differentiate this person from Judas Iscariot, but in Greek it is the same name (*Ioudas*). Judas/Jude was a common Jewish name based on the Hebrew name Judah. The person referred to in verse 1 (Jude) is the brother of Jesus and James (Matt. 13:55; Mark 6:3). Christian tradition suggests that Jude became an apostolic missionary (cf. 1 Cor. 9:5) whose grandsons became leaders in the churches of Palestine (Eusebius, *Historia ecclesiastica* 3.19.1–20.8). Although recent research has reopened the question of authorship, making plausible arguments for Jude's authorial authenticity, most scholars regard the letter as pseudonymous. The historical perspective reflects a time beyond first-generation Christians (3, 17). The recipients of the letter are not geographically identified (1), but a Jewish Christian community (or communities) in Palestine is most probable.

The Letter of Jude addresses a situation in which false teachers ("intruders" [4]) have introduced a version of Christianity that leads to immorality (4, 7, 15–16, 18), denies apostolic authority (8; cf. 18), and threatens Christian unity (19). The letter exhorts the readers to "contend for the faith that was once for all entrusted to the saints" (3) and to keep (1, 21, 24) themselves faithful in prayer and love (20–21).

Notably, the author draws from both canonical and noncanonical texts while articulating his points. In addition to the scriptural texts of Genesis (7, 11) and Numbers (5, 11), the author of Jude also utilizes the noncanonical Jewish texts of 1 Enoch (6, 14–15) and the Assumption of Moses (9, perhaps 16). These noncanonical texts and others like them were known and read widely by Jews in the first century, and as evidenced by Jude, some communities deemed them quasi-authoritative even though their popularity and use never translated into canonical status.

2 Peter

Though 2 Peter has an introductory salutation (1:1–2), the genre is more akin to a "last testament," in which a well-known figure gives final instructions to his disciples or family members as he nears death (cf. 2 Timothy). In antiquity last testaments, such as *The Testaments of the Twelve Patriarchs*, were almost exclusively pseudonymous writings, and 2 Peter is likely no exception. The text portrays the apostle Peter as facing death and offering his final teaching as an enduring message (1:13–15). Like Jude, 2 Peter simultaneously warns against false teachers (2:1–3:7) and encourages its readers to maintain the faith in the face of this threat (1:3–11, 19; 3:14–18).

The Johannine Letters

The Johannine letters consist of 1, 2, and 3 John. The name John does not appear anywhere in these texts. Instead, the author of 2 and 3 John is identified simply as "the elder" (2 John 1; 3 John 1). These letters are named after

John in part because they are associated with the Gospel of John; all four texts likely originated within the same Christian community. The three letters address similar contexts and were most likely written and sent at about the same time. Some interpreters also wonder whether the letters circulated together as one "package." If one reads them as a package of materials, the letters would function as follows: (a) 3 John is a letter of commendation for Demetrius (12), who is the letter bearer; (b) 2 John is a "cover letter" to 1 John, addressing the church as a whole, describing the situation, and introducing the major topics of 1 John; and (c) 1 John is a written homily that presents in full rhetorical force the teaching of "the elder."

Occasion

The Johannine letters reflect a Christian community that became deeply divided over theological debates about Jesus. Some members eventually separated from the rest of the community, creating a deep schism (1 John 2:19; cf. 2 John 7). The author refers to these defectors as "antichrists" (1 John 2:18, 22; 4:3; 2 John 7), because they deny that "Jesus is the Christ" or that "Jesus Christ has come in the flesh" (1 John 2:22; 4:2–3, 15; 2 John 7). Most likely these opponents espoused an early form of **Docetism** (from Greek *dokein*, meaning "to seem"), which emerged in the late first or early second century CE. Docetism denied the humanity of Jesus Christ; its adherents believed that Jesus only "seemed" to be human, and some attempted to distinguish between a spiritual Christ and a human Jesus.

Contemporary scholars generally envision the Johannine community as a network of house churches in a limited regional area, possibly Roman Asia (or Asia Minor), with a base church in the vicinity where "the elder" resided. The divided community, then, refers to various house churches that either accepted or rejected the authority and teaching of the elder. Third John provides a particularly helpful window into this situation. The elder writes to a certain Gaius (1), who presumably hosts a church in his house. Gaius is commended for the hospitality that he has extended to those messengers from the elder (5–8). Gaius stands in contrast to a certain Diotrephes (9), who hosts another house church but does not receive the elder's delegates (10). Diotrephes is one of the defectors; he "does not acknowledge [the elder's] authority" (9), and he spreads "false charges against [the elder]" (10). Second John reiterates the importance of hospitality and its role in the community's conflict: "Do not receive into the house or welcome anyone who comes to you and does not bring this teaching; for to welcome is to participate in the evil deeds of such a person" (10–11). This command also reveals that the conflict includes traveling messengers from the defectors.

1 John

Though traditionally designated as a letter, 1 John does not contain the formal features of a letter. It does not have the conventional salutation or concluding remarks, nor does the text resemble what one would expect in the body of an ancient letter. The genre of 1 John is best understood as a homily (or sermon) that exhorts readers to embrace ethical and theological teachings based on an outside authority (e.g., Scripture or tradition). In the case of 1 John, the author relies on the authority of eyewitness tradition, which the author received and now preserves (1:1–4).

First John alternates between ethical exhortation (1:5–2:17; 2:29–3:24; 4:7–12; 4:16b–5:4a) and christological exhortation (teachings about Christ) (2:18–28; 4:1–6, 13–16a; 5:5–12). The two forms of exhortations are intended to complement each other: a correct belief about Jesus will correlate with correct behavior, and vice versa. Furthermore, these exhortations are specific to the situation of the Johannine community.

Christological exhortations. The christological exhortations emphasize the confession that "Jesus is the Christ" (2:22; cf. 5:1), that "Jesus Christ has come in the flesh" (4:2), and that "Jesus is the Son of God" (4:15; cf. 5:5). The defectors deny these teachings (2 John 9). They proclaim a Christology that separates the human Jesus from the divine Father and the divine Christ. As a result, the author of 1 John instructs the house churches to examine traveling teachers to see if their spirit-inspired messages contain the correct confession (4:1–6).

Ethical exhortations. The ethical exhortations revolve around the theme of love (2:10–11, 15–17; 3:11–22; 4:7–12), which is best understood here in terms of fidelity or loyalty. To love one another means to be faithful to the community and its christological tradition. Because of their disloyalty, the defectors "hate" their brothers and sisters (2:9–11; cf. 3:10, 12–15). Similarly, to love God means to "abide" in God's love (fidelity), which was manifested in the sending of his Son "to be the atoning sacrifice for our sins" (4:7–12, esp. 10). Unity of fellowship is underscored throughout: unity between the Father and the Son, unity between the Father/Son and the community, and unity in the community. The language of "abiding" defines this fellowship (2:6, 10, 24, 27–28; 3:6, 24; 4:12–16).

The Revelation to John

With its bizarre images, both monstrous and celestial, the book of Revelation has enticed diverse readers, spawning a multiplicity of interpretations and controversy in both ancient and modern times. Revelation has also deterred readers, who are confused and put off by its strange and enigmatic symbolism. Much of the confusion and controversy surrounding Revelation has to do with readers' expectations and preconceived ideas about the nature and function of Revelation. A very popular interpretation of Revelation assumes that the book is about forecasting the future, more specifically the end times. According to this interpretative approach, the symbols and images are essentially coded language that refers to actual events and persons in the generation living during the "last days"—and in most cases the readers relying on this approach imagine that they are living in the end time. This predictive approach is problematic for two reasons. First, it restricts the relevance and message of Revelation exclusively to the end-time generation. If Revelation is only about forecasting events and persons in the end times, what use is it for the myriad of generations that have come before? This approach fails to take seriously that Revelation was intended for and addressed to fledgling churches in Roman Asia (or Asia Minor) some nineteen hundred years ago (see below) and therefore its message was actually relevant to their situation. Second, up to now this predictive approach has always been wrong. For example, those who read Revelation in this predictive manner have often identified the "beast" of Revelation 13 with a figure in their own time (e.g., the pope, Adolph Hitler, Ayatollah Khomeini, Mikhail Gorbachev, and Saddam Hussein, just to name a few), but none of these figures has ushered in the end of time. A predictive approach to Revelation misunderstands the purpose of Revelation.

The approach we take in this book is consistent with what we have done with other writings of the Bible. We attempt to understand the text in its historical and literary contexts. In other words, how was Revelation read and understood by its intended audience, the seven churches of Roman Asia named in Revelation 1–3? Certainly there are future aspects found in Revelation, but these refer to either the audience's future ("to show his servants what must soon take place," 22:6; cf. 1:1, 3; 22:10) or the ultimate future of God's grand intervention, which is conveyed at numerous points throughout the Bible. Our assumption is that the message and purpose of Revelation are inextricably connected to, but not exhausted by, its historical context.

Author and Audience

The author identifies himself simply as "John" (1:4, 9; cf. 1:2), who has been exiled to the island of Patmos "because of the word of God and the testimony of Jesus" (1:9). Early Christian tradition was actually divided on John's identity. Many ancient writers held that the author was John the apostle, one of the twelve disciples. Others, however, claimed that he was John the elder, perhaps the same elder who wrote 2–3 John. The text itself suggests a third

Figure 8.2. Location of the seven churches of Revelation and the island of Patmos

alternative, a Christian prophet (1:3; 22:9, 18–19). Christian prophets were Spirit-inspired messengers who delivered God's (or Christ's) word to churches (cf. Acts 11:27–28; 21:9; 1 Cor. 14:29–32; 1 Thess. 5:19–20). They could minister in the context of one church (1 Cor. 11:4–5; 14:29–32; cf. Rev. 2:20), or they could be itinerant prophets, traveling from church to church (Acts 11:27–28; cf. Rev. 2:2). The author of Revelation was most likely an itinerant prophet whose preaching circuit included the seven churches addressed in Revelation. These seven churches (1:4, 11; 2:1–3:22) located in the western region of the Roman province of Asia were the intended audience for John's Revelation.

Genre

The book of Revelation is a "word of prophecy" (1:3; 22:18–19) written in the form of an apocalypse with a letter framework. The message of Revelation originates from the author's vocation as a Christian prophet: "I was in the spirit on the Lord's day" (1:10). Because he is exiled, John can no longer travel to the churches to deliver his Spirit-inspired message; he has to communicate it to them in writing.

One can discern the letter framework at the beginning and the end of Revelation (1:4–8; 22:21). The author sends a long-distance correspondence identifying both the sender and recipients. The introductory chapters also reveal the occasional nature of this writing; the author addresses the particular situation of seven churches in Roman Asia (Rev. 1–3).

Finally, the author presents his "word of prophecy" in the form of an apocalypse. This literary form is the same as that of the book of Daniel and is related to the tradition of biblical prophecy. As stated in the discussion of Daniel, apocalyptic literature is characterized by elaborate visions/dreams, symbols, numerology, and eschatology, including final judgment, resurrection, and eternal salvation. An apocalypse is revelatory literature, and its visions and related symbols purport to unveil the future or the realm of heaven or both. These revelations, however, are intended to connect with and interpret the circumstances of the intended readers in order to give them the proper perspective on reality. For example, some of the churches that John addresses are presumably participating in events that include worship of the emperor. Perhaps these churches considered these acts to be meaningless (cf. 1 Cor. 8:4–13; 10), or perhaps they thought their participation would "honor the emperor" (cf. 1 Pet. 2:17) and gain the goodwill of the city. By contrast, John's vision of the dragon and the two beasts in Revelation 12–13 reveals in dramatic fashion that such participation is nothing less than an unholy alliance with Satan and ultimate treason against God and Christ (Rev. 14). These churches might understand their actions as constructive accommodations and religious ambiguities, but John's vision starkly exposes their behavior as blasphemous. The vision interprets their circumstances and reveals the reality of their actions.

Situation

Earlier scholarship interpreted Revelation as a response to persecution, and this persecution was perceived as being orchestrated on an empire-wide scale by the emperor Domitian (81–96 CE), who demanded that all inhabitants worship him as "lord and god." Recent scholarship has questioned this interpretation for two reasons. First, we do not possess any evidence of an empire-wide persecution of Christians during the reign of Domitian. Moreover, there is no evidence that Domitian persecuted Christians as a matter of policy. If Christians experienced persecution during the reign of Domitian, it was likely sporadic and local. Second, John envisions a multitude of martyrs (Christians who die because of their faith) in the future, not the present (6:9–11; 12:11; 14:3; 16:6; 17:6; 18:24). John knows that one person has been martyred (Antipas [2:13]), that a few churches are experiencing some harassment (2:3, 9, 13), and that he himself has been exiled (1:9). But these are simply precursors to the onslaught against faithful Christians that John perceives from his prophetic visions.

Instead of a context of empire-wide persecution, most scholars now understand Revelation to be addressing a situation in which the readers are accommodating to their Roman culture to the point of compromising their Christian identity. Though the concrete details of this accommodation are lacking, the issue of idolatry is at the forefront of John's concern. Sacrifices and other forms of religious offerings were ubiquitous in the ancient world. Both public and private events usually involved some form of offering to a god or gods. Moreover, in Roman Asia the practice of emperor worship was growing steadily, promoted by civic leaders (rather than the emperor himself) in order to gain the goodwill of the emperor. In order to participate fully in the life of the city, Christians constantly faced the prospect of participating in pagan acts of worship. The seven letters to the seven churches (2:1–3:22) reveal that most of the churches were compromising in this regard (2:3–5; 3:1b–3, 15–18) and that they were being threatened by a false teaching of radical accommodation (2:14–16, 20–23). John's prophetic message and visions expose the reality of this accommodation that violates the first commandment and its prohibition against idolatry. Notably, there are two exceptions to this unfaithful accommodation: the churches at Smyrna (2:8–11) and Philadelphia (3:7–13) have not compromised. Because of their faithfulness, these churches are experiencing hardships and affliction from local civic leaders or residents or both. John's visions affirm their faithfulness and encourage them to endure.

Content

Interpreters conceive of Revelation's structure in various ways. The following outline represents one approach to seeing the overall flow of Revelation.

> 1:1–8—Title and letter salutation
>> Revelation gets its title from 1:1, "The revelation of Jesus Christ . . . to his servant John." The Greek word translated "revelation" is *apokalypsis*. Thus, scholars sometimes refer to Revelation as the Apocalypse.
>
> 1:9–3:22—Vision and messages of the exalted Christ
>> 1:9–20—Vision of the exalted Christ
>> 2:1–3:22—Prophetic messages to the seven churches
>> These prophetic messages are given in a quasi-letter form and are often designated the seven letters to the seven churches. These prophetic letters follow a similar pattern: command to write, titles/ description of the exalted Christ, message with praise or censure,

word of exhortation, and conclusion with promise of victory and proclamation formula.

4:1–22:5—Symbolic visions of heavenly scenes and the end

4:1–5:14—Vision of the heavenly throne room

6:1–8:1—Opening of the seven seals, with interlude (7:1–17)

8:2–11:18—Blowing of the seven trumpets, with interludes (10:1–11; 11:1–14)

12:1–14:20—The dragon, the beasts, and the Lamb

15:1–16:21—Seven bowls of wrath

17:1–19:10—Judgment of Babylon (Rome)

19:11–22:5—Coming and victory of Christ; new heaven and new earth

The visions of the seven seals, the seven trumpets, and the seven bowls all deal with similar subject matter. They incorporate traditional ideas about the end time: the suffering of the righteous and their subsequent vindication, divine judgment, and eventual eternal peace and salvation. Repetition with variation is key to understanding these visions. Next, John combines the visions of traditional end-time scenarios with visions about how Rome plays a part in this drama, both in the suffering of Christians (chaps. 12–13) and as a recipient of divine judgment (chaps. 17–18). Finally, most of the visions begin with a heavenly scene (e.g., chaps. 4–5) where worship serves as the dominant activity. This exemplary worship in heaven calls the audience to participate in the true worship of God and Christ rather than the idolatrous worship of the emperor and pagan deities. Thus, these visions interpret the earthly situation of the seven churches in light of the divine drama that is happening in heaven and will happen in the end.

22:6–21—Epilogue

Theological Reflection: A Fitting Conclusion

The General Letters and Revelation are noteworthy in terms of their collective function within the canon of Scripture. In particular, they help to round out and conclude the biblical witness.

Catholic Epistles

As noted earlier, James, 1–2 Peter, 1–3 John, and Jude became part of the New Testament canon as a collection known as the "Catholic Epistles." These texts certainly had an existence and use before they were brought together, so why did the early Christians compile this collection with these particular texts? If the Pauline and Gospel collections coalesce around common authorship (Paul) and common content (Gospels), what is the purpose or logic behind assembling the catholic collection? Many scholars believe that the catholic collection was crafted primarily in response to the Pauline collection.

Impetus for the catholic collection. The development of the New Testament canon had at its core the thirteen (or fourteen if Hebrews was included) letters of Paul and the four Gospels. Perhaps some desired additional "apostolic balance." Paul was not the only apostle. Early Christians likely found additional texts representing the larger apostolic tradition to be essential. Moreover, the Pauline letters were open to misinterpretation and distortion, which is evidenced both explicitly (2 Pet. 3:14b–17) and implicitly (James 2:14–26) in the catholic collection. This distortion of the Pauline tradition included some Christians pitting Paul and the other apostles against one another. The catholic collection functioned as a complement to Paul's letters, demonstrating that Paul and the other apostles were in agreement in their apostolic witness to the faith.

Constitution of the catholic collection. The shape and framework of the catholic collection appear to have been influenced by the Pauline collection. The apostles represented in the catholic collection are James, Peter, John, and Jude. The first three names (James, Peter, and John) match the names and order of Christian leaders that Paul mentions in Galatians 2:9, where he refers to them as the church's "pillars." Jude is never mentioned by name in Paul's letters, but Paul does mention "the other apostles and the brothers of the Lord" in 1 Corinthians 9:5. So the brothers of Jesus (James and Jude) bracket the apostles Peter and John. The inclusion of Jude also brings the number of letters in the catholic collection to seven (James; 1–2 Peter; 1–3 John; Jude). This seven-letter collection, then, corresponds to the seven churches that constitute the Pauline collection (Rome, Corinth, Galatia, Ephesus, Philippi, Colossae, and Thessalonica).

Revelation

The book of Revelation not only concludes the New Testament canon but it also provides a proper conclusion to the Christian Bible as a whole. Its vision of a new heaven and new earth (21:1–22:5) evokes the beginning of the canon and the creation accounts of Genesis 1–2. What God began in creation is consummated with the new heaven and new earth. Although the garden of Eden (Gen. 2) is replaced with a city (the new Jerusalem [Rev. 21:2, 9–21]), a river still runs in its midst and the tree of life remains (Gen. 2:9–10;

Rev. 22:1–2). Moreover, the darkness and watery chaos (Gen. 1:2) that God subdued and ordered is now banished altogether. In the new creation, the threatening waters and darkness simply do not exist (Rev. 21:1, 25; 22:5). As a result, the new creation does not need the sun or moon (21:23; 22:5); the very presence of God gives light (21:23; 22:5). Revelation gives witness to the divine accomplishment of redeeming all creation.

SUGGESTED READING

Gorman, Michael J. *Reading Revelation Responsibly: Uncivil Worship and Witness.* Eugene, OR: Cascade Books, 2011.

Koester, Craig R. *Revelation and the End of All Things.* 2nd ed. Grand Rapids: Eerdmans, 2018.

Peeler, Amy L. B., and Patrick Gray. *Hebrews: An Introduction and Study Guide.* T&T Clark Study Guides to the New Testament. New York: T&T Clark, 2020.

Puskas, Charles B. *Hebrews, the General Letters, and Revelation: An Introduction.* Eugene, OR: Cascade Books, 2016.

Skinner, Matthew L. *A Companion to the New Testament: The General Letters and Revelation.* Waco: Baylor University Press, 2018.

Conclusion

Overarching Story of the Christian Scriptures

The Bible is in essence an anthology that contains many different kinds of literary texts from different time periods. These texts are not uniform in their purposes or meanings. The Bible gives witness to a diversity of voices, some affirming and expanding traditions, and others challenging and reinterpreting those traditions. And yet, while still acknowledging the diversity within the Bible, one can also detect an emerging, overarching story. The God of Israel creates a good creation, including the creation of humanity. Humanity's sin, however, corrupts and distorts God's good creation. God does not abandon humanity but continues with the divine intention to bless and restore. This divine intention finds expression in a covenant relationship with Israel, whose story is a complex plot of calling, disobedience, judgment, and redemption. The nations (or Gentiles) are never far from this story, being held accountable for their own acts of injustice and idolatry. Even then, hope remains that the nations will be included in Israel's salvation. All of God's redeeming efforts— for both Israel and the nations—are fulfilled and accomplished in the central event of Christ's ministry, death, and resurrection. The Christ event represents the beginning of God's end-time action to reconcile all creation to God's self. As it awaits the consummation of this redemption in the coming of Christ, the community of Christ followers gives witness to this divine action in its life together and its proclamation. This overarching story, of course, provides another context in which to interpret the texts of the Bible.

Glossary

acrostic A type of poem in which the first letter of each line or paragraph follows a particular pattern. Several biblical texts are acrostics in which the first letters of successive verses spell out the Hebrew alphabet in order (e.g., Ps. 119, parts of Lamentations and Nahum).

Alexander the Great King of Macedonia who consolidated the Greek armies, conquered the Persian Empire in 332 BCE, and gained control of territories in Egypt and Palestine. Alexander's conquests furthered the spread of Hellenism throughout the ancient world.

allegory An interpretive approach that identifies hidden meanings and symbolic values in texts. For example, an allegorical interpretation of the book of Jonah would identify Jonah's encounter with the great fish as an allegory for Jesus's death, burial, and resurrection.

amanuensis A secretary who aided in the production of texts in the Greco-Roman world. An amanuensis did not merely take dictation but sometimes drafted, edited, or composed texts.

Amarna Age A period of Egyptian history in the fourteenth century BCE characterized by radical change under Pharaoh Akhenaton. Changes included the move of the capital city to Amarna and the introduction of a monotheistic religion.

Amenemope, Wisdom of An Egyptian wisdom text that has many points of comparison with Proverbs 22:17–24:22, likely indicating a literary relationship between the two.

amphictyony A term originally applied to archaic Greek tribes that organized around a religious center. Martin Noth appropriated the term to describe the twelve tribes of Israel in the days of Joshua and Judges, but the Israelite organization was looser than that of the Greek amphictyony.

ancestral narratives The narratives of Genesis 12–50 that recount the story of Israel's ancestors, beginning with Abraham.

ancient Near East   The cultural setting of the OT narratives. Geographically, the ancient Near East comprises the general area of the modern-day Middle East. The ancient Near East is known as the "cradle of civilization," because it was home to great civilizations such as the Sumerians, Egyptians, Assyrians, and Babylonians.

Antiochus IV Epiphanes   Seleucid king who came to power in 175 BCE and took the title Epiphanes ("god manifest"). Antiochus IV brutally forced Hellenism on the Jewish people and desecrated the Jerusalem temple, which prompted the Maccabean Revolt. Many scholars see the book of Daniel as a reflection of Jewish persecution under Antiochus IV.

apocalypse   A type of literature, influenced primarily by the prophetic tradition, that is characterized by elaborate visions/dreams, symbols, numerology, angels, cosmic upheavals, and an emphasis on the end time, including the final judgment, resurrection, and eternal salvation. The term comes from the Greek word *apokalypsis*, which means "revelation." This revelatory literature, with its visions and related symbols, purports to reveal the future or the heavenly realm, or both, in order to interpret the circumstances of its readers. The books of Daniel and Revelation are the two biblical books that represent the apocalypse genre, but other biblical texts, such as Isaiah 24–27, Zechariah 9–14, Mark 13, and 2 Thessalonians 2:1–12, are often identified as "apocalyptic."

apocalyptic, apocalypticism   A complex of ideas that includes ethical (good/evil dualism, existence of angels and demons), spatial (supernatural world, levels of heaven, eternal places for the wicked and the righteous), and temporal (end-time perspective and events) dimensions. These ideas come together in an end-time perspective that sees reality in terms of two ages: the present evil age, which is dominated by sin and death and is hostile to God's ways and God's people, and the age to come, which is a new heaven and a new earth where sin and death no longer exist. The transition from the present evil age to the age to come is facilitated by God's grand intervention (for early Christians this is Christ's return), which includes resurrection of the dead and subsequent judgment of the wicked and vindication of the righteous.

Apocrypha   A collection of Jewish religious writings that were included in the Septuagint and give insight into Jewish perspectives and practices during the Greek and Roman time periods. The word *apocrypha* means "hidden texts." Though Jews eventually excluded these texts from the Hebrew Bible, some Christian groups came to regard them as part of the Christian canon and labeled them "deuterocanonical" ("second canon"), because they became canonical later than the other writings. The Apocrypha includes Tobit, Judith, Additions to Esther, Wisdom of Solomon, Wisdom of Ben Sirach, Baruch, Additions to Daniel, 1–2 Maccabees, 1 Esdras, Psalm 151, 3 Maccabees, 2 Esdras, and 4 Maccabees.

apodictic law A type of law given on the authority of the lawgiver that takes the form of a basic, universal statement. Most of the Ten Commandments are examples of apodictic laws.

apostle One closely associated with Jesus, particularly as a witness to his resurrection, who has been sent (Greek, *apostellō*, "to send") to continue Jesus's work.

apostolicity A criterion early Christians used in the process of determining the parameters of the New Testament canon. A text meeting the criterion of apostolicity would have apostolic connections: it was written by an apostle, written in the time of the apostles, or written in agreement with apostolic teaching.

archaeology The study of human history through the excavation of material remains. Archaeology is a critical tool for interpreters, because it gives insights into the culture and lives of the people the biblical texts portray.

ark of the covenant The most important visible symbol of YHWH's divine presence with the Israelite community. The ark was a golden box decorated with winged cherubs that contained the Decalogue, Aaron's blossomed rod, and manna. It rested first in the tabernacle (mobile sanctuary) and later in the holy of holies within the temple.

Assyria, Assyrians One of the great empires of ancient Mesopotamia, which had its capital city at Nineveh. Assyria conquered the Northern Kingdom of Israel in 722/721 BCE and laid siege to Jerusalem in 701 BCE. The Assyrian Empire fell to Babylon in the late seventh century BCE.

Atrahasis Epic A Mesopotamian flood narrative that may be the basis for the Gilgamesh Epic.

Authorized Version *See* King James Version.

autographs The original manuscripts written by the biblical authors, which are no longer in existence.

Babylon, Babylonians One of the great empires of ancient Mesopotamia that rose to power after defeating the Assyrians. Babylon first sacked Jerusalem in 598/597 BCE and sent many of the city's inhabitants into exile. Judah fell completely to Babylon in 587/586 BCE, and another wave of Judeans went into exile. The Babylonian Empire fell to Persia in 539 BCE.

Bar Kokhba Revolt Led by Simon bar Kosiba (later known as Simon bar Kokhba) in 132 CE, this was the last notable attempt by Judean Jews to oust the Romans. In response, the Romans leveled Jerusalem and forbade Jews from living in Judea. This revolt is also known as the Second Jewish War/Revolt.

beatitude A proverb-like saying that announces a blessing or congratulation. The most famous examples are Jesus's Beatitudes (Matt. 5:3–12) in the Sermon on the Mount.

benediction A brief word of blessing and thanksgiving to God.

biography, ancient   A literary genre that selectively narrates a person's sayings, deeds, and death in order to portray the essence of that person. Ancient biographies were not intended to be objective but rather were meant to persuade readers to adopt a particular perception of the subject and imitate the subject's life. An ancient biography is referred to as a "life" (Greek, *bios*; Latin, *vita*).

Book of the Twelve   The twelve Minor Prophets that scribes gathered together as a single prophetic collection arranged in roughly chronological order and connected with catchwords and similar themes. It comprises Hosea, Joel, Amos, Obadiah, Jonah, Micah, Nahum, Habakkuk, Zephaniah, Haggai, Zechariah, and Malachi.

books of Moses   A way of referring to the first five books of the Bible (Pentateuch) that reflects the traditional association of these books with Moses.

Canaan   The region along the eastern Mediterranean coast that consists of modern-day Syria, Lebanon, Israel, and Jordan.

canon   Coming from the Greek word for a measuring rod, the identification and listing of texts that function as scripture (i.e., authoritatively) for a religious group.

canonical criticism   A variety of approaches that emphasize the final form of a biblical book and how that book has been received and interpreted as authoritative (or "canonical") by the believing community (Jewish or Christian). A text's historical process of canonization and its location in the canon are also contexts for interpretation.

casuistic law   A type of law that applies basic principles to various contexts in a community's life. This type of law often takes the form of "If this thing happens, then this consequence follows." Much of the Covenant Code (Exod. 20:22–23:19) is made up of casuistic laws.

catholic   A term for something "universal" or "general."

Catholic Epistles   A canonical collection that coalesced in the late third century and included James, 1–2 Peter, 1–3 John, and Jude. The modern category "General Letters" is based on the Catholic Epistles, though the General Letters also includes the book of Hebrews.

central hill country   A major geographical division of Palestine that lies between the coastal plain and the Jordan Rift. This region includes—from north to south—the Galilean hills, the Plain of Megiddo, the Shephelah, and the plateau of Jerusalem.

Christology   Theological reflection that explores the significance and identity of Jesus of Nazareth.

Chronicler   The proposed compiler and editor of 1–2 Chronicles, Ezra, and Nehemiah whose work reflects the Second Temple period and its theological-political concerns.

circumcision   The procedure of removing the foreskin from male genitals. Circumcision was a sign of God's covenant with Abraham (Gen. 17) and became a major Jewish identity marker.

coastal plain   The geographical region of Palestine that runs along the shore of the eastern Mediterranean Sea.

Code of Hammurabi   An eighteenth-century-BCE Babylonian law code that reflects rigid social stratification and the principle of *lex talionis*.

codex, codices   An ancient book form constructed by stacking sheets of vellum or papyrus and binding them along one edge.

composite document   A document constructed by bringing together multiple smaller texts or fragments of texts and editing them into a unified whole. For example, see the discussions about the formation of Isaiah or 2 Corinthians.

covenant   A formal agreement that binds two parties together in a relationship. Covenants were often formed between parties of unequal power where a stronger party would promise to provide security for a weaker party that promised to provide loyalty. Biblical covenants often emphasize either the responsibility of the stronger party (e.g., God's promises in the Abrahamic covenant) or the responsibility of the weaker party (e.g., Israel's obligations in the Sinaitic/Mosaic covenant).

Covenant Code   The law code following the Ten Commandments that expands those ten basic statements and applies them to daily life (Exodus 20:22–23:19).

cult, cultic   A term referring to organized worship, often occurring in a temple setting.

Cyrus   The Persian ruler who in 538 BCE issued an edict that allowed the exiled Israelites to return to their homeland. The book of Isaiah refers to Cyrus as the chosen one of YHWH.

Day of Atonement   An annual feast day in Israelite worship that had to do with the cleansing of impurity for the purpose of restoring and renewing the relationship between YHWH and Israel. The feast involved purification offerings, confession of sin, and the removal of a scapegoat from the community.

Day of YHWH   In the tradition of the Latter Prophets, the day of victory and reign of YHWH over those who oppose the divine will. At times, Israel is included among those who oppose YHWH, because of corrupt religious and social systems.

Dead Sea Scrolls   A collection of scrolls discovered in the mid-twentieth century in caves near the Dead Sea. The collection includes Hebrew biblical manuscripts dating from the mid-third century BCE to the first century CE, which draw from a variety of text types and represent the oldest known Hebrew manuscripts of the Hebrew Bible / Old Testament.

Decalogue   *See* Ten Commandments.

Deutero-Isaiah   *See* Isaiah, book of.

Deuteronomic, Deuteronomistic   Language or theology that reflects the perspective of the book of Deuteronomy, especially ideas of obedience to the Sinaitic/Mosaic covenant and centralization of worship in Jerusalem.

Deuteronomistic History   A name for the books of Deuteronomy, Joshua, Judges, 1–2 Samuel, and 1–2 Kings, which tell the history of Israel up until the exile from a Deuteronomistic perspective.

Diaspora   A Greek term, meaning "the dispersion" or "the scattering," commonly applied to Jews who lived outside Palestine. Frequently, Diaspora Jews had different theological and cultural practices (temple worship, food laws, circumcision, relationship to Greco-Roman culture) from Judean Jews.

diatribe   An ancient literary technique that involved voicing a theoretical opponent's position before stating one's own opinion.

Docetism   A Christian heresy that emerged in the late first or early second century CE and denied the humanity of Jesus Christ. Docetists believed that Jesus only "seemed" (from the Greek *dokein*, "to seem") to be human. Some adherents distinguished between the spiritual Christ and the human Jesus.

Documentary Hypothesis   The theory that the Pentateuch developed when editors combined several preexisting documents. The classic statement of this hypothesis came from Julius Wellhausen in 1878 and was accepted by scholars for the next century. Wellhausen referred to the different documents as J, E, D, and P.

dynamic equivalence   A translation method that focuses on the function of the original language and attempts to re-create that reading experience in the target language so that the meaning of the original language is faithfully expressed. Accordingly, this method is often described as a "meaning for meaning" translation.

Eden, garden of   The garden into which God placed Adam and Eve to live and provide care for. After they ate from the forbidden tree, God expelled Adam and Eve from the garden of Eden and placed angelic guards at its entrance.

emperor cult   Worship of the Roman emperor as a god, which became increasingly important in the Roman Empire after the death of Julius Caesar in 44 BCE. Emperor worship was closely associated with political loyalty to the Roman Empire.

Enuma Elish   The Babylonian creation epic, which takes its name from its opening words. The epic dates back to the Akkadians in the third millennium BCE and describes creation as the result of war among gods and goddesses; the earth is shaped from the defeated body of the goddess Tiamat.

Epicureans, Epicureanism   A Greek philosophy that aimed to free humans from the fear of death and the fear of the gods by arguing that the gods do not exist and that humans are free to pursue the best possible life.

Essenes   A sect of Judean Jews in the first century CE who believed that in the afterlife a person's soul would experience reward or punishment based on how that person lived. Accordingly, they strove to live pure and righteous lives without the distractions of wealth and, in some cases, marriage. They criticized the temple establishment for being corrupt and often isolated themselves into their own communities.

etiology   An explanation of a current reality through the narration of its origins.

exile, Babylonian   The period from 587/586 BCE (the fall of Jerusalem to Babylon) to 538 BCE (edict by Cyrus of Persia allowing the return of the exiles to their homeland) during which large numbers of Judeans were in exile in Babylon. This period prompted significant theological reflection and religious-political shifts due to the destruction of the temple and end of the monarchy.

exodus event   The story of how God used Moses to lead the Israelites out of bondage in Egypt using miraculous signs and supernatural events.

Farrer Theory   Austin Farrer's solution to the synoptic problem that postulates that Matthew used Mark and that Luke used both Mark and Matthew. This solution maintains Markan priority without Q.

feminist criticism   An approach to the text that emphasizes the perspectives and experiences of women. Feminist readings detect forms of patriarchy in the text and in the history of interpretation, but they also highlight positive portrayals of the feminine in the text that have often been ignored or even deliberately suppressed in the history of interpretation.

Fertile Crescent   The name given to the arable region that curves from the Persian Gulf westward toward Syria and down through Palestine into Egypt. The name derives from the crescent-like shape of this area.

Five Scrolls   *See* Megilloth.

formal correspondence   A translation method that takes a literal approach to translation by staying as close as possible to the form of the original language in both its grammar and word order. This method is often described as a "word for word" translation.

form criticism   The analysis and classification of literary types according to their form. These literary types—such as hymns, laments, sagas, parables, and miracle stories—are studied for their rhetorical functions within a text. Older form-critical approaches attempted to reconstruct the history of a literary form within various settings of Israel's institutions or the various activities of early Christianity.

Former Prophets   A division of the Hebrew Bible that consists of the books Joshua, Judges, 1–2 Samuel, and 1–2 Kings.

General Letters   A modern designation for a group of New Testament writings comprising Hebrews, James, 1–2 Peter, 1–3 John, and Jude. These writings tend to address a general Christian audience. This collection is based on the ancient collection known as the "Catholic Epistles," which did not include Hebrews.

Gentiles　The term for non-Jewish peoples. Gentiles were sometimes referred to as "the nations."

Gilgamesh, Epic of　A Mesopotamian epic poem about a hero named Gilgamesh, a ruler who searches for eternal life. The poem includes a flood story comparable to the Genesis story of Noah.

gnosticism　A movement in antiquity that took root among a variety of religious adherents, including some early Christians. Gnosticism focused on a saving knowledge (Greek, *gnosis*) that was only given to an elite few. This special knowledge espoused a dualism that considered the physical or material realm to be evil, whereas good could only be found in the spiritual realm.

gospel　Meaning "good news," this term initially referred to an oral announcement or proclamation but came to be associated specifically with the message of and about Jesus Christ. In the second century CE, *Gospel* became a designation for the literary texts that tell the story of Jesus's life and ministry.

Gospel　Writing that narrates the life and ministry of Jesus. The biblical Gospels are Matthew, Mark, Luke, and John. The genre of the Gospels is best understood as ancient biography: portrayals of Jesus that reflect the theological and literary concerns of their authors. The four Gospels coalesced into a collection no later than the latter half of the second century and quickly gained wide acceptance as authoritative.

Habiru　Groups who caused various kinds of conflict in Egypt, Palestine, and Mesopotamia during the fourteenth century BCE. Some of these conflicts could have involved rebellious elements among enslaved people.

Hasmonean dynasty　Established after the success of the Maccabean Revolt, these Jewish rulers reigned over an independent Judea between 142 and 63 BCE.

Hebrew Bible　The collection of Jewish Scriptures, which is arranged into three parts: the Law (*Torah*), the Prophets (*Nevi'im*), and the Writings (*Ketuvim*). The Hebrew Bible is also known as the "Tanakh," which is an acronym based on the Hebrew titles for the three parts.

Hellenism　Greek culture and ideas; usually associated with the spread of the Greek Empire by Alexander the Great.

hermeneutics　The art and process of interpretation.

Herod Antipas　The ruler of Galilee and Perea during the time of Jesus. He reigned from 6 to 39 CE. The son of Herod the Great, Herod Antipas was a client ruler of Rome.

Herod the Great　Ruler of Judea at the time of Jesus's birth. He reigned from 37 to 4 BCE. A client ruler of Rome, Herod the Great is known for his expansion of the Jerusalem temple and, according to the Gospel of Matthew, ordering the mass execution of male babies around Bethlehem in an effort to eradicate the threat to his throne.

historical Jesus   The term for the "Jesus of history" who stands behind the interpretive narratives of the Gospels. Scholars use a variety of methods and criteria to determine which material in the Gospels is historical and which is fictional. Scholarly conclusions about the historical Jesus exhibit tremendous variety.

Holiness Code   The material in Leviticus 17–26 comprising instructions to the community on how to reflect the holiness of YHWH in their worship and community life.

holy   The state of being distinct. Holiness in Scripture is based on the holiness of YHWH and is not a way to separate from the world but a way to relate to the world based on the distinct covenant relationship between YHWH and YHWH's people.

homily   A term for a sermon.

household code   Instructions addressing relationships within the Greco-Roman household, such as those between husbands and wives, servants and masters, and parents and children. Biblical examples of household codes appear in Ephesians 5:22–6:9; Colossians 3:18–4:1; and 1 Peter 2:18–3:7 and are reflected in 1 Timothy 3:1–13; 5:1–6:2; and Titus 2:1–10.

Hyksos   A Semitic group who came to power in Egypt between 1700 and 1550 BCE. The story of Joseph is often related to the period in which the Hyksos were in power.

idolatry   The worship of idols, which were material figures or images that represented deities. Idolatry was widespread in the ancient world and is strictly prohibited in the biblical tradition. In addition, the biblical tradition forbids the fashioning of any kind of image to represent YHWH.

inclusio   A literary device in which similar material (e.g., words, phrases, or images) brackets or frames a section of text.

intercalation   A literary device in which one story is framed by another. This "sandwich" storytelling style is particularly prominent in the Gospel of Mark.

Isaiah, book of   An Old Testament book included in the Latter Prophets. Scholars typically argue that the book originated in stages. Chapters 1–39 (Proto-Isaiah) relate primarily to the eighth-century prophet Isaiah of Jerusalem; chapters 40–55 (Deutero-Isaiah) come from an exilic prophet who carries the Isaianic tradition into the sixth century; and chapters 56–66 (Trito-Isaiah) relate to the time after the return from exile.

Israel, kingdom of   The Northern Kingdom after the division of the united monarchy. The kingdom of Israel fell to Assyria in 722/721 BCE. The name "Israel" can also refer to the nation of Israel as a whole or to the ancestor Jacob whom God renamed "Israel."

JEDP   *See* Documentary Hypothesis.

Jeroboam I   The first ruler of the Northern Kingdom of Israel after the division of the united monarchy. Jeroboam I established sanctuaries with golden calves at Bethel and Dan to prevent Israelites from associating with the Davidic ideology in Jerusalem at festival time and to support the northern economy. He reigned from 922 to 901 BCE.

Jerusalem Council   The assembly of Jewish Christians in Jerusalem that met to debate the question of how Gentiles come to receive salvation. Accounts of the Jerusalem Council are found in Acts 15 and Galatians 2:1–10.

Jordan Rift   The geographical region of Palestine that runs from Mount Hermon in the north down to the Dead Sea. The Jordan Rift provides the location for the Jordan River, which flows from the Sea of Galilee to the Dead Sea.

Judah, kingdom of   The Southern Kingdom after the division of the united monarchy. The kingdom of Judah fell to Babylon in 587/586 BCE.

judge   An Israelite tribal leader during the period from Israel's entry into Canaan until the establishment of the monarchy. The judges were primarily military leaders who periodically delivered the Israelites from various oppressors.

King James Version   Also called the King James Bible. This translation of the Christian Scriptures first appeared in 1611 and exerted tremendous influence on British and American cultures for centuries. Translated from Hebrew and Greek by a committee of translators from Oxford, Cambridge, and Westminster, the King James Bible is also known as the "Authorized Version."

King's Highway   One of the major highways between Damascus and Egypt in the ancient Near East. It ran through the Transjordan Plateau east of the Jordan River and was valuable for military and trade purposes.

lament psalms   A major type of psalm characterized by a cry out to God, a description of a crisis, a plea for help, and a statement of trust that God has heard the prayer. Lament psalms often conclude with a vow to praise the God who comes to deliver.

Latter Prophets   A division of the Hebrew Bible that consists of the books Isaiah, Jeremiah, Ezekiel, and the Book of the Twelve (Hosea, Joel, Amos, Obadiah, Jonah, Micah, Nahum, Habakkuk, Zephaniah, Haggai, Zechariah, Malachi).

Levites   The priestly clan tasked with caring for the tabernacle, and later the temple, and its worship regalia.

lex talionis   The law of retaliation, which is defined by the principle that punishments should fit the crimes, or "an eye for an eye."

logos   A Greek term that carried a variety of meanings in antiquity (e.g., word, statement, thought). Stoic philosophers used the term *logos* to refer to the unifying agent or logic of the universe, and Jewish writers used the same term to refer to God's creative and redemptive work in the world. The author of the Gospel of John builds on these preexisting conversations in the prologue to his Gospel (John 1:1, 14).

Luther, Martin   The Protestant Reformer who translated the Bible from Hebrew and Greek into German between 1522 and 1534. Luther's German Bible became greatly influential in German literature and theology.

LXX   *See* Septuagint.

Maccabean Revolt   The twenty-five-year Jewish uprising that began in 167 BCE under the leadership of the priest Mattathias and his five sons. The revolt was a response to Seleucid pressure to offer pagan sacrifices and enforce Hellenistic culture in Judea.

magi   Based on the Greek word *magoi*, a term for Eastern wise men who studied the stars, dreams, and other forms of divination.

Magnificat   The traditional name for the Virgin Mary's song in Luke 1:46–55. The name derives from the Latin translation of the song's opening words ("My soul magnifies the Lord").

Manual of Purity   The material in Leviticus 11–16 that addresses preparation for worship in terms of clean (a state acceptable for worship) and unclean (a contagious state unacceptable for worship).

Manual of Sacrifice   The material in Leviticus 1–7 that presents the ritual for five sacrifices for both laity and priests that constitute a large part of ancient Israel's worship.

manuscripts   A term that means "handwritten" and refers to copies of the biblical text produced before the invention of the printing press.

Mari Tablets   A collection of texts from Mari, a capital city in northern Mesopotamia on the Euphrates River, which reveal third- and second-millennium-BCE customs of people who were ancestors of the Hebrews.

Masoretic Text   The text of the Hebrew Bible that serves as the base text for Old Testament textual criticism. The Masoretic Text (MT) is named for the generations of Masoretic scribes who worked between 500 and 1000 CE to standardize and preserve the Hebrew text.

Megilloth   The collection of "brief scrolls"—also known as the "Five Scrolls"—consisting of Ruth, Esther, Ecclesiastes, Song of Songs, and Lamentations. These books are part of the Writings, and each has some association with a Jewish festival.

Mesopotamia   Part of the ancient Fertile Crescent. Mesopotamia is the region that begins on the east at the Persian Gulf and moves north and west toward the Mediterranean Sea. The name means "in the midst of rivers" or "between rivers," which is a reference to the centrality of the Tigris and Euphrates Rivers to this region.

messiah   A Hebrew term meaning "anointed one," which is most often used in the Old Testament for kings. It comes to be associated with an ideal, future Davidic king. The term translates into Greek as *christos* and becomes the dominant title used for Jesus.

messianic secret   Primarily found in Mark's Gospel, the term for Jesus's practice of keeping his identity a secret until after his arrival in Jerusalem. Jesus commands both demons (Mark 1:24–25, 34; 3:11–12) and his disciples (Mark 8:29–30; 9:7–9) not to share their knowledge of his identity.

Mount Sinai   The place where Moses encountered YHWH in a burning bush and to which he and the people of Israel returned to receive the Torah and enter the Mosaic covenant. At times this location is also known as Mount Horeb.

narrative criticism   An analysis that pays close attention to the way narrative features such as character and characterization, narration, plot development, point of view, and literary techniques (e.g., irony and hyperbole) shape meaning in the text.

Nazirite   A segment of the Hebrew community that was to embody the community's holiness by following the vow of not cutting their hair, avoiding strong drink, and avoiding the uncleanness of corpses. In the initial taking of the Nazirite vow, their hair was cut and offered to YHWH as a symbol of the giving of their life to the deity.

Olympian gods   The gods and goddesses of classical mythology (e.g., Zeus/Jupiter, Poseidon/Neptune, Athena/Minerva) who resided in a hierarchical society on Mount Olympus.

Omri   A king of the kingdom of Israel who established Samaria as the northern capital and founded a brief dynasty of economically and militarily successful rulers. He reigned from 885 to 874 BCE.

oracle   Short prophetic speech that typically includes a proclamation from God about coming trouble or hope and a reason for that proclamation related to the loyalty or disloyalty of the people or the loyalty of YHWH.

Palestine   A name for the land between the Mediterranean Sea and the territory east of the Jordan River. The name Palestine derives from the name "Philistine," the people group who lived on the coast, which the Greeks applied to the whole region.

papyrus, papyri   A paper-like material made from papyrus plants that was used for writing in the ancient world. Papyri fragments of New Testament writings are very important witnesses to the earliest forms of these texts.

parable   A brief, fictional story that teaches a lesson or principle. Though found in the Old Testament, parables are most often associated with Jesus's teachings in the Gospels.

paraenesis   A style of rhetoric in which familiar, traditional moral instructions are grouped together in order to encourage audiences to continue living in a particular way.

parallelism, antithetic   A type of parallelism in Hebrew poetry in which the second line articulates a contrast to the first.

parallelism, stair-step   A type of parallelism in Hebrew poetry in which the second line takes the thought a step further than the first.

parallelism, synonymous   A type of parallelism in Hebrew poetry in which the sense of the second line is similar to that of the first.

parousia   The Greek word for the "presence" or "arrival" of an individual that the New Testament writings apply to Jesus's expected return.

Passover   Combined with the Feast of Unleavened Bread (which lasted seven days), this special one-day feast in the worship of ancient Israel was celebrated in the spring as a reminder of God's deliverance of the Hebrews from Egypt.

Pastoral Letters   The collection of New Testament writings comprising 1–2 Timothy and Titus. The letters are part of the Pauline corpus, though their Pauline authorship is disputed. They are called "Pastoral Letters" because they offer instruction and advice to Timothy and Titus for effective pastoral leadership in their respective churches.

Pentateuch   The name for the first five books of the Hebrew Bible / Old Testament: Genesis, Exodus, Leviticus, Numbers, and Deuteronomy. This section of the Hebrew Bible is also known as the Law or Torah.

Pentecost   Also known as the Festival of Weeks; one of three major festivals in Israel's calendar. It originated as a celebration of the first fruits of harvest but eventually came to include the commemoration of the giving of the Torah. This festival is significant in the Christian tradition because of its association with the giving of the Holy Spirit to Jesus's followers (Acts 2).

Persia, Persians   One of the great empires of ancient Mesopotamia. The Persians succeeded the Babylonian Empire in controlling Mesopotamia in 539 BCE and allowed the Israelite exiles to return to their homeland. Persia fell to the Greeks in 332 BCE.

pharaoh   The term for the ruler of ancient Egypt.

Pharisees   A sect of Judean Jews that probably emerged in the second century BCE who strove to embody the virtuous life the Mosaic law prescribed so that they would be rewarded for their faithfulness with bodily resurrection in the afterlife. They were skillful interpreters of Scripture and revered the oral traditions. After the destruction of the Jerusalem temple in 70 CE, the Pharisees morphed into rabbinic Judaism.

Pontius Pilate   A Roman official who served as the governor of Judea from 26 to 36 CE. In the biblical account, Pilate is the official who ordered the crucifixion of Jesus.

postcolonial criticism   An approach that pays attention to issues of imperial power and domination in both the text and the history of interpretation. The books of the Bible were compiled or produced in times and circumstances of imperial domination (Babylonian, Persian, Greek, or Roman). It considers how these texts reflect the reality of imperial oppression, whether in terms of resistance, negotiation, or accommodation. In contemporary terms, it looks at how postcolonial populations interpret these texts differently from their colonial masters who used these texts to promote their domination.

postexilic   Relating to the period of Israelite history following the return from the Babylonian exile in 539 BCE.

priest   A religious figure whose role centered on worship and sacrifice in the tabernacle or temple. In Second Temple Judaism, priests took on considerable political power and often came to be associated with oppressive imperial figures.

primeval history   The material that narrates the history of the first age, beginning with creation and concluding with the tower of Babel, in Genesis 1–11.

prophecy   Speech on behalf of a deity. Prophecy in the Hebrew Bible / Old Testament can involve speech about the future acts of God but more often is preaching about God's will for the present. Prophecy often uses shocking language to get the attention of a crowd.

prophet   A messenger from a deity who speaks on behalf of the deity. Israelite prophets bring ancient Israel's faith traditions to bear in interpreting life for the people of faith and apply these traditions to the present relationship of the community with YHWH.

Prophets   One of the three major divisions of the Hebrew Bible. The Prophets, or *Nevi'im*, consists of the books Joshua, Judges, 1–2 Samuel, 1–2 Kings, Isaiah, Jeremiah, Ezekiel, and the Book of the Twelve.

Proto-Isaiah   *See* Isaiah, book of.

proverb   A compact, memorable, applicable teaching about life. The etymology of the Hebrew term for proverb (*mashal*) suggests that such sayings in ancient Israel include a comparative element.

psalm   A song or poem used in worship. The book of Psalms contains psalms of various types (e.g., laments, hymns, thanksgivings).

pseudonymity   The practice of writing under a false name. This practice was common in the Greco-Roman world, especially in philosophical traditions in which a disciple would write in the name of the philosophical founder.

Ptolemies   The Greek descendants of Alexander the Great's general Ptolemy who gained control of Egypt—and, at some points in time, Palestine—after Alexander's death.

Q source   Based on the Two-Source Hypothesis solution to the Synoptic Problem, the hypothetical source reconstructed from the approximately 220 to 230 verses shared by the Gospels of Matthew and Luke but not Mark. It gets its name from the German word for "source" (*Quelle*).

rabbinic Judaism   The Judaism that developed out of Pharisaic Judaism after the fall of the Jerusalem temple in 70 CE. The predecessor of modern forms of Judaism, rabbinic Judaism focused on the study of the Hebrew Scriptures in synagogues and the leadership of teachers or rabbis.

reader-response criticism   An approach that emphasizes the construction of meaning by the reader as opposed to the text itself or its historical circumstances. Attention is given to a reader's social location, gender, and ideology.

redaction criticism   The analysis of how a text's sources have been adapted and edited, so that an author's literary and theological emphases can be detected.

Red Sea   Traditionally the sea across which Moses led the Hebrews as they were leaving Egypt in the exodus. The more accurate translation of the Hebrew is "the sea characterized by reeds or vegetation."

Rehoboam   The son of Solomon who became the first king of Judah after the division of the kingdom. He reigned from 922 to 915 BCE.

rhetorical criticism   An analysis of how a text persuades or affects its readers. Attention is given to rhetorical features such as structural patterns, repetition, wordplays, forms of argumentation, and type scenes.

Roman Empire   The ancient civilization that at its height held territories in Europe, Africa, and Asia. The Roman imperial period began in 27 BCE, when the Roman Senate made Octavian Caesar emperor and gave him the title "Augustus." The western half of the Roman Empire fell in the late fifth century CE, and the eastern half fell to the Ottoman Turks in 1453.

Rosetta Stone   A black granite stone bearing an inscription in three languages that, upon its discovery around 1800, made it possible to translate previously undecipherable Egyptian inscriptions by comparing the Greek version to the two Egyptian languages of demotic and hieroglyphics.

sacrifice   Something a worshiper offers to a deity as a sign of devotion and means of securing divine favor.

Sadducees   A sect of Judean Jews that probably emerged in the second century BCE and was often associated with the Jerusalem temple and the upper classes of society. They did not believe in the resurrection of the dead, an afterlife, or the authority of oral traditions about the law.

Samaritans   A branch of Judaism that developed during or soon after the Babylonian exile and continues into the modern era. The Samaritans held the Pentateuch as authoritative Scripture, but their temple was on Mount Gerizim, and there was often cultural and religious tension between them and the Jews from Galilee and Judea.

Satan   A Hebrew term meaning "accuser." By the time of the New Testament, this title came to be associated with the supernatural adversary of YHWH and Jesus who leads humans to sin.

scapegoat   A key part of the Hebrew Day of Atonement festival. Priests would confess the community's sin over the goat, and then the goat would be removed from the community, symbolizing the removal of the community's sin and the restoration of the community's relationship with YHWH.

scripture   Those writings that function authoritatively for the faith and practice of a religious group.

second temple   The Jewish temple in Jerusalem that was built in the late sixth century BCE at the end of the Babylonian exile. The period of Israelite history after the reconstruction of the Jerusalem temple after the Babylonian exile until the Roman destruction of the temple in 70 CE is known as the "Second Temple period."

Seleucids   The Greek descendants of Alexander the Great's general Seleucus who gained control of the Syrian region north of Judea after Alexander's death. By 198 BCE, the Seleucids had become the established overlords of Palestine as well. The Seleucids were viewed very negatively by most Jews.

Septuagint   The Greek translation of the Hebrew Scriptures, often abbreviated as "LXX," which served as the primary form of the Scriptures for many Jewish and Christian communities in the first centuries BCE and CE. The translation process probably began at the beginning of the third century BCE in Alexandria, Egypt, with the Pentateuch. By the end of the second century BCE, the Septuagint expanded to include the Prophets, most of the Writings, and some additional Jewish religious texts.

sign act   The term given to prophecies that take the form of symbolic actions the prophet performs.

source criticism   The analysis of a biblical text to determine what sources (usually written) were used in its composition. Identifying a text's sources (along with their possible "authors" and dates) allows interpreters to reconstruct the text's compilation history or analyze the intent of the biblical author(s).

Stoics, Stoicism   A Greek philosophy that sought the inner peace that comes from living in accordance with reason and the divinely ordered universe as opposed to the fear of the gods or other aspects of life beyond one's control.

synchronistic dating   The biblical practice, primarily in 1–2 Kings, of dating a king's reign during the time of the divided monarchy. The time of a king's reign is given alongside the time period of the reign of the king of the other (northern or southern) kingdom.

syncretism   The blending of rituals and worship practices of two or more religions.

Synoptic Gospels   The name given to the Gospels of Matthew, Mark, and Luke, because these Gospels share similar structure, content, and wording. The term *synoptic* means "seen together."

synoptic problem   The term for the question about the literary relationship between the Synoptic Gospels (Matthew, Mark, and Luke). It has prompted numerous theories about which Gospel was written first and what source material the Gospel writers used.

Syro-Ephraimite Crisis   The name given to the events surrounding the Northern Kingdom's unsuccessful efforts to pressure Judah into a military alliance with Syria and Egypt against the Assyrian Empire (736–732 BCE). Assyria suppressed the alliance and established vassal kings to prevent future resistance.

tabernacle   The mobile wilderness sanctuary that the Israelites built after the exodus event. The tabernacle served as the site of worship and sacrifice and the home of the ark of the covenant.

Ten Commandments   The "ten words" of commandment that YHWH gave to Moses on Mount Sinai following the exodus event (Exod. 20). Also known as the "Decalogue," the Ten Commandments are central to the shape of Old Testament faith.

tetragrammaton   The term for the divine name YHWH, because of the four letters that compose the name. The name became so holy to ancient Israel that they developed the practice of not pronouncing or writing out the whole name.

textual criticism   The work of reconstructing the earliest forms of a text through analyzing and comparing diverse manuscripts.

theodicy   The term given to the questions and attempted answers related to the justice of God. The traditional articulation of the issue is how one can claim the existence of an all-good and all-powerful God in the face of evil and suffering in the world.

Torah   One of the three major divisions of the Hebrew Bible. The Torah, also known as the "Pentateuch" or "Law," comprises the books Genesis, Exodus, Leviticus, Numbers, and Deuteronomy.

tradition history   The study of the development and reconfiguration of key events, institutions, and ideas in the Old and New Testaments.

Transjordan Plateau   The geographical region of Palestine that lies to the east of the Jordan River and was home to people groups such as the Moabites and Edomites.

Trito-Isaiah   *See* Isaiah, book of.

Two-Gospel Hypothesis   A solution to the synoptic problem that argues that two Gospels—one of which is Matthew—serve as sources for the last Synoptic Gospel written. In the fourth century, Augustine proposed that Matthew was written first, Mark was an abbreviation of Matthew, and Luke used both Matthew and Mark as sources. Nineteenth-century scholar J. J. Griesbach modified this theory by positing that Mark drew on both Matthew and Luke.

Two-Source Hypothesis   A solution to the synoptic problem that argues that the authors of Matthew and Luke independently used Mark's Gospel and a hypothetical source known as "Q" as written sources of information for composing their Gospels.

Tyndale, William   The translator of the first printed English Bible, known as the Tyndale Bible, which appeared between 1526 and 1530. Tyndale translated from Greek and Hebrew rather than Latin.

variant readings   Discrepancies among biblical manuscripts that came about because of both unintentional errors on the part of scribes while copying and intentional changes created by scribes for literary, theological, and political reasons.

Via Maris   One of the major highways between Damascus and Egypt in the ancient Near East. This "Way of the Sea" followed the Mediterranean coast and was valuable for military and trade purposes.

Vulgate   Jerome's fourth-century Latin translation of the Christian Scriptures, which served as the Bible for Western Christianity for nearly a thousand years. The term *vulgate* means "common," and so that title refers to the common version of the Latin Bible that was used in the Western church. The Roman Catholic Church designated the Vulgate as the official canon of the Bible at the Council of Trent (1545–63).

Wisdom literature   The name commonly given to the books of Proverbs, Job, and Ecclesiastes. These books are related to the Israelite wisdom movement, which was concerned with finding the order of the universe and the best way to live a good life within that order. The wisdom tradition is associated with instruction and guidance both within family contexts and in the royal courts.

Writings   One of the three major divisions of the Hebrew Bible. The Writings, or *Ketuvim*, comprises the books Psalms, Proverbs, Job, Song of Songs, Ruth, Lamentations, Ecclesiastes, Esther, Daniel, Ezra, Nehemiah, and 1–2 Chronicles.

Wycliffe, John   The producer of the first English translation of the Bible in manuscript form, which he translated from the Latin Vulgate (1384).

YHWH   *See* tetragrammaton.

Zealots   A revolutionary Jewish movement in the first centuries BCE and CE that sought to expel the Romans from Judea. The Sicarii were a splinter group of Zealots who were especially radicalized.

Scripture Index

Subject Index